Corporate Strategy

This book takes a fresh look at corporate strategy, exploring it from a feminist perspective. Challenging male-dominated theory, *Corporate Strategy* looks at unquestioned assumptions held about strategy in practice and academia, including whether women approach strategy differently from men, and if so, how their approach differs.

Reviewing the histories of strategy and feminism, the book explores the reasons why so few serious works on strategy have been written by women, and investigates the continued lack of women at senior levels within many organizations. Angélique du Toit draws on postmodern arguments to illustrate the claims made for the necessity of diversity within organizations, and challenges the fact that positions of power, both in society and organizations, remain the exclusive right of men. *Corporate Strategy* argues that if an organization is to survive and succeed in the global economy, it has to pay more than lip service to issues surrounding diversity.

Angélique du Toit combines Executive Coaching with academia, running a Postgraduate Diploma in Organizational Coaching for senior managers at the Sunderland Business School, UK. She has worked as a senior manager in both blue chip and medium-sized organizations, and also spent a number of years as a fashion designer.

Routledge Research in Organizational
Behaviour and Strategy

Corporate Strategy

A feminist perspective

Angélique du Toit

Routledge
Taylor & Francis Group

LONDON AND NEW YORK

First published 2006
by Routledge
2 Park Square, Milton Park, Abingdon, Oxon OX14 4RN

Simultaneously published in the USA and Canada
by Routledge
270 Madison Ave, New York, NY 10016

Routledge is an imprint of the Taylor & Francis Group, an informa business

© 2006 Angélique du Toit

Typeset in Garamond by
Newgen Imaging Systems (P) Ltd, Chennai, India
Printed and bound in Great Britain by
Biddles Ltd, King's Lynn

British Library Cataloguing in Publication Data
A catalogue record for this book is available from
the British Library

Library of Congress Cataloging in Publication Data
A catalog record for this book has been requested

ISBN10: 0–415–36561–9 (hbk)
ISBN10: 0–203–01817–6 (ebk)

ISBN13: 978–0–415–36561–1 (hbk)
ISBN13: 978–0–203–01817–0 (ebk)

Contents

Acknowledgements

We do not achieve anything in life without the support and encouragement of others. In fact, some of the best things we achieve in life are thanks to some very special people in our lives. This book is no exception. First and foremost, my heartfelt thanks go to Professor Stewart Sim. Without his continued support over the last few years, I would not have had the courage to complete the journey. As always, a special thanks to my family and in particular, my brother Eugene and his partner, Pieter. Their continued belief in my abilities has been a source of support when needed. Finally and of most importance has been the support from my partner, Laurence Davies. Only he will know how much his presence has facilitated the inspiration for the completion of this book.

1 Introduction

The inspiration for writing this book came from my research into the field of strategy, which started some years ago. It struck me some way into the process that there were very few journal articles or books of note written by women on the subject of strategy. I found this puzzling and decided to discover the reason for it. After some time it finally dawned on me that it was not mysterious at all and, in fact, it was quite obvious. My personal experience as a manager has been no different from that of many other women; the majority of senior positions in organizations are dominated by men. This is confirmed by Rodgers *et al.* (2003) who observed that leadership continues to be the exclusive domain of the white male.

Interestingly enough, I found this to be the same in academia, as certain subject areas are also dominated by men, strategy being one of them. In fact, in a recent academic newspaper, an adviser to the European Commission was quoted as saying that the way research was structured as well as the criteria used for measuring excellent research were seriously biased against women. Committees with the authority to appoint and award research funding and accolades are dominated by men who favour the approach and type of research carried out by men. Bottom line, women get a raw deal when it comes to competing with male colleagues for limited funding and prestigious research awards. This very much reinforced my own experience, as I had great difficulty in getting any of my ideas on strategy published in the mainstream journals, as this posed too much of a challenge to the traditional paradigms of strategy. It may not come as a surprise that most of the articles in those journals are published by men.

If we therefore perceive strategy to reside at the senior levels of an organization and if the majority of the senior managers are male and equally, the majority of academics in the field of strategy are male, then both the practitioners and academics will approach strategy from a masculine perspective. The next question I then asked myself was whether women would approach strategy from a different perspective to that of men? The journey I embarked on to discover the answer took me down some very interesting roads. I encountered studies into the science of complexity, which as a matter of interest has been called a feminine science by some authors. The reason will become clear later. I also found inspiration in the discourse of postmodernism, particularly social constructionism which advocates that our reality is pretty much of our own doing. How different would our strategic realities be if we approached them from a feminist perspective, if in fact a feminist perspective does exist? This is what I set out to discover and I invite you to come on the journey with me as described in the following chapters. Allow me to set the context.

Despite the vast array of publications on strategy, from the most intellectual of debates to the most practical of applications, we can sum strategy up in one sentence. It is a process, albeit an elaborate one, that helps us to make sense of our organizational realities. Furthermore, it is an activity that everyone in the organization participates in and contributes to, despite the reified state strategy is held in by those seeking to protect their positions and domains of power. The sense we make determines the meaning we assign to our experiences. In the same way as a scientist is perceived as the objective observer, there is a belief in both the practice and the theory that strategists are equally able to detach themselves from their organizations and make decisions devoid of personal agendas. However, this is not the case and our personal need to assign meaning to our lives is intricately connected with the meaning we try and make of our organizations.

It is interesting to note that the strategic sense an organization makes tends to be dominated by a small group of people in the organization and, we can therefore argue, reflects a limited point of view. We tend to assume that the act of strategic formulation is the domain of the chief executive and/or the senior management team. If we stop for a minute and think about the fact that those senior managers are more often than not white (in the West), middle-aged men, we can argue that the sense they make and the meaning assigned to their experiences, are from a rather limited perspective and do not necessarily reflect the rich diversity of their organizations.

Although the body of literature on strategy for both academics and practitioners spans many years, no publication has examined strategy from a feminist perspective or, indeed, any other diverse perspective for that matter. In fact, the practice of strategy in organizations is reserved for the board room and as with the bedroom, what goes on in there is not often talked about beyond its walls, shrouding it in mystery. In the case of the board room it is inhabited by a small group of the elite, an elite, as Rodgers points out, that is more often than not white middle-aged males.

As I mentioned earlier, we observe the same imbalance of genders in the field of academia where the theoretical pontification of strategy takes place and which is also dominated by men. The domination of modernism and its associated assumptions continues to exclude the voices of diversity in much of the literature. It cannot be otherwise as the theoretical reflects the practical and the practice is protected for the few by the old-boy network. It is as a result of my own frustrations with the limitations of the strategic literature that I decided to draw on an eclectic collection of disciplines to challenge the absence of diversity from the strategic literature.

As with the field of strategy, there is a long history of literature covering all aspects of feminism. Yet never the twain has met hitherto and the purpose of this book is not only to achieve such a meeting, but also to explore the reasons why this has not been done before. As strategy is activity associated with the senior echelons of an organization and there are very few women present at this level, this may be one reason why a feminist perspective has never entered the debate and equally therefore, the publication of strategy. It can be argued that organizations are the product of men, designed by men for men and are therefore dominated by masculine characteristics from strategy to management, not to mention leadership.

As a female manager of SMEs as well as blue chip organizations, a consultant and an academic, I feel well qualified to express my views on corporate strategy. Not only will I express such views boldly, but they will reflect a feminist perspective to redress the balance and offer an alternative view of strategy. The purpose of this book is to specifically challenge the functionalist and mainly male-dominated perspective of organizational strategy. I will argue that if we approach strategy from a postmodernist and feminist perspective it will be more inclusive and creative and will more accurately reflect the diverse nature of organizations and the communities they aim to serve. My experiences working as a manager in different countries, and with culturally diverse colleagues, have led me to conclude that the strategies of organizations, both small and large, remain largely the domain of the inner sanctum of senior managers. As the majority of senior managers are men, I conclude that it is predominantly a male-dominated perspective.

Many who belong to groups other than the small group of elite, middle-aged men who run and control our organizations experience the effects of inequality in many ways, some subtle and some not so subtle, such as ageism, sexism and racism. Diversity of all kinds – cultural, sexual orientation, values and beliefs – are marginalized within organizations. Even the phrase 'diversity' has an underlying assumption that everything we label as diverse is in fact different from what is perceived as the norm – a norm that predominantly reflects the beliefs held by the male population of the world. Anything outside this reality is *the other*. Diversity is not embraced within organizations and remains an enigma. Diversity scares us because it challenges the way we perceive the world and our particular version of the truth.

Gender bias occurs frequently in many spheres of life and in both overt and covert ways and the study of strategy is one such example. The concept of a *glass ceiling* is the metaphor often used to describe such prejudice and discrimination and can be perceived as one reason why the voice of feminism has not influenced the field of strategy. Mainstream organizational theorists and writers have traditionally written from a rational and male-dominated perspective, with perhaps the exception of authors such as Stacey. Feminine ontology is intrinsically marginalized in many discourses, especially the discourse of organizations and leadership (Shildrick, 1997). This denial of the female existence runs deep in our societies and is also reflected in the renditions of history. The history of a class society, such as most historical societies were, is a history about the rulers and the rulers have predominantly been men.

Throughout the history of strategy, certain schools of thought have emerged, tentatively moving away from the traditional presuppositions of strategy. The move away is influenced by approaches such as postmodernism which has been associated with feminism by numerous writers. Interestingly, managerial thinking has always been influenced by scientific discovery. The science of chaos and complexity theory has also found its way into organizational literature and that of strategy in particular. The theories of complexity promote an understanding of the relatedness of organizations to others within the context of their existence. The science of complexity is also described as a feminine science since it demands a holistic way of thinking, a characteristic normally associated with women. If organizations are perceived as complex adaptive systems, the traditional command-and-control, mechanistic style of management will be totally inappropriate.

Society and the products of society are, according to a constructivist philosophy, the result of the interaction of those who comprise a particular society. The core of my challenge is based on the fact that organizational *reality* is created by a minority population for a majority population, namely men, and the rest of the organization colludes in upholding their fantasies of reality. I am reminded of the Emperor's new clothes. Despite the fact that he is naked, everyone colludes with the illusion that he is clothed.

Legislation and the need for political correctness have merely driven a bias against that which is different underground. It is not possible to change the hearts and minds of people through legislation. Discrimination is alive and well, but is now mainly expressed covertly as opposed to overtly. As a woman trying to make my way to the upper level of the organizational hierarchy, my personal experiences testify to the existence of barriers to prevent the status quo from being challenged. The social rules by which we govern our organizations and societies become the norms by which we are all governed and allow ourselves to be governed. Žižek advises us that, 'Only to the already enlightened view does the universe of social customs and rules appear as a nonsensical "machine" that must be accepted as such' (1989: 80).

The organizational theories by which we govern our organizations are often linear and one-dimensional and seem far removed from reality as we experience it. Nor do they adequately capture the dynamic and ever-changing environment of the manager. Wider social and ethical debates are conveniently omitted from the management agenda and continue to place decision making in the hands of a self-elected group of *experts*. Furthermore, organizational literature does little to prepare you for the pressures, frustrations, contradictions and double standards you come to associate with the role of manager. In order to stimulate debate I challenge what I perceive the dominant organizational paradigm to be, namely that of functionalism. I propose an alternative model and advocate an approach to organizational management very different from the political systems we attempt to duplicate in organizations.

We observe and experience functionalism in organizations by the obsessive need for measurement and as managers we don't feel comfortable if we don't have the latest ratios, sales statistics and any relevant analysis to satisfy our illusion of being in control. The deluded state of control provides us with the equally deluded state of being able to predict the future, hence the need to formulate a strategy. The game of strategy depends on a number of beliefs. The strategic games we engage in assume that whilst we carry out our analysis, both the organization and the environment will bow to our will and remain in an unaltered state until we have completed our analysis. However, we all know from experience that organizations and their environments are dynamic and in a constant state of changing and becoming. The eventual conclusions we draw are therefore based on erroneous information that may have changed many times over.

Managing a dynamic organization is beyond the perceived control of the functionalist and often beyond the limits of the known. The dichotomy of control and freedom to explore requires the light hand of a conductor or facilitator. The intuitive nature of decision making contradicts much of the organizational literature, which is based on prediction and control. There is an increase in management development programmes to assist managers in developing their intuitive abilities. Retreats are perceived as one way of getting in touch with one's subjective or creative nature. Such skills require managers to transcend their need for control and certainty and to come to terms with uncertainty and unpredictability. As a manager, many of my intuitive decisions were dressed up in the familiar management speak and backed up by numbers to make it palatable to my superiors, especially if it did not follow the espoused, logical and linear path to decision making – a masculine perspective of the world.

As mentioned earlier, management theory is hugely influenced by the science of the day and the associated paradigm dominating science. The staple diet of science is to view society as ontologically prior to man and attempts to place man within that wider context – man as observer rather than as participant and, therefore, attributing an independence to man. A deep-seated view is that of order and the need to provide an explanation of what is observed. Organizational literature reflects a functionalist assumption that it holds the answers to the challenges faced by organizations – answers that not only exist outside of the organization, but can and should be imposed externally.

Strategy formulation reflects a further belief which leads managers to delude themselves into thinking that they can, in a wise and all-knowing manner, detach themselves from their organizations, environment and positions, and make decisions based on pure and untarnished information. However, my experience and the experience of others contradict such a belief in many ways. We have a tremendous influence in what we experience as our actions significantly contribute to what we ultimately come to experience. Decisions we made, or did not make, come back to haunt us in one shape or another, often long after the event. We are both part of our own problems as well as the solutions. However, the functionalist paradigm continues to advocate the manager's need and ability to predict future outcomes based on sound analysis by distancing himself/herself from his/her organization and his/her environment. Predictability is the very essence of strategy formulation and reflects the intrinsic and unquestionable need of management to control the future. My experience of organizations is that people, and that includes managers, are not the rational and predictable creatures science has led us to believe. Herein lie many of the difficulties faced by managers and organizations. The erroneous belief that managers operate from a logical and rational basis, devoid of personal bias, is continuously reinforced by organizational literature, especially that of strategy.

Organizational reality

What my personal experience has led me to conclude is that we continue to reinforce a perspective of *reality* that doesn't reflect the experiences of organizations. My personal frustrations with organizational literature mounted as it contradicted the reality of my day-to-day experiences of organizational life. The histories of organizations are littered with the tombstones of those who doggedly clung to a strategy that reflected a reality which had long since evaporated. Many Fortune 100 organizations that dominated their industry and at the time of their rule appeared immune to failure, became extinct.

Many managers share my disillusionment with organizational strategies. We spend endless hours producing a plan for our departments with predictions and forecasts we know are a far cry from the chaos of our day-to-day activities. So we all continue to collude in reinforcing the illusive reality that gives an equally illusive feeling of being in control. In my experience, strategy formulation is more akin to the way jazz musicians create their music – extemporaneously creating compositions together without prediction or control.

Strategy is a tool to support managers in making sense of the constant stream of new information they have to deal with. It helps us to make sense of that which is unknown and to integrate it into our existing paradigms, no more no less. It is part of an ongoing process of negotiation and conversation in which every individual member of the organization participates. Strategy is seen as being synonymous with planning and control upon which the success of the organization depends. However, this is rather paradoxical. Managers conspire to create the illusion of control, and yet on many occasions as a manager one feels totally out of control. The consequence of denying uncertainty is to limit the organization's peripheral vision, the source of awareness and openness to change and opportunities outside and beyond the norm. The process of formalizing strategy denies the informal and unplanned process of planning – the conversation in the corridor or the hunch to follow a road less travelled.

Organizations the product of men

Organizations are the products of men, designed by men for men and are dominated by masculine characteristics from strategy to leadership. The dominant paradigms of control and prediction have built paternalistic and hierarchical organizations that have protected the seat of power for the select few, the select few being predominantly male. Management presumes to have the wisdom and clarity to make decisions for and on behalf of the rest of the organization. Control is vital and often, so is fear. Organizations are mechanisms of control and organizational structures and practices perpetuate and reinforce control under the banner of rationality.

It has only been in recent years, with the rapidly changing environment and unpredictability of industries, that the hierarchy have had to concede that they are not all knowing and possibly not as much in control as they once thought. Tentative steps have been taken to introduce changes to management styles and to include approaches more akin to female characteristics such as participation and consultation (Oshagbemi and Gill, 2003; Regine and Lewin, 2003). I say tentative, as the changes remain firmly in the control of the select few middle-aged males. The masculine view of reality is reinforced and perpetuated by the selection and recruitment of those similar to the existing power base. One can therefore argue that strategy remains wedded to a one-sided, pro-managerial perspective that aims to rationalize the functionalist masculine values of how strategy should be done. Diversity of any kind, in particular the voice of feminism, is not heard when it comes to strategy formulation – a domain protected for men by the old-boy network.

The power of language

The power and influence of language on organizational behaviour are significantly underestimated and ignored. As managers, we are constantly engaged in language games of one sort or another, coupled with implicit assumptions and meanings we attempt to convey through our use of language. Language is employed in many ways to aid the construction of organizational reality and to maintain and reinforce that reality. The war-like vocabulary of strategy creates the image of battles to be fought with competitors representing the enemy. The male-dominated environment of management is reinforced through the use of sports metaphors which, of course, exclude anyone not familiar with sports such as rugby or football, not to mention the quintessential English game of cricket, referred to in more genteel circles. Management speak is constantly changing and sometimes also employed in sinister ways to make the unpalatable nature of organizational control more palatable. For example, laying off or firing employees has been labelled as 'outplacement', rationalization' or 'downsizing'. The danger is that these terms assume a reality outside of the individuals exercising their control and which therefore exonerates them of responsibility.

The illusion of diversity

We are subconsciously, although continuously, adjusting our behaviour and beliefs to conform to what is acceptable both in society at large and more specifically, in our organizations. Something as trivial as clothing is hugely influenced by the industry, organizational culture and position. Adhering to a particular dress code is in many industries an unwritten rule for both men and women if you want to be taken seriously. Cultural differences are suppressed even if you are part of a multicultured team. Creative opportunities are lost because mainstream organizational visions have only one window through which they observe the outside world. We are indoctrinated, soon after joining the organization, into a culture that frowns upon questioning the status quo.

Organizational ideology is influenced by the change of governments and the values and beliefs held by society. During the 1980s in Britain we had the Thatcher era, with its individualistic ideology resulting in the downfall of the union stronghold in organizations. The lack of women in the boardrooms of many organizations from many diverse industries supports my own experience. Many talented women give up and leave to start their own organizations. The labels we attach to people, or the group they represent, influence our behaviour towards them and ultimately our expectations of them. Women in certain industries are rarely promoted to any level of management, let alone senior management, and then only as a token. The subjective assumptions of the place of women in society significantly influence the way organizations are run, people are managed and decisions are made.

I propose that strategy remains the domain of men probably because there are so few women allowed into the inner sanctum of organizations where strategies are formulated. It is difficult to name well-known female strategists or even authors of strategy. Alternative views are rejected as they challenge the dominant male assumptions and the status quo. The complexity of organizations at all levels has increased a hundred fold over the last decade or so and the one-dimensional solutions that may have applied to stable and traditional industries of the past are no longer appropriate or relevant. Such an approach is totally unsuited to the dynamic and ever-changing world of organizations where uncertainty reigns: hence the need for diversity.

The collusion in maintaining the status quo

Our Western culture privileges action over discourse, a conviction underpinned by notions such as *talk is cheap* and *actions speak louder than words*. Organizations therefore emphasize and favour action. Activities such as debate, consultation and discussions are considered secondary to action. Yet, it is through dialogue and discussions that meaning is negotiated and given form and potential problems identified and avoided. Talk is devalued and real work is considered action. As Western managers we tend to scorn the more participative nature of the East as being time consuming. However, when solutions are implemented, this is done in a much smoother and more elegant way if it has the support of those who have to implement them. This is true empowerment and not the watered down and often manipulative version of the American model we adhere to in English-speaking countries.

Organizations have an enormous impact on society and the lives of those working for them. To many, the organization and their colleagues are their family and the main focus of their lives. Perhaps managers would be wise to lift their vision from the pragmatic to the political and the philosophical. Often, so-called 'pragmatic actions' may be political motives in disguise. However, organizational reality needs the collusion of both the management and the workers. In order to sustain the illusion, workers have to relinquish their freedom and potential partnership status to the perceived superiority and wisdom of management. In return they will be taken care of by the organization and provided with a job.

Ideological beliefs become internalized by all who participate in this collusion to the point where they are no longer questioned and are accepted as the norm. The result is that some of these shared beliefs will sometimes mean that employees willingly participate in their own demise like lambs going to the slaughter, believing that it is best for them and the collective whole of the organization. How often are plants and divisions closed down, not because of below-standard production and output, but because some person at head office perceives it to be the most rational decision as part of downsizing or rationalization? Very often the rationalized are the very people who have helped make the organization successful.

The use or abuse of power

An organizational reality which has in recent years gained momentum, certainly in the Western world, is the necessity to keep shareholders happy. The result is that employees are often treated as secondary to the financial well-being of the organization. Everyone in the organization conspires in reifying the management elite. Historically, the foundations of a paternalistic relationship were established between the organization and its employees. Such a hierarchical relationship within an organization continues to dominate, often reflecting the command structure of an organization.

In recent times, organizations may have been surprised to find that we as the public are not prepared to accept or condone some of these management practices. The outcry against *fat cats* being rewarded for driving their organizations to near extinction is an example of the rejection of some management practices. There is an increasing need for transparency and a wider ethical approach in the way organizations are managed. In my experience as a manager and a consultant, it is difficult to bring about change as fundamental as cultural change if it is not endorsed by the senior management. Often, such attempts are viewed with cynicism by the employees as nothing changes at the top and hollow values are espoused without any conviction. It is my personal belief that the paternalistic and controlling style of management is not appropriate to contemporary organizations, nor will it be suited to organizations of the future.

Leaders who inspire do not represent the American model of the charismatic lone hero who will ride into town and solve all the organization's problems whilst sweeping everyone along with *him*, fired up by total commitment, of course. I emphasize 'him' as the myth requires the role of hero to be filled by a male. Strategy in particular has been locked into the assumptions of its place of origin and a particular time frame, namely that of the 1960s in the USA, which have acted as a muzzle on the discipline ever since (Whittington, 2004). Instead, those who inspire are often unassuming in their ways with a knack of making others believe in themselves. In the self-managed teams organizations are moving towards, leadership can emerge at many different levels. We have an outmoded view in organizations that leadership has to come from the top of the organization. The challenge for modern leaders is to balance the paradox of being task focused with demonstrating an awareness and sensitivity to the social aspect of organizations and a concern for their people.

The above are renditions based on my own experiences and interpretations of those experiences. They may not be yours, but they are mine. However, I invite you to explore with me in the pages and chapters that follow the bold statements that I have made through further discussions and explorations.

Chapter outlines

Chapter 1 – introduction

I gave a brief outline of the arguments and challenges against the functionalist and mainly male-dominated perspective of organizational strategy which will be discussed in detail in the following chapters.

Chapter 2 – the dominant paradigms of strategy

I will introduce the paradigms and assumptions that continue to dominate strategy from both an academic and a practitioner's point of view. The unquestioned assumption of strategists is that it is planning and preparation for a game or a battle that has to be won. A number of disciplines will be used to describe what constitutes strategy from a functionalist perspective and what the subject may look like if viewed through the lenses of postmodernism. I will argue that a functionalist approach has dominated most of the schools of strategy that have evolved over the last 50 years.

Despite tentative attempts to sever the ties attached to a functionalist approach, the underpinning paradigm of strategy remains firmly wedded to that of functionalism and by default, that of a male perspective. This is only one definition of the *reality* constituting strategy. However, I will argue in this chapter that there are numerous other *realities* hidden behind the traditional monolithic approaches to strategy. Different realities are suppressed by the minority white males who dominate senior positions in organizations, close off debate and prevent people from incorporating their differing ideas and networks of relationships.

Chapter 3 – the illusion of planning and control

As mentioned, an overarching assumption of strategy is that of control; control of the organization, its resources as well as the environment. The need for control says a lot about the assumptions we hold about the employees of our organizations and the perceived power and ability of those who run the organization. Control actually masks a fear of the unknown and possibly our own inability to truly exercise control over circumstances and events.

Hand in glove with control is the belief of prediction. It would be impossible to formulate a strategy for the future if we are not in some way able to predict what that future is likely to look like. Predictions are very much reliant on the past as we tend to predict the future based on an extrapolation of the past and events that have already taken place. It is impossible for us to foresee and predict events of which we have had little or no experience. It is a bit like driving with your focus on the rear view mirror with obvious consequences.

Chapter 4 – strategy and complex adaptive systems

A scientific renaissance influencing contemporary management thinking is that of complexity science. The theories of complexity promote an under-standing of the relatedness of organizations to others within the context of their existence. Such theories support the criticisms levied against a functionalist approach to strategy and associated assumptions, discussed in Chapter 2. The study of complex dynamic systems has uncovered a funda-mental flaw in the analytical method that is inextricably linked with the functionalist paradigm. A complex system is not constituted merely by the sum of its components, but also by the intricate relationships between these components. Science has come to realize that nature at the atomic level does not appear as a mechanical universe of fundamental building blocks, but rather as a network of relations, and that ultimately, there are no parts at all in this interconnected web. With the new sciences comes a shift from thinking in terms of structure to thinking in terms of process. In fact, the very structure under observation is a manifestation of an underlying process.

If organizations are perceived as complex adaptive systems, the traditional command-and-control, mechanistic style of management will be totally inappropriate. In fact, according to Regine and Lewin (2003: 347) such management styles '... inevitably will impair their efficacy, in terms of creativity and adaptability'. A management style guided by the principles of a complexity science is seen to be hierarchically flat, embracing diversity and supportive of open communication – traits traditionally associated with a feminine style of leadership. In this chapter I will put forward the ongoing debate as to whether or not the feminine characteristics expressed by women place them in a better position to be more natural at leading with interactive and transformational styles. Relationships are seen to be the bottom line for business success in a complex environment. This is in stark contrast with the recent exposure of a number of hyper-masculine-led organizations and their greed-driven cultures. Such big egocentric leaders perceive the purpose of their organizations as vehicles for enriching the few at the expense of the many.

Chapter 5 – breaking the mould

I will introduce the nature of diversity and identify the consequences of denial of diversity in organizations. Denial of diversity continues to reinforce a reality that belongs to a small group of the population, namely men. People subconsciously, but continuously, adjust their behaviour and beliefs to conform to what is acceptable. Cultural differences tend to be suppressed or marginalized even if one is part of a multicultural team. To be a 'company man', one is expected to accept without question. The various strategies organizations employ in dealing with diversity will be put forward as well as the consequences of ignoring difference. I will argue that the espoused practices of diversity within organizations are often window dressing only and that voices advocating difference continue to be suppressed. The promotion of minorities is seen merely as a token activity in order to satisfy the statistics and to appease the voices of criticism who argue for inclusion. This is very different from the recognition that comes from a belief that truly values and acknowledges difference.

Chapter 6 – cultural diversity

The values and the norms of our cultures will dictate the place individuals will occupy in society, how they are treated and how they will view themselves in relation to other members of their society. Furthermore, these beliefs go unquestioned. It is a fact that in many cultures, women are valued much less than men and in some cultures they are seen as no more than the chattel of men, to be used and abused at their whim.

It is only to be expected that organizations will reflect the norms and values of the cultures from where they came. Should that culture not recognize diversity, organizations are likely to reflect the same rejection of anyone who does not fit the right mould. Globalization has to some extent put pressures on organizations to deal with diversity. In fact, internationally successful organizations claim that the recognition and inclusion of diversity is a vital factor in achieving such success.

Chapter 7 – the silent voice of feminism

In order to survive and compete in a male-dominated society, many women find it necessary to suppress their feminine values. Being successful, particularly in the corporate world, requires women to develop and express their masculine qualities at the expense of what many perceive as their weaker side – that of the feminine. This chapter will argue that women, not only for their own benefit, but also for their societies, need to rediscover and reclaim their feminine side and to become liberated from the constraints that silence their feminine voices.

The gender debate should go much deeper than merely the narrow gender vocabulary that dominates organizational issues. Values deeply embedded within the capitalist and market economy, such as growth, exploitation of nature, hedonism, affluent consumption and careerisms are major barriers to reform. Within the history of Western philosophy, masculine and feminine have always been depicted as mutually exclusive with opposing traits. The core characteristics depicted by masculinity are the traits associated with leadership, such as objective, action-orientated, linear, assertive, independent, rational control. However, these traits are not fixed and are subject to meanings ascribed to them culturally. Women reflecting the traits associated with masculinity are more likely to be perceived as successful managers and are accepted more easily by their male colleagues. The price of masculine hegemony is the denial by both women and men of the characteristics associated with the feminine – characteristics such as nurturing, emotions, needs, empathy and compassion.

Chapter 8 – the imbalance of leadership

Leadership continues to be dominated by deeply held beliefs and values of paternalism. It is therefore not surprising that the majority of senior management positions continue to be dominated by men. The preferred leadership style of women is more collaborative as opposed to the more transactional approach exhibited by men, which contributes to disadvantaging women when competing for leadership positions.

There is an assumption that women lack the experience and psychological make up of what is required of a leader. If the deep-seated values of paternalism are used to measure leaders, women will certainly fall short of the mark. The image of heroism in most modern cultures is dominated by the male gender. Men are seen as being natural to the hero role, hence the image of the organizational leaders being men.

Chapter 9 – the sexuality of women

The ways in which we express our genders are established at a very early age through socialization. Rules are established as to which is the dominant and which the more submissive of the genders. These rules cause women difficulties within the organization. Does a woman express assertive qualities associated with a masculine approach or the more inclusive and therefore softer feminine characteristics? Either way, she will be in a no-win situation.

There is a deep-seated belief that women should be more submissive and defer to the more dominant male. Even the clothes you wear have to be given more thought than that of your male counterparts. Your dress is seen as either too butch or you come across as being a seductress. Unfortunately, sexuality in the workplace may lead to the extreme of sexual harassment. In most societies, harassment and abuse of varying degrees towards women are tolerated. As the dominant sex, it is seen as the right of the man to exercise his will over a woman.

Chapter 10 – power and hegemony

Historically, the foundations of a paternalistic relationship were established between the organization and its employees. I will draw on Transactional Analysis to demonstrate the various relationships between employer and employee and how all the players within the organization collude to maintain the status quo.

The roles of men and women which determine the place and status of women is not a given of nature, but decided on by history. The roles assigned to women are therefore defined socially. The right to rule is intrinsic within the paternalistic nature of society. The model of the authoritative father supports the division of leadership in favour of the wise father. This reinforces the hegemonic nature of organizations and the taken-for-granted right of men to rule those organizations. Dominance is not only achieved through the formal lines of authority, but also through the supportive networks, or 'old-boy networks' that protect the camaraderie of men in organizations. The very nature of management is based on obedience and, often, coercion. Many organizational practices support these assumptions, no matter how they are dressed up, the concept of empowerment being one example.

Chapter 11 – the challenge from postmodernism

I will consider the implications of applying postmodern theory to strategy. Postmodernism is committed to pluralism in all areas of life, and does not believe in 'essential' truths or facts. It treats all truths and facts as interpretations expressed from a particular viewpoint. Instead of truths and facts, postmodernism encourages the idea of there being a plurality of narratives. Postmodernism is sceptical of all types of authority, on the grounds that they tend to suppress those narratives which query their own 'meta-narrative' – the means by which authority exerts control. As far as a thinker like Lyotard is concerned, postmodern science is a series of discrete narratives lacking any dominant meta-narrative, and it produces the unknown rather than the known.

A fundamental element in the method of analysis of postmodernism is aimed not at closure, but at opening up discourse to a multiplicity of divergent voices. This has significant importance to feminism and the opening up of organizations to reflect the many voices they represent. Social, as well as organizational cultures, have created a one-dimensional man with the emphasis on *man*. It is the one-dimensional man who decides whose voice is to be heard. Postmodernism posits that it is through relationships that those claiming power are granted such power. Permission is granted by those engaged in the relationship through their acceptance of imposed power. The reciprocity of relationships demonstrates the interdependence of communities.

Chapter 12 – identity, the product of social constructionism

Social constructionism argues that identity is socially created (Gergen, 1999; 2001). Post-structuralism has rescued feminism from the naïve essentialism which perceived women as homogenous units with a common identity to be buried by patriarchy. Social constructionism argues that identity is discursively constructed, fluid and constantly in a state of becoming. Equally, the categories of male and female are defined within cultures rather than being biological givens.

In fact, it is irrelevant whether identities are essential or socially constructed as organizations continue to reinforce the dominance of one identity, that of the male identity over many others, whether it be feminism or differences posed by national cultures. Appropriating postmodernist theories for a feminist ethic is to challenge the way in which society constructs values and to suggest new ways to configure such values, not to deny the possibility of values. In the corporate world in particular, perceptions as to the behaviour of male and female are filtered through a gender lens, tapping into a subconscious image of leadership being a masculine construction.

Chapter 13 – conclusion

The strategic reality that the organization ultimately experiences is as a result of the collectively negotiated process in which all members of the organization should be engaged. However, if the sense of an organization is made predominantly from a masculine perspective, the strategic result will not embrace the differences represented within an organization. The essence of organizational identity is based on the premise of competitive individuality – the individual leader, the worker and so on, again a masculine characteristic. The entire field of strategy rests on the assumption of individual and competitive rationality. Yet, what postmodernism and feminism have demonstrated is that individuality is not only subservient to the relational, but is a result of community. Furthermore, that community is composed of different individuals with differing ideas and beliefs. Therefore, organizations need to relinquish their masculine obsession with planning and control and instead, become sensitive to the whispers of change that herald the opening of new windows of opportunity.

2 The dominant paradigms of strategy

Strategy is an organizational activity that has historically been in control of the senior management of the organization. Senior management, as the statistics will bear out, is dominated by middle-aged men. The elitism of strategy has meant that decisions, which not only affect everyone in the organization but often society, remain in the hands of the few. The few do not represent the whole and yet we are at the mercy of those decisions and as some of the recent failures of the dotcoms and organizations such as Enron highlighted, decisions taken are not always for the better. It is in the interest of the elite to maintain the myth that strategy can only be engaged in by the few. If, however, we follow the advice of Whittington (2004) and perceive strategy as any other social activity in which everyone participates, the myth will disappear and the house of cards will come tumbling down. The demystification of strategy will also mean the inclusion of all and the recognition and acceptance of diverse perspectives and ideas.

Much has been said and written about the various approaches to strategy and Meyer and Preston (1995) neatly describe two camps that divide the field of strategy. The first group devotes considerable time and energy in protecting very clear and solid boundaries. They demonstrate a belief of strategy from a functionalist and elitist perspective which is dedicated to producing an intellectual superstructure true to the scientific and functionalist tradition. Needless to say, this camp is dominated by the male species. The opposing view, and the basis for the hypothesis of this book, is based on low and permeable boundaries that reflect a pluralistic view. This view recognizes that other disciplines have a great deal to contribute to the challenges senior managers face when deciding on the strategic direction of the businesses.

There is an unease in the field of strategy, a sense that the unquestionable truths it has been built on are about to come tumbling down. This is because these truths are unable to deal with contemporary organizations and their ever-changing landscapes. The fact that organizations are enormously complex challenges the unitary perspective often associated with strategy.

This unitary perspective seldom acknowledges the diverse nature of our organizations and the continuous dynamic interactive relationships that shape and influence the strategic process. Yet it is difficult to find any significant reference to diversity in the mainstream literature on strategy – diversity of either kind, cultural or gender. It is hardly recognized nor is its relevance to strategy acknowledged. I suppose one could ask just why literature should reflect diversity of any kind. When we look at the average profile of the occupiers of the boardrooms and the owners of the strategic domain, it is predominantly inhabited by men. How can it therefore be anything other than a limited view?

We find a clue in the nature of strategy through the language that continues to dominate the field of strategy. It is a view that only acknowledges with very little room for cooperation – hence the *game* of strategy. We play many *games* within organizations: power games, political games, competitive games, military games and, of course, games of domination. It is part of the male psyche to compete in order to prove that *mine is bigger and better than yours* and strategy is no exception. Competing is very much perceived as a virtue (Alvesson and Willmott, 1995), which leaves little room for collaboration or cooperation, unless it is part of the winning strategy. We have an obligation, to challenge the competitive nature of the strategy story and instead write a story that reflects the diverse nature of organizations and the representation of different values and assumptions.

However, competition continues to dominate the field of strategy. Not only does it dominate, it is also perceived as a virtue. The thrill of the chase and the need for victory reflect the male-dominated games played by managers within organizations. The very nature of the strategic language is aggressive and warlike. Competition is likened to battles that have to be won and markets that need penetrating. Penetration from a male perspective equals domination and possession. A succinct description of strategy is as follows:

> to the extent that the discourse of strategy is successfully introduced and disseminated by a powerful managerial elite, it serves to construct (or reinforce) the (commonsense and masculinist) understanding that organisations are engaged in a competitive struggle.
>
> (Alvesson and Willmott, 1995: 100)

I found trawling through the literature a pattern of sameness – one of order, prediction, structure, planning and control, control of the environment and control of resources, competition and analysis. The purpose of a strategic plan is to eliminate uncertainty and this is considered the result of a rational process. Plans of diverse ideas are not often tolerated. It is fascinating to observe the extent to which organizations will go to resist difference, even in the way they compete with others. Especially during times of turbulence, organizations seek comfort in similarities rather than in striving to be different. Achieving that winning strategy is not only about obsessively measuring yourself against your competitors, but also the ability to engage in introspection and recognize and develop the unique abilities and competencies within the organization. Such introspection requires acknowledging and valuing differences and a willingness to question our views of the world.

Our organizations and their related theories are dominated by an American culture that finds it difficult to deal with the complex nature of organizations and the diverse values and beliefs represented therein. This is especially true of strategy which had its origin in the USA during the 1960s, with a particular mindset that advocates detachment. This mindset continues to haunt both the practice and the theory of strategy. The strategic literature continues its obsession with the leaders of the organization and their ability to manage the long-term planning and control of their organizations.

Pettigrew *et al.* counsel that 'in an increasingly interdependent and multicultural world it is crucial to recognize differences in institutional and cultural context and diversity in intellectual traditions in different societies' (2002: 4). Organizations are social units that are comprised of much diversity, which is mostly ignored by organizational literature and practitioners alike. Strategy then becomes the product of a particular rationality which is not necessarily representative of all or the majority of organizational members. The progression of our thinking and understanding of organizations should be based on inclusion, not exclusion and exclusivity. Why? Because organizations and institutions serve diverse communities with diverse expectations and values.

Throughout the history of management theory, science has had a powerful influence on both the theory and the practice. This is also true of the scientific research into complex adaptive systems which is beginning to influence management theory quite significantly. However, the practice is less influenced by such theories at the moment. A key theme of complexity theory is that diversity is a prerequisite for change. I will discuss strategy in relation to the theories of complexity in the following chapter.

Despite the importance of diversity, the literature continues to ignore the wider aspect of strategy formulation and focuses on a simplistic view of the organization and the nature of its relationship with the environment. The dynamic nature of strategy is reduced to the need for being in control of the organization's destiny, or rather the delusion of being in control. As I will discuss, the new sciences of chaos and complexity theory caution against excessive control which may lead to a resistance to change and, more importantly, stifle creativity and innovative thinking. Furthermore, the importance of the many relationships within and without the organization is not even mentioned in much of the strategic literature. Strategy remains the exclusive domain of the board or senior management team.

However, experience questions the notion of strategy being a detailed plan, arrived at through careful analysis and prediction. Instead, it is more of a theme which, if successful, is shared by all in the organization. Indeed, the complex and chaotic nature of organizations and their environments challenge the assumption that integrated planned strategies are possible, whereas a unified theme will provide the organization with the guidance to decision making and what it should focus on. It should engage not only the intellect, but also the hearts and emotions of those within the organization. It is the collective legacy the organization will leave behind. Strategy is not the exclusive domain of the senior echelon of the organization. Senior managers arrogantly and erroneously labour under the belief that they could at any moment in time have a 360 degree vision and understanding of the organization and its activities.

Is it not ironic that despite the literature on strategy advocating the need to be different in order to compete effectively, organizations continue to marginalize difference within the organization rather than harnessing the creativity of such difference? I think we all agree that life is constructed of endless variety. So too is the environment which organizations inhabit and the options open to the organization with which they could respond. However, the very nature of strategy denies experimentation, playfulness or the opportunity to explore. Such activities build an ability within the organization to be more creative and resilient in dealing with complexity and change. In fact, those on the periphery of the organization or the *other* to the organizational elite, are often more informed as they are exposed to ideas that are different and challenging to the dominant beliefs.

In order to deal with the complexity of the environment, instead of attempting to simplify the complexity and respond with one or two solutions, the law of requisite variety states that in order to deal successfully with external complexities, organizational solutions need to reflect the same level of complexity. The one or two simple solutions will fail as they will not be able to deal with any of the unforeseen events likely to occur. Hence the reason why embracing and harnessing diversity is so important is that it multiplies the solutions available to the organization.

As mentioned earlier, an unquestioned assumption of strategy is that of planning and preparation for games to be won. This assumption of planning reflects the deep-seated belief in the dominant functionalist paradigm of order and pattern. Synonymous with this paradigm are fundamental organizational beliefs of planning, a command-and-control style leadership and efficiency: all fundamental beliefs that dominate the activity of strategy in organizations. The word strategy is used interchangeably with the word planning. Strategy is reduced to a linear formalized process engaged in by strategists to systematically and logically determine the future direction of the organization. An important emphasis of the planning approach is that of rationality. Furthermore, the notion of planning separates the implementers of strategy from those who formulate the strategy, thereby denying a vast majority of the organization any input or voice in the process.

There has been a tendency in organizations to confuse planning and control with order. If organizations are machines, control makes sense and, of course, the machine metaphor has long dominated strategic planning. The future success of the organization is not to be found within the limited boundaries of rational analysis and planning. The underlying assumption of the machine metaphor is that an organization is based on rationality and logic. The maintenance of order, stability and equilibrium is viewed as being of paramount importance. Evidence to support the success of a planning approach to strategy remains elusive. It is ironic that the strategic process actually undermines the achievement of order the organization so actively strives for through a division of thinking and doing. Despite tentative attempts to sever the ties attached to a functionalist approach, the underpinning paradigm of strategy remains firmly wedded to that of functionalism and by default, that of a male perspective. The view of the strategist or strategists being omnipotent continues to persist, even in those who recognize the flaws in the traditional assumptions of strategy.

The traditional functionalist perspective is one definition of strategy. However, I argue that there are numerous other definitions and approaches to strategy, although alternative approaches are prevented from posing any serious challenge to the dominant storyline of organizations. As stated earlier, the senior positions within most organizations are occupied mainly by middle-aged men and in Western countries, by white middle-aged men who close off any debate which may challenge their dominance of the organization.

An alternative perspective to this one-sided view of reality is that of an interpretivist paradigm, the essence of which is in understanding reality from the perspective of the participant. Furthermore, reality is based on collective assumptions and shared meanings. Contained within this paradigm is the work of proponents of social constructivism which will be discussed in greater detail in the following chapters. Constructivists argue that the perceived reality of our experiences is the result of socially created processes of interaction.

Furthermore, this process is of an ongoing nature. The premise of this paradigm therefore challenges the deeply held views of organizations and the study of organizational activities such as strategy.

The above introduces two diametrically opposing views of how we may describe and understand what we perceive as reality. Such differing views clearly result in wide-ranging perspectives as to the definitions of and approach to strategy. A common definition acceptable to both theorists and practitioners therefore remains elusive. The dictionary definition of strategy perceives it as the art of a commander-in-chief and the art or skill of careful planning: planning for successful action based on rationality and interdependence of the moves of opposing or competing participants.

I referred to strategy in terms of the military at the beginning of this chapter, and to the militaristic overtones of strategy, likening it to the art of war, reflecting the underlying assumptions held by so many in the field of strategy. The strategic literature is peppered with references to battles and advice on how to conduct yourself on the battlefield, judging the right moment for attack or withdrawal.

Most of the literature on strategy advocate the tradition of strategy as a deliberate process. The study of strategy has reached a crossroad and the question is whether to stay with the familiar or whether to venture into new territories. The latter will require letting go of traditional paradigms and traditionally accepted wisdom to allow for innovative and new ways of defining and solving organizational problems. The motivation to break from tradition can only come from a perspective that brings a different set of values and assumptions, such as the inclusion of a feminist approach.

The history of strategy has been dominated by certain schools of thought, which have emerged over the evolution of strategy. The design school has dominated strategy with its fundamental beliefs in the logical and rational approach to the planning and control of strategy. In later years, some have tentatively moved away from the traditional presuppositions of strategy, such as the cognitive and learning schools. Mintzberg, who has led the revolt, argues that strategy is an emergent phenomenon that can be initiated from anywhere in the organization through a learning process that is collective. He argues that strategy is not carefully designed or planned for, but is made up as the organization conducts its activities. His observations led him to believe that the outcomes achieved by management are emergent and do not often correlate with a manager's initial intentions.

Then there is the pluralistic school that introduces an understanding of strategy less dominated and coloured by the views of the senior management. Its influence comes from Critical Theory and the assumption that the discipline of management is researched, practised and understood from an intellectually narrow perspective. This perspective is dominated by the social values, interests and views of the organizational elite, the elite view, I argue, being predominantly that of a male perspective. Furthermore, strategy reflects a one-sided, pro-managerial perspective which reinforces and rationalizes the masculine values of how strategy should be conducted. The domination of masculine values is perpetuated through the powerful strategic rhetoric that elevates those and their opinions of strategy as a masculine, militaristic pursuit, reinforcing a patriarchal approach to organizations (Alvesson and Willmott, 1995).

The literature also reflects the power and political struggles that permeate organizations. These struggles exert influence not only on the process of strategy formulation, but also on the selection of strategies. The influence of power games on strategy formulation is expressed in the form of bargaining, compromises and tradeoffs amongst individuals and groups vying for power and the protection of personal agendas and fiefdoms. Having the power to present arguments based on the personal preferences and ambitions of those in decision-making positions will naturally influence the strategic process. It would be naïve to separate these political tradeoffs and coalitions from the strategic process. It therefore raises the question of how strategy can be the product of a logical, linear process from which strategists are supposedly detached.

This political influence on strategy hints at the messiness and unpredictability of the nature of strategy as opposed to the logical and detached perspective we are led to believe is the norm. Insistence on applying only logical reasoning to strategy creates an intellectual straitjacket, which excludes the views of those who dare pose a challenge to such a view of the world. The imposition of authority and control associated with strategy reflects a game of politics and power. I have introduced challenges to these traditional paradigms.

A further challenge to many of the functionalist assumptions and activities traditionally associated with management is in the form of postmodernism. Postmodernist beliefs challenge the assumption of order as a rigid state and instead perceive it as a dynamic energy swirling around us, and which is beyond the control of the individual or the elite group of strategists. Postmodernism further rejects the underlying authoritarian ideologies and political systems that underpin many organizational ideologies of which strategic planning is only one example.

It stands to reason that whichever strategy the organization pursues will influence and determine not only the behaviour of the organization, but the behaviour of individuals within the organization. Eventually, an organizational personality will develop. As with an individual personality, it has the potential of resisting alternative views and different ways of behaving. Ignoring diversity may deny the organization access to vital information that could influence the future success of the organization. Strategy formulation is merely a map to guide the organization on its journey of evolution and problems arise when the map is confused with the territory.

3 The illusion of planning and control

An underlying assumption of strategy is the perception of it being a linear, step-by-step activity through which one logically moves from problem identification to diagnosis and problems solution, concluding with the implementation of the solution. However, any manager would testify that the espoused linear view of strategy is far from the messy and creative reality of management. An erroneous belief associated with strategy is that planning is perceived as synonymous with organizational success (Bresser and Bishop, 1983); without planning the organization will not succeed in its endeavours. Planning is further erroneously assumed to be based on logic and rationality (Ansoff, 1965; Alvesson and Willmott, 1995; Johnson and Scholes, 1999; Lynch, 2000; Stacey, 2000; Whittington, 2000; Bailey and Johnson, 2001; Cummings, 2002).

Furthermore, control is seen as the domain and responsibility of the chief executive who is perceived as the strategist of the organization. Control directly impacts on the behaviours of others and the need for control is based on an assumption that people cannot be relied upon to behave in the best interest of the organization. Furthermore, it is only the strategist who is capable of understanding the bigger picture and is therefore responsible for translating the overall strategy to those further down the hierarchy. The identity of the strategic planner came into being during the 1950s when management discovered quantitative analysis. However, strategy remains overly prescriptive with little resemblance to the reality.

The need for control reflects a fear of the unknown and is the antithesis of the ambiguity that surrounds organizations. Ambiguity is a constant companion in every walk of life. Furthermore, planning assumes control and an obsession with control leads to an aversion to risk and creative thinking and stifles responsiveness to changing circumstances. Planning, as we know, is carried out at the higher echelon of the organization where power is held and controlled. The lower end of the organization is responsible for the implementation of the strategies, its activities often subjected to constant control and monitoring.

Without the support of the majority of the members of the organization, planning of any kind is a futile activity. Planning by its very nature promotes inflexibility and denies the instinctive and creative element of strategy.

A further danger associated with planning is that planners become so wedded to their plans that change is unthinkable. An underlying assumption of planning and prediction is conformity, eliminating any challenges to the status quo or denying the existence of diversity. Strategists intrinsically assume that the formulation and control of the strategic process take place away from the activities and influence of all the members of the organization. Instead, strategy is in fact the result of relationship building at all levels of the organization leading to a joint discovery of meaning and destiny. It is not an activity for the privileged few.

Detached observer

Associated with the ability to predict an unknown future is an assumption that strategists are able to detach themselves from the world around them. Such detachment would then allow them in a logical and value-neutral way, to carry out their analysis (Cummings, 2002). This belief has been influenced by science through the perception of the scientist as the detached observer, able to understand subject matter from a distance. The assumption of this approach is that the manager is able to detach him or herself from the very environment of which they form a part. Of equal significance is the assumption that others within the organization lose their humanity and become objects without choice and voice and therefore subject to prediction and control, hence the paternalistic image of senior management as they wisely plot the future course of the organization. The scientific approach to management in the early twentieth century perceived management science as objective and therefore subject to the same scientific laws and principles. The manager was seen as an objective scientist, deciding on the objectives and goals of those in the organization who were expected to carry these out with mechanistic precision. As discussed earlier, an interpretivist perspective of reality perceives organizations as the result of the interactions of all individuals within the boundaries of the organization. If we accept this view, we also accept the need of a shared responsibility for the direction the organization will follow. It is not an activity reserved for the select few who represent an equivalent minority group of the organization, namely men.

Strategy continues to labour under the beliefs and assumptions of its scientific roots that it is a rational activity akin to that of a detached scientist. As with science, it was held up as an activity for the intelligent elite of the organization. The reality is that it is a practical process the whole of the organization engages in to make sense of its organizational life. If the organization is the product of the interaction of all who participate in the organization, then everyone has the right and the responsibility to either have his or her voice heard or to be represented where decisions that affect everyone are taken – a representation of the diversity of views within the organization. Whittington (2004) points out that this move towards the more practical element of management research is led by European scholars and can be seen as an extension of the European challenge of the postmodern on the Enlightenment stronghold.

Predicting the unpredictable

If we accept the view which advocates that we are able to predict and forecast the future direction of our organizations, we assume compliance from an acquiescent environment. Otherwise, how could we possibly make accurate predictions? Perhaps because prediction is an elusive mirage which doesn't in any way reflect the reality of the strategic process which, as I mentioned before, is messy (Stacey, 2000) and reflects the ambiguity everyone in the organization lives with. Furthermore, forecasts are based on descriptions of the past rather than predictions based on future aspirations and which may very well be unrelated to past experiences (Ackoff, 1983).

We cling to the erroneous illusion that the future will necessarily resemble the past. This is reinforced by matching solutions with which we are familiar to new problems rather than discovering new solutions for new problems. The old ways are very often inadequate when dealing with new circumstances and new problems. This behaviour pattern erects barriers against diversity. It is human nature to seek the familiar and that includes people who share our own views of the world and who speak the same language as us. The same language is both the language of our nationality as well as the language of the social groups we belong to. We can see how a simple thing such as language will exclude not only those from a different nationality, but also those belonging to a different social group. We have often heard it being said that we employ those in our own image because it feels comfortable and familiar. Is it therefore surprising that men find the language used by women as being alien and therefore to be marginalized?

Returning to the fundamental principle of forecasting, in order to forecast, past data are projected along a straight line from a state of now to a future state of then. The very nature of this activity denies the opportunity to exercise choice or even to allow for the unexpected. Formal forecasting techniques are incapable of predicting discontinuous changes within the organization or changes within the environment. The linear process of planning and prediction can only be successful if the future remains static.

The planning and prediction carried out by the charismatic leader continues to be reinforced by gender-specific historical beliefs. The myth perpetuates the reliance of the organization on one or two individuals while the rest of the organization is enthusiastically swept along by their vision. The myth of leaders as heroic figures continues to be reinforced by the strategic process. It also reflects the chimera that these heroic figures are the intelligent thinkers of the organization and the remainder have to follow and implement their visions. As corporate strategy is perceived to be the domain of the boardroom, it is shrouded in mystery and secrecy. The whole organization colludes in the reification of strategy and therefore the superiority of those who engage in it.

At the heart of strategy is the expectation that it will provide organizations and management with consistency, not only in defining a consistent organizational identity, but more importantly, in reducing the ambiguity we constantly face in all aspects of organizational life. In order to ensure consistency, we believe that the process should be analytical and deliberate. It stands to reason that if the process is deliberate and consistent, those who are responsible for the process also have to exhibit consistency in their behaviour and identity. If not, the process will be fundamentally flawed. However, postmodernism poses serious questions of the beliefs held in relation to identities and the essentialist nature of identities. The manifested reality is but one of many potential realities. Every decision provides us with choice and if we choose differently, what we experience will also be different. The flawed belief therefore that strategy represents stability is refuted by the fact that much of the study of strategy is about change and how to deal with such change. Consistency also assumes a continued existence. Strategists assume the continuation of the organizational existence and its environment in a particular state or form. We know from experience that this is not the case. Many organizations have come and gone and the environment is often subject to radical change overnight.

Relatedness

I referred earlier to the assumption of the detached and independent existence of the organization from that of the environment in which it operates. If we perceive our organization as an independent and solitary unit, we deny the intricate and intimate relationship and, indeed the partnership, it has with its environment. Instead the expectation is that organizations have to adapt and conquer a faceless environment.

The separation of the organization from its environment has led to a central theme in the strategy doctrine: the *fit* between the internal capabilities of the organization and that of external opportunities. However, the truth is that organizations are engaged in a relationship of continuous exchange with other organizations and the environment. This creates a complex web of interdependency, contradicting the view of an existence independent from the environment. Therefore, the identity of the organization stems from the reciprocal interdependent relationships in which the organization engages. The act of relating develops the distinctive capabilities of the organization. Without such relationships, these capabilities would not exist nor have any meaning. This demonstrates the importance of both the internal and external relationships in which organizations are engaged.

Furthermore, such relationships are difficult to direct or control. The meaning of an organization is the result of such interactive relationships and the imaginary lines that can be drawn between events, situations and objects. The organization and its environment are therefore the result of *making* as opposed to the *perceiving* of independently existing phenomena. This pattern of continuous action–reaction reflects the underpinning need of the organization to deal with and make sense of the ambiguity and change it constantly faces. The need for an organization to adapt to the trends of an independent environment becomes futile as the organizational actions contribute to the creation of those trends. Furthermore, as the postmodernist perspective advises, those events and trends are open to multiple interpretations leading to choice. Organizations are not the controllers of events, but they have the ability to influence such events through the choices they make.

The postmodern perspective encourages and urges an understanding of the multiple and interdependent relationships in which the organization has its existence. Such relationships are influenced by the diverse nature of the participants in the relationships. Different views of the world represented by either a feminist or culturally diverse perspective bring many influences to bear on the organization.

Denying the existence of the variety inherent in strategic formulation, as has been the tradition, is damaging and deprives the organization of the infinite choices available to it. However, organizational strategy rarely recognizes or gives credence to the value or even existence of such diversity. The result is that decision makers rarely see a complete picture of the world and therefore operate with a blurred image of their perceived reality, influenced by their own preferences, desires and mental pictures of the world.

Accepting a belief that what the organization experiences is as a result of their actions and reflecting on those actions and the paradigms that influence those actions will be paramount. These paradigms and their associated assumptions, will act as filters through which the organization makes sense of future ambiguities and change. Organizational science is based on the assumption that organizations have to be investigated in relation to the independent external environment. This perspective is at the heart of the prescriptive schools of strategy, seeking to match the internal strengths of the organization with the opportunities that exist outside of the organization (Joyce and Woods, 2001): Hence the motivation to uncover the ideal strategy to be pursued under a given set of conditions. The perception of strategy being a science has been vehemently attacked by Mintzberg (1976) who perceives strategy more as an art.

Meta-strategy

Consistent with the above dominant assumptions associated with strategy, is the search for an ultimate strategy akin to the functionalist's search for a meta-narrative: the answer to all of life's questions. As discussed earlier, the assumption is that the ultimate strategy can only be discovered through planning. Organizations devote vast amounts of resources in an attempt to discover the ultimate or meta-strategy that will provide them with the answer to all their questions and ambiguities. However, on closer inspection, the multidimensional nature of strategy formulation reveals the infinite possibilities open to organizations.

There is no one strategy, but many choices and options, each with its own consequences. Such rigidity denies the fluid nature of our polymorphous organizations. The dynamic interactions between the organization, competitors and customers will eventually result in objectives and plans of action, denying the existence of a meta-strategy. Furthermore, an underlying assumption of an ultimate strategy is a sense of dissatisfaction. The current state an organization finds itself in is seen as negative and a state to move away from or to overcome. An ultimate strategy leading to total success is a mirage organizations fruitlessly pursue.

The strategic storyline

Strategy as an act of planning, prediction and control has lost its lustre. Strategy can be seen as fiction determined and created by organizational writers who face the same challenge as other authors do – how to write a compelling and convincing account, one which the readers are willing to support and implement. Whatever story the strategist tells, it is merely one of many story lines, plots and themes.

The importance of the understanding and inclusion of organizational relationships may influence the success of a strategic story and its power of engagement and persuasion rather than the tools of scanning and objective planning organizations so doggedly cling to. Strategic storytellers employ elaborate arguments and narrative tactics to give credibility and persuasiveness to the strategic arguments put forward by them. Increased diversity dictates the need to make a narrative shift from the traditional male-dominated role of the strategic author and to give way to the many voices that will through joint authorship shape and narrate the strategy of the organization. Such narration will by necessity be of a dialogical nature in order to accommodate the diversity of authorship, thereby reflecting the interdependent relationships referred to above.

Organizational knowledge

We can define the strategy of an organization as that of a specific type or uniqueness of knowledge that the organization possesses. It is unique to the organization as no two organizations are the same. However, as I have challenged in this chapter, strategy or the knowledge of the organization, is not the privilege of the senior management. The knowledge or strategy of the organization is the product of the relationships and interactions within and without the organization and is both tacit and explicit. Collectively, members of the organization create a shared understanding through cognitive processes resulting in what we may define as the tangible aspect or strategy of the organization.

The knowledge which forms the basis of an organizational strategy evolves through the process of dealing with and making sense of new stimuli which are then absorbed into the existing knowledge of the organization. It is not the possession of one individual or a small group of individuals, but the property of all within the boundaries of the organization. Knowledge is the culmination of the diverse views and values of the organizational members shared through formal and informal activities and relationships. Creating a winning strategy requires the integration and valuing of such diversity.

Creating reality extemporaneously

Strategy can be compared to the improvization practised by jazz musicians. Improvization comes from a standpoint of working with the unexpected, relinquishing any prior expectations. Of importance to the strategic process is that it surrenders the need for control. Jazz musicians effectively produce a piece of music on the spur of the moment as a result of their collective creative process. They enter this activity without any preconceived ideas or expectations of what the result is likely to be. In addition, the resulting melody may bear no resemblance to the original piece of music with which they may have started off. Drawing on experiences, techniques, interpretations and responsiveness, the musicians collectively create a previously unimagined and improvized melody. So too, the organization collectively creates through improvization the appropriate strategy of the moment.

This would mean that the organization will be able to harness and draw upon the diverse competencies of a much wider representation of the organization than hitherto. The strategy is also likely to assume a meaning that reflects the circumstances and ability of the organization. The strategy of the moment will closer resemble strategy as an emergent phenomenon. The reality is that organizations formulate their strategy after implementation. We can only impose meaning after the event when we are able to review our actions. We can only assign a label to a situation once it has been experienced and we have had the opportunity to reflect on it. Understanding is the outcome of reflection on action that has already taken place, and hence the benefit of hindsight.

Drawing on the analogy of an iceberg, we can conclude that the success of an organization's strategy relies on what lies beneath the surface and not merely on that which we can see. We therefore need to give due attention to the intangibles or the glue that keeps the organization together and not only to the plans and forecasts. The complexity and unpredictability of organizations and their environments challenge the assumption that chief executives and the small teams of senior management are able to formulate strategies based on rational logic and objective analysis. It also challenges the simplistic relationship between problem and solution and therefore planning and implementation.

Organizations are not simplistic by nature, nor are the environments they inhabit. In addition, planning is only possible if we can predict the future or imagine what such a future state might look like. However, the future often brings the unimaginable which makes a mockery of our carefully laid plans.

A common theme emerging from the multitude of studies of complexity is the constant change of competitive landscapes through interaction. Small changes may lead to major consequences and it would be impossible for one individual to be aware of all of the trends and minute changes which could lead to radical events. The theories of complexity to be discussed in Chapter 4, argue for co-evolution above that of a directed and hierarchical approach. Recognizing the value and, indeed, influence each member has on the organization allows the organization to harness the value each one can contribute. Instead of focusing on the control and management of strategies, organizations would benefit more from creating a context within which the organization can evolve and excel. Strategy is the creative outcome of interactive relationships within and without organizations, based on collective reflection and judgement.

4 Strategy and complex adaptive systems

This chapter briefly introduces the ideas of the science of complex adaptive systems. It does not purport to offer an in-depth understanding or critique of the intricate and varied arguments covering the field. Other writers such as Stacey, do so much more eloquently. However, it is a broad introduction to an area of science that has significantly increased its influence on management from both the theoretical and practical perspectives.

Managerial thinking and theories related to organizations have always been influenced by scientific thinking. A recent scientific renaissance which is influencing the way we view organizations is that of complex adaptive systems. Complexity theory can assist us in understanding the nature of unpredictability that is a particular feature of the process of formulating organizational strategies. Both chaos and complexity theories have their origin in the study of natural systems such as weather patterns and biological organisms. One of the key messages of complexity theory is that of non-linearity which we can also perceive within organizations (Tetenbaum, 1998). The difficulty we have is to let go of the linear and predictable thinking of the Newtonian and Cartesian era associated with the Industrial Age. The non-linear path of complexity is the antithesis to predictability and can be considered as the natural, organic way. Rather than describe, complexity guides. Predictability erroneously assumes a stable and direct relationship between the past and the future.

The mechanical view of the world made sense of the Industrial Age, but these truths are no longer applicable to the organic world which is emerging. The dualism of this age persists in influencing our thinking of what is out there and how we can control and compete with it. As discussed in previous chapters, these two are not separate entities, but part of the same process of emergence. The one influences the other which in turn engenders new responses in a process of co-evolution. What we perceive as being out there is subjective and is influenced by our interactions with it. Although from a mathematical and scientific perspective complex systems behave in complex and unpredictable ways, simple underlying equations can be identified. Some writers claim that organizations and their environments are unpredictable and mainly chaotic. Instead of the simple cause-and-effect perspective of the world, complexity requires us to look for patterns and small leverage points.

Traditional theories to strategy advocate that change occurs as a result of the choices made by the senior management. According to the theories of complexity, members of the senior management are not detached observers who can objectively make choices and therefore predict the long-term outcomes of those choices. Instead, they are active participants of the systems, and organizational change emerges not only from choices made but also the responses these choices generate in others, both internal and external to the organization. In fact, change is a natural state for a system to be in and resisting and stifling change leads to stagnation and the ultimate death of the system. Strategy can therefore be perceived as one activity that helps us to deal with the constant state of change that our organizational systems find themselves in. The theories of complexity support a different approach to the management of change and the way we therefore view the strategic process.

A central theme of systems theories is that a system has an inherent propensity towards order and stability. The caveat is that it is sufficiently in touch with and open to interaction with its environment and other systems. Interaction within and without is fundamental. The language of interaction supersedes the language of efficiency. Interaction requires the sharing of meaning and collective sensemaking. Furthermore, the natural state of order can be achieved from a number of different places and is not dependent on the history of the system. Without knowledge or certainty about the future state of the system, local and self-organizing interaction amongst those who compose the system generates new forms. However, this is only possible where diversity is present. Diversity is a key aspect of complexity within an organizational context.

Sustainability of a system is dependent on creativity which is rooted in diversity of all kinds and the willingness to take risks. The emphasis is therefore on the relationships of those within the system rather than the elusive knowledge of the whole. In the quantum world, relationships are more than nice to have, they *are* reality. No one individual or group of individuals controls or defines the behaviour or shape of the overall system. Yet, we persistently attempt to create barriers and metaphorical walls to control what we perceive the chaos out there to be.

Furthermore, complexity theory challenges a fundamental assumption of traditional organizational beliefs, namely that of the detached observer. No member of the organization can step outside of the system, nor can he directly influence or predict the future state of the system. He can only influence it through local interaction with others within the system. Collectively, everyone in the organization is part of a co-creative process which will eventually determine future states. The belief of collectivism is fundamental to complexity theory and promotes an understanding of the relatedness of participants within organizations and, in turn, organizations with their environment.

A further significant theme of complex systems is that order emerges spontaneously in a system. Such order is the result of the collective interaction of those who comprise the system. Fluctuation and change are necessary elements of the very process by which order is created. However, organizations fiercely resist ambiguity and the need for order and control results in a failure to see ambiguity as a precursor for potential and novelty. Yet organizational reality is that of change and uncertainty, and not the illusion of control we console ourselves with.

Organizations tend to be run by those whose reality of organizations does not include variety. For them it is inconceivable that there is a multiplicity of ways in achieving their purpose. In fact, letting go of control will bring it about naturally. Stability is a product of interaction because through interaction we create mutual understanding and a common purpose.

Order can appear quite suddenly, as if by magic, but it results only after numerous small pieces of the whole have set the stage. The participation and interaction of every member of the system is vital, which questions the essence of strategy formulation as an activity reserved for a small group of people. The fittest are not as the popular belief go, those who compete, but in fact those who co-operate.

The new sciences advocate a shift in thinking from perceiving form in terms of structure to thinking of process and the notion that structure is a manifestation of an underlying process. They also recognize that systems often operate at what has been termed the edge of chaos. However, the edge of chaos is not seen as an abyss, but rather a state or condition which holds the potential for innovation and change. Yet, the very essence of strategy is to reduce chaos and uncertainty.

Within this system of co-creation, endless possibilities exist. Potential possibilities emerge if the elements are willing to adapt, learn and co-create with the other elements or players within their system. Innovation is only possible if we are willing to question our existing assumptions and beliefs. Doing what we have always done is a recipe for extinction.

The sacred cows that control our organizations and our behaviours are temporal. They have a shelf life and must therefore constantly be updated. A complex adaptive system is therefore always in the process of unfolding and becoming. It does, however, make prediction of the outcome impossible, as it is difficult to predict how the players within a system are likely to respond to each other. The reality or existence we therefore experience in organizations can be said to emerge from this process of interaction.

Emergence is, however, reliant on the intelligence in every part of a complex system, and within organizations, this would mean not only the intelligence, but the participation of every member within that organization. Together the elements learn through experience from both the other connected elements as well as the system of which they form a part. One can therefore argue that the elements thus connected are accountable for the system that emerges as a result of their individual co-creation. Complexity theory focuses on the relationship the organization has with the environment as well as the dynamics of the internal relationships.

No organization is an island and organizations are interdependent with their environment, not necessarily in the competitive manner that we traditionally associate with organizational relationships, but in a more co-operative manner. The emergent system is truly greater than its parts as the whole has a grasp of a *larger* picture that is unavailable to the parts. Order emerges because of the interaction of all of the members within the system. If we translate this into what it means for the strategic formulation process, we begin to see how important the inclusion of all the members is and more importantly, the diversity they represent.

By marginalizing diversity and restricting the behaviours of people within the organization managers stifle the very source of organizational creativity, namely the collective knowledge of the members of the organization. It is not possible to approach new challenges with old solutions. Organizations need to constantly evolve in their approach to new opportunities and that requires the brainpower of everyone.

The order organizations so persistently try and create through carefully planned and controlled strategies will in fact emerge spontaneously and not because someone or some thing expends energy to create it. Order will inevitably emerge from the natural consequences of interaction of all members in the organization. The theories of complexity advocate a joint responsibility for what we come to understand the organization to be. Every one of us contributes to our organizational environment and that includes a responsibility and the opportunity to share in the direction and ultimate strategy the organization decides to pursue. Collectively everyone in the organization makes sense of the shared environment and the reality experienced. One person or a small group of people can not do that on behalf of the organization. It is very much a joint and participative activity.

We can see how the philosophies and beliefs of complexity theory may challenge the traditional assumptions of how to manage organizations. It will shake the very foundations upon which the whole discipline of strategy formulation is built. Instead of senior management decreeing the strategic direction of the organization, there is a need for a shared understanding of purpose and a clearly communicated set of values – values and purpose which are inclusive of the diversity of the members who compose the organization.

Evolution and co-evolution mean that the organization is not fixed, but constantly changing and evolving. Change is therefore not seen as a necessary state in between periods of stability, but the natural state of the organization. Stability is but the fleeting breath between sighs of change. From a complexity perspective, one may reach the conclusion that the future is truly unknowable and that creative futures emerge unpredictably from self-organizing interactions between members. In addition, learning is part of the constant flow of adaption, experimentation and co-creation within the system as we automatically adjust our understanding and knowledge. Learning is basically our collective way of making sense of the sea of change. Furthermore, through action and experimentation we collectively create reality.

Knowledge and information sharing must be one of the primary preconditions for emergent change. However, information is impossible to pin point or to isolate. It is somewhere within the system and all of the constituents of the system are therefore important in the transference of information. Resistance to thinking or the view that it is the privilege of only the elite few is a hangover from the mechanistic and Newtonian Industrial Age. As with the jazz metaphor, each player takes responsibility for the collective performance of the orchestra. This is achieved through a continuous co-evolutionary process through a convergent interest, namely to collectively create music. In the complex environments of the postmodern organization, the arrogant assumption that one person or a small group of elite managers could know it all hints at delusions of grandeur. The know-how and diversity of everyone is required.

Strategy formulation is very much based on a linear view of the world, but non-linearity is also a part of reality although mostly ignored by science up until recently. The science of quantum physics however, advises that there are no predetermined ends or truths to be discovered. There are only possibilities that will manifest as ideas, depending on what the discoverer focuses on. Probably the reason why we feel uncomfortable with non-linearity is that it is much less easy to predict. Without prediction we feel vulnerable, for it provides us with a life vest.

There is an assumption or hope that through prediction we can in fact dictate what the future should be and how everyone and everything should behave – man (please note!) the ruler of nature. A critical difference is that predictability and linearity is about stasis, stability within what we perceive to be chaos, whereas non-linearity is about movement and change, the very thing we fear and try and avoid at all costs within organizations. Our fear of the unknown and unpredictability stems from the Darwinistic belief that if you do not get it right you die. Life is perceived as competition for limited resources where the fittest will survive. However, life is about innovation, invention and creativity and above all, endless possibilities.

A characteristic of non-linear systems is that small inputs can lead to dramatically large consequences. We have all heard the saying that it is the last straw that broke the camel's back. Unfortunately, we do not know when it will be the last straw or which straw is likely to be the last. Life therefore becomes much more open to possibilities and that requires everyone in the system to participate. It is impossible for one person, or a small group of people, to constantly be aware of the changes in environment, of the trends that may be emerging or to identify small opportunities that could possibly lead to major wins later on. It is impossible for one person or a small group of people, inside or outside of the organization, to determine how the organization will evolve. It is only through interaction at the individual level that the organization emerges.

Complexity appears to be connected to the ability of the system to switch between different modes of behaviour as the environmental conditions change. Such flexibility and adaptability of the system come with the ability to choose. The order we desire to achieve through our planning and control processes actually emerges naturally if the system is left to processes of self-organization. The very foundation upon which management theory and practice is built relies on the existence of control, prediction and planning.

Synonymous with planning and control is measurement. However, in a quantum world the very act of measurement denies us the knowledge and information it sets out to achieve. By measuring, we inadvertently shut the door on possibilities and variety. By challenging these fundamental historical truths of management, we question the very identity of management and organizations as we know it. If we apply complexity theory to human systems such as organizations, we come up against our biases and assumptions held by traditional views of management.

For over 50 years, organizational science has focused on controlling uncertainty and strived to eliminate the unknown. The need for control is a key theme within organizations and with their masculine leaders. Removing the need for a plan and a strategy castrates the manager and makes him feel powerless and useless. How is he supposed to manage if he is not in control? However, in a postmodernist organization power is to be found and identified in a network of relationships that are systematically interconnected and interdependently create order. The world is inherently ordered and does not need us to enforce it. Structures emerge, but only as temporary solutions that in turn facilitate further change. Organizations lack faith that their purpose and vision can be accomplished in various ways and that the most elegant way of achieving it is not to resist change, but to allow transient forms to emerge and disappear. Such a state requires openness and fluidity, but also joint responsibility and from directions that arise from natural processes of growth and self-renewal.

The organizational environment becomes a reality when an organization interacts with it. Abstract planning without interaction and action remains a cerebral activity of conjuring up a world that does not and could not exist until we interact with it. In this way, organizations have the flexibility to create structures that not only fit the moment, but that mean the organization is able to maximize the opportunities that present themselves at a given time. They also means that an organization has the freedom to evolve into different forms so as to create an order best suited to new demands without being locked into a structure that is not fit for its purpose.

The failure to predict does not mean a failure to understand or to explain. Restrictive and outmoded structures are not only physical, but also mental. Outdated mental beliefs and assumptions and preconceived ideas have the same restrictive effect on the organization. As we approach the boundaries of our limiting beliefs, we bump against the edge of our comfort zones which, if we can transcend, guarantee that we will emerge as something more than what we were before we started the journey.

A complex adaptive system is in a continuous state of flow and creativity, of changing and becoming. Change and fluctuations, instead of being avoided, should be embraced as they are the source of innovation and new potential form. The fixation organizations have with predicting the right way or the ultimate strategy denies experimentation or trial and error. The equilibrium we seek through our predictions and control implies an end point, whereas the essence of emergence is in the journey, the endless unfolding.

Emergence is the result of the complex interactions within the organization, which as we have seen, are impossible to control or predict. The lifeblood of emergence is the flow of information which includes knowledge of patterns, collective sensemaking and ways of learning. We continue to persist with the futility of exercising control on the organization and its people and restricting the flow of information and sharing through structures and lack of trust. Yet the organizational reality is that organizations live with the paradox of control and chaos.

Equilibrium within systems thinking inevitably leads to the death of the system (Waldrop, 1992; Kauffman, 1995) and is not supportive of movement or experimentation. The system therefore becomes unable to adapt to a changing environment. Control is not only unnecessary, but it also strangles creativity and starves the system of the options open to it through serious play and experimentation. It does not follow that by letting go of control we invite chaos. It is about allowing patterns to emerge and possibilities to be identified, which had not existed before.

A key element of experimentation and the robustness the system develops is its ability to harness the inherent diversity. Diversity ensures that the system is able to recognize and match the complexity of the environment in which it operates. Diversity is to be encouraged within organizations, not marginalized. Control is highly dispersed and coherent behaviour within the system arises from competition and co-operation among the participants within the system. The paradox of co-operation and competition is a phenomenon which seems to be characteristic of industries. Whilst competition encourages specialization and innovation, co-operation provides joint advantages such as shared infrastructures or sharing of cost and risk.

5 Breaking the mould

Many of the Western business models and theories we continue to practice in organizations and teach in Business Schools are outdated products of a bygone era. They are representative of a time when the white male minority dominated and diversity did not even exist in the minds or vocabulary of the organization. The very structures of our organizations, leadership styles and practices are women and cultural diversity unfriendly. They are governed by practices that suit and have suited the white male who has not had the responsibilities or practices of other minority groups. The one size does not fit all and to accommodate diversity, organizations have to question and address outdated and inflexible working practices.

In a global competitive market place, to remain successful requires international expansion. The value of an organization is increasingly measured by the success of its international activities. International success requires an understanding and inclusion of diversity. Statistics continue to emphasize the need for organizations to have a much more diverse workforce if they are to ensure their success in the future. The emphasis is on having the most talented people within the senior team and that includes women and members from cultural groups other than the traditionally male-dominant group.

Those who dismiss the importance of cultural diversity draw particularly on two erroneous claims that permeate organizations. The first claim is that the world is getting smaller and cultures are therefore merging. However, anyone who has lived or worked in a culture other than the culture of his birth will know that the influence of culture is as powerful and submerged as the currents of the ocean. The recent crisis in the EU community is further proof that cultures are by no means merging and strong differences remain. The second claim put forward is that management is management irrespective of the cultures we represent. This is an assumption that is in itself based on cultural assumptions and, in particular, the scientific management ideas that so strongly influenced management in the early twentieth century. It is a further example where organizations from one culture invade other cultures with their business philosophies and ideologies with the erroneous belief that if it works in one culture, it is automatically right for another culture.

However, the transactional masculine approach is to ignore diversity and to bully everyone into conformity – conformity reflecting the opinion and beliefs of the dominant group. Despite the long history of legislation in various Western countries, equal opportunities remain a myth for women, for people with disabilities and for minorities from ethnic groups. Women and other minority groups face discrimination and bias leading to barriers in career advancement. The white fist continues to strangle the throat of diversity, silencing its cry. The ideals, both political and social, which govern our lives are the ideals of this elite group. Is it surprising therefore that minority groups remain cynical about the tokenism to equal opportunities organizations attempt to introduce?

I once again draw inspiration from science to support the need for not only acknowledging diversity within our organizations, but also to actively draw on the benefits diversity brings. The benefits of sexual reproduction above that of asexual reproduction is that by reshuffling our genetic material, we avoid the dangers of uniformity. Genetic variation allows a species to cope better with a changing environment and may prevent extinction. That should act as a jolt to those who continue to resist anything that is different from their entrenched ways and views of the world. Diversity allows an organization to increase and expand its knowledge of competitors, markets, customers, investors and other vital matter necessary for organizational survival. However, diverse communities remain unrepresented at the board level, which continues to be dominated by the male minority as the statistics reveal only too clearly.

There are many dimensions of diversity such as locations, gender, culture, age, industry experience, occupation and values and beliefs. We are not uni-dimensional and Gergen purports in his many writings on social constructionism that we are composed of multiple identities (Gergen, 1991; Sim, 2000b). However, a multiplicity of identities also leads to a multiplicity of discrimination. Women who may be experiencing domestic violence may feel reluctant to report such abuse as they may face a different kind of discrimination outside their domestic situation.

Whatever forms of difference we care to name, the underlying assumption of difference has always meant inferior and less equal. Those of us outside the inner circle, such as female managers, collude in maintaining the status quo by our silence and failure to challenge our organizations. Many women would react quite strongly to being identified as women and how their careers may or may not have been hindered or helped by the fact that they are women, preferring to see themselves as 'persons'. Of course, as a woman you are a person, but you can not change the fact that you are a female person. This denial of our diversity and difference keeps discrimination alive and well as the recognition of the value of others remain uncelebrated.

It is a taboo within organizations to talk about the advantages and privileges men have over women, and women themselves play a role in the collusion and perpetuation of the taboo. The result is that the occupation of men within positions of power, remain protected at the expense of women. Although we are taught about the negativity of discrimination, we are not necessarily taught about the advantages of being white. Equally, we have not been taught to recognize the advantages enjoyed by men in all areas of society, organizations being no exception.

The political correctness of our society prevents an understanding of diversity and the value different groups can bring to organizational debates. The understanding of different beliefs is enhanced by the opportunity to challenge the beliefs and assumptions of diverse groups. The reasons for avoiding the acknowledgement of one's difference other than being a 'person' are valid in some cases as one might have to look for another job if one publicly opposes the opinions of the senior management of the organization. Nevertheless, it amounts to collusion and the maintenance of the status quo. This is, of course, one aspect of a complex web of interaction within the organization.

Organizations are very hostile and unfriendly places for diversity. If one has any needs outside the norm of the dominant male minority, organizations are experienced as very rigid. For example, anyone who has care responsibilities for family members knows the difficulty of fitting in around the rigid hours of work. We have dabbled with flexible hours within organizations, but it has mainly been superficial and at the margins and does not offer any real flexibility for anyone outside of the norm.

For any organization that operates in the international arena, an understanding of cultural differences is vital. However, the frameworks available to both academics and organizations to facilitate such understanding are not gender specific. Globalization puts pressures on national cultures, creating changes in long-held values and beliefs. Proponents of cultural dimensions, such as the well-known model by Hofstede, do not identify gender differences within their cultural dimensions. However, much of our mental programming is determined by the fact of whether we were born as male or female.

In developing countries, the rules are very much made by the men whereas in developed countries, the changes in economic conditions have resulted in a reconsideration of the role of women. Culture is a significant factor to be considered when addressing the success of women in business. In some cultures, women are at a distinct disadvantage without any or with little career prospects, no matter how competent or intelligent they may be.

Many women continue to find themselves suppressed in low-wage and often abusive jobs due to cultural beliefs of class and gender roles. Legislation has indeed brought pressure to bear on organizations to address the gender equality balance. Although the changes that have taken place over recent years have greatly impacted on the roles of women in society, they have, in my opinion, not gone far enough.

Many industries continue to be dominated by men or masculine characteristics, expressed by either gender, at the expense of a more feminine approach. The legal profession in the UK recently announced tentative steps towards addressing the imbalance of representation at the Bar. There are virtually no minority groups of any kind represented. How can an institution that claims to serve the nation and communities within that nation so totally lack in the representation of the communities they purportedly serve? Many institutions and industries reflect the same imbalance.

Not many multinational organizations recognize the fact that their competitive success depends on their most talented people being included in the senior management team. The most talented people are also to be found within the ranks of the minorities. The low representation of diverse groups at senior management level reflects the denial of diversity within organizations. The denial of diversity reflects an ethnocentric approach to leadership reflecting a belief that the minority view is the only view. The discomfort with diversity is reflected in early science, which perceived diversity as a disease and then set out to find the cause and subsequent cure for such diversity.

Statistics reveal dramatic changes to demographics and predict that by the year 2008 the new workers of the majority of countries will in fact comprise people from groups currently classed as minorities, such as women and minorities from ethnic groups. The ruling class of white, middle-aged men is dying out. This must act as a wake-up call to organizations that have, up until now, at best shown a passing interest the diversity debate, using it as a public relations exercise, or at worst totally ignored it. The shift in demographics has got to mean changes to business models and strategies.

However, despite the obvious necessity for substantially increasing diversity within organizations and the benefits of diversity, organizations remain resistant to it and will only pay attention to diversity if the bottom line is visibly affected by it. Diversity does in fact positively impact the bottom line as it helps the organization maintain a competitive edge. Diversity also improves corporate culture and enhances employee retention. A diverse workforce also ensures that the organization is in touch with the communities it aims to serve. Needless to say, a diverse workforce ensures creativity and allows organizations to recruit the best and the brightest. For organizations who continue to ignore the need for diversity, the result is a loss of business in growing and changing markets. Creating a single work ethic among a diverse workforce is indeed a challenging prospect for an organization, but to ignore diversity is not the answer, and it can only reduce the competitive nature of a business.

As I mentioned before, cultural values and upbringing play a significant role in our attitudes towards equality and diversity. Most cultures have constraints and social inequalities even though they are often unconscious. Social groups collectively construct what the group will perceive as being valuable. However, these values may and certainly do change over time. An example is the older workforce. In Eastern cultures, the older generation is almost revered for their wisdom and knowledge, whereas in Western cultures in particular, older workers are discriminated against in favour of youth and attractive physical appearance. Many people will testify that if you lose your job over the age of 45, you will find it very difficult in securing another permanent position. The excuse is normally that you are too experienced which is shorthand for being too old and expensive.

The suppression of diversity within organizations is as a result of avoiding disagreements and ensuring conformity. Cooperative and collaborative behaviour may be easy to manage, but it does not encourage differences of opinion and opportunities to challenge traditional assumptions and behaviours within organizations. The very nature of diversity creates new opportunities. Diversity within organizations is too often seen as a problem that needs to be eliminated rather than as a rich vein of new ideas and new choices.

Within society and the institutions of society, systems have evolved to create and protect the privileges of men. The old-boy network is one such example, which ensures the promotion and inclusion of men in the most inner sanctums of power. These systems provide men with unearned opportunities and privileges and put women and other minority groups at an immediate disadvantage. Such male hegemony opens doors of opportunity for men whilst keeping them firmly shut to outsiders. When challenged, and all arguments exhausted, the eventual fall back will be that evolution or religion has meant that men are the chosen and natural leaders and providers, placing women in the supportive and nurturing roles. Such privileges are not only assigned to race and sex as examples, but also to physical ability, religion and sexual orientation. Heterosexual couples enjoy many privileges denied to homosexual couples.

Masculinity is synonymous with power, whoever may express it. The expected behaviour of those in power is toughness, dominance, competitiveness, assertiveness and being in control. To be anything else is perceived as weakness. Exhibiting such dominant masculine characteristics has always been equated with success. The result is that men have always been overrepresented in positions of power and decision making. Social constructionism challenges the biological rights associated with being male and views their dominant systems as the product of social relations. Furthermore, a social constructionist perspective removes the inevitability of dominance by one group over another. It does however consider the contribution of everyone in society in maintaining the status quo and in order to create a new social order, requires the participation and responsibility of both men and women.

Discrimination and extreme harassment against homosexuals, bisexuals and transgendered people remains a very powerful force in society and organizations. In some societies, discrimination ranges from instant dismissal to murder once their sexual orientation is discovered. Many organizations are adopting anti-discrimination policies. However, as I mention elsewhere, you can not legislate against the hearts and minds of people, and discrimination remains in both overt and covert ways.

Our cultures socially construct the beliefs and values we carry around with us and which influence our behaviours within organizations. Our cultural influences are very strong even if we travel and work across cultures. It is true to say that most cultures assign women to what is perceived as inferior roles to that of men and perceive women to be submissive to men. In some cultures that is taken to the extreme with women not being allowed the opportunities of an education nor participation in the workforce. Women who do not obey the laws laid down by men are often abused to the point of death.

There are numerous strategies organizations can employ in dealing with diversity. The first approach is dismissive of difference and guided by a belief that everyone wants to be equal. It is a numbers game and the success of the diversity policy of the organization is measured by way of numbers. Difference is not at all understood or valued, but the organization accepts the notion of fairness towards all. The second approach is an acknowledgement that minority groups represent profitable opportunities for organizations and employing members of such minority groups will ensure access to these profitable niche markets, such as the pink dollar and latterly the grey dollar. However, very few organizations have a true acceptance and understanding of the value of diversity for learning, creativity and innovation.

Our societies observe the physical matter that people are comprised of and then place them into various categories such as race and gender. We then assign characteristics to them based on our expectations and beliefs as to the nature of those groups. These include our beliefs about their abilities, intelligence and expected behaviour based on those categories we have assigned them to. We therefore expect women to be caring, fat people to be jolly, men to be aggressive, black people from Africa to be good at athletics, people with disabilities to be incapable of holding down a responsible job, older people to be slow and out of touch with the modern world, people from the Indian sub-continent to be excellent shop keepers, young people hanging around to be yobs and up to no good and in the West, leaders to be white, middle-aged men!

We therefore draw unequivocal assumptions about people and their abilities, preferences and place in society based on the bodies they occupy. The meanings we assign to these bodies contribute to the inequalities and lower status of some groups in comparison to others, thereby excluding them from certain domains in society. Our assumptions will in turn influence what we notice and the interpretations we assign to what we notice. Our individual assumptions are not a description of the world, but merely our own interpretations of a small part of the world we inhabit.

6 Cultural diversity

Members of a particular cultural group create a meaning system which assists them in adapting to their particular cultural group and helps them to function effectively within that group. Collectively, the group develops a language, values, norms, art and expectations as to the behaviour of individuals. Cultural groups develop their own particular themes such as individualism or collectivism which influence the individual and collective behaviour of the culture.

Within our cultures, we create assumptions that go unquestioned. They dominate how we view the world and the role of people within that world. The role of women varies from culture to culture and in some cultures, women are literally slaves to the males within their culture. In these cultures, the lives of women have very little value, other than how well they serve men. Our cultures programme us to assign meanings to the behaviours of people. Differences are often a source of conflict and miscommunication across cultures.

The way many organizations choose to deal with cultural and gender differences is to ignore them. Rather than celebrating differences and integrating the value of differences for the benefit of the organization, they assume there is only one way of doing things. Normally that way is the way of men, leadership being an example. The result is that everyone is treated the same. To a certain extent, women contribute to the situation as their unconscious fear is that should they be seen as different, they will automatically be seen as inferior to men, particularly when judged against masculine measurements. The denial of difference in turn denies the organization the value such difference brings to organizations. However, organizations that recognize the value of difference do so not because those that are different are successful in behaving like white middle-aged men, but because they behave as themselves and therefore contribute a different perspective.

Many organizational texts advocate that knowledge is the most important element in creating and sustaining competitive advantage. It is a logical conclusion therefore that organizations operating internationally have to equally embrace international knowledge. A further logical conclusion is that such knowledge has to extend beyond the knowledge of the ruling minority who continue to run most larger and international organizations. I mentioned earlier that the law of requisite variety demands the same level of complexity within the organization as that to be found outside of the organization if it is to deal with the external complexity effectively and creatively. The knowledge and learning that organizations acquire through cultural diversity helps them to maintain their competitive position in the international arena.

The denial and suppression of differences make it easier for organizations to deal with diversity. However, this leads to a denial of many opportunities for collective learning. In turn, our learnt culture shapes and influences our behaviour. If we look at culture from a constructionist perspective, culture can be perceived as something we create together within the groups we belong to. There is an ethnocentric tendency in some cultures to expect their particular cultural ways to represent people in general and their behaviour to be seen as the 'right' way of behaving in given situations. Every one of us embodies beliefs from our respective cultures and the norms of the various groups we belong to and our beliefs are further complicated by our own personal experiences.

The knowledge organizations are able to create and disseminate across their structures is what competition is all about in contemporary organizations. Harnessing cultural diversity supports the process of knowledge creation. A key aspect of knowledge creation is that it is a collective activity and to marginalize diversity is therefore to deny the organization access to an enormous amount of knowledge. Where we hold on to knowledge as sacred, it leads to grooved thinking which means any new perspective or way of thinking will merely bounce off the fortress walls of existing knowledge and rigid behaviour. New perspectives and ways of approaching organizational activities will simply not penetrate these impenetrable walls. No group or culture can claim to possess pure or superior knowledge, but each diverse perspective contributes to the collective body of knowledge.

However, organizational knowledge remains overwhelmingly the interpretations and knowledge of the dominant group, at the senior levels in particular because that is where diversity is the least represented. The underlying assumption within organizations is that knowledge is both universal and unitary and that cultural, gender and other diversity are put to one side. Within an international organization, the acquisition and sharing of knowledge are generated by cross-cultural teams and networks. Globalization demands new ways of working and challenges many of the traditions which have dominated organizations in the past. The only way new practises will be achieved is to harness the wealth of knowledge diversity offers.

Cultural beliefs clearly influence both the practice and the research of management. Each culture has its own beliefs and assumptions as to what constitutes management. Often, groups or individuals from one country find that their beliefs are not easily transferable to another cultural group without adapting to the norms of that particular culture. Management theories tend to be dominated by the American culture. However, globalization requires the ability to hold and integrate a multiplicity of perspectives without any one necessarily being perceived as superior.

The recognition and acceptance of differences do not come easy to some cultures or some groups within cultures. I am here referring to North American cultures and the dominant group of men who run North American organizations. This assumption is based on my own experiences of working for North American companies and also the vast evidence from organizational literature. This group does not necessarily have the breadth of experience and exposure to other cultures that European managers have. It could be argued that diversity is not necessarily accepted at home where sameness and equality is advocated. It is impossible to separate management and organizations from the societies within which they operate. They are influenced by the cultural norms, politics and religion of those societies, which will influence the rules by which those organizations will be managed.

The differences in our respective cultural groups can be observed by the behaviours, practices and rituals we express. These cultural artefacts are there for all to see. However, what is of significance are the values and beliefs of our cultures that lead to the creation of these behaviours and practices in the first place. These are further influenced by the assumptions and mindsets of our cultures and are the powerful influencers and drivers of how we perceive the world and our place within that world. An important fact about the behaviours we observe is that different behaviours have different meanings within cultures. To complicate matters even further, the additional groups we belong to such as gender, locations, religion and interest groups all add to differences of behaviours, values and beliefs. Interpreting the behaviours of others according to the meanings assigned to them in our own cultures leads to misunderstandings and discrimination.

The meanings of rituals are hugely underestimated, particularly by the Western mentality. This is particularly evident within organizations where the assumption is that business is business first and foremost and that culture does not and should not interfere with this activity. Such an erroneous assumption has cost many organizations dearly and the denial of cultural differences within the making of business has had a significant impact on the success of organizations and therefore the bottom line.

The cultural artefacts we observe in different cultures are powerful expressions of the underlying assumptions and beliefs of those cultures. They are also very powerful in maintaining the status quo and discrimination that may be part of a particular culture. I am thinking in particular of dress code. Anglo women tend to dress in a very masculine way in order to blend in and be as visually representative of the dominant group as possible. The French find this perplexing and consider Anglo women to be 'masculine'. However, an Anglo woman who wants to be taken seriously within her organization will never dream of dressing in the way of women within a French or Latin organization, who consider personal style to be important. Dress code is just one example of how different cultures approach the whole notion of work and business.

The assumptions and belief systems of our cultures therefore influence how we approach business, tasks and the management of people. Our internal and external relationships are also subject to the influence of our cultural beliefs. This affects whether we operate in a hierarchical society and if so, what the pecking order is within that hierarchy. In some cultures, the building of relationships take precedence over business. In fact, you will not consider doing business with a stranger. This is so alien to the beliefs of the Anglo culture which clearly separates business from personal relationships. In masculine cultures, the emphasis is on competitiveness, assertiveness, promotion and materialism as opposed to a feminine culture that values the well-being of people expressed through welfare programmes. These opposing values will lead to the creation of very different types of organizations and associated business activities.

It is also necessary to take into account the sub-cultures within cultures and the differences amongst these sub-cultures. On the other hand, some regional sub-cultures may have stronger similarities with cultures from other countries. Furthermore, the complex layer of cultures is added to by our genders, personalities, religions, organizational cultures, functional cultures as well as strong professional cultures. These cultures all influence behaviour and dictate as to what is considered appropriate behaviour.

It is interesting how society will dictate which professions, for example, are more valued than others. Such value will influence the status assigned to individuals of that particular profession and indeed the financial rewards attributed to them. In addition, it also dictates who will and will not be allowed entry into such professions. Entrepreneurs are the new heroes and frontier men in American culture. I deliberately emphasize men, as the hero role in this culture has been dominated by the masculine, cowboy image of what a hero should look like. In other cultures, entrepreneurs are perceived as pushy and not necessarily to be trusted. No matter how successful you may become in France, if you do not have the appropriate education you will never quite have made it.

Management training and development is used by organizations, consciously or unconsciously, to not only provide consistent technical or conceptual skills amongst its managers, but also as a way of creating a company-wide mentality. Such a company-wide mentality is heavily culture biased and not necessarily transferable across all cultures. Organizations tend to accept the fact that they can expect cultural differences when operating abroad, albeit begrudgingly for some. However, at home we expect the foreigner to abide by our rules and integrate with the dominant group. Having said that, colonialism is an example of members of one culture having invaded another and forcing their perceived superior culture on that of the host culture whether this was wanted it or not.

Many organizations are moving towards self-managed teams and many of those teams are multicultural. It is important for those teams to manage not only their tasks and outputs, but also the process of being a team. The definition and purpose of a team will vary significantly across cultures. Successfully integrated and performing teams, especially multicultural teams, do not just happen, and are fraught with conflicts and frustrations. If groups from diverse cultures and backgrounds can overcome and value their differences, they are far more able to generate alternatives than teams from mono-cultures.

A truly global mindset requires the ability to recognize, appreciate and learn from the diversity of others. As well as differences, there will also be similarities. A global mindset requires a level of comfort with ambiguity, recognizing that there is more than one way of doing things and developing a capability of peripheral vision. It is interesting that we actually get to know ourselves and our own cultures better by exploring and learning to understand and appreciate the differences of others. Finally, diversity starts at the top. If the senior managers remain from the same mould, the organization is unlikely to encourage and value diversity other than as a public relations exercise.

Making sense of our environment

The groups we belong to, whether that be our cultural or gender groups, create a meaning system which helps us to make sense of our world. According to Weick, the process of making sense of our world and our organizations is an ongoing conversation without beginning and end. Our societies, including our organizations, are therefore products of our ongoing sensemaking processes. Sensemaking is the process through which we reduce the complexity of our environment to a level we can understand and accept. It is therefore a meaning creating activity through which information, insights and ideas coalesce into something useful or come together in a meaningful way. An important element of sensemaking is that it is a collective and shared activity. The members of an organization collectively make sense of their organizational events.

Thinking about sensemaking as an ongoing process is also to see reality as an ongoing and flowing activity. As different groups and cultures will arrive at different realities through their own sensemaking activities, the idea of an ultimate reality or truth is therefore challenged. Identity is a core preoccupation in the sensemaking process and as sensemaking is an ongoing activity, then so too is the discovery and creation of identity. Our individual identities are also closely linked with the groups we belong to and how others may perceive those groups. The sensemaker is influenced and shaped by what is external, which in turn is influenced by the sensemaking process of the sensemaker. We therefore both shape and react to our environment. In fact, our interpretation of what we perceive the reality of our environment to be is probably more powerful than the environment itself.

Sensemaking is a retrospective act and meaning is always imposed after the event when action is available for review. A situation can only be named and labelled once it has been experienced and reflected upon. Understanding is the result of reflection on action that has already taken place. Furthermore, actions can only be known once they have been completed. We base our current thinking and beliefs on what we have experienced in the past. This will in turn act as filters in determining what we notice and become conscious of in the future. The context within which we make sense of our world is also an important factor as it has a strong influence on sensemaking and what we will experience as reality.

As discussed in the previous chapter, the social and cultural contexts provide the norms and standards by which we measure new experiences. When there are differences of opinion as to what constitutes common events, conflict results. New information will, therefore, reinforce and deepen existing patterns and beliefs. In societies and organizations where information is treated as sacred, routines and grooved thinking will prevent the society or organization from processing new information and adapting past knowledge to accommodate changed circumstances.

Presumed events are given substance when enacted upon through faith. We experience what we believe reality to be thereby creating our own self-fulfilling prophecies of the world and others. As we act out what we believe the prophecy to be, we create the event according to our faith and what our perception of reality is. As the sensemaking process is set in motion, it confirms the faith through the effect it has on our actions which in turn confirm what we had only previously envisioned or believed in. We discover and experience the reality we expect. We also discover and experience people and groups of people in the same way. We assign characteristics and expectations to individuals based on the culture or group they represent. We then interpret their behaviour in a way that reinforces our expectations and biases about them. Women and minorities are constantly subjected to such interpretation of their behaviours, as we will discuss in other chapters. Sensemaking is therefore about plausibility, creation and invention, and is not reliant on accuracy.

As part of the sensemaking in organizations, we create roles and social networks within organizations which in turn generate scripts and expectations that help shape the reality we experience in our organizational lives. These roles and scripts are overtly and covertly gender based. When there is a change from the norm, ambiguity results as the familiar scripts and roles are no longer able to deal with the change and we then need to engage in a renewed process of sensemaking to integrate the change. New ways of thinking, behaving and acting sometimes take time to integrate as our old scripts have been with us for a long time and are comfortable and familiar. As men and women, we have for so long acted according to the roles assigned to us by society that it will take time to rewrite the scripts.

We develop highly structured knowledge or meaning systems also called a schema, in order to manage and deal with multiple information-processing demands. Such a schema helps us to interpret the world around us, including our organizations and also generates appropriate behaviours without having to devote much conscious thought to it. They provide the rules by which we deal with information. Our schemas evolve as a result of our experiences and interactions with others in our social environment. Schemas thereby provide a readymade knowledge system for the interpretation and storing of new information. Our schemas assume the status of reality and we rarely question their validity. We use our schemas to make judgements about ourselves, others and the world around us without much forethought and question whether there may be a different way of perceiving all around us. Through the process of organizational sensemaking, a shared understanding of values and assumptions emerges, and is established over time by the members of the organization. These values and assumptions will encourage certain behaviours that are seen as being for the benefit of the organization through conformity.

In society and organizations, it is necessary for a consensual agreement as to what is seen as real and what is illusory. We then collectively create an organizational grammar that acts as rules and conventions which guide and determine the behaviours and social processes within the organization and which the members of the organization can subscribe to. Organizations with access to varied images and vivid words will be more adaptive in their sensemaking than organizations with a limited vocabulary. The richness of the sensemaking process is dependent on the ability to embrace novelty and an expanded vocabulary, leading to increased possibilities and choices, hence the need for the inclusion and acceptance of diversity at all levels of the organization.

7   The silent voice of feminism

The traditional role model representing a successful manager encompasses aggression and a competitive, forceful, self-confident, logical and independent nature, plus a high need for control. No wonder women don't seem to fit the bill as female managers are perceived as being submissive, nurturing, illogical, emotional and with a much lower need for control. Not only do such stereotypes put women at a disadvantage in the eyes of men, but it erodes the way women see themselves and their ability to perform as effectively as men.

There is much evidence in the literature that women's performance measurement suffers from gender bias. Their competence is often denied or negated due to the stereotypical assumptions applied to women and their ability to match the expected qualities associated with certain male-dominated roles. Even if a woman has demonstrated her competence in managing a 'man's work', she is still likely to suffer from biased judgements and have less promotional opportunities than her male colleagues. Not only are gender stereotypes descriptive, but they are also prescriptive. The result is that specific norms and behaviours are ascribed to how women and men are expected to be as well as not be.

Many organizational activities such as strategy and the management of change have hardly been researched from a gender perspective. Such organizational activities within organizations are dominated from a male perspective. Women and their differing approach are given the rare token mention. An implicit assumption as to what is perceived the 'right' way of managing dominates in organizations and goes unchallenged. The 'right' way is associated with the masculine transactional way and women play a role in colluding to maintain it as being the only way.

Most organizational assumptions and theories have their origin in a masculine perspective. Is it therefore surprising that women experience real barriers in achieving equal status? The different perspectives women represent are more often than not ignored, to the point that a female perspective is not given acknowledgement or taken seriously.

Organizations are historically designed by men for men, dominated by male values and goals and the male career pattern of long hours and very little, if any, time off for family commitments. These values continue to dominate organizations and those involved in the recruitment of senior managers. On the other hand, there is no typical working pattern identified for women. This may also be another motivating factor in women becoming entrepreneurs. By running their own businesses, they have greater flexibility in designing a career path to suit their lifestyle. Although, even within the small business literature, we once again come up against the fact that business owners are perceived as being male, with women business owners virtually being ignored. This assumption raises barriers for women when seeking support limiting the entry of women into enterprise. With organizations adopting changes to traditional practices such as flatter organizational structures and a more team-managed approach, this might be the time and opportunity to rewrite the traditional male-dominated career model.

Historically, career progression was seen as linear with the person moving through the ranks in a predictable manner through variously related jobs which led to increased prestige and financial reward. The need for flexibility to allow for responsibilities outside of a career does not feature at all. Biases such as these put women at a disadvantage with men when competing for more senior positions.

In recent years, there has been a negative connotation associated with the term *feminism*. This is reflected in the decline of attention gender issues have received over the last few decades. This may very well be attributed to groups who do not wish to see women escape the boxes they have been placed in, thereby threatening the status quo and their positions of power. Women themselves feel that in order to get on in their organizations, they should not be labelled as feminists and admit that they change the way they manage in order to be accepted within the dominant organizational paradigm, which I will argue is dominated by a masculine perspective. However, gender discrimination is alive and well in society and in organizations.

Equally, the lack of a feminine representation in subjects such as strategy within academia is probably because Universities reflect the same lack of diversity at senior level than what organizations do. Furthermore, as with the practice, certain subjects are assumed to be the exclusive property of men. The gender blindness within business schools mirrors the male domination of organizations and the world of work. The institution where managers therefore come to learn and discover new ways of managing reinforces male paradigms of management and leadership rather than challenging outmoded models and beliefs. The academic literature on management activities such as strategy and leadership continue to reinforce gender blindness. Traditional literature is dominated by male perspectives, reinforcing male paradigms. The output of business schools, whether in teaching, research or publications, reinforce the paradigm that management and leadership equal male.

Not only is the road to positions of seniority for women an arduous journey, but if they do make it to such positions, they earn considerably less than their male counterparts. Role socialization continues to influence and restrict the roles women assume in their lives and in particular their careers. This process continues within organizations and we soon learn which roles are acceptable for women and which are not, thereby restricting our career choices. The domain of senior management remains a role very few women manage to achieve. However, women collude with men in perpetuating the myth that women are less competent than men in some careers, especially those associated with the hard sciences and as we have seen, science has played a major role in the shaping of management. This myth is reinforced by women creating self-fulfilling prophecies due to their lack of self-efficacy which is seen as important in high achievement. If women are then also socialized to be 'nice girls' and not to be too loud and forward, they will not have the same sense of self-belief as men who are socialized to be brash and forward.

Organizational cultures continue to reinforce a culture whereby corporate masculinity is a requirement of senior management, whether you are male or female. It is true that the number of women running businesses, particularly small enterprises, is growing, but nevertheless, organizations remain patriarchal domains.

The conceptualization of the role of women within society and organizations remains firmly rooted in outdated beliefs and creates conflict for both women and for those who make decisions that will influence their careers. The perception of the role of women influences the lack of international assignments offered to women, for example.

Women continue to receive conflicting messages as they grow up and my personal experience testifies to that. Many women are taught by their parents to be independent and strong-minded, able to make up their own minds, but on the other hand, they would dismiss certain activities or careers as being the domain of men. Furthermore, as you grow up, these characteristics of assertiveness, intelligence and speaking your own mind are perceived as less feminine and therefore discouraged. The tension of role conflict is then inevitable based on the beliefs women have of themselves as well as the weight of the beliefs held by their societies.

The perceived incompatibility of work and family roles remains a significant factor for women who aspire to fulfil their career ambitions, burdens men do not normally have to wrestle with. There remains an unspoken assumption that a woman will only work, and do any other activities for that matter, if the day-to-day management of the household is taken care of. The traditional routine of work and weekend relaxation, is designed around the lives of men and does not suit the responsibilities of women if they have childcare responsibilities. However, flexible working arrangements or part-time work is seen as inferior and in many instances deprives women of rights associated with 'normal' career patterns. That which is perceived as a normal day's work does not include domestic work. Women will not be able to claim complete equality with men until their levels of income are comparable with that of men and there is a true and equal partnership in the sharing of childcare and household labour.

According to Greer (1999), the imbalance related to the division of labour between men and women reflects the fact that not only do women do all of the work in human reproduction, but they have, throughout history and in numerous cultures, also done all the hard labour. Whilst man has tradition-ally been the hunter, the female has been burdened by the daily drudgery of taking care of future generations and the responsibility associated with the feeding and sheltering of the tribe. Women continue to be burdened with heavy and repetitive labour in many cultures. Greer also reinforces the fact that much of women's work remains outside the realm of what is perceived as work and remains hidden as unpaid contribution to societies. Furthermore, unpaid work is heavily gender biased. Greer (1999: 127) argues that 'Women are worker bees; males are drones'. The male of the animal kingdom is much less busy than the females. However, the male with the colluding support of the female, has created the myth that he is the real worker and that what the female does is not real work, but merely supportive of the real work being carried out by the male.

Social capital is defined as social networks and the associated trust that results from such connections. It is such networks that are perceived as key in coordinating and achieving goals and objectives. It is seen as creating collaboration, commitment and facilitating the sharing of information, lead-ing to greater success and effectiveness of an organization. Social connections are seen as a prerequisite in achieving individual and group success. Organizations with high levels of social capital also share common frames of reference amongst those within the network. Research further suggests that the success of an individual within an organization relies as much on his ability to access social capital within the organization as on his human capital which consists of education, skills and experience. Human capital contributes more to career success at the lower levels of the organization whereas social capital is associated with success at the senior level of the organization and career advancement.

Positions in manufacturing and operations for example are often denied women managers, which, women find later on, excludes them from the upper ranks. A significant factor in utilizing social capital for career advancement is in gaining membership status of networks. Networks allow individuals to establish their connection with others and to develop a sense of belonging and recognition from colleagues. Networks also engender loyalty and commitment amongst the members of that particular network.

Being a successful member of an organization requires the individual to understand the organizational values and norms which are achieved through membership of organizational networks. The stark reality for women is that they continue to have little access to those networks and contacts that are necessary for advancement and positions of power. Exclusion denies women the access to the benefits connection to such networks brings, these being valuable information and support. These male-dominated networks consider anyone different from themselves as being outsiders and through exclusion deny them legitimacy within the organization. One way of gaining entry to such an exclusive club is to be introduced by a sponsor. The support of a sponsor is fundamental to women reaching the senior levels of an organization and thereby access to the inner sanctum.

For women to become truly liberated and with access to the same opportunities as men, there will have to be a significant shift in the beliefs of society regarding the perceived roles and positions of women and men. Barriers which include sexist attitudes and racism continue to create obstacles for women in their pursuit of career goals. Men have traditionally been supported and nurtured during their careers by role models and mentors. Many successful senior managers cite the importance of a mentor as part of their success.

Having access to a mentor is an often-quoted barrier for women. This is due to the fact that informal networks are based on racial and gender lines thereby reinforcing the divide. Having successful role models or being the protégée of someone who has gone before remains a limited option for women and they are often excluded from such mentoring due to the old boys' network. Women who rise to the top of their professions get there very much on their own steam and as the statistics reveal, remain in the minority. To find yourself outside of the inside group makes it much more difficult to achieve success and recognition.

A cognitive gender difference we observe and which influences management roles in particular is that of competitive achievement styles. Men tend to score higher on these whereas women score higher on the cooperative achievement styles (Farmer *et al.*, 1997). The debate as to whether it is due to nature or nurture will not be solved here. However, a significant factor worth mentioning is that since men dominate senior management roles, the acceptable management style continues to be that of competition and achievement as opposed to a more co-operative style of management. Indeed, the latter is perceived as weak and in order to demonstrate my own experience of this, I quote a comment made by a senior manager in an all-male meeting I recently chaired. We were discussing the different management styles attributed to different cultures and his assumption of a Scandinavian style of management was that 'it is very much a feminine style of management which means they are a pushover and allow everyone to walk all over them', to which I replied that had he worked for me, he would not have considered a feminine style of management a pushover! However, this Freudian slip demonstrates how strongly a more inclusive and co-operative style of management, whether exhibited by a female or male manager, continues to be perceived as weak and therefore ineffective; real men are tough! It is a fact that feminine values and femininity are perceived as being incompatible with being a successful high-flyer.

The style of management one adopts is a particularly important issue for women in management. In order to survive and compete in a male-dominated society, as women we find it necessary to suppress our feminine values. Success in a masculine environment requires women to develop and express their masculine qualities at the expense of what many perceive our weaker sides to be – that of the feminine. The lack of female senior executives on corporate boards, especially in large, Fortune 500 organizations, is testimony to the denial in organizations of including both soft and hard approaches. Instead, the majority of CEOs are white and male. Rodgers *et al*. (2003) claim that the role of leadership remains the exclusive domain of the white male despite the fact that organizations espouse values of diversity and equality. The softer, interpersonal skills traditionally associated with women are increasingly seen as a vital leadership skill required to build and strengthen company relationships.

The changes to the way we manage have also meant the requirement of different competencies. Instead of a directive approach to management, a new facilitative style is called for. A manager is required to be flexible and to use influence as opposed to force when persuading and negotiating – competencies women tend to exhibit naturally.

Gender bias occurs frequently in many spheres of life and in both overt and covert ways (Oakley, 2000). The *glass ceiling* metaphor is often used to describe such prejudice and discrimination (Carli and Eagly, 2001). Many women opt to get off the treadmill and start their own businesses before they bang their heads against the glass ceiling too often. Gender stereotyping and associated expectations play an enormously influencing role in determining the behaviour of women. Metaphors and narratives are powerful in framing meanings we hold about ourselves and our organizations. Mainstream organizational theorists and writers have traditionally written from a rational and male-dominated perspective. Feminine ontology is intrinsically marginalized in many discourses, especially the discourse of organizations and leadership. This denial of the female existence is also reflected in the renditions of history. The history of a class society, as of most historical societies, is a history about the rulers, and the rulers were predominantly men.

I recognize and support the argument that feminism may be based on essentialist assumptions of identity, therefore posing a challenge to feminist politics. As Gergen (1999; 2001) would argue, identity is socially created and that includes gender identities. Social constructionism views gender as relational and therefore identities and the roles various identities assume are not seen as fixed. Identities from this perspective are then perceived as being fluid, ever-changing and multiple due to numerous associations. A social constructionist perspective is also concerned with social changes that will influence the nature of identity. This may be problematic to some readers. However, feminist post-structuralism recognizes the need of an illusion of the subjective in order to engage with and participate in the world (Charles and Hughes-Freeland, 1996).

The tension within feminism as to whether an identity is discovered or socially developed parallels the tension between social constructionism and essentialism. I support the argument by Roseneil (1996) who is of the belief that women will only be able to challenge patriarchy and dominant modes of thinking effectively if identities are transgressed and transformed. Patriarchy is deeply embedded within the division of labour based on gender. She goes on to say that post-structuralism has rescued feminism from the naïve essentialism which perceived women as a homogenous unit with a common identity to be buried by patriarchy. The arguments of post-structuralism resonate with the arguments of Gergen who purports that identity is discursively constructed, is fluid by nature and is in a constant state of becoming.

Furthermore, a number of theorists argue that the categories of male and female are defined within cultures and are not biological givens (Segal, 1999; Billing and Alvesson, 2000). Whether identities are essential or socially constructed is basically irrelevant in practice as organizations continue to reinforce the dominance of one identity, namely the male identity over many others, whether it be feminism or differences associated with national cultures. Furthermore, if one continues the debate of constructionism and accepts that truth is a socially constructed phenomenon as opposed to the view held by functionalism that perceives it as a phenomenon to be discovered, one can deduce that the preferences and views of the dominant group will influence the nature of such truth. Appropriating postmodernist theories for a feminist ethic is about challenging the way in which society constructs values and to suggest new ways to configure such values. The purpose is therefore not to deny the possibility of values.

We observe in the corporate world in particular how perceptions regarding the behaviour of male and female are filtered through gendered lenses. These perceptions therefore tap into a subconscious image of leadership as being masculine by nature (Billing and Alvesson, 2000; Olsson and Walker, 2003). Men are unable to recognize leadership skills that differ from that of the traditional masculine perspective of leadership. Power is central to masculinity in whatever way it is conceptualized and whoever so practices that power.

Our views of the world are filtered through gendered lenses and the subsequent language and discourse we then create potentially distort judgements of men and women. Archetypes of leadership are examples of the influence the gendered lens has and they reinforce the continued association of men with leadership. This is clearly seen in the differing linguistic style between the genders. Women are much more likely to request rather than command, which is seen as a weakness by men who perceive women as lacking in control and authority. This, of course, leads to the leadership double-bind women encounter.

The existence of both toughness and femininity is a difficult concept to accept in most areas of power, be that of organizations or the political environment. Is it therefore surprising that successful corporate leaders, whether they are male or female, will adhere to the masculine traits associated with the stereotypical image of competitiveness, logic and self-confidence? Furthermore, there will certainly be no room for any perceived emotional weaknesses of any kind.

Cognitive research suggests that men's brains are designed to follow a logical step-by-step approach to problem solving, focusing on one thing at a time. Whereas women process information in a more holistic manner, demonstrating a more intuitive approach, which is viewed with suspicion by the male brain as it does not follow the logical and linear path. It is interesting to note that organizational literature increasingly challenges the logical and linear approach to management and calls for the need of a more creative and intuitive approach, drawing on the knowledge and creativity of all within the organization. The conclusion is that the ability to multi-task is the way to managing our increasingly complex organizations.

8 The imbalance of leadership

The exclusion of diverse representation within organizations can clearly be traced back to the deep-rooted patriarchal processes and beliefs that underpin the concepts of leadership (Rodgers *et al.*, 2003). Practices within organizations contribute significantly to support and encourage the imbalance between male and female. Examples include closed promotional practices and certain experiences that are predominantly given to men, such as operational and line management positions referred to earlier. Women are consistently placed in support roles due to erroneous assumptions regarding them and their level of ambition as it compares to that of men. Commitment to the organization and one's career tend to be measured by the hours you devote to work and the priority it has in your life above everything else, including your family.

Should women therefore take time out to have a family, it reinforces the masculine belief that they are not as reliable or committed as men are to the organization or their careers. The idea of a balanced life and a therefore different career model does not enter the equation and women are found wanting when compared with the dominant male version of careers. It goes without saying that it is in the interest of men to perpetuate and reinforce the role of women as house keeper and the one responsible for the raising of children. Even if a woman is without children and not married, she remains the nurturer in the eyes of men and therefore inferior and unsuitable to the traditionally privileged roles reserved for men. A challenge to their taken-for-granted right to certain positions and roles has not even entered the reality of the world according to a male view. This is only too apparent in both research and practice.

Vinnicombe and Singh (2003) found from their study that women tend to receive less training than their male counterparts despite the fact that evidence suggests women value training highly. Senior positions remain the exclusive right of men, reinforced through organizational practices such as a lack of diversity initiatives or policies that will remove the obstacles women face in an attempt to ascend through the ranks. If such policies are introduced, they are often only paying lip service to the cause and have no impact other than tokenism. Women continue to be disadvantaged through financial rewards that remain higher for men than for women. This puts women in a weaker position than their male colleagues as pay scales are often perceived as an indicator of success. In the corporate world, one's compensation remains a major indicator of a successful career. Other rewards are also denied women or offered to a lesser extent than it is for men. They also receive less perks such as time off for training and education and they are also likely to receive less by way of stock options and other senior management perks. Family commitments are often held up as a perceived barrier as to why women find it more difficult to reach senior positions. It has to be said that men will experience the same resistance if they take a more active role in family commitments.

Another area where women are grossly under-represented is within the international arena. Organizations increasingly attach importance to international assignments as a significant method of developing the senior managers of the future, especially for international and global organizations. It is interesting to note that international hotel chains are only just accepting that the obligatory trouser press in the rooms are augmented with an iron or a skirt press, hangers that can accommodate both trousers and skirts and a wardrobe that accepts space for long skirts and dresses! In addition, some also provide floors and rooms for women only, which are strategically placed for the purpose of their security.

It is a sad fact that women should need such preferential treatment, but it reflects the perceived right of some men to threaten the physical and mental well-being of lone women in hotels (Davies, 1998). I doubt whether any male away on business would give a second thought to having a pre-dinner drink in the bar or a meal on his own. Yet, most of my female colleagues chose to remain in their rooms, using room service, the reason being that you can guarantee, as a female alone in a bar or restaurant, that you will be pestered by men who perceive you as either being on the game or an easy pick up. Personally, I make the point of doing exactly that as I consider it my right as much as anyone else, to have a drink or a meal where and whenever I choose, unaccompanied.

Despite the increased demand for internationally experienced managers, women in such positions remain depressingly low. Worldwide, it varies from 2 to 15 per cent. Many reasons and justifications are offered by way of excuses. As mentioned earlier, the active role of women in the raising of families again features significantly as a reason. Other explanations proffered are the lack of interest on the part of women although I find this hard to believe. Prejudices are offered by way of an excuse which women may experience in certain societies, like concern for personal safety, to mention but one. Even in the most liberalized industrial societies, the expectation is that women will have a greater responsibility in the raising of the family. The balance between work and family demands are therefore greater, which makes expatriation less of an option for women as it is for men.

Women often find themselves in a no-win situation as they are either accused of being too aggressive, even though the same behaviour by men is applauded and labelled as assertive, or alternatively, they are also perceived as too feminine and therefore weak. Research suggests that women who are confident and self-promoting are more likely to be rejected as they are seen to be a threat to men. If women are modest, they reinforce the male view of women as being weak and less competent than men.

Gender differences in leadership styles reinforce the divide between the genders. The preferred leadership style of women tends to be more equal and transformational, like sharing of information, supporting and nurturing of those they lead (Oshagbemi and Gill, 2003), whereas the leadership style associated with men is more transactional, using their situational power to lead from the front (Vinnicombe and Singh, 2003). It is therefore suggested that women are more comfortable than men with a participative style of management, for men find it more difficult to interact with people in the same way.

Both men and women are restricted by a masculine straightjacket advocating models of power and authority, which does not allow for diversity. The leadership styles of men are often described as directive and bureaucratic, whereas the leadership styles adopted by women are perceived as collaborative. Women are also more aware of the impact of their decision on others than men. This connection with others may be perceived as stronger within women and will therefore influence the more participative and inclusive nature of female leadership.

The very nature of women's roles in society is the active development of others. Women are also better equipped in understanding and using emotional data. Men on the other hand find dealing with emotions tedious at best or are completely dismissive of its value, which may reflect their own fears in dealing with emotions. However, relational activities are not rewarded in most traditional organizations. The expression of different types of emotions is clearly gender-specific.

Women are socialized at a very early age not to express emotions such as anger and aggression, which is perceived as coarse within a woman. Nice girls do not behave in an aggressive manner. Men on the other hand are very much encouraged as boys to display acts of aggression. Emotions that facilitate the building and maintaining of social relationships such as warmth and friendliness are associated with and encouraged in women, but not seen as manly enough, and thus as less desirable in men. It is interesting to note that it is exactly such unmanly type emotions that are increasingly seen as imperative in leaders and senior management. Take, for example, New Labour and their touchy–feely sentiment regularly portrayed by Tony Blair which started with the Princess Diana death speech. The venue for one of his political broadcast was from his family kitchen whilst he casually wore rolled up shirt sleeves surrounded by pots and pans. Similarly, President Clinton was known for his more personal down-to-earth approach.

However, women who are progressing towards senior positions find that they may suppress certain emotions within the workplace as these would be considered typically female and therefore inappropriate. So, instead, they suppress their more natural emotional states and fake the more acceptable masculine emotions which may lead to feelings of inauthenticity and emotional dissonance as well as possible long-term psychological harm.

Furthermore, leadership also reflects different communication styles and it is suggested that women use more verbal communication in relationship building and offer more emotional support to colleagues than men. On the other hand, men tend to emphasize the dissemination of information and the demonstration of competence. This also reflects the differences between the sexes as to how language itself is perceived. Women tend to use language to build rapport and build relationships whereas men use language to maintain their status and position through negotiation and vying for centre stage. The jury is still out as to whether preferences in leadership styles among men and women do in fact exist. It is true to say that there are many examples of male leaders who use a relations-oriented approach as of women leaders who practise a command-and-control approach. Different organizational scenarios require different approaches and both styles are necessary.

Some of the theories that have been developed in order to explain the lack of representation by women in management, especially that of senior management are first based on the gender-centred approach that assumes women lack the skills, knowledge and abilities required by a senior management role. Needless to say, men are seen as possessing the necessary qualities. If the role requirements are judged from a masculine perspective, then it could not be otherwise, could it? It is a perspective that continues to prevail in the minds of men. Many writers have demonstrated how organizational practices reinforce the inequalities and divisions of labour between paid and unpaid work, the way work is designed and evaluated, what opportunities are available and to whom and which roles are labelled as male or female roles.

Organizational boundaries between functions, divisions, professions and occupations correspond with the boundaries between perceived male and female work. The stereotypical segregation between femininity and masculinity has reinforced and supported the myths of differences between men and women as being natural. The result is hierarchy with men at the top and masculine values given higher value than feminine values. It is not possible to understand people in organizations separate from the society in which they live, and when the social system changes, the other components such as organizations will also change.

The nature of third possibility leaders

The image of the heroism of the male appears to be a universal aspect of human culture. People who have achieved public status as heroes are predominantly male. In Western tradition, the earlier heroes included deities of both sexes with equal power. However, over time male deities assumed a superior role and female deities migrated to a more subservient role. Medieval chivalric codes of conduct as well as changes in religion, meant that men assumed the leading role as far as heroism was concerned. This belief continues to dominate society and organizations and is particularly evident in the beliefs and assumptions regarding the heroic nature of leadership. Despite the increase of women in management roles, they remain in the minority. As men are perceived as superior to women and the natural heroes, they assume the right to limit the access of women to positions of power and to restrict their roles and lifestyles.

In every sphere of society outside that of the home, women lag behind men. It is a well-documented fact that a wage gap exists between the genders, favouring men. Men assume the higher status roles with women in roles with less status. The roles women find themselves in have less power and prestige and are therefore less valuable in terms of remuneration than the role occupied by men. The dominant paradigm within society that perceives men as the providers and heroes therefore places more value on the work they do as opposed to the work done by women that is perceived as being of lesser status and therefore lesser value. After all, women's wages are the 'second wage', are they not?

The decision makers within organizations influence the decisions made regarding the rates of remuneration and how roles will be rewarded. The stereotypes of women's inferiority to men and their subordinate role influence the decisions made by those in power with regard to rewards. As those decision makers are predominantly male, is it any wonder that women remain undervalued in comparison with male colleagues? There seems no other logical reason why a woman should be rewarded less for the same job as that of her male counterpart.

The unquestioned belief which continues to dominate our view of leadership is the American model of the larger-than-life, charismatic white male who inspires unquestioned devotion and following. As with leadership, entrepreneurship is essentially perceived as more masculine than feminine. It is a conception of reality that represents only a small proportion of the world's population. We only have to look at the Bush and Blair governments to see a large-scale example of what happens on a smaller scale within organizations across much of the Western world. Feminine values are not represented and rarely are the values and beliefs of other cultures reflected or represented other than as a token to pacify critics.

Leadership is dominated by a small group of elite who impose their views on others and who do not even attempt to consider the possibility that organizations and their activities may actually be perceived differently by different groups and different cultures. The arrogance of their ethnocentric beliefs as being the only way is such an intrinsic part of their cultural fibre that it is beyond consciousness and therefore question.

The powerful and dominant view of leadership is as a result of a socially constructed concept by a small minority of the world's population. It is a myth that the most successful companies have been led by the stereotypical hero model (Regine and Lewin, 2003). It is debatable that with more women entering the inner chamber, change will come about and that organizations will move towards a more inclusive model. It remains to be seen. My experience of organizations is that they continue to have a healthy disregard for diversity and differing views held by members of non-dominant groups in society, such as women. Equality appears to be synonymous with similarity or sameness and Greer (1999: 308) argues that 'The denial of real difference can be as cruel as forcing different-sized feet into a single-size shoe'.

As I mentioned in my introduction, Žižek (1989) reminds us that we all contribute and collude to the perpetuation of such beliefs and it is reinforced when we take a closer look at the leadership roles women construct for themselves. As we discussed earlier, the female leadership role does not reflect the same characteristics as that of the male leadership model. The construction of femininity and what was perceived as the natural place of women in family groups, was also applied to exclude women not only from senior management positions, but also from political power.

It is only in recent years that the significance of masculinity in the workplace has come under scrutiny and up until then it has been a taken-for-granted reality. The position of men in organizations and the assumptions regarding their influence and domination of organizations has been such a significant part of socially held beliefs of gender roles that they were beyond explanation or questioning. As the male gender was perceived as the norm, the appearance and presence of women were perceived as being out of place and therefore troubling.

I argued in the section on complexity theory that such theories are more in keeping with the reality experienced by managers and that the ambiguity and dynamic nature of complex systems provide a better reflection of contemporary organizations. Furthermore, the science of complexity is described as a feminine science by some as it demands a more holistic way of thinking – a trait women are perceived as being better at than men. If we approach organizations from a complexity perspective, the traditional command-and-control, mechanistic style of management will be totally inappropriate. In fact, according to Regine and Lewin (2003) such a management style '... inevitably will impair their efficacy, in terms of creativity and adaptability' (p. 347). A management style guided by the principles of a complexity science is seen to be hierarchically flat, embracing diversity and requiring supportive and open communication – traits traditionally associated with a feminine style of leadership. This view highlights the ongoing debate as to whether or not feminine characteristics expressed predominantly by women might place them in a better position to be more natural at leading through interaction and participation.

As we saw from the theories of complexity, success in such an environment relies heavily on the quality of relationships. Regine and Lewin (2003) posit that those men and women who are able to balance the masculine and the feminine in a dynamic manner are equipped to become powerful leaders. They label women who are capable of such a balance between the masculine and feminine as 'third possibility leaders', applying a different model of leadership than hitherto seen. Leadership from this perspective is not exclusively about individual success, but recognizes success as being collective, giving credit where it is due.

However, quiet leaders do not dominate the front covers of leading business publications as they are not sensational enough. The success of the quiet leader is often attributed to luck rather than skills and competencies. If leaders do not exhibit the traditional masculine characteristics of leadership discussed here, they are labelled as ineffective leaders. Masculine qualities are seen as being synonymous with leadership. It is apparent therefore, why deeply ingrained views of leadership will dismiss feminine behaviours as powerless and ineffective.

Until very recently in the history of humankind, women have been dominated by men and their world of rules based on male values. If women are to be represented equally with men in various roles within society and organizations, their perception of themselves will be a powerful catalyst to change. It is imperative that women perceive themselves not as victims but as having the same opportunities as men. The victim archetype reinforces the collusion referred to by Žižek and from a constructionist perspective, it is apparent why the male advantage over women is therefore maintained.

Gender stereotyping prevents the exploration of different ways of being and in particular, different styles of leadership which both men and women can express. A leadership style which transcends the either/or model will not perceive male and female qualities as essences contained within the bodies of men and women, but qualities to which both sexes can and should have access. Social constructionism demonstrates that identity is complex and multifaceted and advocates that traits associated with masculinity or femininity are not static, but subject to change over time and within the lifetime of individuals. This view is supported by Foucault who perceives the body and sexuality as cultural constructs as opposed to natural and given phenomena.

The physical bodily differences between the sexes have served to legitimize inequality amongst the sexes. Women are classed as inferior to men based on their physical differences with men. Furthermore, it is also subject to factors of class, race, values and beliefs, occupation, organizations, age and individual conditions. It is therefore not a given, but is socially created.

9 The sexuality of women

Feminism has challenged the unquestioned belief that organizations are a-sexual. However, women find themselves in a difficult situation at work in the way they present themselves and their gender. Women face many double-bind behavioural norms, which act as barriers to their career advancement. For example, women are expected to be as tough and authoritative as men if they are to be taken seriously. However, if they succeed they are often accused of being 'bitches' and certainly too aggressive. On the other hand, being feminine means a woman will be dismissed as being incompetent.

This dichotomy is firmly established at a very early age through socialization. There is a deep-seated assumption in society that it is natural for women to be submissive and an equally accepted belief of the dominance of men. Not only is it seen as natural, but essential to sexual pleasure. In fact, the orgasm of a woman is perceived as a sign of the sexual prowess of the man. It is inconceivable that a woman can achieve sexual satisfaction without the presence of a man. The inevitability of male dominance over women is a powerful force in the acceptance of the subservience of women.

Girls are told to be nice and not to be too outspoken or to sound too sure of themselves as they will not be liked. Boys on the other hand are expected to be assertive and to stand up for themselves. The result is that women are much less self-promoting than men and lack the same level of confidence and self-belief as men.

To be taken seriously and to be seen to be as competent as male colleagues, they have to dress in a fairly masculine way so as not to be too feminine and therefore seen as a 'temptress' or being the type that sleeps its way to the top. On the other hand, they may be accused of being too 'manly' and not feminine enough and labelled as a ball-crushing dyke.

I challenge the view that women have to suppress their femininity, particularly in the workplace, as it represents the very essence and strength of who we are as women. Do men repress their masculinity in the event that women may accuse them of flaunting their manliness and be the subject of female banter and sexual innuendos? Of course not. At the very heart of organizational paternalism and hegemony is the male essence of masculinity, and women have the right and, I would go so far as to say, an obligation to balance it with their own essence of femininity. Otherwise, the only thing women achieve is being a paler version of the male. This will not lead to a situation where we truly value and embrace the strengths and compensate for the weaknesses of both sexes, whether that is expressed by either gender.

Sexuality at work is unfortunately expressed in various forms of harassment. Victims of sexual harassment, an act of aggression, tolerate it in the workplace as it reflects the paternalism of organizations and the dominance of men and subordination of women. The nature of sexuality, and in particular the sexuality of women, varies enormously from culture to culture and is also hugely influenced by our upbringing. Research suggests that individuals with less or little social power are more likely to suffer abuses of power. As women have less social power than men, they are seen as less deserving of status and are ignored within relations of power.

Physical abuse, harassment and hostility towards women are tolerated in most societies and, in fact, in some cultures perceived as the norm and the privilege of the man to enforce. As violence against women often goes unreported and undetected, the statistics reporting violence against women may very well be extremely conservative and only the tip of the iceberg. We find the ultimate form of female suppression in some cultures carried out through unthinkable acts of barbarism such as female circumcision.

In contrast, in other cultures women are encouraged to find out and explore their own sexuality at an early age. Women collude to a different form of barbarism against them. As women, we continue to feed the myth that physically we have to be perfect. It is a multi-billion dollar industry which we continue to feed. As Greer (1999) points out, the majority of cosmetic surgery for the purpose of creating the perfect physical appearance is done on women by men. Women continue to subject themselves to the myth that they have to be perfect. They are not allowed grey hairs or droopy breasts and cellulite is enough to fill the hearts of most women with despair.

For women to feel comfortable in and with their own unique bodies, complete with their own strengths and weaknesses, they will have to exhibit the same level of confidence in themselves as men do. The power lies with us to ensure that men take us seriously and see all of who we are, not merely our appearances. We need to break the cycle and stop colluding with this illusion.

The statistics make grim reading for those seeking change in society as well as organizations. According to 2001 figures, women occupy only 10.9 per cent of board seats in the top Fortune 1000 companies and almost 40 per cent of the Fortune 500–1000 companies had no women on their Board of

Directors at all. Judging by the figures, can we truly say that we have moved beyond tokenism in the number of women that occupy senior positions? As a result of the barriers women experience, many women opt out and set up their own organizations. In the USA, one-third of businesses are owned by women. One has to ask that if they are capable of running their own organizations, why are so few women found on the boards of corporate businesses in the USA and many other businesses elsewhere?

Despite the fact that male power dominates in boardrooms, women have managed to carve out a niche for themselves in some societies. Women have learnt to take control of their relationships and establish their own identity and individuality within those relationships. Some women have chosen to go it alone and support their children on their own, drawing on emotional strength which is typical of our gender. Others have made the conscious decision not to have children, something which would have been socially unacceptable not so long ago. More often than not, women earn their own money within or without relationships and sometimes even earn more than their partners.

An interesting fact about our emotional well-being is revealed through research. Women have a greater sense of well-being if they choose to remain single, whereas men do not fare as well and have a higher sense of well-being when within a relationship. An interesting point for reflection is whether men are able to cope with confident and successful partners without feeling threatened in any way, especially if their partner has a career which requires entertainment outside of work or just long hours to meet deadlines. The tables have turned and one wonders how well men cope with it.

Stereotypes associated with women play a significant contributing factor to the limited representation of women in senior positions. Stereotypes can be a useful starting point in assisting us in understanding groups and cultures we have little knowledge of. However, it is imperative that we update our stereotypes as we get to know more about a certain group of people. Unfortunately, stereotypes associated with women and their role within society and organizations have not been sufficiently updated. The media plays a significant role in reinforcing the stereotypes of women being associated with home activities, casting women in submissive roles as opposed to the dominant role for men. As we have seen, the stereotypes associated with men promote men in favour of women in positions of power, whether that be in organizations or society. However, power is something we as women find difficult to deal with. We are socialized not to be aggressive and competitive and we therefore struggle with the traditional male concept of power. As women, we tend to seek and facilitate relatedness and do not feel comfortable with being in conflict with those around us. However, our preference for cooperation over competition has done us no favours in our battle for leadership positions.

Although individual incidents of discrimination may be relatively small, their cumulative effect is huge. Discrimination fuelled by stereotypes continues to dominate beliefs regarding the commitment of women to work and their suitability for certain roles. Such negative stereotyping plays an influential role in recruitment policies and promotional decisions. This is true even in industries and careers that are perceived as 'women's work'. Senior positions and positions of power continue to be dominated by men. Positions of power and authority equal masculinity.

It may be that when the younger generation of men have replaced the old dinosaurs who doggedly cling to outdated stereotypes women and other diverse groups may finally break through the glass ceiling successfully. Many women are coming out from under the glass ceiling to become entrepreneurs and thereby creating their own rules and opportunities of career advancement. Within their own organizations, women are free of the cultural influences and stereotypes regarding the accepted expectations of leadership and management.

Women also have more flexibility to manage caring roles within their own organizations. Family responsibilities continue to be a powerful barrier for women on their way to senior positions as women are traditionally perceived as being responsible for the care of the family. Furthermore, there is an assumption that this role will take precedence over any work roles they may have. Men who assume family responsibilities face the same dilemma, but seeing how the burden of caring for the family falls mainly on the shoulders of women, they experience it as a greater disadvantage than men do. Family-friendly policies are not perceived as less and less feasible the more senior the role.

10 Power and hegemony

The French philosopher, Michel Foucault (1972), has made a significant contribution to the field of power and hegemony through his writings and his analysis of the ways in which society has exercised control over its members. This is achieved through the creation of various institutions such as law, medicine, education and of course organizations. Organizations are both experienced and perceived as institutions that suppress conflicting interests and are active in 'the perpetuation of corporate and societal hegemony' (Ogbor, 2001: 591). A patriarchal society has ensured the devaluation and subordination of women to men. It has also locked women into the role of unpaid labourer within the household. Paternalism and power have always been a feature of mankind and history and tradition are conventions of enduring paternalism. Power and politics are part of the very essence of our capitalist society as well as our organizations which, as mirrors, reflect the societies within which they operate.

Common to a capitalist exploitative persona are unquestioned assumptions about the nature and existence of diversity. True gentlemen lived according to a strict code of conduct as to what was done and what was not. This code included gentlemanly behaviour in terms of a benevolent responsibility and concern for those of a lower status and order within society, particularly within rural society. Power was seen as justified as long as it was accompanied by service. The landless working class was seen as deserving of governance by the upper classes. It was inconceivable that those of lower status would be involved in regulating matters that concerned them collectively. It was the responsibility of the gentry to carry out this activity on their behalf. Those of a lower class were not required to think for themselves and in fact, they were encouraged not to do so. Once again, this was seen as the responsibility of the paternal higher classes.

The upper classes were responsible for guiding and restraining the working classes in the same way as a parent would do with and for his or her children. The social needs of the working class would be taken care of by their superiors in exchange for their labour and attachment. An assumption of such paternalism and control was that it ensured stability and order and we continue to observe this assumption within our modern-day organizations. Furthermore, such relationships of power and hegemony became moral ones, legitimizing hierarchy within the social order.

Hegemony requires the consent and collusion of society for the ruling classes to maintain their control over society. The hegemonic conditioning we find in our organizations goes unchallenged and the workforce continues to support exploitation and domination. Ironically, we perceive it to be a normal state of affairs. The traditional perspective of the ruling class, as it applies to organizations, can be likened to that of the management elite. The right of managers to control and rule the organization goes unquestioned.

Power permeates organizations and will therefore influence organizational activities such as strategy both explicitly and implicitly. Power is often exerted through coercion and may not necessarily reside with the position of the person. The chief executive and the senior management team are thought to be the most powerful people in the organization. We perceive them as the ultimate decision-makers of the organization and with the power to influence and direct the lives of those further down the organization. This assumption is supported by all the players in the organization and in fact everyone colludes to maintain this status quo or organizational belief.

In a paternalistic way the senior team, and especially the chief executive, is perceived as the all-knowing and all-seeing one with the wisdom to decide on behalf of everyone in the organization. In a childlike fashion, people in organizations often give their power away to those they perceive as being wiser than themselves. Such a belief is distilled in us from an early age and the wisdom we associate with our parents, teachers and others in authority is carried into our adult life and that of our organizations. Patriarchal relations continue to structure power in favour of men, ensuring male dominance over female subordination.

The American culture appears to set great store on charismatic power and looks to its leaders, both within the political arena and in organizations, to engender inspiration and devotion. This need leads to referent power or the need to be associated with such charismatic leaders. The many faces of power permeate the very fibre of organizations and play an enormous role in influencing and dictating the behaviours of those within the organization. Such ways of behaviour become part of the organizational culture and when you first join an organization, you very quickly become indoctrinated and socialized into acceptable behaviour patterns and the areas where the echelons of power lie.

It is an illusion that the roles of men and women, determining the place and status of women, are a given of nature. It is, instead, decided on by history. We find that in some cultures, women may not do any heavy work at all and within other cultures their role is associated with heavy work only. Historically, women in the West have been seen as too physically fragile to be employed in heavy engineering posts or where physical strength is required. An example would be the fire services which have only recently allowed women into their very male-dominated environment. In Africa on the other hand, it has traditionally been the role of women to till the fields. The roles that are assigned and accepted as being suitable for women are therefore defined socially and are not a given. Equally, the right to rule is intrinsically associated with the paternalistic nature of society. The model of the authoritative father supports the division of leadership in favour of the wise father and not the wise mother. The mother is perceived as the nurturer and not the ruler. This reinforces the hegemonic nature of organizations and the taken-for-granted right of men to rule our organizations.

Dominance is achieved through a number of routes other than the formal lines of authority, such as the supportive networks, or the 'old boys' network' that protects the camaraderie of men within this network. It also protects the exclusivity of male-dominated positions in organizations. The very nature of management is based on obedience and often coercion. We can identify many organizational practices that support these assumptions irrespective of how they are rephrased, the empowering of employees to name but one. The traditional image we have of entrepreneurship, reinforced by the media especially in the 1980s, portrays a vision of the 'self-made man', macho and flamboyant, exhibiting an abrasive and autocratic leadership style, characteristics exclusively associated with men. One can observe the supporting language employed which is highly (hetero) sexualized – penetration of markets, getting into bed with competitors as well as the hackneyed sporting metaphors.

There are various explanations put forward for the under-representation of women in leadership positions. Some attribute it to the lack of leadership traits in women. Even if they happen to achieve leadership roles, they are invisible. It stands to reason that such assumptions will be made in relation to the ability of women to lead if mainstream research into leadership is conducted in the positivist tradition rather than ideologically focused on interpretive approach. In a study carried out by Olsson and Walker (2003), participants reinforced the gendered lens in the construction of the executive world unthinkingly as the domain of men. The under-representation of women at executive level was not raised as an issue in the male executives' constructions of a desired future organizational state. Women are stereotyped into the 'caring' or 'people-oriented' roles, not roles associated with leadership, but as a support to leaders, roles occupied by men, of course.

The stereotyping of gender is both descriptive as well as prescriptive, creating not only the differences between men and women, but also reinforcing the norms associated with different behaviours between men and women. Stereotypes portray women as being less effective in leadership roles than men because they are being measured by and compared with male values. Senior management positions are characterized in male terms which can only lead to discrimination against women and the stereotypical feminine characteristics associated with women. The result is prejudice that erroneously assumes that men are better suited to leadership positions than women (Carli and Eagly, 2001).

Women find it difficult to gain experience needed for senior positions in areas such as operations, manufacturing or marketing as access to such positions is often denied to them. This contributes to the difficulties women face in reaching the top as these experiences are perceived as essential prerequisites for senior management positions. Furthermore, these deeply held assumptions and beliefs regarding the male characteristics associated with senior management and the perceived characteristics associated with women and their related behaviour all add to the difficulties of women fitting into the role of senior management.

In the minds of society and the male population in particular, there exists a dichotomy between the masculine perception of who and what a senior manager is and the unquestioned expectations of who and what women are. Therefore, if a woman reaches the privileged position of a senior manager, confusion reigns in the minds of men. As already mentioned, such a woman is then often labelled as being aggressive or a 'super bitch' if she is effective at exhibiting male characteristics and behaviours. It is a taboo to include the traditionally associated female characteristics in the scope of the senior management role. The violation of the gender stereotypes inevitably leads to disapproval and penalties for the violator. Advancement is not only dependent on competencies, but also on social acceptance and the situation described above often leads to non-acceptance of women.

According to Billing and Alvesson (2000), the gender debate should go much deeper than merely the narrow gender vocabulary that dominates leadership issues. They consider values deeply embedded within the capitalist and market economy, such as growth, exploitation of nature, hedonism, affluent consumption and careerism, to be the major barriers to radical reform. Throughout the history of Western philosophy, masculine and feminine have always been depicted as mutually exclusive with opposing traits and never the twain shall meet. Indeed, the core characteristics depicted by masculinity are the traits associated with leadership. Such characteristics include objectivity, action orientation, linearity, assertiveness, independence, rationality and control. These traits are not a fixed given and are dependent on the meanings ascribed to them by a specific culture.

Should women successfully reflect the traditional traits associated with masculinity, they are more likely to be perceived as successful managers and be more easily accepted by their male colleagues. The price of masculine hegemony leads to the denial by men of their characteristics associated with the feminine – characteristics such as nurturing, emotions, needs, empathy and compassion.

The mechanisms by which a class or economic system maintains its existence are institutions such as the family, culture, political and legal systems, religious and educational systems and organizations. These institutions all contribute to our integration and indoctrination into a particular economic system and the maintenance of the dominant ideology. We accept their values and beliefs as being representative of the truth and the way of the world. I have already referred to the power of language in previous chapters and these institutions employ language as a tool to help maintain their positions of power.

Language is equally used in organizations in subtle ways to exclude the majority from the powerful inner circle. One example is the use of sports metaphors, which unless you understand the games referred to, would have no meaning to you. The exercise of power is present in every sphere of our lives and every decision we make contributes to the exercise of power somewhere in the world. Think about everyday decisions such as the type of coffee you will purchase. Your choice contributes to the power of organizations over the growers of the coffee beans, depending on which brand you choose. We all collude to the use and abuse of power in our society.

Power over us is exercised in so many ways, for example through the abundance of laws that govern many of our daily actions. Ideology is a powerful tool with which to control our behaviour as we voluntarily behave in ways that are acceptable to such an ideology. We accept the beliefs of an ideology as being the right way and representative of truth and reality. The natural state of affairs therefore means that we voluntarily contribute to our own suppression and exploitation because that is the way things are. We voluntarily work long hours or overtime without reward to increase the profits for shareholders even further. As women, we accept that very few of us will reach the top of our professions and that the care of our families is mainly our responsibility. Ideology is responsible for the suppression of many women throughout the world and in some cultures, for an exclusion from society and associated activities.

It is difficult to question the continued existence of a paternalistic world society and balance of power being in the favour of men when you read the statistics. The statistics reveal that women work two-thirds of the working hours worldwide, and yet earn only 10 per cent of the income and own less than 1 per cent of the property worldwide. Only 1 per cent of executive positions within the largest international corporations are held by women. The 'common sense' of our ideology keeps women firmly in their subordinate positions through the maintenance of erroneous stereotypes.

With postmodernism came a rejection of the old imperialist grand narratives and the suppressive regime of communism, and a new dawning rose lifting the old shackles of oppression. Or so we thought. Sim (2004) warns that a new order of oppression is taking hold on world societies, namely that of fundamentalism. Furthermore, fundamentalism is not limited to the political arena, but is very much a reality in markets with its 'one size fits all' philosophy. We recognize fundamentalists by their lack of acceptance of anyone outside of their select group. Challenge to the status quo is not acceptable. What hope could you possibly have of having your voice heard if you happen to belong to the 'other'? Fundamentalism throughout history has always been aligned with masculine characteristics and has had very definite ideas as to the role of women in society. These ideas did not include the equal participation of women in what was perceived as masculine domains. Women were firmly placed and kept in the role of subordination. Fundamentalists have particularly strong and narrow views on sexuality and any deviation from this such as homosexuality would surely mean not only exclusion, but damnation.

One could argue that the Western policies and philosophies as expressed through the IMF and World Bank are the fundamentalist beliefs of the West being imposed on developing countries. They are fundamentalist philosophies that will inevitably fuel counter fundamentalism in turn. It is the poor who are held down and with nothing to hope for and therefore nothing to lose who will turn to extremism to oppose extremism. It is ironic that the staunchest supporters of the so-called 'free market' beliefs are the most protective of their own industries. However, they will be the most vocal when it comes to imposing policies and principles on those who are least able to defend themselves or resist their unfair and unequal treatment.

Globalization runs the risk of coming across as being fundamentalist, bent on persuading the world that we are becoming this global village with homogenous lifestyles, preferences and beliefs. It is a denial of diversity on a grand scale, where once again the select few will save the rich pickings for themselves. A free global market, as with Marxism, denies the existence of diversity, insisting on the one size to fit all approach – totalitarianism by a different name.

Fundamentalism is essentially about imposing the world view of one group on others and this is no more apparent than in the political arena. This is not only to be found in theocratic states, but Western democracies are also guilty of imposing their will on others. You need look no further than Northern Ireland for the fundamental beliefs held by all parties and which has made resolution to their disputes seem impossible. American Imperialism embodied within American organizations imposes their definitions and belies of management and management practices on the rest of the world. Whether they are culturally transferable is irrelevant.

Surely, democracy by its very nature means confrontation and disagreement that prevent the very possibility of an authoritarian order emerging. Our so-called 'democratic societies' exert overt and covert pressures on their members to conform. I mentioned earlier that I consider politic correctness to be one such mechanism which leads to the stifling of healthy debates and challenges. With the death of Marxism there is no counter balance to Western fundamentalism except the extreme theocratic fundamentalism which leaves death and destruction in its wake. In Britain, it is almost impossible to distinguish the different political parties from one another. They are all blending into one another to become this bland homogenous mass. Unanimity is the goal of all fundamentalist beliefs. Both Christian and Islamic fundamentalists have as central to their ideologies, an overriding belief in the justice of God. The current state our societies find themselves in is, as Žižek (2002: 52) puts it, 'a clash of fundamentalisms'. One would have thought after three centuries of so-called 'Enlightened thought' the power of the God hypothesis would have waned somewhat. The most powerful relationship in humankind is the relationship with the creator or what particular religions or spiritual beliefs may perceive God to be. And guess what? God is a man!

The drive towards unanimity is no less apparent than in market fundamentalism. The Western seats of power see no reason for any change to their economic paradigm. The belief of market fundamentalism is that we have reached our ultimate destiny. Furthermore, it will ensure that others follow and obey the rules with the IMF and the World Bank being the guardians of the truth. It is very difficult for weaker and less-developed regimes to oppose these truths and survive to tell the tale. The Western utopian view of a single market assumes that economic life throughout the world can and, more importantly, should be fashioned on the American model of what constitutes a free market.

Dare I ask the question that has been in the back of my mind since researching fundamentalism in our societies? Why are most, if not all, fundamentalist movements founded and supported by men with women often being suppressed and the victims in such societies? Sadly, the pluralistic celebration of diversity, particularly cultural diversity, is not likely to be cultivated or even tolerated under the current climate of fear associated with suicide bombers. In fact, there is a backlash in our Western cultures and a renewed questioning of multiculturalism. Ultimately, fundamentalism is about power, the power and suppression of others.

11 The challenge from postmodernism

It may be unclear to you as to why I chose to include this discourse on postmodernism. Many feminist writers, including myself, are of the opinion that feminist theory has always dealt with postmodern issues. The essence of postmodernism is to challenge the dominating single voice and to argue for the inclusion of diversity. I therefore see postmodernism as significant in helping us understand the role of diversity and the importance of it to our organizations.

The method of analysis of postmodernism is therefore not aimed at closure (Shildrick, 1997), but instead seeks to open up debates to include all of the divergent voices that make up society. In essence, the overarching purpose of feminism is for the voice of women to have equal status with that of the masculine voice. This is of significant importance to feminism and the opening up of organizations to reflect the many voices they represent. Social, as well as organizational cultures have created a one-dimensional man with the emphasis on *man*. It is the one-dimensional man who decides whose voice is to be heard.

Ogbor confirms the experiences of many that organizations are a socially constructed ideology that 'legitimize the power relations of managerial élites within an organization and society at large' (2001: 591). Such elitism was fuelled by Darwinism which referred to the 'lower races' and accepted the claim that whites had the greater intelligence. Indeed, the comparison of women with such 'lower races' were widespread in earlier society (Bland, 2001) and one can argue that it continues to be very much a fact of many societies. Such deeply rooted assumptions of superiority continue to influence organizations and society and the place different people in society might be allowed to occupy. In essence, postmodernism rejects the idea that an ultimate *truth* is possible and that the world as we experience it is as a result of hidden structures. As we will see, such an ultimate truth is the truth created by men for men throughout the ages. Postmodernism rejects many of the truths of the modernist era such as that of *grand theories* and *meta-narratives*. Instead, postmodernism invites multiplicity and endless variety.

As mentioned, modernist philosophy is the search for an ultimate truth or knowledge whereas the postmodernist approach is towards a polysemic model of knowledge, seeking and valuing the voice of everyone. Postmodernism was born from the perceived failure of and disillusionment with modernism. As will be discussed later, developments within postmodern science would suggest that the universe is not as deterministic in its unfolding as the nineteenth century would have people believe. Nor is it as predictable as previously thought. The quest for absolute knowledge or a *meta-narrative*, which will bring with it prediction and control, is shown by science to be a futile waste of energy.

Control as we have seen, is important to the male of the species. Furthermore, despite its revered status in Western culture, science is unable to produce a consistent view of the world (Sim, 2000b). On the other hand, postmodern thinkers invite exploration into those areas where knowledge is as yet unknown and challenge existing systems of beliefs in the light of the missing knowledge. In essence, postmodernism challenges the truths and certainties which have supported Western culture for the past two centuries. These truths and certainties, as I will argue, are the truths of men and have not taken into account what the truths of women might look like. Postmodernism is also identified by its scepticism of perceived wisdom, authority and political norms. Once again, these reflect the view of men only.

We observe a sense of erosion of what might until now have constituted the *self*. Traditional values are being questioned and as mentioned earlier, the confidence in the *grand narratives* of the past is fast disappearing (Shildrick, 1997). Political power has centred around the ability of governments and other political groups to insist on obedience from society without an understanding as to what discourse informs the justification of obedience. Such power was seen as the birthright of the white male within the Western world. How can we have trust in governments, economic planners and scientists who purport to create a better world for the future if that future would be skewed by the desires of some men and not be inclusive of others within that society.

The modernist philosophy has been one of separation, whereas postmodernism is about integration, seeing society as a whole. A postmodernist perspective considers such boundaries as artificial and created by man, man being males, not mankind. Postmodernism is a debate about *reality* and what constitutes the phenomenon called reality. However, as I claimed earlier and have supported with further arguments in other chapters, such reality has mainly been the reality of men. In essence, postmodernism embraces ambiguity and paradox and dismisses the need of modernism to assign clarity and an ultimate truth to phenomena. The modernist approach is about closure of conversations, by suppressing the *other* and difference.

Organizational science continues to be conducted within a modernist framework whilst organizational theorists maintain their allegiance to modernist principles such as rationality and individuality. Organizations established during a modernist era reflect a style and structure wedded to logic and reason. A modernist organization is a product of the industrial era which was certainly dominated by men – a new world designed by men for men. Processes are rigid and policies and procedures provide strict guidelines for actions and behaviour and the roles of everyone within the organization. The industrial revolution, an achievement of modernity, brought significant changes between the sexes.

The roles of women were firmly associated with domestic labour whereas the roles of men were of a public nature. Such a divide reinforced patterns of domination and subordination which have been carried forward into organizations, a subordination women continue to battle with. In the modernist organization, power is very much held at the top of the hierarchical structure and reserved for the privileged few, the few invariably being white, middle-aged men. In contrast, power in the postmodernist organization is identified in a systematically interconnected network of relationships.

Postmodernism advises us that it is through the power of language that we collectively create and maintain the ideologies of our societies. It is through language that we think and without language, we will be unable to express concepts or ideas. We come to know ourselves through the language of our culture. The act of living is synonymous with participating in language – to ask questions, to heed, to respond, to agree. Language and thought are, therefore, inseparable and it is through language that we come to know what constitutes self. It is through language that social and cultural roles and identities are created.

Not only do people of different cultures speak a different language, but also the way in which the language is applied varies significantly between cultures. The context within which language is employed is as important and multi-layered as the language itself. The traditional view of language is that it is the vehicle that transmits and reflects the world as it is. This belief is a deep-rooted assumption that language is able to convey truth. Furthermore, certain languages have been seen as superior and more truthful than others. Western cultures in particular, have viewed their language as being superior to that of other cultures, which led to colonization and the suppression of the other, *other* being those who hold a different view of truth to that of the dominant culture. The dominant truth of the West is mainly truth as perceived by men.

Language in itself does not represent any pictures or maps as to what constitutes reality, but achieves meaning through the exchange between people within relationships. Without language, through which people are able to express their internal states and characteristics, social life as we know it would not exist. It is through the application of language that the world is arbitrarily carved up into categories, arbitrary because these categories are different for different cultures and different groups of people.

Traditionally, knowledge has been associated with that stored within intangible renderings such as books, journals and, increasingly, electronic means of storage. However, such renderings are the creations of social interactions. Knowledge is not the property of the individual, but rather the product of an activity people engage in together. Sounds and symbols constituting language have no meaning *per se* other than the meaning assigned to them by those who use them. Learning a language is therefore not merely learning different symbols and sounds, but also a different way of perception as to what reality means to that particular society. Meaning is transitory and constantly evolving and changing, with no permanence or substance, and is different from person to person. A postmodernist perspective of language reflects a belief that the world is constituted and created through a shared language. That shared language should include the voices of everyone in society and not merely the language of the dominant group.

Language plays a significant role in the creation of our identities. Our social identity is not only displayed by various social codes such as our behaviour and the way we dress, but also by the way we speak. For a constructionist perspective, our identities are always in a state of becoming and are something we constantly negotiate with others through our interactions with them. The use of language is a strong indicator of our identities and the social groups we belong to. The accent we speak with carries a tremendous amount of information as to the social groups we belong to, our education and how we will be judged by others. Your accent can immediately set you apart from a group if you speak with an accent different from the dominant group.

As language evolves, so does our understanding of what the world consists of. Not only does reality and meaning differ from culture to culture, but also from group to group. Whereas modernism suppressed that which was different from the male-dominated Western perspective, postmodernism invites the difference of others, recognizing that difference contributes to the dialogue of meaning. Meaning is dependent on the collective understanding which has evolved within relationships over a period of time. Shared meaning is the invisible bond that holds communities together. Communities share sets of assumptions that guide action, behaviours and the place the individual will occupy within that community. The same is true of organizational communities. To reach a collective understanding, various interactions are required, such as conversations.

Conversations contain elements of both dialogue and discussions. The purpose of a discussion is to persuade and get a particular opinion accepted. On the other hand, the overriding purpose of partners in a dialogue is to investigate and to allow meaning to unfold without a predetermined idea as to the nature of that meaning. Dialogue also contains a sense of exploration, a willingness and openness to discover the unexpected. It is a way of interaction that collectively constructs meaning. An assumption of dialogue is the willingness of partners to understand each other (Bohm, 1996). Each partner listens with that willingness and, in turn, communicates in order to be understood. Each participant demands from the other a conversational attitude that will facilitate understanding.

Dialogue provides the opportunity and freedom for participants to contribute their ideas and holds the individual responsible for their contribution. It is however not a license to impose the ideas of one person on the others. One can argue that the transactional nature of a masculine preference reflects the qualities of conversation whereas women approach conversations in a more transformational way which is akin to that of dialogue.

Each word used in language names a perceived object. Meaning is assigned to each of these words which are then combined to form sentences. Sentences are therefore a complex and subtle array of meanings that reflect the beliefs and assumptions of a certain group of people. Postmodern philosophy suggests that the world is constituted by our shared language and that we can only know the world through the particular forms of discourse our language creates. The knowledge and meaning we assign to the world are as a result of our interactions and do not take place in isolation.

The absolute nature we have assigned to self has contributed to the suppression of women. The perceived traits and characteristics that have been assigned to men and women are seen as 'natural' to the genders. This has meant that certain roles and status within society have been attributed with the exclusive privilege or right of either gender. Men have claimed the positions of power in politics and organizations and the place assigned to women has been the home and a supportive role to men. Social constructionism argues that self is not a given, but that it is a product of society and the tool of language we employ to create self with.

With the passing of the certainty of self, and the world of truths, the infallibility of an objective world is being eroded and questioned. Central to all Western traditions is the existence of the individual self and to question such a fundamental belief is to invite a barrage of scorn.

Historically, the self has been as a mirror for what we have perceived to be *out there*. The traditional view of personality, or self, is that every person has his or her own, individual personality which remains relatively unchanged throughout his or her life, exhibiting the essence of the person. Such a belief has reinforced and maintained the chains that have bound women to their perceived natural selves. Their natural selves have meant they were bound to the roles of carers of the family and the supporters of their husbands. However, some philosophers would argue that there is no logical justification for such an enduring identity. There is no evidence which can demonstrate the existence of personality.

The modernist being is also perceived as a rational one, reliable and predictable. Central to the modernist theme of the individual thinker being the centre of knowledge, is the dictum by Descartes – 'I think, therefore, I am'. This is the rock of certainty upon which the modern world approaches things. However, if we begin to understand that the mind is not an accurate reflector of what is out there, but instead makes things up, then the very idea of what constitutes the natural self begins to crumble. It is from the material of everyday life that narration creates and assembles the self. The stories individuals tell about themselves are part of their becoming. These stories hold the possibilities of who and what one might become. In the postmodern era, the self is open to construction and reconstruction. All knowledge and understanding are as a result of direct experiences.

Historical assumptions about what constitutes the self are the product of a particular culture at a particular time. Narrative is the vehicle through which meaning is created in the moment of telling (Luhman and Boje, 2001), and the narrative in society has been that women are inferior to men. Our sense of self is dependent on the perception others have of us and how that is reflected back to us as individuals. It is therefore very difficult for women to have a sense of self and to express the nature of that self if it is not shared by others in society.

There is an agreement within the postmodern and post-structuralist domain that the Western concept of the individual self has passed its sell-by date. In our postmodern world of uncertainty, there is increasingly a need for multiple personalities. The individual has to express many different selves and juggling many different personalities and different demands on those personalities is something women are particularly good at. The busy career woman is also the carer of her family, amongst many other roles. The pastiche personality is born – a personality that is able to flex and borrow from multiple selves to suit a particular moment in time, creating a kaleidoscopic self that responds and adapts to the moment. Identity is formed by social processes and once it is established, maintained and modified by social relations. It is time as a society that we update the identity and self of women to recognize their equal status with men and it is the responsibility of women not to collude with the erroneous views held of the identity of women.

As I have outlined, language is the provider of structure to everyday life. It also provides everyday life with meaningful objects. This everyday life is also perceived as being *the* reality. However, the border between fact and fiction is blurring and new realities are constantly emerging. From a constructionist perspective, whatever the nature of reality, there is no single array of words which is able to uniquely portray such a reality. There are many interpretations as to what constitutes reality and as we have already discovered, the genders do not always share the same reality.

Organizations do not escape the ever-changing and evolving landscape of perceived realities, and postmodernism is seen as being better equipped in dealing with the paradoxes and ambiguity of contemporary society. It allows flexibility and invites the inclusion of everyone necessary to create and develop new forms in order to evolve. Terms such as truth, reality, rationality and objectivity serve a purpose and can be very useful within organizations in that they affirm the culture of the organization and maintain consistency throughout, ensuring certain modes of operation.

However, the danger is when such terms are perceived as the only way and thereby subjugating other perspectives and ways of being. The purpose of realism is striving for unity and solidarity, whereas constructionism encourages a state of ambiguity and creativity.

The truth each one of us experiences is very much dependent on the culture within which we find ourselves. In order to make sense of information and experiences, we divide our experiences into categories. However, these named subdivisions are mere abstractions and labels are assigned for the purpose of understanding and convenience. These labels do not within themselves constitute a reality which exists external to us, but are merely reflections of a communal process of sensemaking. The danger arises, of course, when we perceive our labels as being immovable and unchangeable truths. The labels we have assigned to genders have been one such example. As a society, we have created gender prisons for both genders, locking them into expected behaviours, roles and characteristics.

Postmodernism concerns itself not only with the social relationships championed or discredited by particular theories, but also with the potential for theories to offer new possibilities for our culture. Organizational studies reflect the modernist perspective that has dominated our society. It has been expressed through the creation of hierarchies that privilege particular readings and voices whilst suppressing and denying alternative articulations. In contrast, a postmodernist approach implies a collectivity of authors that would oppose, overturn and re-negotiate the established hierarchies of a modernist organization. The modernist version of what constitutes the truth is decided on by an authority that assumes superiority in its ability of knowing what is best. Such knowledge is then imposed by the elite on others, demanding their acceptance of reality. Hierarchies and laws are produced from such knowledge and used to control others, silencing and suppressing the voices of dissent.

One of the fundamental attacks of postmodernism on modernism is on the belief in a *grand narrative*. The grand narrative has determined the role of everyone in society and for generations has led to the suppression of many divergent groups within society. Generally, postmodernism is not regarded as a unified theory, but the overarching philosophy is that of a rejection of the rational discourses that lay claim to a grand narrative. Modernism is the search for a totalizing meta-narrative. Postmodernism on the other hand, directly opposes this and views meaning not as universal, but fragmented and experienced locally. Such a grand narrative seeks to dominate and suppress discourses which may be in opposition to its ideology.

The very nature of a meta-narrative leads to annihilation of what is perceived as different and in opposition to it. We see many examples where in our society we very often suppress those that are different, using extreme measures. Instead, at the heart of postmodernism is the inclusion of all the narratives within society. Through the inclusion of all narratives, we accept difference and the transient nature of knowing, which is in opposition to the modernist structure of opposites. Postmodernist knowledge then becomes a reflection of everyday life, inviting a multitude of alternative voices. What is important is not whether they are true or false, but whether they serve a purpose at a given time.

The postmodern environment is characterized by diversity and conflict as society is complex and filled with uncertainties. The grand narrative is seen as the oppressive force of authoritarianism and the death of an overarching meta-narrative reveals knowledge as not universal, but as the product of everyone.

The very idea of a grand narrative has to lead to the rejection of difference. Postmodernism recognizes truth as fluid and ever-changing and the most which is to be hoped for is a snapshot at a particular time which, of course, changes at the very moment the snapshot is taken, further illustrating the illusion of truth. Postmodernism forms the intellectual backdrop for social constructionism which I will discuss in Chapter 12.

12 Identity, the product of social constructionism

Why is it that within every culture you care to name, the value society places on women is much less than that for men? Who determines what the place is of a woman? As there is no logical biological origin for this, it can only be a result of social and cultural influence. The essentialist natures of genders have remained unquestioned and seen as a given and have served to keep genders locked into the traits and personalities assigned to each one. Such an imbalance has been kept alive via patriarchy throughout the history of (hu)mankind. Western history has been about the white, propertied and Christian male as the head of the household. History has therefore been about 'his' story and 'his' idea of truth and reality, obliterating the voices of groups other than 'his' dominant group. Not only do patriarchal values lead to the devaluation of women, but they also suppress the feminine characteristics within men, albeit subconsciously.

Men are socialized from birth to reject their emotions as being inferior and to rely on the superior qualities of their logic and tough manliness. The underlying assumption of feelings and emotions being inferior to logic has played a significant role in the perceived inferiority of women in society. Emotions and feelings have always been associated with women and motherhood. Good old Freud played a significant role in reinforcing the belief of society that women were the enemy of civilization and order. Is it surprising therefore that most women spend a big portion of their lives fighting a sense of inferiority and unworthiness? Freud naturally concluded that civilization is not only the achievement of men, but that it is also their natural birthright.

As with most theories and philosophies, there are always differences in terminology including associated meanings. Social constructionism is no exception. However, discussing the nuances within the movement is not the purpose of this book. We will seek to generate a general understanding of constructionism and how it might help us in turn to understand how the suppression of diversity within society and organizations came about. The essence of constructionism is that whatever we perceive as knowledge or having existence is the result of the creative process between all of us. Nothing exists 'out there', and the realities we experience are of our collective making. We influence each other in our thoughts and feelings and over time we create a collective paradigm which we can all believe in and express. If this is the case, then as women, we also need to understand what our contribution is and has been to facilitate the creation of an institution that leads to our suppression. How do we collude with the status quo? More about this later.

Social constructionism advises us to be ever critical of our assumptions about the world and our taken-for-granted beliefs as to how it should operate, including ourselves. The anti-realism belief of social constructionism is very important to the argument for the inclusion of diversity within society and organizations. As a belief system, it challenges the monolithic beliefs that have kept men and women imprisoned in their respective towers for centuries. The identities and characteristics traditionally assumed as being our 'natural' state are challenged by social constructionism that holds that our identities are also part of the socially created process and therefore always open to change. Identities are not fixed, but they are dynamic by nature. Social constructionism argues that our identities are not givens but created by the linguistic conventions at a particular moment in time and place and result in the truth we accept without challenge about our own place in that culture or the nature and place of others.

Social constructionism facilitates a dialogue from the many voices representing all the cultures of humanity, in an attempt to understand how realities are constructed (Campbell, 2000). We have delved into the contemporary science of complexity and how it demonstrates that everything is related and interconnected. The theme of relatedness is also fundamental to constructionism as it supports the relatedness of everything. Moreover, such relatedness leads to the central premise of social constructionism, namely, that knowledge is a product of this relatedness and is constructed between individuals. Constructionism is an outcome of postmodern thought and it views the world as the product of communal interchange.

Our individual renditions of truth and reality are constructed between ourselves and others with whom we engage to form various types of relationships. Irrespective of what our socially constructed perspective of the world might be, it requires a related action. As our perspectives of the world and people within it change, so do our corresponding actions. The objective of constructionism is not to negate traditional epistemology, but rather to invite new forms of enquiry through challenge and debate. As with postmodernism, social constructionism does not claim, nor does it offer, a replacement meta-narrative, and instead of removing or opposing difference, it sees the inclusion of difference as paramount in understanding the world afresh.

Social constructionism challenges the taken-for-granted beliefs about the world and the outmoded perception that knowledge about the world is acquired through observation alone. Instead, our experiences are seen as the result of active interchange between people engaged in reciprocal relationships. The emphasis is therefore on the necessity of communal interdependence and relationships (Gergen, 1994). Consciousness from a constructivist perspective is reflexive in nature as it realizes its contribution in establishing cultural assumptions by which things will eventually be judged.

The traditional approach to human relations is that they are a by-product of autonomous individuals and that these relations are secondary to the needs of the personal. However, from a constructivist perspective the identity of the individual is known only when juxtaposed with others. The social therefore creates the individual and is not at the mercy of the individual (Gergen, 2001). In an attempt to understand the self, attention is given to the vehicles used by the community to construct what is experienced, such as language, dialogue, ritual, traditions and distribution of power.

Contrary to popular belief by those within power, it is not a quality reserved for the select few, but is rather a body of knowledge which allows an individual to define the world in a way of his or her choosing. Power can only emerge when certain social and cultural conditions are conducive to the realization of such power. A community will represent the world and its place within that world in a way that not only gives rise to power, but also sustains that power over a period of time or until the representation changes.

As with postmodernism, constructionism advocates the multiplicity of ways in which the world may be constructed and interpreted and rejects any attempt at establishing universal first principles. Cultures create the norms and rules which determine the assumptions and subsequent human activity to be found in their specific orbit. The rules of a particular society reflect the truth of the community and are subject to change and evolution as the beliefs of the community change. Rules are culture specific and not necessarily transferable. Equally, organizations are also communities who create their own specific rules for operation and despite popular management theories, are not necessarily transferable across cultures and organizational structures. Constructionism insists on the appreciation and validity of how and why other cultures will construct a world which differs from the reality of our own. It therefore seeks not only the tolerance and understanding of difference, but also the equality of difference.

What happens when our realities become objectified is that it leads to closure of arguments (Gergen, 2001). Options are then dismissed and relationships are frozen and voices of difference go unheard. It is to be expected that the challenges levelled against traditional assumptions of knowledge by constructionism are to be resented. The view that such knowledge is the product of social creation further shakes the foundations of traditional epistemology. It is not easy to accept that the truths we held dear for generations have in fact got feet of clay. The rejection of constructionism is based on a belief in an obdurate reality. A further challenge brought by constructionism to the traditional views of truth and reality is that it is never complete, but in a continuous flow of becoming. Knowledge and truth are evermore open to redefinition and interpretation. Equally, the interpretation of events is open to infinite interpretation and modification (Gergen, 1999) and future events are also likely to influence the interpretation we may have of current events in a retrospective manner. With hindsight, current events may assume very different meanings.

Critics of social constructionism see the concepts as annihilating truth, objectivity, science and morality. However, constructionism allows one to reconstitute the past in far more promising ways and we may even be able to rewrite the history of humankind to acknowledge and include the contribution of women. If we accept that we live in a world that is socially constructed, it is important to be aware of the sources of construction and to assume responsibility for our own reality. The media plays a crucial and significant role in the creation of the reality we all experience. The media saturates everyday life and stimulates desires, creates values and generates ideals and is influential in how we construct our individual self. The language and the images used by the media, infiltrate our thinking and influence the reality our societies end up creating and expressing. As soon as we begin to articulate what is objective and what isn't, what is real and what isn't, we choose a particular tradition and way of life that will reflect a set of values and preferences. The very nature of choosing will exclude the values and preferences of others.

The question as to whether there is a real world out there reflects the Western reality of dualism – a separation between a world *out there* and a world *in here*. It is the very nature of this dualism that has created and reinforced the inferiority of women to men and their exclusion from many positions and roles within society and organizations. The very moment one identifies something as real, from that moment on one excludes other possibilities as to what might be real.

The social construction of organizations

An understanding of the generation of organizational realities is as important to the well-being of the organization as it is with any other community. Organizations also have to make sense of the ever-shifting sands of *realities* of their environment. An organization, as any other community, is an entity that is constantly changing, being reinvented as a result of the interacting relationships within and without the organization. The challenge of constructionism to perceived organizational realities is that they are the products of the fictions of our minds. All institutions, including organizations are objectified human activities. Despite the perceived power and size of many organizations, they remain the result of human interaction and construction (Berger and Luckmann, 1991).

The power of language in the creation of reality and particularly within organizations, has been of significant interest to organizational theorists in recent years. In communicating what we think the reality is, we are in fact in the process of creating that very reality. We filter out, justify and reason away the information that challenges and opposes the particular views that we may have as to what constitutes the reality of the organizations. We can think of many arguments that have been put forward as to why women are not suited to certain roles within organizations. I have put forward many of these arguments throughout earlier chapters.

The women struggling for equal acknowledgement, not only equality, can also testify to the many 'positive' stories told within organizations as to how the opportunities for women have improved and about all the efforts the organization put in to promoting diversity. I have raised the debate of equality in previous chapters, but briefly pose a question we need to answer for ourselves, whether women are or should be equal to men or whether we should celebrate and promote our differences and obtain equal recognition and acceptance because of our differences? So many women who are successful in male-dominated environments achieve their success by being able to reflect the persona and masculine characteristics of the male narrative as opposed to achieving success for bringing a different narrative.

Traditionally, organizations have been attributed with a reality and existence external to those who inhabit the organization. As discussed earlier, language is the vehicle we use to maintain a community of understanding and organizations are no exception. The logic we normally attribute to institutions is not an intrinsic characteristic of our institutions, but is provided through the application of language. It is apparent from the discussions regarding social constructionism that culture influences the assumptions we hold about a particular social environment. Equally, organizational cultures influence the assumptions held about the nature of organizations or industries. To enable an organization to move beyond its current reality and discover new realities, it may be necessary for an organization first to understand the nature of its collective beliefs and assumptions.

The participation within organizational conversations acknowledges individuals and their particular value to the organization. The act of acknowledgement by others provides individuals with the ability to influence those relationships around them. Women go unacknowledged in many areas of organizational life, particularly in the places of power, and have therefore little ability to influence.

In order to achieve acceptance within institutions, roles are created. The institution becomes embodied within an individual through the enactment of such roles. Through role playing, individuals contribute to the objectifying of their institutions. Roles are very clearly defined within organizations, those of leaders and those of the workers, and both need the other to stay within role to secure the continued existence of the other. The metaphor chosen to describe or make sense of the organization will influence the way in which it is structured. It will also affect how members within that organization are treated and how they may conduct themselves. It is worth considering the paradoxical nature of metaphors.

When individuals communicate within the organization, it is not merely for the clarification of the next task or to maintain their place within the organization. They are also involved in the process of creating meaning. According to a constructivist perspective, the ills that trouble an organization are directly a result of their negotiated reality. With the postmodernist organization comes uncertainty about the future. Such uncertainty could be painful as the human need for security is eroded. The transitory nature of organizations reflects the ephemeral and equally transitory nature of the self and personal identity.

As postmodernism and social constructionism advocate, there are different ways of defining and perceiving our organizational realities. Different approaches will reveal a different reality and a different way of making sense of the experiences we encounter within that reality. Each of these realities express its own justifications for its particular view of the world. However, as we have seen, the very need of modernism is to discover the grand narrative which dismisses the inclusion of other views and perspectives. In contrast postmodernism embraces such differences and advocates inclusion. It is through value judgements that are assigned to a particular point of view that blindness to other realities is created. This state also robs us of the sense of adventure that entertains different interpretations of reality. The strength of postmodernism in general, and social constructionism in particular, is its philosophical and practical inclusion of difference.

On a micro level, organizations wrestle with the same debates as those on the macro level. Organizations are communities creating a meaning to which all members can and should subscribe. The members of an organization should be allowed to contribute their voices to the debates and negotiations which will determine what organizational truth to is to them, a truth they can support and defend and which will inform their actions and decisions.

Drawing on the inspiration of social constructionism and postmodernism, I have therefore argued that an organization does not have a reality external to its members. It is the product of the interaction between the individuals within the organization. Organizations therefore do not have a static identity, but are in the process of being created every moment of the day through the interactions of those within the organization. Organizations are therefore dynamic and ever-changing and each one of us has the opportunity and responsibility for the reinvention of our organizations. The question is whether we constantly invent and reinvent organizations for the benefit of a small elite or whether we create organizations that are supportive of the many voices within their boundaries.

As we have seen, postmodernism advocates that knowledge is contextual and pluralistic with no absolute truths and supports the feminist challenge of essentialism. The challenge on essentialism therefore questions truths such as the true nature of male and female. The arguments of postmodernism, whether one agrees with them or not, support my argument that we should not restrict the movement of women to a single entity or universalism. People, irrespective of their gender, are far too rich and beautiful in their diversity to be reduced to a single classification.

The Enlightenment has a lot to answer for, creating a world of dualisms. The dichotomy created by the Enlightenment puts a woman between a rock and a hard place. She can either conduct herself in the manner expected of her and be labelled 'feminine' or she can express male qualities and be labelled 'unfeminine'. Not only was the male/female dualism created, but it also reinforced the less than male status of the female. The inferiority of women is attributed to the fact that she lacks the qualities of men. The inferiority of women are created and maintained by the language society employs. The power of language is so underestimated and we just have to spend a few hours in an organization, especially the boardroom, to become aware of the masculine nature of the language that permeates our organizations. A consequence of a world and organizations based on a male version of reality is that the experiences of women become invisible at best.

13 Conclusion

As I have argued and supported with various discourses, organizational reality is ultimately the result of a collectively negotiated process in which all members of the organization are engaged. Instead, organizational sensemaking is dominated by a masculine perspective, as men hold most of the senior positions within organizations. Their privileged positions also afford them the power to impose their strategy on the organization, a strategy that will not necessarily have included a diversity of opinions. Why, because diversity is not represented at senior levels where strategic discussions take place.

The very nature of strategy resists the inclusion of a feminine perspective. It is the domain of senior management and as the research and statistics have demonstrated is very much dominated by men. The games and language of strategy are designed to keep the transformational approach out. They reek with competitiveness, domination and control. The notions of collaboration and cooperation seldom feature. The language of strategy reflects the aggressive competitive nature of the 'game' of strategy.

The lack of a feminine perspective at the strategic level of organizations reflects the deeply held assumptions concerning leadership. A leadership role is very much perceived as the ownership of men and their exclusive right. The gender differences in terms of the way we approach leadership make it difficult for men to perceive leadership from a more transformational point of view as their transactional approach has always been perceived as superior.

Chiles and Meyer (2001) advise organizations that it is time to relinquish their masculine obsession with planning and control and instead, become sensitive to the whispers of change that herald the opening of new windows of opportunity. However, the awareness of such opportunities will only emerge if the organization is willing to embrace diversity.

The need for collaboration and operating collectively has been a key theme. As we have seen, collaboration is a characteristic attributed to women by numerous authors. I have drawn on the theories of complexity and postmodernism to challenge the traditional assumptions we hold regarding organizational realities. These have demonstrated that reality is the outcome of interdependent relationships, based on inclusion and cooperation. This does, however, require the participation of everyone. Furthermore, diversity is in fact the essence of creating a reality that reflects the true nature of the organization, and it is also the source of creativity. Postmodernism further challenges the unquestioned beliefs our societies hold regarding identities. Our identities are seen as biological givens which, of course, has been a key factor in keeping women locked into certain roles. However, what we have seen is that identities are socially constructed and not natural givens.

The realities created within organizations evolve almost accidentally through conversations and storytelling. It is impossible to predict, control or force the direction these stories will take. These stories do not necessarily reflect a feminist perspective or a feminine consciousness and the majority of organizational stories reflect a masculine perspective and are created and nurtured within the old-boy network. Women seldom have access to such networks despite the agreement by both practitioners and theorists that membership to such networks greatly enhances career prospects. I argued forcefully that the masculine perspective throughout society is treated as superior and has dominated the formulation of organizational strategies.

I have put forward the arguments that a feminist approach to management is more holistic and transformational whereas a masculine approach is more transactional. However, what I am not advocating is that one approach is superior to the other. Both approaches are necessary and are very much dependent on the given situation. Therein lies the secret. If women are perceived as inferior to men, a more transformational and inclusive approach will not be seen as an option to a more transactional approach. We are a long way from giving both approaches equal status, irrespective of who exhibits those traits. Neither approach is the exclusive right of a particular gender.

Whether the different approaches to strategy and leadership are the result of the roles and characteristics we are socialized into from birth or whether they are innate to our particular genders is irrelevant. What is relevant is the need for the recognition of diversity and the strengths and weaknesses of both genders to be given equal status in the running of our organizations, providing a much more balanced perspective. If organizations are to succeed within a global market place, the recognition and inclusion of diversity is vital as is the need to employ the best talent available, irrespective of the gender label the talent comes with.

Bibliography

Abrahamsson, L. (2002) Restoring the Order: Gender Segregation as an Obstacle to Organisational Development, *Applied Ergonomics*, 33: 549–557.

Ackoff, R. L. (1983) Beyond Prediction and Preparation, *Journal of Management Studies*, 20 (1): 59–69.

Adams, C. (1994) The Sexual Politics of Meat in *The Polity Reader in Gender Studies*, Cambridge: Polity Press.

Agars, M. D. (2004) Reconsidering the Impact of Gender Stereotypes on the Advancement of Women in Organizations, *Psychology of Women Quarterly*, 28: 103–111.

Aldrich, H. (1999) *Organizations Evolving*, London: SAGE Publications Ltd.

Altman, Y. and Shortland, S. (2001) Women, Aliens and International Assignments, *Women in Management Review*, 16 (3): 141–146.

Alvesson, M. and Willmott, H. (1995) Strategic Management as Domination and Emancipation: From Planning and Process to Communication and Praxis in Shrivastava, P., Huff, A. S. and Dutton, J. E. (Eds) Vol. 12 (Part A) *Advances in Strategic Management*, Hampton Hill: JAI Press Ltd.

Ansoff, H. I. (1965) *Corporate Strategy*, New York: McGraw-Hill.

Astley, G. W. (1984) Toward an Appreciation of Collective Strategy, *Academy of Management Review*, 9 (3): 526–535.

Bailey, A. and Johnson, G. (2001) A Framework for a Managerial Understanding of Strategy Development in Volberda, H. W. and Elfring, T. (Eds) *Rethinking Strategy*, London: SAGE Publication Ltd.

Bak, P. (1997) *How Nature Works: the Science of Self-Organized Criticality*, London: Biddles Ltd.

Barr, P. S., Stimpert, J. L. and Huff, A. S. (1992) Cognitive Change, Strategic Action, and Organizational Renewal, *Strategic Management Journal*, 13: 15–36.

Barry, D. and Elmes, M. (1997) Strategy Retold: Toward a Narrative View of Strategic Discourse, *Academy of Management Review*, 22 (2): 429–452.

Bateson, G. (1972) *Steps to An Ecology of Mind*, Chicago, IL: University of Chicago Press.

Becker, S. W. and Eagly, A. H. (2004) The Heroism of Women and Men, *American Psychologist*, 59 (3): 163–178.

Benhabib, S. (1994) Feminism and the Question of Postmodernism in *The Polity Reader in Gender Studies*, Cambridge: Polity Press.

Berger, P. and Luckmann, T. (1991) *The Social Construction of Reality: A Treatise in the Sociology of Knowledge*, London: Penguin Books.

Billing, Y. D. and Alvesson, M. (2000) Questioning the Notion of Feminine Leadership: A Critical Perspective on the Gender Labelling of Leadership, *Gender, Work and Organization*, 7 (3): 144–157.

Bland, L. (2001) *Banishing the Beast: Feminism, Sex and Morality*, London: Tauris Parke Paperbacks.

Bohm, D. (1996) *On Dialogue*, Nichol, L. (Ed.) London: Routledge.

Boland, R. J. Jr (1984) Sense-Making of Accounting Data as a Technique of Organizational Diagnosis, *Management Science*, 30 (7): 868–882.

Boucher, C. (1997) How Women Socially Construct Leadership in Organizations: A Study Using Memory Work, *Gender, Work and Organization*, 4 (3): 149–158.

Bradley, H. (1994) Gendered Jobs and Social Inequality in *The Polity Reader in Gender Studies*, Cambridge: Polity Press, 157–158.

Braidottie, R. (1994) Radical Philosophies of Sexual Difference: Luce Irigaray in *The Polity Reader in Gender Studies*, Cambridge: Polity Press.

Bresser, R. K. and Bishop, R. C. (1983) Dysfunctional Effects of Formal Planning: Two Theoretical Explanations, *Academy of Management Review*, 8 (4): 588–599.

Broekstra, G. (1998) An Organization is a Conversation in Grant, D., Keenoy, T. and Oswick, C. (Eds) *Discourse and Organization*, London: SAGE Publications Ltd.

Brown, L. (Ed.) (1983) *The New Shorter Oxford English Dictionary*, 5th edn, London: Oxford University Press.

Brown, R. H. (1994) Reconstructing Social Theory After the Postmodern Critique in Simons, H. W. and Billig, M. (Eds) *After Postmodernism: Reconstructing Ideology Critique*, London: SAGE Publications Ltd.

Bruner, J. (1986) *Actual Minds, Possible Worlds*, Cambridge, MA: Harvard University Press.

Bruni, A., Gherardi, S. and Poggio, B. (2004) Entrepreneur-Mentality, Gender and the Study of Women Entrepreneurs, *Journal of Organizational Change Management*, 17 (3): 256–268.

Burgelman, R. A. (1983) A Model of the Interaction of Strategic Behaviour, Corporate Context, and the Concept of Strategy, *Academy of Management Review*, 8 (1): 61–70.

Burgess, R. G. (1984) *In the Field: An Introduction to Field Research*, London: Unwin Hyman Ltd.

Burkitt, I. (1999) Relational Moves and Generative Dances in McNamee, S. and Gergen, K. J. (Eds) *Relational Responsibility: Resources for Sustainable Dialogue*, California: SAGE Publications Ltd.

Burr, V. (1995) *An Introduction to Social Constructionism*, London: Routledge.

Burrell, G. and Morgan, G. (1979) *Sociological Paradigms and Organisational Analysis*, London: Heinemann Educational Books Ltd.

Buttner, E. H. (2001) Examining Female Entrepreneurs' Management Style: an Application of a Relational Frame, *Journal of Business Ethics*, 29: 253–269.

Caldart, A. A. and Ricart, J. E. (2004) Corporate Strategy Revisited: a View From Complexity Theory, *European Management Review*, 1: 96–104.

Caligiuri, P., Lazarova, M. and Zehetbauer, S. (2004) Top Managers' National Diversity and Boundary Spanning, *Journal of Management Development*, 23 (9): 848–859.

Cameron, D. and Frazer, E. (1994) Masculinity, Violence and Sexual Murder in *The Polity Reader in Gender Studies*, Cambridge: Polity Press.

Campbell, D. (2000) *The Socially Constructed Organization*, London: H. Karnac (Books) Ltd.

Cardenas, R. A., Major, D. A. and Bernas, K. H. (2004) Exploring Work and Family Distractions: Antecedents and Outcomes, *International Journal of Stress Management*, 11 (4): 346–365.

Carli, L. L. and Eagly, A. H. (2001) Gender, Hierarchy and Leadership: An Introduction, *Journal of Social Issues*, 47 (4): 629–636.

Carter, P. and Jackson, N. (1994) Modernism, Postmodernism and Motivation, Or Why Expectancy Theory Failed to Come Up to Expectation in Hassard, J. and Parker, M. (Eds) *Postmodernism and Organizations*, London: SAGE Publications Ltd.

Charles, N. and Hughes-Freeland, F. (1996) *Practising Feminism: Identity, Difference, Power*, London: Routledge.

Chiles, T. H. and Meyer, A. D. (2001) Managing the Emergence of Clusters: An Increasing Returns Approach to Strategic Change, *Emergence*, 3 (3): 58–89.

Chodorow, N. (1994) Gender, Relation and Difference in Psychoanalytic in *The Polity Reader in Gender Studies*, Cambridge: Polity Press.

Choo, C. W. (1996) The Knowing Organization: How Organizations Use Information to Construct Meaning, Create Knowledge and Make Decisions, *International Journal of Information Management*, 16 (5): 329–340.

Choo, C. W. (2000) Working With Knowledge: How Information Professionals Help Organisations Manage What They Know, *Library Management*, 21 (8): 395–403.

Cilliers, P. (1998) *Complexity and Postmodernism: Understanding Complex Systems*, London: Routledge.

Clegg, S. R. (1990) *Modern Organizations: Organization Studies in the Postmodern World*, London: SAGE Publications Ltd.

Clegg, S., Carter, C. and Kornberger, M. (2004) Get Up, I Feel Like Being a Strategy Machine, *European Management Review*, 1: 21–28.

Colgan, F. and Ledwith, S. (Eds) *Gender, Diversity and Trade Unions*, Abingdon: Routledge.

Colville, I. D., Waterman, R. H. and Weick, K. E. (1999) Organizing and the Search for Excellence: Making Sense of the Times in Theory and Practice, *Organization*, 6 (1): 129–148.

Connell, R. W. (1994) Gender Regimes and the Gender Order in *The Polity Reader in Gender Studies*, Cambridge: Polity Press.

Cooksey, R. W. (2001) What is Complexity Science? *Emergence*, 3 (1): 77–103.

Cullen, D and Gotell, L. (2002) From Orgasms to Organizations: Maslow, Women's Sexuality and the Gendered Foundations of the Needs Hierarchy, *Gender, Work and Organization*, 9 (5): 537–555.

Cummings, S. (2002) *Recreating Strategy*, London: SAGE Publications Ltd.

Daft, R. L. and Weick, K. E. (1984) Toward a Model of Organizations as Interpretation Systems, *Academy of Management Review*, 9 (2): 284–295.

Das, T. K. and Teng, B.-S. (1999) Cognitive Biases and Strategic Decision Processes: An Integrative Perspective, *Journal of Management Studies*, 36 (6): 757–778.

Davies, H. L. (1998) *The Hotel as a Crimogenic Place*, Masters Dissertation, University of Derby.

Davies, P. G., Spencer, S. J. and Claude, M. Steele (2005) Clearing the Air: Identity Safety Moderates the Effects of Stereotype Threat on Women's Leadership Aspirations, *Journal of Personality and Social Psychology*, 88 (2): 276–287.

Davis, N. Z. (1994) Gender and Sexual Temperament in *The Polity Reader in Gender Studies*, Cambridge: Polity Press.

De Cock, C. (1998) Organisational Change and Discourse: Hegemony, Resistance and Reconstitution, *Management*, 1 (1): 1–22.

Deleuze, G. and Guattari, F. (1984) *Anti-Oedipus: Capitalism & Schizophrenia*, London: The Athlone Press Ltd.

Deleuze, G. and Guattari, F. (1999) *A Thousand Plateaus*, London: The Athlone Press Ltd.

Delphy, C. and Leonard, D. (1994) The Variety of Work Done by Wives in *The Polity Reader in Gender Studies*, Cambridge: Polity Press.

Denzin, N. K. (1983) Interpretive Interactionism in Morgan, G. (Ed.) *Beyond Method: Strategies for Social Research*, California: SAGE Publications, Inc.

De Weerdt, S. (1999) Dialoging: Exploring the Dialectics, *Emergence*, 1 (3): 64–70.

de Wit, B. and Meyer, R. (1998) *Strategy: Process, Content, Context*, 2nd edn, London: International Thomson Business Press.

Donnellon, A., Gray, B. and Bougon, M. G. (1986) Communication, Meaning and Organizational Action, *Administrative Science Quarterly*, 31: 43–55.

Dougherty, D., Borrelli, L., Munir, K. and O'Sullivan, A. (2000) Systems of Organizational Sensemaking for Sustained Product Innovation, *Journal of Engineering and Technology Management*, 17: 321–355.

Dutton, J. E. and Dukerich, J. M. (1991) Keeping an Eye on the Mirror: Image and Identity in Organizational Adaptation, *Academy of Management Journal*, 34 (3): 517–554.

Easthope, A. (2001) Postmodernism and Critical and Cultural Theory in Sim, S. (Ed.) *The Routledge Companion to Postmodernism*, London: Routledge.

Eddleston, K. A., Baldridge, D. C. and Veiga, J. F. (2004) Toward Modelling the Predictors of Managerial Career Success: Does Gender Matter? *Journal of Managerial Psychology*, 19 (4): 360–385.

Eden, C. and Ackermann, F. (1998) *Making Strategy: The Journey of Strategic Management*, London: SAGE Publications Ltd.

Eden, D. (1992) Leadership and Expectations: Pygmalion Effects and Other Self-Fulfilling Prophecies in Organizations, *Leadership Quarterly*, 3 (4): 271–305.

Ellinor, L. and Gerard, G. (1998) *Dialogue: Rediscover the Transforming Power of Conversation*, New York: John Wiley & Sons, Inc.

Ericson, T., Melander, A. and Melin, L. (2001) The Role of the Strategist in Volberda, H. W. and Elfring, T. (Eds) *Rethinking Strategy*, London: SAGE Publications Ltd.

Fagenson, E. (1993) Diversity in Management: Introduction and the Importance of Women in Management in Fagenson, E. (Ed.) *Women in Management: Trends, Issues and Challenges in Managerial Diversity*, Newbury Park, CA: SAGE Publications.

Farmer, H. S. and Associates (1997) *Diversity & Women's Career Development: From Adolescence to Adulthood*, California: SAGE Publications, Inc.

Feyerabend, P. (1987) *Farewell to Reason*, London: Verso.

Fielder, S. L. and Dawe, A. (2004) Entrepreneurship and Social Inclusion, *Women in Management Review*, 19 (3): 139–142.

Foucault, M. (1972) Power and Strategies in Gordon, C. (Ed.) *Power/Knowledge: Selected Interviews and Other Writings, 1972–1977*, New York: Pantheon Books.

French, R., Simpson, P. and Harvey, C. (2001) 'Negative Capability': the Key to Creative Leadership [Web Page] Accessed 2004 Sep. 1. Available at: http://www.sba.oakland.edu/ispso/html/2001symposium/french.htm

Friday, E. and Friday, S. S. (2003) Managing Diversity Using a Strategic Planned Change Approach, *The Journal of Management Development*, 22 (10): 863–880.

Frost, P. J. and Morgan, G. (1983) Symbols and Sensemaking: The Realization of a Framework in Pondy, L. R., Frost, P. J., Morgan, G. and Dandridge, T. C. (Eds) *Organizational Symbolism*, 1: 207–236.

Gannon, M. J. and Newman, K. L. (Eds) (2002) *Handbook of Cross-Cultural Management*, Oxford: Blackwell Publishers Ltd.

Gatens, M. (1994) The Dangers of a Woman-Centred Philosophy in *The Polity Reader in Gender Studies*, Cambridge: Polity Press.

Gaudet, T. (2004) *Consciously Female*, London: Vermilion.

Gergen, K. J. (1985) The Social Constructionist Movement in Modern Psychology, *American Psychologist*, 40 (3): 266–275.

Gergen, K. J. (1991) *The Saturated Self: Dilemmas of Identity in Contemporary Life*, New York: Basic Books, 6–10, 119–122, 144–145, 150–151.

Gergen, K. J. (1994) *Toward Transformation in Social Knowledge*, 2nd edn, London: SAGE Publications Ltd.

Gergen, K. J. (1997) *Realities and Relationships: Soundings in Social Construction*, Cambridge, MA: Harvard University Press, 191–193, 205–209, 218, 220–221, 265.

Gergen, K. J. (1999) *An Invitation to Social Construction*, London: SAGE Publications Ltd.

Gergen, K. J. (2001) *Social Construction In Context*, London: SAGE Publications Ltd.

Giddens, A. (1994) Men, Women and Romantic Love in *The Polity Reader in Gender Studies*, Cambridge: Polity Press.

Gioia, D. A. and Chittipeddi, C. K. (1991) Sensemaking and Sensegiving in Strategic Change Initiation, *Strategic Management Journal*, 12: 433–448.

Gioia, D. A. and Pitre, E. (1990) Multiparadigm Perspectives on Theory Building, *Academy of Management Review*, 15 (4): 584–602.

Glover, S. H., Bumpus, M. A., Sharp, G. F. and Munchus, G. A. (2002) Gender Differences in Ethical Decision Making, *Women in Management Review*, 17 (5): 217–227.

Goddard, C. and Wierzbicka, A. (1997) Discourse and Culture in van Dijk, T. A. (Ed.) *Discourse as Social Interaction*, London: SAGE Publications Ltd.

Golding, D. and Currie, D. (Eds) (2000) *Thinking About Management: A Reflective Practice Approach*, London: Routledge.

Goold, M. and Quinn, J. J. (1990) The Paradox of Strategic Controls, *Strategic Management Journal*, 11: 43–57.

Grant, D., Keenoy, T. and Oswick, C. (Eds) (1998) *Discourse and Organization*, London: SAGE Publications Ltd.

Grant, R. M. (1991) *Contemporary Strategy Analysis: Concepts, Techniques, Applications*, 4th edn, Oxford: Blackwell Publishers Ltd.

Gray, J. (1998) *False Dawn: The Delusions of Global Capitalism*, London: Granta Publications.

Greenleaf, R. K. (1977) *Servant Leadership: A Journey into the Nature of Legitimate Power and Greatness*, New York: Paulist Press.

Greenleaf, R. K. (1996) *On Becoming a Servant-Leader*, Frick, D. M. and Spears, L. C. (Eds) San Francisco, CA: Jossey-Bass, Inc.

Greenleaf, R. K. (1998) *The Power of Servant-Leadership*, Spears, L. C. (Ed.) San Francisco, CA: Berrett-Koehler Publishers, Inc.

Greer, G. (1999) *The Whole Woman*, London: Doubleday.

Gunnarsson, B.-L. (1997) Applied Discourse Analysis in van Dijk, T. A. (Ed.) *Discourse as Social Interaction*, London: SAGE Publications Ltd.

Haberberg, A. and Rieple, A. (2001) *The Strategic Management of Organisations*, Harlow: Pearson Education Ltd.

Håkansson, H. and Snehota, I. (1989) No Business is an Island: The Network Concept of Business Strategy, *Scandinavian Journal of Management*, 5 (3): 187–200.

Hall, C. (1992) *White, Male and Middle Class: Explorations in Feminism and History*, Cambridge: Polity Press.

Hall, C. (1994) Competing Masculinities in *The Polity Reader in Gender Studies*, Cambridge: Polity Press.

Hall, L. (1994) Deconstructing the Monolithic Phallus in *The Polity Reader in Gender Studies*, Cambridge: Polity Press.

Hampden-Turner, C. and Trompenaars, F. (2000) *Building Cross-Cultural Competence: How to Create Wealth from Conflicting Values*, Chichester: John Wiley & Sons Ltd.

Hardy, C., Lawrence, T. B. and Phillips, N. (1998) Talk and Action: Conversations and Narrative in Interorganizational Collaboration in Grant, D., Keenoy, T. and Oswick, C. (Eds) *Discourse and Organization*, London: SAGE Publications Ltd.

Hardyment, C. (1994) The Domestic Mystique in *The Polity Reader in Gender Studies*, Cambridge: Polity Press.

Harris, H. (2004) Global Careers: Work-Life Issues and the Adjustment of Women International Managers, *Journal of Management Development*, 23 (9): 818–832.

Harrison, J. S. (2003) *Strategic Management of Resources and Relationships*, USA: John Wiley & Sons, Inc.

Harvey, C. P. and Allard, M. J. (1995) *Understanding and Managing Diversity*, New Jersey: Pearson Education, Inc.

Hassard, J. (1994) Postmodernism and Organizational Analysis: An Overview in Hassard, J. and Parker, M. (Eds) *Postmodernism and Organizations*, London: SAGE Publications Ltd.

Hassard, J. and Parker, M. (Eds) (1994) *Postmodernism and Organizations*, London: SAGE Publications Ltd.

Hayes, J., Allinson, C. W. and Armstrong, S. J. (2004) Intuition, Women Managers and Gendered Stereotypes, *Personnel Review*, 33 (4): 403–417.

Hayward, S. (2005) *Women Leading*, Basingstoke: Palgrave MacMillan.

Heilman, M. E. (2001) Description and Prescription: How Gender Stereotypes Prevent Women's Ascent Up the Organizational Ladder, *Journal of Social Issues*, 57 (4): 657–674.

Heilman, M. E., Wallen, A. S., Fuchs, D. and Tamkins, M. M. (2004) Penalties for Success: Reactions to Women Who Succeed at Mal Gender-Typed Tasks, *Journal of Applied Pscyhology*, 89 (3): 416–427.

Hekman, S. (1994) The Feminist Critique of Rationality in *The Polity Reader in Gender Studies*, Cambridge: Polity Press, 51–52.

Holden, N. J. (2002) *Cross-Cultural Management: A Knowledge Management Perspective*, Harlow: Pearson Education Ltd.

Hosti, K. J. (1985) *The Dividing Discipline: Hegemony and Diversity in International Theory*, Massachussets: Allen & Unwin, Inc.

Hultin, M. and Szulkin, R. (2003) Mechanisms of Inequality: Unequal Access to Organizational Power and the Gender Wage Gap, *European Sociological Review*, 19 (2): 143–159.

Hume, D. (1962) *A Treatise of Human Nature* in Macnabb, D. G. C. (Ed.) Glasgow: William Collins.

Inkpen, A. and Mchoudhury, N. (1995) The Seeking of Strategy where it is not: Towards a Theory of Strategy Absence, *Strategic Management Journal*, 16: 313–323.

Jackson, N. and Carter, P. (2000) *Rethinking Organisational Behaviour*, Harlow: Pearson Education Ltd.

James, M. and Jongeward, D. (1996) *Born to Win*, Reading, MA: Addison-Wesley Publishing Company.

Jenkins, M. and Ambrosini, V. (Eds) (2002) *Strategic Management: A Multi-Perspective Approach*, Basingstoke: Palgrave.

Johnson, G. and Scholes, K. (1999) *Exploring Corporate Strategy*, 5th edn, Harlow: Pearson Education Ltd.

Johnson, P. (1994) *Feminism as Radical Humanism*, NSW, Australia: Allen & Unwin Pvt Ltd.

Jones, D. (2004) Screwing Diversity out of the Workers? Reading Diversity, *Journal of Organizational Change Management*, 17 (3): 281–291.

Joyce, P. and Woods, A. (2001) *Strategic Management*, London: Kogan Page Ltd.

Juarrero, A. (1999) *Dynamics in Action: Intentional Behavior as a Complex System*, Cambridge, MA: MIT Press.

Kanter, R. (1977) *Men and Women of the Corporation*, New York: Basic Books.

Kappeler, S. (1994) Art and Pornography in *The Polity Reader in Gender Studies*, Cambridge: Polity Press.

Kark, R. (2004) The Transformational Leader: Who is (S)he? A Feminist Perspective, *Journal of Organizational Change Management*, 17 (2): 160–176.

Kauffman, S. (1995) *At Home in the Universe*, Oxford: Oxford University Press.

Kerby, A. P. (1991) *Narrative and the Self*, Indiana: Indiana University Press.

Kiesler, S. and Lee, S. (1982) Managerial Response to Changing Environments: Perspective on Problem Sensing from Social Cognition, *Administrative Science Quarterly*, 27: 548–570.

Knights, D. and Mueller, F. (2004) Strategy as a 'Project': Overcoming Dualisms in the Strategy Debate, *European Management Review*, 1: 55–61.

Kristeva, J. (1994) James Joyce between Eros and Agape in *The Polity Reader in Gender Studies*, Cambridge: Polity Press.

Lane, H. W., DiStefano, J. J. and Maznevski, M. L. (2000) *International Management Behaviour*, Oxford: Blackwell Publishers Ltd.

Lane, N. and Piercy, N. F. (2003) The Ethics of Discrimination: Organizational Mindsets and Female Employment Disadvantage, *Journal of Business Ethics*, 44: 313–325.

Latour, B. (1993) *We have Never been Modern*, Porter, C. (Trans.) Hemel Hempstead, NY: Prentice Hall/Harvester Wheatsheaf.

Lawson, C. and Lorenz, E. (1999) Collective Learning, Tacit Knowledge and Regional Innovative Capacity, *Regional Studies*, 33 (4): 305–317.

Legge, K. (1995) *Human Resource Management: Rhetorics and Realities*, London: Macmillan Press Ltd.

Leonard, P. (2002) Organizing Gender? Looking at Metaphors as Frames of Meaning in Gender/Organizational Texts, *Gender, Work and Organization*, 9 (1): 60–80.

Lévinas, E. (1991) *Otherwise than Being or Beyond Essence*, Lingis, A. (Trans.) Dordrecht, Boston and London: Kluwer.

Lewin, R. (1993) *Complexity: Life at the Edge of Chaos*, New York: Macmillan Publishing Company.

Lewis, R. (1994) From Chaos to Complexity Implications for Organizations, *Executive Development*, 7 (4): 16–17.

Linstead, S. (1994) Deconstruction in the Study of Organizations in Hassard, J. and Parker, M. (Eds) *Postmodernism and Organizations*, London: SAGE Publications Ltd.

Looney, J., Robinson Kurpius, S. E. and Lucart, L. (2004) Military Leadership Evaluations. Effects of Evaluator Sex, Leader Sex, and Gender Role Attitudes, *Consulting Psychology Journal: Practice and Research*, 56 (2): 104–118.

Luhman, J. T. and Boje, D. M. (2001) What Is Complexity Science? A Possible Answer from Narrative Research, *Emergence*, 3 (1): 158–168.

Lynch, R. (2000) *Corporate Strategy*, 2nd edn, UK: Pearson Education Ltd.

Lyon, D. (1999) *Postmodernity*, 2nd edn, England: Open University Press.

Lyotard, J. F. (1979) *The Postmodern Condition: A Report on Knowledge*, UK: Manchester University Press.

Lyotard, J. F. (1988) *The Differend: Phrases in Dispute*, Van Abbeele, G. (Trans.) UK: Manchester University Press.

Lyotard, J. F. and Thebaud, J. L. (1985) *Just Gaming*, Godzich, W. (Trans.) USA: The University of Minnesota Press.

McCarty Kilian, C., Hukai, D. and McCarty, C. E. (2005) Building Diversity in the Pipeline to Corporate Leadership, *Journal of Management Development*, 24 (2): 155–168.

McCuiston, V. E., Wooldrige, B. R. and Pierce, C. K. (2004) Leading the Diverse Workforce, *Leadership & Organization Development Journal*, 25 (1): 73–92.

McDowell, L. (2001) Men, Management and Multiple Masculinities in Organisations, *Geoform*, 32 (2): 181–198.

MacLean, D., Mayer, M., MacIntosh, R. and Francis, A. (1998) *Managing Metaphors – Differing Interpretations and Implications of Complexity Theory*, 14th EGOS Colloquim, Maastricht University.

McNamee, S. K. J. and Gergen, K. J. (1999) *Relational Responsibility: Resources for Sustainable Dialogue*, California: SAGE Publications, Inc.

Mann, M. (1994) Persons, Households, Families, Lineages, Genders, Classes and Nations in *The Polity Reader in Gender Studies*, Cambridge: Polity Press.

Mano-Negrin, R. and Sheaffer, Z. (2004) Are Women 'cooler' than Men during Crises? Exploring Gender Differences in Perceiving Organisational Crisis Preparedness Proness, *Women in Management Review*, 19 (2): 109–122.

Marion, R. (1999) *The Edge of Organization: Chaos and Complexity Theories of Formal Social Systems*, California: SAGE Publications, Inc.

Marion, R. and Bacon, J. (2000) Organizational Extinction and Complex Systems, *Emergence*, 1 (4): 71–96.

Marshak, R. J. (1998) Talk and Action in Grant, D., Keenoy, T. and Oswick, C. (Eds) *Discourse and Organization*, London: SAGE Publications Ltd.

Martin, L. (2001) Are Women Better at Organisational Learning? An SME Perspective, *Women in Management Review*, 16 (6): 287–297.

Mattis, M. C. (2004) Women Entrepreneurs: Out from Under the Glass Ceiling, *Women in Management Review*, 19 (3): 154–163.

Mavin, S. (2000) Approaches to Careers in Management: Why UK Organisations should Consider Gender, *Career Development International*, 5 (1): 13–20.

Mavin, S., Bryans, P. and Waring, T. (2004) Unlearning Gender Blindness: New Directions in Management Education, *Management Decision*, 42 (3/4): 565–578.

Merali, Y. (2000) Individual and Collective Congruence in the Knowledge Management Process, *Strategic Information Systems*, 9: 213–234.

Meyer, A. and Preston, D. in Shrivastava, P., Huff, A. S. and Dutton, J. E. (Eds), Vol. 12 (Part A) (1995) *Advances in Strategic Management*, Hampton Hill: JAI Press Ltd.

Miner-Rubino, K. and Cortina, L. M. (2004) Working in a Context of Hostility Toward Women, Implications for Employees' Well-Being, *Journal of Occupational Health Psychology*, 9 (2): 107–122.

Mintzberg, H. (1976) Planning on the Left Side and Managing on the Right, *Harvard Business Review*, July–August: 49–58.

Mintzberg, H. (1978) Patterns in Strategy Formation, *Management Science*, 24: 934–948.

Mintzberg, H. (1987) Crafting Strategy, *Harvard Business Review*, July–August: 66–75.

Mintzberg, H. (1990) The Design School: Reconsidering the Basic Premises of Strategic Management, *Strategic Management Journal*, 11: 171–195.

Mintzberg, H. (1994) *The Rise and Fall of Strategic Planning*, Hemel Hempstead: Prentice Hall Europe.

Mintzberg, H., Ahlstrand, B. and Lampel, J. (1998) *Strategy Safari*, Hemel Hempstead: Prentice Hall Europe, 4–8.

Mintzberg, H., Quinn, J. B. and Ghoshal, S. (1998) *The Strategy Process* (Rev Ed) Harlow: Pearson Education Ltd.

Mir, R. and Watson, A. (2000) Strategic Management and the Philosophy of Science: The Case for a Constructivist Methodology, *Strategic Management Journal*, 21: 941–953.

Moderez, I. (1999) Freedom and Uncertainty, *Emergence*, 1 (3): 84–91.

Moore, H. (1994) The Cultural Constitution of Gender in *The Polity Reader in Gender Studies*, Cambridge: Polity Press.

Moran, D. (2000) *Introduction to Phenomenology*, London: Routledge.

Morgan, G. (1983) *Beyond Method: Strategies for Social Research*, California: SAGE Publications, Inc.

Morgan, G. (1997) *Images of Organization*, California: Sage Publications, Inc.

Mumby, D. K. and Clair, R. P. (1997) Organizational Discourse in van Dijk, T. A. (Ed.) *Discourse as Social Interaction*, London: SAGE Publications Ltd.

Newby, H., Bell, C., Rose, D. and Saunders, P. (1978) *Property, Paternalism and Power: Class and Control in Rural England*, London: Hutchinson & Co. (Publishers) Ltd.

Ng, E. S. W. and Burke, R. J. (2004) Cultural Values as Predictors of Attitudes Towards Equality and Diversity: a Canadian Experience, *Women in Management Review*, 19 (6): 317–324.

Nicolis, G. and Prigogine, I. (1989) *Exploring Complexity*, New York: W. H. Freeman & Co.

Nonaka, I. and Takeuchi, H. (1995) *The Knowledge-Creating Company*, Oxford: Oxford University Press.

Oakley, J. G. (2000) Gender-based Barriers to Senior Management Positions: Understanding the Scarcity of Female CEOs, *Journal of Business Ethics*, 7: 321–334.

O'Dwyer, J. and Carlen, P. (1994) Women in Prison: Surviving Holloway in *The Polity Reader in Gender Studies*, Cambridge: Polity Press.

Ogbor, J. O. (2001) Critical Theory and the Hegemony of Corporate Culture, *Journal of Organizational Change*, 14 (6): 590–608.

Ohmae, K. (1982) *The Mind of the Strategist: The Art of Japanese Business*, New York: McGraw-Hill, Inc.

Olesen, V. L. (2000) Feminisms and Qualitative Research At and Into the Millennium in Denzin, N. K. and Lincoln, Y. S. (Eds) *Handbook of Qualitative Research*, 2nd edn, California: SAGE Publications, Inc.

Ollson, S. and Walker, R. (2003) Through a Gendered Lens? Male and Female Executives' Representations of one Another, *Leadership & Organization Development Journal*, 24 (7): 387–396.

Ollson, S. and Walker, R. (2004) 'The Women and the Boys': Patterns of Identification and Differentiation in Senior Women Executives' Representations of Career Identity, *Women in Management Review*, 19 (5): 244–251.

Oshagbemi, T. and Gill, R. (2003) Gender Differences and Similarities in the Leadership Styles and Behaviour of UK Managers, *Women in Management Review*, 18 (6): 288–298.

Ostroff, C. and Atwater, L. E. (2003) Does Whom you Work with Matter? Effects of Referent Group Gender and Age Composition on Managers' Compensation, *Journal of Applied Psychology*, 88 (4): 725–740.

Pacey, P. (1994) Homemaking in *The Polity Reader in Gender Studies*, Cambridge: Polity Press.

Parpart, J. L. and Marchand, M. H. (Eds) (1995) *Feminism/Postmodernism/Development*, London: Routledge.

Pascale, R. T., Millemann, M. and Gioja, L. (2000) *Surfing the Edge of Chaos*, New York: Crown Publishers.

Pateman, C. (1994) The Disorder of Women in *The Polity Reader in Gender Studies*, Cambridge: Polity Press.

Paton, R. and Dempster, L. (2002) Managing Change from a Gender Perspective, *European Management Journal*, 20 (5): 539–548.

Pettigrew, A. M. (1977) Strategy Formulation as a Political Process, *International Studies of Management and Organization*, Summer: 78–87.

Pettigrew, A., Thomas, H. and Whittington, R. (2002) *Handbook of Strategy and Management*, London: SAGE Publications Ltd.

Phillips, A. (1994) The Representation of Women in *The Polity Reader in Gender Studies*, Cambridge: Polity Press.

Porter, M. E. (1980) *Competitive Strategy: Techniques for Analyzing Industries and Competitors*, New York: Free Press.

Porter, M. E. (1981) The Contributions of Industrial Organization to Strategic Management, *Academy of Management Review*, 6: 609–620.

Porter, M. E. (1990) *The Competitive Advantage of Nations*, New York: Free Press.

Porter, M. E. (2000) Location, Competition and Economic Development: Local Clusters in a Global Economy, *Economic Development Quarterly*, 14 (1): 15–34.

Purvis, J. (1994) *Hidden from History* in *The Polity Reader in Gender Studies*, Cambridge: Polity Press.

Regine, B. and Lewin, R. (2003) Third Possibility Leaders: the Invisible Edge Women Have in Complex Organisations, *The Learning Organization*, 10 (6): 47–352.

Rindfleish, J. (2002) Senior Management Women and Gender Equity: A Comparison of Public and Private Sector Women in Australia, *Senior Management Women and Gender Equity*, 21 (7): 37–55.

Rindfleish, J. and Sheridan, A. (2003) No Change from Within: Senior Women Managers' Response to Gendered Organizational Structures, *Women in Management Review*, 18 (6): 99–310.

Rodgers, H., Frearson, M. Holden, R. and Gold, J. (2003) *Equality, Diversity and Leadership: Different Journeys, Variegated Landscapes*, Proceedings of British Academy of Management Annual Conference held in Harrogate, 15–17 September 2003.

Roering, W. D. and Lad, L. J. (1995) The Thrill of Victory, and the Agony of Having to Compete: An Ethical Critique of a Myth about Competition in Shrivastava, P., Huff, A. S. and Dutton, J. E. (Eds), Vol. 12 (Part A) *Advances in Strategic Management*, Hampton Hill: JAI Press Ltd.

Roseneil, S. (1996) Transgressions and Transformations: Experience, Consciousness and Identity at Greenham in Charles, N. and Hughes-Freeland, F. (Eds) *Practising Feminism: Identity, Difference, Power*, London: Routledge.

Roughgarden, J. (2004) *Evolution's Rainbow: Diversity, Gender, and Sexuality in Nature and People*, California: University of California Press.

Saraga, E. (Ed.) (1998) *Embodying the Social: Constructions of Difference*, London: Routledge.

Schein, V. (1994) Managerial Sex Typing: a Persistent and Pervasive Barrier to Women's Opportunities in Davidson, M. and Burke, R. (Eds) *Women in Management, Current Research Issues*, London: Paul Chapman.

Schein, V., Mueller, R., Lituchy, T. and Liu, J. (1996) Think Manager – Think Male: a Global Phenomenon? *Journal of Organizational Behaviour*, 7 (4): 33–41.

Schneider, S. C. and Barsoux, J. L. (1997) *Managing Across Cultures*, Harlow: Pearson Education Ltd.

Schwenk, C. R. (1988) The Cognitive Perspective on Strategic Decision Making, *Journal of Management Studies*, 25: 41–56.

Segal, L. (1999) *Why Feminism?* Cambridge: Polity Press.

Semler, R. (1993) *Maverick!* London: Arrow Books Ltd.

Sherman, H. and Schultz, R. (1998) *Open Boundaries: Creating Business Innovation Through Complexity*, USA: Perseus Books.

Shildrick, M. (1997) *Leaky Bodies and Boundaries*, London: Routledge.

Shotter, J. (1993) *Conversational Realities: Constructing Life through Language*, London: SAGE Publications Ltd.

Shrivastava, P., Huff, A. S. and Dutton, J. E. (Eds), (1995) *Advances in Strategic Management*, Vol. 12 (Part A) Hampton Hill: JAI Press Ltd.

Sichtermann, B. (1994) Rape and Sexuality in *The Polity Reader in Gender Studies*, Cambridge: Polity Press.

Sim, S. (2000a) *Contemporary Continental Philosophy: The New Scepticism*, Aldershot: Ashgate Publishing Ltd.

Sim, S. (2000b) *Post-Marxism: An Intellectual History*, London: Routledge.

Sim, S. (2001) *The Routledge Companion to Postmodernism*, London: Routledge.

Sim, S. (2004) *Fundamentalist World: The New Dark Age of Dogma*, Cambridge: Icon Books Ltd.

Sim, S. and Van Loon, B. (2001) *Introducing Critical Theory*, Cambridge: Icon Books Ltd.

Simmie, J. and Sennett, J. (1999) Innovative Clusters: Global or Local Linkages, *National Institute Economic Review*, 170: 87–98.

Simons, H. W. and Billig, M. (Eds) (1994) *After Postmodernism: Reconstructing Ideology Critique*, London: SAGE Publications Ltd.

Simpson, P. A. and Stroh, L. K. (2004) Gender Differences Emotional Expression and Feelings of Personal Inauthenticity, *Journal of Applied Psychology*, 89 (4): 715–721.

Sims, H. P. Jr and Gioia, D. A. (1986) *The Thinking Organization*, New York: Jossey-Bass, Inc.

Smircich, L. and Stubbart, C. (1985) Strategic Management in an Enacted World, *Academy of Management Review*, 10 (4): 724–736.

Spencer, L. (2001) Postmodernism, Modernity, and the Tradition of Dissent in Sim, S. (Ed.) *The Routledge Companion to Postmodernism*, London: Routledge.

Spender, J. C. (2001) Business Policy and Strategy as a Professional Field in Volberda, H. W. and Elfring, T. (Eds) *Rethinking Strategy*, London: SAGE Publications Ltd, 26–40.

Stacey, R. D. (1995) The Science of Complexity: An Alternative Perspective for Strategic Change Processes, *Strategic Management Journal*, 16: 477–495.

Stacey, R. D. (1996) *Complexity and Creativity in Organizations*, San Francisco, CA: Berrett-Koehler Publishers, Inc.

Stacey, R. D. (2000) *Strategic Management & Organisational Dynamics*, 3rd edn, Harlow: Pearson Education Ltd.

Stacey, R. D. (2003) *Complexity and Group Processes*, Hove: Brunner-Routledge.

Stacey, R. D., Griffin, D. and Shaw, P. (2000) *Complexity and Management: Fad or Radical Challenge to Systems Thinking?* London: Routledge.

Stanworth, M. (1994) Reproductive Technologies and the Deconstruction of Motherhood in *The Polity Reader in Gender Studies*, Cambridge: Polity Press.

Stedham, Y. E. and Yamamura, J. H. (2004) Measuring National Culture: Does Gender Matter? *Women in Management Review*, 19 (5): 233–243.

Steier, F. (1991) *Research and Reflexivity*, London: SAGE Publications Ltd.

Stewart, I. and Joines, V. (1987) *TA Today: A New Introduction to Transactional Analysis*, Nottingham: Lifespace Publishing.

Strauss, A. L. (1987) *Qualitative Analysis for Social Scientists*, Cambridge: Cambridge University Press.

Susskind, L. and Elliott, M. (1983) *Paternalism, Conflict and Coproduction*, New York: Plenum Press.

Sutcliffe, K. M. (1994) What Executives Notice: Accurate Perceptions in Top Management Teams, *Academy of Management Journal*, 37 (5): 1360–1378.

Sutherland, J. and Canwell, D. (2004) *Key Concepts in Strategic Management*, Hampshire: Palgrave MacMillan.

Swann, P. and Prevezer, M. (1996) A Comparison of the Dynamics of Industrial Clustering in Computing and Biotechnology, *Research Policy*, 25: 1139–1157.

Taylor, S. S. (1999) Making Sense of Revolutionary Change: Differences in Members' Stories, *Journal of Organizational Change Management*, 12 (6): 524–539.

Tetenbaum, T. J. (1998) Shifting Paradigms: From Newton to Chaos, *Organizational Dynamics*, Spring: 21–32.

Theweleit, K. (1994) The Military Academy and the Mal Body in *The Polity Reader in Gender Studies*, Cambridge: Polity Press.

Thomas, H. and Pollock, T. (1999) From I-O Economics' S-C-P Paradigm Through Strategic Groups to Competence-Based Competition: Reflections on the Puzzle of Competitive Strategy, *British Journal of Management*, 10: 127–140.

Thomas, L., Wareing, S., Singh, I., Stilwell Peccei, J., Thornborrow, J. and Jones, J. (1999) *Language, Society and Power: An Introduction*, London: Routledge.

Thornton, A. P. (1966) *The Habit of Authority: Paternalism in British History*, London: George Allen & Unwin Ltd.

Tierney, W. G. (2000) Undaunted Courage: Life History and the Postmodern Challenge in Denzin, N. K. and Lincoln, Y. S. (Eds) *Handbook of Qualitative Research*, 2nd edn, California: SAGE Publications, Inc.

Timberlake, S. (2005) Social Capital and Gender in the Workplace, *Journal of Management Development*, 24 (1): 34–44.

Townsley, N. C. and Geist, P. (2000) *Western Journal of Communication*, 64 (2): 190–217.

Tsoukas, H. and Hatch, M. J. (2001) Complex Thinking, Complex Practice: The Case for a Narrative Approach to Organizational Complexity, *Human Relations*, 54 (9): 79–1013.

Tushman, M. L. and Anderson, P. (Eds) (1997) *Managing Strategic Innovation and Change*, 2nd edn, London: Oxford University Press.

Van de Ven, A. (1993) The Development of an Infrastructure for Entrepreneurship, *Journal of Business Venturing*, 8: 211–230.

Van Dijk, T. A. (1997) *Discourse as Social Interaction*, London: SAGE Publications Ltd.

Vinnicombe, S. and Singh, V. (2003) Locks and Keys to the Boardroom, *Women in Management Review*, 18 (6): 325–333.

Volberda, H. W. and Elfring, T. (2001) *Rethinking Strategy*, London: SAGE Publications Ltd.

von Foerster, H. (1984) On Constructing a Reality in Watzlawick, P. (Ed.) *The Invented Reality*, New York: W. W. Norton & Company.

von Glasersfeld, E. (1984) An Introduction to Radical Constructivism in Watzlawick, P. (Ed.) *The Invented Reality*, New York: W. W. Norton & Company.

von Glasersfeld, E. (1995) *Radical Constructivism: A Way of Knowing and Learning*, London: The Falmer Press.

Wajcman, J. (1994) Technology as Masculine Culture in *The Polity Reader in Gender Studies*, Cambridge: Polity Press.

Walby, S. (1994) Towards a Theory of Patriarchy in *The Polity Reader in Gender Studies*, Cambridge: Polity Press, 22–25.

Waldrop, M. M. (1992) *Complexity: The Emerging Science at the Edge of Order and Chaos*, New York: Simon & Schuster.

Wallemacq, A. and Sims, D. (1998) The Struggle With Sense in Grant, D., Keenoy, T. and Oswick, C. (Eds) Discourse and Organization, London: SAGE Publications Ltd.

Watzlawick, P. (1984) *The Invented Reality*, New York: W. W. Norton & Company.

Weeks, J. (1994) The Body and Sexuality in *The Polity Reader in Gender Studies*, Cambridge: Polity Press.

Weick, K. E. (1979) *The Social Psychology of Organizing*, New York: McGraw-Hill, Inc.

Weick, K. E. (1993) Organizational Redesign as Improvisation in Huber, G. P. and Glick, W. H. (Eds) *Redesigning Organizations*, 346–379.

Weick, K. E. (1995) *Sensemaking in Organizations*, London: SAGE Publications Ltd.

Weick, K. E. (1999) That's Moving Theories That Matter, *Journal of Management Inquiry*, 8 (2): 134–142.

Weick, K. E. (2001) *Making Sense of the Organization*, Oxford: Blackwell Publishers Ltd.

Wheatley, M. J. (1992) *Leadership and the New Science: Learning about Organization from an Orderly Universe*, California: Berrett-Koehler Publishers, Inc.

Wheatley, M. J. and Kellner-Rogers, M. (1996) *A Simpler Way*, California: Berrett-Koehler Publishers, Inc.

White, C. (2004) *Strategic Management*, Basingstoke: Palgrave MacMillan.

Whittington, R. (2000) *What is Strategy and Does it Matter?* 2nd Edn, London: International Thomson Business Press.

Whittington, R. (2004) Strategy after Modernism: Recovering Practice, *European Management Review*, 1: 62–68.

Whorf, B. L. (2000) *Language, Thought and Reality* in Carroll, J. B. (Ed.) Cambridge, MA: The MIT Press.

Wilson, D. C. and Jarzabkowski, P. (2004) Thinking and Acting Strategically: New Challenges for Interrogating Strategy, *European Management Review*, 1: 14–20.

Wilson, F. M. (2003) *Organizational Behaviour and Gender*, 2nd edn, Aldershot: Ashgate Publishing Ltd.

Winn, J. (2004) Entrepreneurship: Not an Easy Path to Top Management for Women, *Women in Management Review*, 19 (3): 143–153.

Wittgenstein, L. (1961) Tractatus Logico-Philosophicus in Pears, D. F. and McGuinness, B. F. (Eds) London: Routledge.

Wittgenstein, L. (2001) *Philosophical Investigations*, Anscombe, G. E. M. (Trans) Oxford: Blackwell Publishers Ltd.

Woodilla, J. (1998) Workplace Conversations: The Text of Organizing in Grant, D., Keenoy, T. and Oswick, C. (Eds) *Discourse and Organization*, London: SAGE Publications Ltd.

Žižek, S. (1989) *The Sublime Object of Ideology*, London: Verso.

Žižek, S. (2001) *On Belief*, London: Routledge.

Žižek, S. (2002) *Welcome to the Desert of the Real*, London: Verso.

Index

W9-DCE-917

OBESITY

OBESITY

Second Edition

Evelyn B. Kelly

Health and Medical Issues Today

 GREENWOOD™

An Imprint of ABC-CLIO, LLC
Santa Barbara, California • Denver, Colorado

Library of Congress Cataloging-in-Publication Data

Names: Kelly, Evelyn B., author.
Title: Obesity / Evelyn B. Kelly.
Description: Second edition. | Santa Barbara, California : Greenwood, [2018] |
    Series: Health and medical issues today | Includes bibliographical references
    and index.
Identifiers: LCCN 2017056252 (print) | LCCN 2017056693 (ebook) |
    ISBN 9781440858826 (ebook) | ISBN 9781440858819 (print : alk. paper)
Subjects: LCSH: Obesity.
Classification: LCC RC628 (ebook) | LCC RC628 .K45 2018 (print) |
    DDC 616.3/98—dc23
LC record available at https://lccn.loc.gov/2017056252

ISBN: 978-1-4408-5881-9 (print)
       978-1-4408-5882-6 (ebook)

22 21 20 19 18   1 2 3 4 5

This book is also available as an eBook.

Greenwood
An Imprint of ABC-CLIO, LLC

ABC-CLIO, LLC
130 Cremona Drive, P.O. Box 1911
Santa Barbara, California 93116–1911
www.abc-clio.com

This book is printed on acid-free paper ∞

Manufactured in the United States of America

Contents

Every day, the public is bombarded with information on developments in medicine and health care. Whether it is on the latest techniques in treatment or research, or on concerns over public health threats, this information directly affects the lives of people more than almost any other issue. Although there are many sources for understanding these topics—from websites and blogs to newspapers and magazines—students and ordinary citizens often need one resource that makes sense of the complex health and medical issues affecting their daily lives.

The Health and Medical Issues Today series provides just such a one-stop resource for obtaining a solid overview of the most controversial areas of health care in the 21st century. Each volume addresses one topic and provides a balanced summary of what is known. These volumes provide an excellent first step for students and lay people interested in understanding how health care works in our society today.

Each volume is broken into several parts to provide readers and researchers with easy access to the information they need:

> Part I provides overview chapters on background information—including chapters on such areas as the historical, scientific, medical, social, and legal issues involved—that a citizen needs to intelligently understand the topic.
>
> Part II provides capsule examinations of the most heated contemporary issues and debates, and analyzes in a balanced manner the viewpoints held by various advocates in the debates.
>
> Part III provides case studies that show examples of the concepts discussed in the previous sections.

A selection of reference material, such as a timeline of important events, a directory of organizations, and a bibliography, serve as the best next step in learning about the topic at hand.

The Health and Medical Issues Today series strives to provide readers with all the information needed to begin making sense of some of the most important debates going on in the world today. The series includes volumes on such topics as stem-cell research, obesity, gene therapy, alternative medicine, organ transplantation, mental health, and more.

Some people have dubbed obesity an expanding epidemic. Judging from the number of products claiming to be the answer to losing weight, many people are interested in the latest fad diet or pill that is "guaranteed to work." Floods of articles in both lay and medical publications announce almost daily that obesity is a disconcerting problem that needs to be addressed. In spite of the multitude of existing programs and emphasis on fitness, no significant changes were seen in either adult or childhood obesity prevalence in the United States between 2003–2004 and 2011–2012. According to the Food and Agriculture Organization of the United Nations, in 2013, the United States was the second most obese industrialized nation with 31.8 percent of Americans falling into the obese category; Mexico was first at 32.8 percent.

Obesity is associated with health risks. In November 2013, the U.S. surgeon general reported an estimated 300,000 deaths per year may be attributed to causes related to obesity. These numbers put two-thirds of all U.S. citizens in at-risk categories. Shocking research has revealed that in 2005 obesity overtook smoking as the leading cause of life-threatening illness and death.

And the problem is not just American. The World Health Organization (WHO) estimates that more than one billion people worldwide are overweight. In fact, the organization coined a new term, *globesity*, to describe the expanding situation.

Why is the incidence of obesity increasing at such an alarming rate? All the essential ingredients for a perfect epidemic are there: Start with technology that produces low-cost, prepackaged, and easily prepared energy-dense foods, and add terrific energy-saving machines, like cars and lawnmowers. To this mix, stir in aggressive advertising and marketing of candy, sweet bubbly drinks, and fast food, and then top with sitting for hours working at the computer or playing video games. Put all these ingredients in the microwave oven of parental influences and environmental factors, and the perfect obesity epidemic emerges.

The dominant factor in this recipe appears to be excessive caloric intake. Fast-food prevalence and super-sizing are potential culprits. According to studies, the average child in the United States will watch nearly 10,000 commercials pushing food and beverages each year. The ads affect the eating habits of both children and adults. Simply stated, people are just eating too much.

A second factor is the lack of physical activity. Non-leisure physical activity has declined both at work and at home. "Accidental exercise" is almost nonexistent. People drive around mall parking lots looking for a space closest to the stores, without thinking that an unplanned walk may do them some good. Few people choose walking up the stairs over taking the elevator. The marvels of technology have enabled the costs of inactivity to go down. Even people in hard-labor jobs like farming and construction can accomplish their tasks with less effort. These great labor-saving devices have become a double-edged sword.

But is the answer just cutting back on food and increasing exercise? Although the answer to obesity appears to be a simple, it is really a very complex problem with challenging issues. For example, scientists are studying the physiology and makeup of fat and finding some surprises. Emerging research of the role of hormones, carbohydrates, and insulin reveals how fat is stored in the body. New information on the role of gut flora on fat is also a field of interest.

Another concept that fat is just sitting in the body doing nothing has been found to be erroneous. Scientists have found that fat is not just a mass of cells occupying space but an active participant in the life and health of the person. In addition, obesity is correlated with a variety of adverse health effects, such as type-2 diabetes, heart disease, stroke, several types of cancer, gall bladder disease, sleeping disorders, arthritis, and many others. Costs of obesity are astounding. Each taxpayer pays about $180 per year on obesity-related medical costs for public-sector health plans.

The interplay of advertising, parental, and environmental influences, social factors, behavior, and genetics affects weight and body mass. Thus, obesity becomes both a personal and societal problem. For the individual, genetics loads the gun, but environment pulls the trigger. And the same factor is part of the societal issues. Solving the issues will involve a concerted effort on many fronts.

This book, *Obesity*, is a revision of the 2006 edition of *Obesity* and contains updated information, coverage of new and emerging topics in the field of obesity research and treatment, and a redesigned Part III that now includes case studies.

PART I

Overview and Background Information

CHAPTER 1

Obesity: A Perfect and Costly Epidemic

If a jetliner crashes into a mountain with 150 passengers on board, dedicated rescuers tromp through dense jungles in a desperate hunt for any survivors. If a tsunami tragically kills large numbers of people, people from all over the world jump into action. They have great pity for the innocent victims of such a disaster. Yet when study after study reports the relationship between health problems and obesity, most people really don't care. Some media hype might accompany the release of a study or new federal guidelines, but that soon disappears.

A typical young person not suffering from any pain or chronic symptoms does not have to worry about something that won't happen for a long time. The condition is typical of those who do not see that decisions they make today will affect the future. It's a case of *I-don't-care-itis*. Why should I care about fixing something that isn't broken?

I-don't-care-itis is a powerful element in the obesity epidemic. Unlike the black death or smallpox plagues, obesity is the first human-made epidemic. It might be called a perfect epidemic—perfect because all the right elements are coming together to create this killer. Someone has described the situation as the genes of survival in a time of plenty. Evolutionary mechanisms are in place to keep weight on to stave off starvation, but when people have plenty of food and little exercise, circumstances create a world of bodies that put on weight and keep it there. Not caring about or realizing the importance of this perfect epidemic perpetuates it.

The United States is the epicenter of the perfect epidemic. According to a 2015 study by the Centers for Disease Control and Prevention (CDC) presented in *the Journal of the American Medical Association* (*JAMA*), more than one-third (34.9%) of U.S. adults age 20 and older are overweight. The study also found a significant increase in obesity, especially among women aged 60 years and older (from 31.5% in 2003 to 38.1% in 2012). Although the prevalence in children has remained stable from a previous 2003 study, the 2012 study showed that 17 percent (or 12.7 million) of youths (ages 2–19) are obese. However, even more troubling from the 2012 data for obesity and severe obesity among people younger than 20 is the projection into the future: overweight children may cause the obesity prevalence to reach 50 percent by 2030.

Why is obesity increasing at such an alarming rate? A number of factors are involved, including the following:

- Environment: Home, work, school, and community encourage overeating and create barriers to an active lifestyle.
- Behavior: Individuals eat too many calories while not getting enough physical activity.
- Genetics: Heredity influences the susceptibility to overweight; genes also determine how the body burns calories for energy and fat storage, as well as appetite and satiety, the feeling of being full or having enough to eat.

Environment is a major determinant of obesity and overweight. Primarily related to food intake and physical activity, environmental influences are powerful. Many strong traditions encourage overeating and consumption of high-calorie foods. For example, in some cultures encouraging people to eat and enjoy meals indicates caring. In the Southeastern United States, feeding people denotes hospitality. Many people in this area grew up with energy-dense foods like fried chicken, fried corn, and pecan pie. Even nutritious vegetables like green beans are overcooked and swim in fatback seasoning from hogs. Remembering mama's cooking is part of the culture. And it is not only in the South: Italians are famous for their "big fat Italian dinners," and the French are known for high-calorie pastries and desserts. In fact, the cuisines of many cultures provide powerful memories associated with food. People cherish these traditions and pass them on to their children.

A second environmental factor is advertising. The food industry mounts an aggressive $12 billion campaign for supermarkets, restaurants, and fast-food businesses. These ads blare at us on television and stare at us from magazines and newspapers. The large portions of food served in restaurants encourage high calorie consumption. The popular super buffets and all-you-can-eat restaurants embrace the psychology that people can eat a lot and get great value for their money. Even when calorie intake does not exceed recommendations and an individual is not overeating, physical activity may not be sufficient to offset consumption. Here is where progress is a two-edged sword. Life is much easier, but increased mechanization limits physical work and activity. Hence, for most of their waking hours, individuals are trapped in sedentary routines at school or work, while riding in a car, or in front of a computer or television. This atmosphere of inactivity promotes obesity.

A number of psychological behaviors influence eating habits. Individuals eat to combat boredom, sadness, or anger. A 1995 study found that 10 percent of people who have mild obesity and try to lose weight on their own have binge eating disorders (BED). Individuals with BED feel they cannot control how much they eat. Most likely, these people have low self-esteem or symptoms of depression. People with binge eating disorders may have more difficulty losing weight and keeping it off than those without BED. Of those who seek professional help, 20 to 30 percent may have BED.

Many fascinating studies have investigated the genetic influences on obesity. A number of these studies have shown that some people are more susceptible to weight gain or loss. Thus, the search is on for a "fat gene." So far, none has been found. Most scientists agree that obesity genetics is multifactorial—that is, several genes are interacting. While investigations continue, nongenetic factors, such as attitudes about food, physical activity, body image, age, gender, income, education, and occupation, will remain strong. In other words, genetics loads the gun, but environment pulls the trigger to make the perfect epidemic.

Often overlooked are other causes of weight gain and obesity. Health conditions such as hypothyroidism (malfunction of the thyroid gland), Cushing's syndrome, and certain neurological problems can lead to overeating. Drugs like steroids and some antidepressants may increase appetite. These medical conditions may not respond to prescribed obesity treatments.

WHAT IS OBESITY?

In 2013, the American Medical Association determined that obesity is a chronic disease. The Obesity Management Association (OMA) provides a technical definition: Obesity is defined as "a chronic, relapsing, multi-factorial, neurobehavioral disease, in which an increase in body fat promotes adipose tissue dysfunction and abnormal fat mass physical forces, resulting in adverse metabolic, biomechanical, and psychosocial health consequences."

That definition is quite a mouthful and simply means that it is a disorder related to the complex forces of environment, genetics, and some unknown causes.

A simpler definition is that obesity is an abnormal increase of fat in the body tissues. Actually, the word *obese* is used more in clinical settings; the term *overweight* is used to describe individuals with a moderate amount of body fat. In 1901, American insurance companies issued idealized weight tables to determine normal weight. At first these charts were based on healthy men, but they were revised in 1959 to include desirable weights for specific heights. In 1998, the National Institutes of Health (NIH) issued unified standards based on body mass index (BMI) to assist scientists in classifying weight. BMI is a measure of body weight (in kilograms) divided by height (in meters) squared:

$$BMI = weight\ (kg) \div height^2\ (m)^2$$

From the number created by the division of weight by height squared, a person is determined to be underweight, normal, overweight, obese, or morbidly obese (see Table 1.1). Normal BMI is 18.5–24.9. A person with a BMI of less than 18.5 is underweight. The BMI range of 25.0–29.9 is designated as overweight. Three classes of obesity are charted: Class I, BMI 30.0–34.9; class II, BMI 35.0–30.9; and class III (extreme or morbid obesity), BMI greater than 40. BMI is only an estimate of the body fat, and it is primarily used for assessing risk for developing a host of diseases. Remember, BMI can be misleading for very muscular people or for women who are nursing. For calculation in common units, see "What's Your BMI in Pounds and Inches?"

Table 1.1 Weight Classifications Based on BMI

Category	BMI (kg/m^2)
Underweight	<18.5
Normal	18.5–24.9
Overweight	25.0–29.9
Class I obesity	30.0–34.9
Class II obesity	35.0–39.9
Class III obesity (extreme or morbid)	>40.0

What's Your BMI?

To figure your body mass index, grab a calculator, pencil, and paper, and follow these steps:

1. Get your weight in pounds and multiply by 703.
2. Get your height in inches and multiply that number times itself.
3. Divide #1 by #2.

Example: A woman is 5'4" and weighs 140 pounds.

1. $140 \times 703 = 98,420$
2. 5'4" is 64 inches; $64 \times 64 = 4,096$
3. $98,420 \div 4,096 = 24$

The woman's BMI is in the normal range, according to Table 1.1.

Don't want to do the math? Find your BMI the easy way by going to one of the following websites:

- BMI Calculator, CDC, http://www.cdc.gov/nccdphp/dnpa/bmi/calc-bmi.htm
- Calculate Your BMI, National Heart, Lung, and Blood Institute, http://www.nhlbisupport.com/bmi/bmicalc.htm

To see how your waist circumference relates to your BMI, check out the NHLBI's Guidelines on Overweight and Obesity: Electronic Textbook, http://www.nhlbi.nih.gov/guidelines/obesity/e_txtbk/txgd/4142.htm.

The OMA does recognize that different BMI cut-off points may be more appropriate for women versus men and may vary in people of different races and ethnicities. They recognize that the cut-off points have not been scientifically validated in all groups.

OTHER WAYS OF ASSESSING FAT

Several other ways of assessing fat are used from time to time. Probably the least scientific and certainly the least accurate is the "eyeball test."

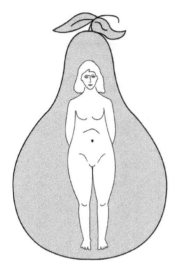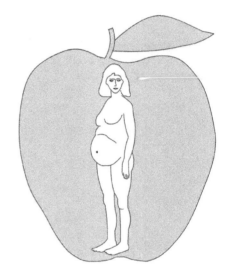

Figure 1.1 Pear and Apple Body Shapes

A person looks at himself or herself or at others and decides according to idealized perceptions about fat. Some ways that professionals use to assess fat are not very accurate either, but other ways attempt to be more scientific, such as the following:

- Body shape and abdominal fat: Where fat accumulates in the body indicates certain things to physicians. There are two kinds of body shapes—apples and pears (see Figure 1.1). People with apple shapes have fat concentrated in the upper part and midsection of the body. This type is seen mostly in men and is called android obesity, from the Greek word *andros* (man). The second type, the pear shape in which fat is accumulated on hips, thighs, and legs, is seen mostly in women. Pear shapes are called gynecoid obesity, from the Greek *gynec* (woman). An apple-shaped person has the greatest health risk because of all the important body activities that take place in the abdominal area. A simple measure of shape is waist circumference. 1998 guidelines state that health risks increase for women whose waists are 35 or more inches and for men whose waists are 40 or more inches (see Chapter 7).
- Calipers: Calipers are devices that measure body fat by pinching the fat in the arm or other areas and then finding the measurement on a standardized chart. Measurements may vary according to who is doing the measuring; using calipers requires training and skill.

- Bioelectrical impedance: In *bioelectrical impedance*, electrodes are placed at various places on the body, or the person may stand on bare electrodes with bare feet. A mild current is sent through the electrodes. Fat is a poor conductor of electricity, whereas lean body mass and bones are good conductors. Body fat percentage is calculated by subtracting the fat-free body mass from the total body weight.
- Water displacement: A person is accurately weighed dry and then is seated in a tank of water on a special chair. A weight belt is attached, and then the person expels as much air from the lungs as possible and is submerged for 10 seconds. A technician calculates the weight under water and the amount of water the body displaces. The process is repeated 10 times, and an average is taken. The procedure is fairly accurate but very cumbersome and expensive. It is used primarily in academic and research facilities.
- Biopod: This procedure uses the same theory of displaced volume as the water displacement method, except it displaces air. All clothing is removed, and a tight-fitting cap controls the hair. The subject sits in a sealed pod and exhales when told. The machine is very expensive and is seen only in specialized research facilities.
- DEXA: Dual-energy X-ray absorptiometry (DEXA) is a type of X-ray that measures both body fat and bone density. Although expensive, the machine is easy to use and suited for a physician's office.
- MRI: Magnetic resonance imaging (MRI) places the subject in a machine that uses atomic nuclei in a strong magnetic field to measure fat. MRI is an excellent source that shows body fat in specific tissues and accurately measures the percentage of fat.
- CAT: Computerized axial tomography (CAT) scans are a computer-driven series of X-rays. They are almost as accurate as MRI in computing body fat percentage.

In thinking about assessment, it is more important for a healthy lifestyle to think of body fat composition rather than just weight.

PREVALENCE OF THE PROBLEM IN THE UNITED STATES

The prevalence of obesity is a major public health issue throughout the United States. Epidemiologists and researchers conduct studies by surveying large groups of people and collecting information. (See "A Short Study of Studies.") Data for the Third National Health and Nutrition Examination Survey (NHANES III) were collected between 1988 and 1994. According to a 2014 study update of the NHANESIII from the Centers for Disease Control (CDC), more than one-third (34.9%) of all U.S. adults age 20 years and older are overweight. This study revealed that overweight conditions are increasing among non-Hispanic whites and blacks, as well as among Mexican Americans. These results also indicate more men have a BMI greater or equal to 25, but more women have a BMI greater than 30. Overweight was more common among men than women, yet more women were obese than men.

A Short Study of Studies

To understand how studies are carried out, one must think numbers. At one time physicians made decisions on anecdotes—"someone got well on a treatment, so it must work for others." There were no numbers to show whether the procedure really worked or whether other factors were involved.

Scientific medicine uses the term *quantitative* to describe how numbers are used to calculate effectiveness and risk. When the term *study* is used in this book, remember that numbers and statistics are driving the results. Scientific studies are based on probability. Here are terms that you must know:

Statistics:	a scientific way of gathering and analyzing data to get information and calculate probabilities
Sample:	a part of a population selected by techniques that represent the whole population
Data:	numbers gathered and fed into a statistical formula
Correlation:	the extent to which two things are related; used interchangeably with the term *association*
Significance:	a very specific term that means that after all the figures are in, there is only a small probability that the results could have been by chance alone
Risk:	an estimate of the degree of hazard to a population
Prevalence:	the total number of cases of a disease or condition in a given population at a given time
Morbidity:	the incidence of a particular disease in a population during a given time period (usually one year)
Mortality:	the incidence of death in a given population during a given time period (usually one year)

According to NHANES III, more female college students think of themselves as being overweight than do their male counterparts; however, the numbers of males and females who were actually overweight according to their BMI were not drastically different. Only in black males was the percentage of persons with excess body weight greater than the percentage that thought they were overweight. These studies indicate that gender and culture differences may play a role in who considers himself or herself overweight.

Some researchers have suggested that the prevalence of obesity is related to social class. Social class indicators include education and income. Overweight and obesity were most common among the least educated and among those living in households earning less than $10,000 a year. Among women, the prevalence of obesity was consistently highest among those with less than 12 years of education. In both men and women, the more educated and those with the highest incomes had the lowest prevalence of obesity.

- Comparing studies over the years shows conclusive trends. Since 1960, the National Center for Health Statistics has tracked height and weight data from studies in the following years: NHESI (1960–1962); NHANES I (1971–1975), NHANES II (1976–1980), NHANES III (1988–1994). Data from the studies show that between 1976–1980 and 1988–1995, the percentage increase in obesity was substantially greater than increases between 1960 and 1975. The dramatic increases were seen in both adults and children. Racial and ethnic minorities, especially non-Hispanic blacks and Mexican Americans, experienced increases greater than non-Hispanic whites.

A 2015 update study of the study reflects the following:

- Percentage of adults age 20 years and over with obesity: 37.9% (2013–2014)
- Percentage of adults age 20 years and over who are overweight, including obesity: 70.7% (2013–2014)
- Percentage of adolescents age 12–19 years with obesity: 20.6% (2013–2014)
- Percentage of children age 6–11 years with obesity: 17.4% (2013–2014)
- Percentage of children age 2–5 years with obesity: 9.4% (2013–2014)

GLOBESITY

At one time obesity was considered a problem of the affluent and self-indulgent countries, with the United States in the epicenter. No longer is this the case. The World Health Organization (WHO), a group that monitors the health of all nations, terms it as a "rising epidemic," and unless steps are taken, the prevalence of obesity could double by 2010.

Dr. Stephan Rossner, an obesity expert at Huddinge University Hospital in Stockholm, Sweden, and president of the International Association for the Study of Obesity, believes that there is no country in the world where obesity is not increasing. So far, nothing has been done to stop it.

The Organization for Economic Cooperation and Development (OECD), a group based in Paris that represents 30 industrialized nations, is a watchdog of worldwide health trends. Using the same BMI classifications as the CDC, the OECD found that in its member countries, the problem is growing. Its study found that obesity in the United States doubled in 20 years to affect 26 percent of the population. In Australia and the United Kingdom, the prevalence of overweight and obesity has tripled to about 21 percent since 1980.

WHO and OECD studies chronicle the rise of the epidemic in country after country, even in developing countries like Zimbabwe and Gambia. These organizations offer some reasons why the problem that originated in Western countries is rapidly being exported to developing countries:

- Modernization: The explosion of industry and technology more than 50 years ago in the Western world has led to an abundance of food—especially high-density foods—and an overall decrease in physical activity.
- Urbanization: The growth of large cities is associated with changes in diet away from more traditional foods and changes from an active, hard-working lifestyle. For example, the rise in car ownership has decreased walking. Rising crime rates in some areas, such as public housing developments, can also discourage women and elderly people from walking. The increase in the use of modern appliances, such as microwaves, dishwashers, washing machines, and vacuum cleaners, has decreased labor. Television viewing has replaced outdoor activities. Computerization in all areas has decreased manual labor. Elevators, escalators, and automatic doors have decreased physical exertion.
- Work outside the home: The number of women in the workforce has increased, making the use of convenience foods more prevalent.

- Globalization: Ethnic groups in many industrialized countries appear to be affected to the degree that they are exposed to the Western lifestyle.

Although a BMI of 27 is classified as moderately overweight, a BMI of 30 or above is the standard of the International Task Force, the CDC, and other national and international health agencies. WHO keeps careful statistics on the obesity epidemic and makes them available on its nutrition website, http://www.who.int/nut/#obs. Consider some specific situations from several databases:

- United States: Alabama and Mississippi, the poorest states, have the highest obesity rates.
- Latin America: Development is correlated with a rise in processed foods in supermarkets, from 20 percent in the 1980s to 60 percent in 2000. Result: obesity.
- Europe: More than half of the food ads in the 10 countries surveyed are for fast foods, candy, and sweetened cereals.
- Africa: In some regions, obesity affects more children than malnutrition does. In Tunisia people are abandoning their traditional whole-grain breads for processed white bread.
- Pacific Islands: The shift to high-fat Western diets has created islands with the world's fattest people.
- Australia: Aborigines have reported high prevalence of hypertension and type-2 diabetes after abandoning their traditional hunter-gatherer lifestyle, which included lots of physical activity and a low-calorie, high-fiber diet, for a Western diet.
- Pima Indians: The Pima Indians of Arizona have a higher prevalence of obesity and type-2 diabetes than the Pima Indians in Mexico. Those in Mexico eat a diet of complex carbohydrates and get lots of physical activity; those in Arizona have a more Western lifestyle.
- Hawaii: Native Hawaiians who once adopted a modern lifestyle have demonstrated a reduction in obesity and improved cardiovascular health by returning to a traditional diet.
- South Africa: Residents are flocking from the townships to cities like Johannesburg looking for work. They leave a life of physical labor for a life where work is sporadic or nonexistent.
- China: Obesity and heart disease are on the rise; many have traded their bicycles for motorized scooters.

A direct link exists between urban sprawl and health. People who live in these areas walk less, weigh more, and suffer from elevated blood pressure. Exportation of fast-food companies, especially from the United States, makes high-fat, calorie-dense foods available. Even in occupations that once demanded intense physical labor, mechanization is decreasing physical activity on the job. Dr. Rossner cited meeting a Swedish lumberjack who, only a year or so ago, expended more than 7,000 calories a day cutting trees. Now his labor is done by machine.

COSTS OF OBESITY

Although the costs of health care and diet aids are substantial, obesity's toll of human suffering cannot be measured. In 2000, the cost of obesity in the United States was more than $117 billion. Poor nutrition and physical inactivity account for more than 300,000 deaths in the United States each year.

Healthcare economic studies have a special terminology to evaluate the burden or cost of illness. Here are some definitions that reflect cost-of-illness studies:

- Cost of illness: an analysis of the total costs incurred by a society due to a specific disease; this estimates the cost to the community, which could be defined as a nation, state, health insurance plan membership, or employer
- Direct costs: the cost of prevention, diagnosis, and treatment related to a disease, including hospital care, physician services, and medications
- Indirect costs: the value of the lost output resulting from stopping of work or other productivity due to the disease
- Morbidity costs: wages lost by people who are unable to work because of the illness or disease
- Mortality costs: value of future earning lost by people who die prematurely

An example of indirect cost would be the decreased physical function and vitality and increased pain of carrying 20 pounds or more. These types of studies are essential to developing public policy about obesity.

RTI International is a group that has studied the obesity dilemma and has developed an obesity cost calculator that can be used for any firm. Dr. Eric Finkelstein presented the following facts about the costs of obesity at the First Annual Obesity Conference (2004):

- Medical costs for obesity total more than $90 billion per year. About 9 percent of medical spending goes to treating obesity-related diseases. Costs are now rivaling those for treating smoking.
- Medicare and Medicaid, government-sponsored health programs, pay about half of the obesity-related dollars. Each taxpayer spends about $180 per year on these medical costs for public-sector health plans.
- Employers and employees also subsidize the costs of obesity for those with private insurance.
- Women with a BMI of 36 missed an average of 3.6 days from work; those with a BMI of 40 or higher missed an average of 9.0 days of work. The financial value of workdays missed per obese woman is about $400.
- Approximately $5.9 billion per year is spent across all firms.

As waistlines grow, healthcare costs catapult, according to D. E. Arterburn, a University of Cincinnati researcher. Writing in the *International Journal of Obesity* (2005), Arterburn described how morbid obesity is associated with substantially increased morbidity and mortality from chronic health conditions and with poorer health-related quality of life. Using data from a study of 16,262 adults in the 2000 Medical Expenditure Panel Survey, he compared normal-weight adults with morbidly obese adults and found that the odds of incurring healthcare expenditures were two times greater. Per capita health expenses for morbidly obese adults were 81 percent greater than for those of normal weight, 65 percent greater than for those that were overweight, and 47 percent greater than for those with Class I obesity. When compared to normal weight adults, those who were morbidly obese were more likely to be female, African American, living in the Southern United States, and living in a household with an income below 200 percent of the federal poverty level. M. L. Daviglus et al. (2004) found that BMI in young adulthood and middle age is correlated with Medicare expenditures in older age. Linking Medicare data from 1984 to 2002 with the Chicago Heart Association Detection Project in Industry of 1967–1973, the researchers found that obesity and overweight in young adulthood and middle age has long-term adverse consequences for healthcare costs in older age.

These and other published reports show the substantial social cost of obesity. Getting the message to the public that the costs of obesity are overwhelming and can bankrupt a nation unless changes are made is a daunting task. However, Arterburn, Daviglus, and Finklestein are convinced that publishing and promoting these financial arguments are probably the best strategies for convincing people to act.

Understanding obesity requires the integration of social, behavioral, cultural, physiological, and genetic factors. Obesity affects millions of American adults and children and represents a challenging public health problem. Labor-saving devices, overconsumption, and the number of people who engage in little or no leisure-time physical activity may partially explain the condition. Studies from the United States and the world show why obesity is the perfect epidemic and why many scientists believe that it is the most prevalent and fatal disease, increasing at rates only seen with infectious diseases. However, controversies rage around what to do. The issues relating to the perfect epidemic are considered in Part II.

CHAPTER 2

Obesity Battles throughout the Ages

Being overweight was not always bad. One of the earliest representations of the human body is a puzzling pint-size sculpture, Venus von Willendorf (see Figure 2.1). If she represented her culture, thin was definitely not in. About the size of a human hand, Venus has no face but sports rows on her head that look like organized kernels on an ear of corn. She has large breasts; a huge round stomach; ample thighs; and tiny, fat feet. This 25,000-year-old limestone replica was discovered in a cave near the Austrian village of Willendorf, hence the name Venus von Willendorf.

In fact, archeologists have unearthed about 100 Paleolithic Venus figurines from southwestern France, Italy, Austria, Turkey, and the north shore of the Black Sea. They are carved in limestone, clay, and ivory, but all the replicas have two things in common: they are all fat, and they all have knee problems. The meaning of the figures frustrates anthropologists. They may represent a fertility cult or a sort of idealized Mother Earth, or they may reflect wishful thinking on the part of their creators. Early man probably understood that large women were valuable to survival and bearing children. During the Ice Age, when glaciers covered most of Europe, people had to hunt and forage for their food; these people certainly had to work for their food or starve. However, the figures suggest that obesity existed even for people in the Stone Age.

Although obesity is projected to be the major epidemic of the twenty-first century, body image and appearance have been on the minds of people throughout history, and ideas about obesity and overweight have varied At

Figure 2.1 Venus of Willendorf

times, being overweight was desirable and a sign of prosperity; at other times, "thin was in."

The desirable body image vacillates from culture to culture and period to period. References to obesity appear in some old Egyptian medical texts, but the bulk of information about body shape and size comes from art history and fashion culture. Only in the twentieth century did the study of obesity and the effects of fat on the body develop into a science.

OBESITY IN ANCIENT HISTORY

About 10,000 years ago, during the Neolithic era, humans experienced the great agriculture revolution. They planted food and domesticated animals. In areas such as the Fertile Crescent of the Middle East, China, Egypt, and Western Europe, the abundance of food allowed small, elite groups of people to grow large and fat. The book *Historic Costumes in Pictures* (1975) has 1,450 illustrations of people in various classes from 2000 BC to the late 1800s. The ruling class and some wealthy businessmen are overweight; the peasants and lower classes are thin.

In Egypt the goddess Isis was depicted as large and fertile; she was even larger than her mate, Osiris. Em Hotep, the creator of the pyramids, appeared overweight by today's standards. However, the Ebers Papyrus, thought to be the oldest extant medical document, dating to 1552 BC, addresses the problem of fat. According to a section from the "Book of the Stomach," if a man suffers stomach ailments, all his limbs are heavy, and his stomach goes and comes like waves under the fingers, then overeating may be the cause. In Egyptian murals, slender high-society women with long arms and legs appear as the beauties of the day. The pharaohs depicted themselves with slender physiques. However, studies of the mummified bodies reveal rolls of body fat, and the pharaohs were not known for denying themselves food or overworking. One historian has surmised that the models for the pictures of the pharaohs were probably their servants. In contrast to the Egyptian ideal of a slender body, the Greeks valued athleticism. Both males and females in paintings appear muscular. For example, according to legend, Pallas Athena, a well-trained athlete, jumped from the head of Zeus. The ancient Greek elites had the resources and leisure time to gain weight and perhaps preferred heavier bodies. Concerned about this trend, Hippocrates (c. 460–377 BC), the great Greek physician, observed that sudden death was more common in those who were naturally fat than in the lean. He encouraged obese people to eat only once a day, take no baths, sleep on a hard bed, and walk naked as long as possible.

In spite of the Greek concern for the athletic body, gluttony or serious overeating existed. Dionysius, a tyrant who lived in Heraclea, stuffed himself so full that he could barely breathe. Often he fell asleep on his throne while making a ruling. His physicians discovered that when needles were jabbed through the sides of his belly fat, he remained asleep, but when they hit firm flesh, he awakened. He expressed the wish to die with his mouth full and rot away in pleasure.

Some Greeks ridiculed those who were obese. Aristophanes, the Greek dramatist, poked fun at those who permitted themselves to get fat and those who were "gouty, big-bellied, heavy of limb, and scandalously stout." The residents of Sparta, a tough and war-like Greek city-state, had little tolerance for overweight citizens. They solved the problem by banishing them from the city. Residents of the island of Crete disdained obesity and claimed they had a secret formula that allowed people to eat as much as they wanted without getting fat. This highly used product was probably some toxic purgative. Cretans may have been the first bulimics.

Although the Romans were famous for gorging at sumptuous banquets, obesity was frowned upon. The Roman physician Galen (c. 129–199) was the first to divide obese people into types. The first type was moderate obesity, which Galen saw as a consequence of life and aging. This type was acceptable and showed economic success. The second type, immoderate obesity, was a character flaw from a life of overindulgence and lust. Galen believed that people with the second type of obesity were impossible to treat and were defiant of nature. He even wrote of his own struggle with overindulgence in his work *On Passions*. Also, some rich Roman women may have been the first anorexics. Documented cases exist where women starved themselves, even to death, to please demanding husbands and fathers.

Other ancient cultures differed in attitudes about body image. Indian paintings of classical beauties reveal hourglass figures with full busts, slender waists, and pronounced hips. However, many Indian gods are fat. Ganesh, the Hindu deity of wisdom and obstacles, is the most lovable of the fat, four-armed gods. According to Hindu tradition, this elephant-headed god holds in his enormous belly the eggs of the entire universe, as well as the power to destroy. Buddha is usually depicted as a smiling obese man perched in thought in the lotus position. Yet in Japan, a traditional Buddhist country, gluttony was related to greed, which indicated a moral failure. In an art museum in Fukuoka, Japan, there is a cut from a twelfth-century picture scroll of an obese older woman and two hefty servant girls. The caption on the picture reads that this woman was a moneylender who became extremely wealthy, and because she ate all kinds of rich food, her body became fat. In Japanese culture, greed and gluttony are moral shortcomings.

Like many other religions, the Judeo-Christian tradition equates gluttony with moral depravity or a moral shortcoming. Yet several of the Proverbs tout that serving God will provide abundant food for the believer. For example, according to Proverbs 28:5, "He that is of proud heart stirs up strife, but he that putteth his trust in the Lord shall be made fat." However, in most Christian teachings, gluttony is ranked with lust, sloth, anger, envy, covetousness, and pride. John the Baptist ate only honey and locusts and never drank alcohol, and the apostle Paul condemned those whose god is their belly.

OBESITY IN THE MIDDLE AGES

During the Middle Ages, most art depicted saints rather than normal men and women. Little attention was given to the body. Yet the writings of Saint Ambrose (c. 330–397) and Saint Augustine (354–430) rank gluttony as one of the seven deadly sins. Morality plays, a popular form of drama in the Middle Ages, described hell as a place where sauces are seasoned with sulfur and devils stuff gluttons with toads from stinking rivers. The reality of this period is that food and being overweight became symbols of wealth and prominence. Peasants, who had to live on meager diets, were skinny. Royalty and the clergy, who were influential during this period, often appear as fat in writings and paintings. For example, Chaucer (c. 1340–1400) in his *Canterbury Tales* writes of a hedonistic monk. Robin Hood's companion Friar Tuck was quite hefty. Peasants usually gorged themselves after a hunt or harvest, but these were not everyday occurrences. Combined with the demands of very hard work, this resulted in little opportunity to become fat.

During the Middle Ages, while most of Europe groveled in ignorance and poverty, the Arabs preserved the medical tradition of the Greeks and Romans. Ibn Sina or Avicenna (980–1037) was a physician who wrote more than 100 medical volumes. In his work *Kitab al-Qānūn fī al-tibb*, he listed obesity as a disease and suggested treating it with hard exercise and lean foods. He differed with Hippocrates in that he did recommend baths.

A Drastic Change in Thinking

The Renaissance changed thought in many areas and laid the foundation for scientific thought. Interest in the human body was awakened. The emphasis changed from religion and saints, and overeating as a sin became less of a focus. Over strenuous objections of the church, some physicians won the right to do autopsies of real bodies rather than studying anatomy from dissection of animals. Johannes Gutenberg (1400–1468) invented the printing press in 1450, and the first textbooks of anatomy were printed that showed how fat was distributed in the body. Artists led the way for the study of the human body. Renaissance paintings and those of the Baroque period (c. 1600–1750) show individuals with more flesh. For example, many of the paintings of Peter Paul Rubens (1577–1640) depict women who probably would have a BMI of 30 or more.

Santorio Santorio (1561–1636), a doctor at the famous medical school at Padua, Italy, became interested in measuring weight. For three decades, he weighed himself in a suspended chair and carefully recorded his weight as it related to the types of food that he ate, what exercise he did, and other bodily functions. He was the first to discover that body mass can be quantified—what is now called *weight*.

The Eighteenth Century

As the Rococo period approached in the eighteenth century, some physicians began to debate anew the problems of obesity, and paintings turned again to more slender body-shape ideals. For women, the waistline was slim, and dresses marked the waistline in about the same position as it is measured today. Most people began to think of obesity as a character disorder.

Following the new eighteenth-century concern about fat, more than 30 doctoral theses were written in both Latin and English on the causes and treatment of obesity. Malcolm Flemyng, a Dutch physician, presented an important paper, "Discourse on the Nature, Causes, and Cures of Corpulency," at the Royal Society of Physicians in London. In England, concern for *corpulency* was growing, so his talk was well attended. Although Flemyng considered obesity a problem, he presented a different and radical proposition: some fat people may inherit a predisposition for the condition that they might not be able to control. He noted how some people put on weight more easily than others. Writing a century before Darwin and Mendel, he approached the idea that corpulence (fatness), like hair or eye color, may have some relationship to biology. Instead of changing the diet, he recommended drinking one-quarter ounce of castile soap every day. His cure did not have the success that he hoped for.

The medical establishment of the eighteenth century believed that all diseases and conditions came from the air, what people ate and drank, their bowel habits, their ability to balance rest and labor, and their emotional state. They believed overweight people chose to be fat. However, some bizarre cases were documented. One example was Daniel Lambert, age 40, who weighed 739 pounds and died in 1809 an extremely happy man. Although today dieting is associated mostly with women, until late in the nineteenth century, it was men who were concerned about being stout. From the 1760s, men made their ways to shops that had large hanging scales and weighed themselves. Records of Messrs. Berry Brothers & Rudd, wine dealers, show that a number of distinguished lords regularly weighed themselves.

THE NINETEENTH CENTURY

At the turn of the nineteenth century, physicians promoted public concern over obesity or *polysarcia* (Greek for "much flesh"). In 1829, William Wadd disagreed with Flemyng's proposal that people may have a predisposition for fat and recommended that weight loss would result from a change in the diet to food with little nutrition. German chemist Justus von Liebig proposed the idea that only fats and carbohydrates were used as fuel in the body and that proteins built and repaired lean tissue. He even developed a high-protein supplement that he claimed encouraged the body to do extra work. His idea of the low-carbohydrate, high-protein diet is seen in several popular diets today.

Another proponent of the low-carb, high-protein diet was a London undertaker, William Banting. As a young man, Banting had been thin, but as he aged, he became so fat that he had to back down the staircase for fear that his huge stomach would topple him over. He could not even bend down to tie his shoes. Banting lost 35 pounds in 38 weeks on a diet of meat, small amounts of fruit, and alcohol. He was so ecstatic over the weight loss that he published a pamphlet, *A Letter on Corpulence Addressed to the Public*. By the time of his death in 1878, over 60,000 copies of his booklet had been sold. *Bantingism* became a popular term for dieting, and to bant meant losing weight. His book popularized a low-carbohydrate, high-protein diet and has been called the first diet book.

During the nineteenth century, the rudiments of scientific medicine emerged. At the beginning of the century, a cure or remedy was strictly anecdotal; it worked for one patient and should work for others. There were no systematic studies. Early in the 1800s, some physicians in France decided to keep records to see whether certain treatments really did make a difference. A Belgian scholar named Adolphe Quetelet (1796–1874), the father of statistics, measured the chests of 5,738 Scottish soldiers and the heights of 100,000 draftees in the French army and then plotted the data into a normal curve. He was the first to develop the idea of the "average man" by averaging the statistics. Another physician, John Forbes, was concerned about the problem of how much fat makes a person morbidly obese. Forbes used the Quetelet Index to quantify the first quantitative assessment of fat. This scale later became the body mass index (BMI) that is now the gold standard.

In addition, the study of nutrition was just beginning. The first understanding of how foods are digested came from the experiments of William Beaumont (1785–1853), a simple frontier doctor. By studying a man who had a gunshot wound in the stomach, Beaumont uncovered the secrets of digestion. Other scientists jumped into the research in this new field. French physiologist Claude Bernard (1813–1878) found that protein could be burned as fuel and converted into lipids to be stored as fat. German physiologist Carl von Voit showed that lipids were formed from proteins, an idea scoffed at by other scientists.

In 1834, Sylvester Graham (1794–1851), a Maine minister, presented a series of four lectures on the evils of tea, coffee, tobacco, opium, and gluttony. He promoted a plain diet: whole grains, vegetables, and pure water. During his appearances, hecklers gathered outside and threw stones. However, he continued to preach his message that gluttony was an arch sin born of civilization, causing indigestion and overexcitement. Followers of Graham, the Grahamites, were the first American weight watchers. They believed that an abstinent diet could make them robust and resilient. Graham also invented the famous graham cracker.

In the antebellum era of Victorian America, people were more obsessed with indigestion or dyspepsia. After the Civil War, the focus shifted to a new disease—nervous exhaustion or neurasthenia. From the late 1870s to the early twentieth century, neurasthenia or nervous exhaustion continued to be a popular diagnosis, and the remedy was to build up a store of fat. In fact, in 1866, the famous Fat Men's Club of Connecticut was founded. In 1901, physicians George P. Wood and E. H. Ruddock published *Vitalogy or Encyclopedia of Health and Home*, which featured a prominent chapter on "How to Become Fat or Plump." In fact, throughout most of the nineteenth century, physicians believed that it was healthy to carry an extra 20–50 pounds. Although they did not favor extreme obesity, they thought a certain amount of fat provided a reserve of vitality.

In 1880, German physiologist Max Rubner put a dog inside a large box and measured heat production as a function of size and diet. He called the device a calorimeter. Rubner found that the metabolic rate within a species is proportional to the surface area of the body. For example, the metabolic rate of a 200-pound man is greater than that of a 150-pound man because the larger body has more surface area. He found that the metabolic rate increased immediately after eating, and he described this occurrence as thermogenic because of the heat burning effect of food.

Building on Rubner's work, William Owen Atwater, an American chemist, developed the idea of food constituents, such as fats, proteins, and carbohydrates, and suggested that diet might improve health. He and physician E. B. Rosa built the first human calorimeter. In addition to calculating the amount of food necessary to do various levels of work, Atwater also figured the energy value of various foods. For example, a gram of bread provided the body with four calories, and a gram of fat provided nine. Then he added a new idea: the social value of food and food values. He estimated that the working class spent 60 percent of its money on food and proposed that people could get high-quality foods at lower prices, but he made one grave error. He advocated that people give up "unnecessary" foods, such as green vegetables and fruits, and fill up on cheap wholesome foods, such as wheat flour. He did not know about vitamins, which were not identified until 1912. But Atwater was a social reformer and contributed to the idea that food—whether fat, starch, sugar, or alcohol—produced tissue and yielded energy in the body. His investigations launched the first nutrition scientists.

Horace Fletcher, an importer of Japanese art, developed another interesting angle for weight loss—chewing. In June 1878, he weighed 205 pounds, and four months later, he chewed his way down to 168 pounds and remained that size until his death in 1919. Called the "Great Masticator," he practiced 100 chews per minute. During a 30-minute dinner, he might chew 2,500 times. Even milk and soup had to be chewed before being swallowed. The term *Fletcherism* was applied to this practice.

The nineteenth century gave rise to new words and expressions. The words *stout* and *fat*, which had become complimentary in the previous century, became ugly words. *Chubbiness* pertained to children and *chunkiness* to runaway slaves and later to street toughs. Other words emerged in the mid-nineteenth century—*dumpy, pudgy, tubby, porky* (1860s), *sodpacker* (1880s), *jumbo* (1880s, from the Gullah word for *elephant*), and *butterball*. Men might have had a *potbelly* or a *bay window*.

Just like today, famous people set the standards of beauty. During the past two decades of the nineteenth century, actress Lillian Russell was the most photographed person of her day. Lillian had golden hair and sweet dimpled cheeks and weighed 250 pounds; she loved to eat and was the epitome of success. But the tide changed around the turn of the century, when Charles Dana Gibson introduced his "Gibson Girl." Still large by today's standards, the Gibson Girl had large breasts, a slim waist, and big hips, but she represented a new ideal body type that emphasized strength and athleticism. Even Lillian Russell went on a diet to fit the changing model. By 1907, actor Fatty Arbuckle summed up the attitude in the ending line of his movie *The Round Up*, "Nobody loves a fat man."

THE TWENTIETH CENTURY

Attitudes about overeating began to change at the turn of the twentieth century. Amazingly, it was not doctors but insurance companies, armed with statistics of health patterns, that drove the change to linking being overweight with poor health and financial burdens. In 1909, Dr. Oscar Rogers of New York Life Insurance reported that 30 percent of the population was overweight, causing early death at the rate of 34.5 percent. He warned that being just 10 percent overweight shortened life. Even presidential candidate William Howard Taft was convinced to lose 60 of his 300 pounds. However, he gained it back after he was elected and supposedly got stuck once in the White House bathtub. This interest by insurance companies led the chief statistician of Metropolitan Life to develop height/weight tables. These charts remained popular for many years.

The insurance companies were joined by fashion designers in the changes in outlook. In 1908, French fashion designer Paul Poiret introduced a new style of clothing that revealed the body and sent the message that fat was unfashionable.

By the 1930s, the medical profession had done an about-face on the value of obesity. One of the important forces was Russell Chittenden, a Yale professor, who wrote *Nutrition of Man* in 1907. In the text he earnestly promoted that overeating was evil. He disagreed with von Voit and Atwater and wrote that it was foolhardy to overindulge in protein. He argued that food intake should never be regulated by hunger but calculated by counting calories. Thus, Americans were introduced to calorie counting, and the idea caught on like wildfire. Lulu Hunt Peters, a physician, wrote *Diet and Health, with Keys to the Calories* in 1917. The book sold 2 million copies.

Although there was an awareness of calorie counting, during the time of the world wars, women were shown with muscular body shapes to help with the physical demands on the home front. But industrialization made work less physical, and food became cheaper. Capitalism and prosperity played a part in the development of obesity. Economic abundance was definitely a double-edged sword. People had money to indulge in fine dining and overeating. But fatness was still frowned upon because it represented greed, excess, and laziness.

As the sciences of nutrition and physiology were developing, pharmaceutical medicines were also primitive and untested. Prescriptions, patent medicines, and home remedies emerged proposing to get rid of fat. These included digestives, such as boric acid, cornstarch, milk sugar, cathartics, emetics, diuretics, and laxatives. In 1910, an obesity tablet was compounded with strychnine, caffeine, and phytolacca, a well-known purgative made from pokeberry. The procedure of developing drugs then is a stark contrast to today's current methods. In the early 1900s, there were no controls, and no tests existed; no agencies regulated pharmaceutical development.

With the new fat-conscious world came frauds and charlatans. In the mid-1890s, thyroid extract became the first obesity drug. It was sold as Frank J. Kellogg's Safe Fat Reducer. It was also called Corpulin and Marmola. Kellogg's ad got more than 100,000 inquiries. However, soon the safe fat reducer was shown to cause osteoporosis, increased heart rate, palpitations, sweating, and chest pain—to which arsenic, digitalis, or strychnine were prescribed as remedies. In 1906, the passage of a law forced nostrum vendors to change their advertising tactics. They did not advertise their medicines as patent medicines but as prescriptions that could be filled at the corner drugstore. Many of these prescription fakes included "Fatoff," which was claimed to cure obesity. In 1909, the *New York Times* ran ads for a multitude of pills and purgatives. Weight-loss schemes were promoted in letters more than three feet high on sides of barns or on rocks — visible to those who were passing in railroad cars.

From the 1920s on, the ideal American woman became thinner and thinner. By the 1930s, after decades of nutrition and metabolism studies, scientists knew about safe and healthy weight-loss diets and were also aware of the moral issues surrounding obesity.

Albert Stunkard, a psychiatrist, completed medical school in the 1940s and ended up in the laboratory of Harold Wolff, a neurologist known for his studies on how emotions affect health. Through well-documented experiments, he showed how emotional conflict could cause the stomach lining to fill with blood and to bleed. Stunkard's interest over a period of 25 years grew from a mild concern to an overriding preoccupation with obesity.

Through the decades of the 1940s, 1950s, and 1960s, a small group of doctors began to specialize in studying obesity. Many were psychologists and psychiatrists, and others studied endocrinology, neurology, and metabolism. However, their numbers were small, and most doctors still considered obesity a matter of choice and a moral issue. In 1958, the Framingham (Massachusetts) Heart Study began to determine risks for cardiovascular fitness; the unexpected findings related to smoking and obesity.

In the 1960s, a model named Twiggy became the rage. Known in real life as Lesley Hornsby, Twiggy draped 99 pounds on a five-foot, six-inch frame. Twiggy was very thin with the shape of a young boy. The anorexic look caused many young women to give up healthy habits in an attempt to look like her. From Twiggy's day on, fashion models have become taller and maybe more muscular, but most are still extremely thin. In the 1990s, Kate Moss revitalized this look in fashion. Even at the beginning of the twenty-first century, the fashion world demands that models have an emaciated "opium look," which has led to eating disorders, such as anorexia nervosa and bulimia.

In 1963, Jean Nidetch, a Long Island housewife, started Weight Watchers International in a storefront to promote a food plan that helped her shed 72 pounds. She was one of the first to promote weight loss as a commercial enterprise. Diets became popular. In 1968, Dr. Irwin Stillman wrote *The Doctor's Quick Weight Loss Book*, which was soon followed by Dr. Robert Atkins and his diet plan. Numerous other books followed and are still popular today.

In 2003, Greg Critser wrote *Fat Land: How Americans Became the Fattest People in the Worldh*, in which he traced the obesity epidemic to the

1970s and 1980s when the Department of Agriculture pushed calorie-laden high fructose corn syrup (HFCS) and palm oil into the diet. HFCS, which is six times sweeter than sucrose, the regular refined white sugar, improves the shelf life of vending machine treats and protects frozen foods from freezer burn. Palm oil is more highly saturated than hog lard. However, both have become staples in the U.S. diet. Critser's book has evoked nutrition wars that are still with us today.

Slowly, some doctors have redefined obesity as a medical condition that demands intervention—an actual disease. These doctors have "medicalized" obesity, abandoning it as a moral problem and instead considering it a malady or sickness. For sociologist Jeffrey Sobal, obesity is both a medical and societal problem. Terms like *corpulence, plumpness*, or *fatness*, which have moral overtones, have been replaced by a term that implies a medical problem—*obesity*. Convincing others that obesity is a disease has not been easy.

CHAPTER 3

What Is Fat?

In 1982, the world's fattest man died. According to the *Guinness Book of Records* (1988), John Minnoch, age 42, of Bainbridge Island, Washington, held the record for the biggest man ever to live. His highest recorded weight was 1,000 pounds when he stopped weighing himself. At the time of his death, his weight was estimated to be over 1,400 pounds, and 80 percent of that was fat. The blue whale, the largest mammal on earth and famous for its blubber, is only about 12 percent body fat. The body fat of human beings ranges from 12 percent to 80 percent.

The next two chapters will discuss the physiology of fat. This chapter discusses the nature of fat at the atomic, molecular, cellular, tissue, and whole body levels, including the basic chemical and physical makeup. Chapter 4 explores how fat is made and how it works in the body.

What is fat to a physiologist, and what role does it play in the human body? Scientists view the mass of the human body at five distinct levels: atomic, molecular, cellular, tissue, and whole body. Each level is different and has specific components (see Figure 3.1).

Atomic Level

Four major elements—oxygen (O), carbon (C), hydrogen (H), and nitrogen (N)—make up most of the human body. These elements, along with calcium (Ca), potassium (K), phosphorous (P), sulfur (S), sodium (Na), and chlorine (Cl), account for more than 98 percent of body mass.

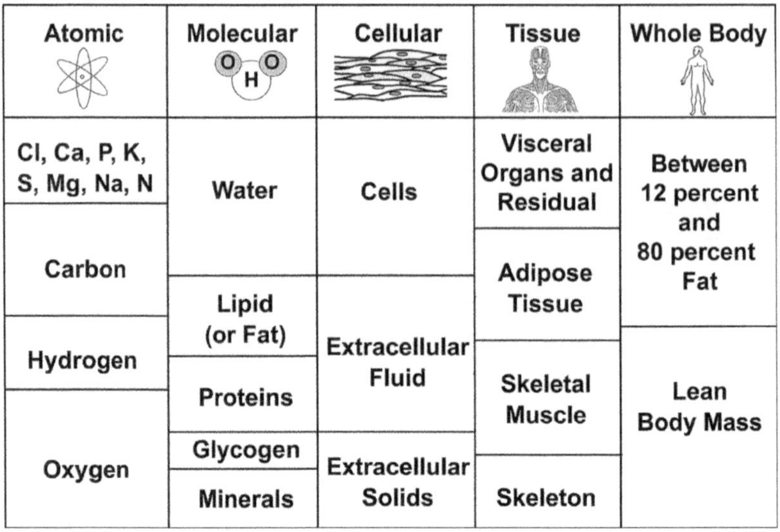

Atomic	Molecular	Cellular	Tissue	Whole Body
Cl, Ca, P, K, S, Mg, Na, N	Water	Cells	Visceral Organs and Residual	Between 12 percent and 80 percent Fat
Carbon	Lipid (or Fat)	Extracellular Fluid	Adipose Tissue	
Hydrogen	Proteins		Skeletal Muscle	Lean Body Mass
Oxygen	Glycogen	Extracellular Solids		
	Minerals		Skeleton	

Figure 3.1 Levels of Human Body Mass

These elements are significant and can be measured to link to higher-level components. For example, measuring total body C, N, and K can result in an estimate of total body fat, protein, and body-cell mass.

MOLECULAR LEVEL

At the molecular level, humans consist of six major components: lipids, water, protein, glycogen, bone mineral, and soft-tissue minerals. When measuring body composition, two components—fat and fat-free mass— apply. The lipids relate to the fat component; the remaining five molecular level components make up the fat-free mass.

Terms relating to the fat mass at the molecular level are often confused. Chemically, a *lipid* is a specific term referring to all material extracted with certain lipid solvents, such as ether or chloroform. Lipids are made up of *triglycerides, phospholipids*, and other small structural lipids. *Fats* refer to the family of lipids that consist of triglycerides, which are found almost entirely in fat cells. Thus, when the word *lipid* is used, it relates to the general family that can be extracted with ether or chloroform; when the term *fat* is used, it means triglyceride. Almost 90 percent of total body lipid in "reference man" is triglyceride. Reference man describes a physiological standard and is established as a white male 20–30 years of age weighing 79 kilograms (174 pounds), measuring 170 centimeters in height (66 inches), living in a climate with a temperature of 10–20 degrees centigrade (50–68 degrees Fahrenheit), and of Western European or American descent.

LOOKING AT LIPIDS

Blood lipids describe the various types of cholesterol and fat found in the bloodstream. The main types are the following:

- Lipoprotein: Protein-coated packages that carry fat and cholesterol throughout the bloodstream. Four general classes are high density, low density, very low density, and chylomicrons.
- Cholesterol: Cholesterol is not a fat but a waxy substance similar in structure. One main property difference from fats is that cells do not burn cholesterol for energy. Essential for health, cholesterol serves many functions in the body, including making membranes for cells, insulating nerve cells, and manufacturing hormones.
- High-density lipoprotein or HDL cholesterol: Often called *good cholesterol*, HDL carries cholesterol back to the liver where it is processed into bile and excreted.
- Low-density lipoprotein or LDL cholesterol: Often called *bad cholesterol* because it carries cholesterol to the tissues of the body, especially the arteries.
- Triglycerides: These tiny droplets of fat are found in the bloodstream and stored as fat in the fat cells.

All triglycerides are made of a forklike structure called *glycerol* with three fatty-acid building blocks, as shown in Figure 3.2. Fatty acids differ in the length of their carbon chains (from 4 to 22) and the number of double bonds they contain. Examples of fatty acids include the following: palmitic acid with 16 chains, which is found in most fats and oils; arachidonic acid with 20 chains, which is found in lard and peanut oil; and linoleic acid with 18 chains, which is mostly from vegetable oil. The vast majority of fatty acids, in both the diet and body, contain 16–18 carbon atoms.

TYPES OF FATTY ACIDS

Fatty acids are classified by the number of double bonds they contain. In chemistry, a double bond occurs when molecules share two common electrons. In the chemical formula, two lines connect the atoms where the electrons are shared. Saturated fats have no double bonds, monounsaturated

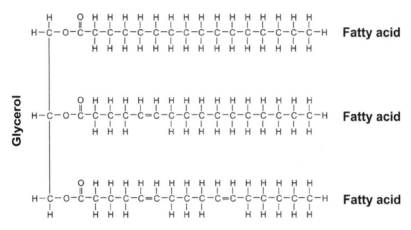

Figure 3.2 Structure of a Triglyceride

fats have one double bond, and polyunsaturated fats have two or more. All fats are made up of a combination of the three types.

Saturated fats with no double bonds have a high melting point and are usually solid at room temperature. Examples are butter and lard. Other sources of saturated fat include cheese, meat, meat products (such as hamburgers and sausage), full-fat milk and yogurt, pies, pastries, hard margarine and baking fats, and coconut and palm oils. The amount of saturated fat in the diet has far greater effect on blood cholesterol, total and LDL cholesterol, than cholesterol-containing foods do. But cholesterol-raising effects appear greater with medium-length chains, such as lauric acid with 12 carbons, myristic acid with 14 carbons, and palmitic acid with 16 carbons, than even longer chains.

Monounsaturated fats are more stable because they have only one bond, and sources include olives, rapeseed, tree nuts (pistachio, almonds, hazelnuts, macadamia, cashew, and pecans), peanuts, and avocados. Most of these oils are liquid at room temperature. Thus, olive oil and peanut oil are more stable and can be reused to a greater extent than polyunsaturated oils. Many people prescribe low-fat diets for weight loss, but recent studies have suggested that moderate amounts of fat help to maintain the HDL, the good cholesterol, and can prevent increases in total blood cholesterol. Diets with monounsaturated fats can also reduce LDL cholesterol levels by displacing saturated fats in the diet.

Polyunsaturated fats, those with more than one double bond, are divided into two families depending on the position of the first double bond:

- *Omega-3 fatty acids* have the first double bond as the third carbon atom along the chain and are mainly derived from alpha-linoleic acid. Omega-3 is found in salmon, mackerel, herring, trout, walnuts, and rapeseed and soybean flaxseed oils. These long chains appear to protect against heart disease. In countries such as Japan, where the people eat a lot of oily fish, rates of heart disease are low. Regular consumption of fish reduces blood triglyceride levels and lowers blood clotting potential.
- *Omega-6 fatty acids* have the first double bond in the sixth carbon atom and are derived from linoleic acid. Foods with omega-6 include sunflower seeds, wheat germ, sesame, walnuts, soybeans, corn, and their oils. These fatty acids have potent LDL-lowering properties to protect against heart disease. However, very large amounts can reduce HDL.

The omega-6 (linoleic acid) and omega-3 (alpha-linoleic acid) families are called essential fatty acids and are necessary for healthy growth and development. They are not made in the body and must be provided in the diet. Although the two acids cannot be made in the body, they can be made from longer chain versions. These longer versions are the building blocks of eicosanoids, the precursors for important hormones such as prostaglandins. Although the conversion can be made from body sources, these are quite limited and the body still needs the direct sources from the diet.

Cis- and Trans-Fatty Acids

Unsaturated fatty acids can be classified in two forms: cis, the bent form, and trans, the straight form. Most unsaturated fatty acids exist in the cis form; however, in the milk of ruminants, such as cattle, and in products that have undergone partial *hydrogenation*, a proportion of the fat is in the trans form. Partial hydrogenation is a process that modifies oils so they will be hard. Trans-fatty acids are found in some frying and baking oils, such as hydrogenated vegetable oils used in biscuits, cakes, and pastries; dairy products; and fatty meats from beef and sheep.

Some nutritionists are concerned about high intake of trans-fatty acids because they are metabolized in a similar way to fatty acids. They appear to raise LDL cholesterol in the same way as saturated fatty acids and lower the level of good HDL cholesterol. Other nutritionists question whether the effect of trans-fatty acids on heart health is comparable to that of fatty acids in general.

Cellular Level

Cells have three main components: extracellular solids, extracellular fluid (ECF), and cell mass. Cell mass is divided into fat cell mass and body cell mass (BCM). BCM uses the energy the fat cells provide to do other cell functions relating to metabolism.

Compared to other cells, fat cells are huge. They are thousands of times larger than most brain cells, red blood cells, or immune stem cells. Each fat cell, called an *adipocyte*, has a round bubble of oil consisting mostly of triglycerides. When the amount of food intake exceeds the expended energy, the excess energy is stored as triglyceride in the fat cell. Fat cells can grow or shrink in size depending on conditions. Like other cells, the adipocyte has a nucleus, cytoplasm, and cell membrane. But the overpowering fat globule shoves the nucleus to the side and fills the membrane so thoroughly that looking at it through the microscope makes it appear empty.

Packing nine kilocalories per gram, fat creates an energy-packed cell. A person of average size carries about one month's supply of fat. Thus, if people had to forage for berries and locusts to eat—like people in some early civilizations—they would be able to survive. These properties of fat cells—cushioning, insulating, and providing fuel—are especially effective when the cells group together to become fat tissue or adipose tissue.

Tissue Level

The tissue system of the body consists of adipose tissue, muscle tissue, visceral organs, and bone. Adipose tissue itself is composed of adipocytes (fat cells), extracellular fluid (ECF), nerves, and blood vessels. Triglycerides make up about 85 percent of adipose tissue. Whereas some tissue systems, such as the heart, brain, and kidneys, are located only in one place in the body, adipose tissue and muscle tissue are scattered throughout the body. Adipose tissue is divided into four major categories:

- Subcutaneous fat tissue: This is found between the muscles and skin.
- Organ fat tissue: This surrounds organs and can be readily separated by dissecting. The organ-surrounding tissue can be perirenal and pararenal (surrounding and beside the kidneys), mesenteric (surrounding the small intestine), or omental (surrounding the viscera). The term *visceral fat* refers to fat in the abdominal area.
- Bone marrow adipose tissue: This is located in the yellow bone marrow.

- Interstitial fat tissue: This is interspersed so tightly in the cells that it becomes part of that body tissue and is difficult to separate at dissection.

Each of these kinds of adipose tissue has specific kinds of metabolic activities.

Two main types of fat tissue are described as white and brown. All subcutaneous fat is usually white adipose tissue (WAT). It stores fatty acids (triglycerides), which in times of starvation can provide fuel for combustion in the liver and muscles. When stimulated by catecholamines, neurotransmitters from the brain, WAT initiates a cascade of reactions that release the fatty acids into the bloodstream, where they provide energy to cells that need it.

Brown adipose tissue (BAT) serves to produce body heat, a process called thermogenesis. It acts in a similar manner to WAT, but it has stable fatty-acid-binding proteins (FABP) that keep the fatty acids that are released inside the cell. Unlike WAT, it can burn the fatty acids to make its own energy and at the same time produce adenosine triphosphate (ATP), the main source of energy in the body. The combustion of fatty acids in these cells does not produce energy efficiently, but it generates heat instead. In most chemical reactions, when heat is produced, energy is a by-product. However, in the bodies of warm-blooded mammals—including humans— BAT is thought to be less efficient in order to create more heat. Hence, this survival mechanism enables the mammal to make extra heat and not depend upon the external environment for its life functions, like a cold-blooded snake or turtle does.

BAT and WAT differ in the ways they treat fat, and understanding their roles is important when looking to diets for weight loss. When WAT takes up fat, it generally leads to weight gain; when BAT takes on fat, it is positive for the body because fat is released and burned for body heat. Also, BAT and WAT are regulated by different mechanisms.

WHOLE-BODY LEVEL

The fifth level of body composition is the whole-body level. The whole body can be divided into regions, such as appendages (arms and legs), trunk, and head. During periods of stable weight and energy balance, the components have steady relationships with one another. However, excessive intake of food greater than the amount of expended energy upsets that balance and may spell trouble for the body. All the action at the whole-body level is coordinated within the brain.

Although excess intake of fats is unhealthy, fat does have important roles in many body functions:

- Along with glucose, fat is a main energy source in the body. One gram of fat provides nine kilocalories, which is more than double the four kilocalories provided by protein or carbohydrates. (A *kilocalorie* is equal to 1,000 calories.) Body fat deposits meet energy demands during times when people may have poor appetite or during times of starvation. Also, fat deposits may meet energy demands for a high level of physical activity in growing babies and children.
- Fat deposits cushion and protect vital organs and help insulate the body.
- In the diet, fat is the carrier of the fat-soluble vitamins—A, D, E, and K—and enables their absorption. Fat also provides the omega-6 and omega-3 essential fatty acids.

CONCLUSION

Understanding the physiology of fat involves body composition at five levels and complex chemical and physical reactions within the body. The atomic, molecular, cellular, and tissue systems, as well as how the whole body interacts, each plays a part in the search for answers about obesity. The serious study of fat is fairly recent, beginning only in the 1960s and progressing rapidly throughout the last part of the twentieth century. However, scientists are slowly unraveling the secrets of the nature of the adipocyte, adipose tissue, and the factors that control deposits of fat. Although much of the obesity epidemic can be controlled with diet and exercise, for some individuals, effective medical intervention is essential. New studies are emerging in the role of hormones and intestinal microbes that provide new targets for understanding the role of fat in the body.

CHAPTER 4

How Is Body Fat
Made and Stored?

It is hard to imagine that fat cells under the microscope could be described as beautiful and organized. Actually, they are shaped like neat, little compartments of a honeycomb. This structure acts in a similar way to the bubble-wrap packing material used for mailing: it insulates and protects. The collection of cells holds in heat and absorbs shock. But they also have surprising other roles.

Chapter 3 described how fatty acids are used as the building blocks of lipid molecules known as triglycerides, the major form of fat in adipose tissue and in food. The body may also synthesize fatty acids from sugar. The organ that acts as Grand Central Station for all the fatty acid storage and distribution is the liver. This chapter describes how body fat is made and stored. It will delve into the chemistry and the role of certain hormones in the process.

In order to trace how fat is made, let us follow the journey of fat after eating:

1. Mouth: Dietary fats as triglycerides, carbohydrates in sugar, starch and fiber, and protein are ingested.
2. Pancreas: The sugars and proteins (now amino acids) stimulate release of the hormone insulin.
3. Intestine: Triglycerides are digested to fatty acids and glycerol.
4. Absorption: Intestinal cells then reassemble fatty acids into triglycerides that are packaged with certain esters of cholesterol,

phospholipids, and apolipoproteins to form chylomicrons, which will be secreted into the bloodstream.
5. Blood: Lipase, an enzyme, breaks down the fatty acids freeing them from the chylomicrons.
6. Adipose, muscle, and heart tissues: Free fatty acids are taken up for storage and oxidation.
7. Liver: Organ takes up the chylomicron remnants for recycling.

How Are Fat Cells Made?

The process of generating fat, or *lipogenesis*, is a complex chemical process. The following process describes how fat is made and stored:

- The hormone insulin starts the process by inhibiting or stopping *lipolysis*, the breaking down of fat cells. Insulin is instrumental in *fat cell differentiation*, that is, the process of making new fat cells.
- A next factor involves fatty acids interacting with a chemical protein receptor called the peroxisome proliferator-activated receptor (PPAR-γ, or PPAR-gamma). This protein acts as a master switch that drives the formation of fat and regulates the storage of fat from the bloodstream, squirreling it away inside the fat cells. Taking fat from the blood encourages the muscles to burn sugar and allows the body to remain sensitive to insulin. Scientists have found a defect in the *PPAR-γ* gene that is related to obesity. The process of how *PPAR-γ* works is the subject of intense investigation (see Chapter 6).
- This complicated chemical reaction forms a compound called a heterodimer with another receptor—the retinoid X receptor (RXR)—to initiate the process of fat cell differentiation.

Fat Cells Do Not Just Sit There

When mature, the 40 billion fat cells in the body do not just sit around doing nothing. They function like little chemical factories absorbing and releasing substances for the body's energy needs. It is a unique system managed by the brain, stomach, liver, pancreas, and thyroid. As the system evolved millions of years ago in our ancestors, it was efficient and critical for survival. That was before fast-food chains, food courts in every mall, and technological advances that do work for us. Obesity results when these mechanisms for survival are exposed to a world of plenty and when one eats more food than is necessary to meet energy demands.

When calorie intake exceeds the energy expended, fat cells swell to six times their minimum size. They also can multiply from 40 billion in an average-size adult to over 100 billion. When a person gains weight and the fat reaches a certain point, the body management system tells the body to generate more fat cells. Compared to other cells, adipocytes live a long time. Losing weight may cause them to shrink and become less active, but their numbers decrease very slowly.

Being overweight and obesity result from increased stores of these fat cells, both subcutaneous (under the skin) and visceral (among the stomach and intestines). The enlarged cells are called hypertrophic, meaning they have increased considerably in size. However, these stores of fat do not just occupy space. They make many powerful products that play an important role in the pathology of obesity.

For decades, researchers just ignored fat cells. But in 1954, Jules Hirsh, an investigator at the Rockefeller Institute for Medical Research in New York City, began to study lipids. He found that obesity was mainly due to having more fat cells than a normal person, but that these cells only got so big—about four times the normal size before reaching the maximum. Later researchers showed that when a person is about 60 pounds over-weight, his or her fat cells have reached maximum size, and the body then makes more fat cells.

A typical fat cell is roughly 0.10 millimeter in diameter, a little larger than a human hair. However, some are small and some are large. Inside are the fatty acids that the body burns to release energy. Each droplet weighs about one-billionth of a pound, and an average adult has 30 billion fat cells or about 30 pounds of fat in storage. This is enough energy to run the body for 40 or 50 days. The extremely obese may carry 300–400 pounds, enough to supply energy requirements for one-and-a-half years. It was reported that one 450-pound man, under medical supervision, went for a year and two weeks on a zero-calorie diet. He lost 280 pounds and had no ill effects.

These cells are actually active little things, secreting hormones and other substances that harm the body. Some biologists call fat an endocrine organ and compare it to glands, such as the thyroid and pituitary glands. However, there is one big difference. Cells of the glands do not grow like fat cells, which have the potential to make more of themselves. Also, too much fat may secrete substances that contribute to diabetes, heart disease, high blood pressure, strokes, and many other illnesses.

The discovery that fat cells were not inert came in 1995 with the discovery that they produce leptin, a hormone that signals to the brain how much fat the body has. The brain then adjusts eating and metabolism, so fat stores are kept at a certain level. The more fat cells one has, the higher the level of leptin.

After the discovery of leptin, other hormones produced by fat were found. The adipocytes make adiponectin, a chemical that makes the body more sensitive to insulin. Obese people appear to make less adiponectin, thus making the person more susceptible to diabetes and heart disease. Another molecule resistin makes the body more resistant to insulin.

Adipocytes are powerful cells—much more than the inert globules that people once thought they were. Researchers are diligently working to decipher the biology of the fat cell. Hopefully, this research will end with the blockbuster drug or silver bullet for obesity and its risks for many diseases.

CHEMICAL CONTROL OF FAT TISSUE

The regulation of adipose tissue is a complex chemical process. If scientists can crack the puzzle of the chemical reactions, then they will have targets for drugs or other interventions. Fat is controlled and regulated by adrenoreceptors, areas on the cells that respond to the chemical norepinephrine (NE). Fat tissue is serviced by a system of blood vessels and nerves. The nerves that are part of the adipose tissue release the hormone NE, which then binds to the adrenoreceptors. NE is a ligand, a molecule that binds to another chemical group. Here it binds to the adrenoreceptors on the surface of the fat cells.

Two main categories of important adrenoreceptors have been identified: beta adrenoreceptors (BARs) and alpha 1 adrenoceptor (A1AR). Each of these works in a different manner and may have subtypes. BARs are numbered 1 to 3. B2AR is the most common and is not present in BAT. B3AR, unique to adipose tissue, is highly expressed in BAT and to a lesser degree in WAT. Thus, B3AR relates mostly to BAT with B2AR relating to WAT. B1AR does not appear important to the formation of white or brown fat.

BARs work in the following manner. Receptors are on the outside of the cell. When NE binds to it, a G-protein located on the inside of the cell membrane is activated leading to a very complex process that eventually releases the energy from the cells. BARs are also in the vascular (blood supply) beds of the fat tissue where they regulate blood flow. NE is the prime regulator of blood flow to organs and the distribution of fatty acids through the body.

BREAKING DOWN THE FAT

The lipid molecule looks like the prongs of a fork. A backbone of glycerol is attached to three fatty acids. Releasing these fatty acids from the glycerol backbone is called *lipolysis*. A protein enzyme called *protein kinase A* (PKA) begins the process. PKA uses two steps: a phosphorus atom activates hormone sensitive lipase (HSL), and HSL then releases a fatty acid from the triglyceride molecule yielding free fatty acids (FFA) and glycerol. Glycerol flows out of the cell and binds with water, improving the blood flow to the cell. To lose weight, lipolysis in WAT is the primary goal, because FFA are transported out of the cell and used for energy. This causes the reduction of fat.

How is fat broken down in BAT? A completely difference process is used. *Mitochondria* are beanlike structures that are the powerhouses that produce energy in the cells and are involved in protein synthesis and lipid metabolism. The term *uncoupling* is used here to describe the breaking down of ATP to produce heat. The body still needs the same amount of energy, thus a reduction of metabolic efficiency leads to a greater need in calories. Therefore, thermogenesis is beneficial to fat loss because more fat is burned for a given amount of food taken in. Mitochondrial uncoupling is induced by an *uncoupling* protein, UCP1. The expression of UCP1 is regulated by both BAR and A1AR. Two other uncoupling proteins—UCP2 and UCP3—have recently been found that may have important effects on energy expenditures and present possible targets for drugs.

One may picture all these chemical reactions like water going over a waterfall. Enzymes or proteins may start the process at the top of the waterfall, but as it cascades down, other powerful forces cause the action to continue. In fact, the term *cascade* is used to describe the process through a series of steps, and each step initiates the next step until the final outcome is reached. The term *downstream* describes a later step in the process.

FAT TISSUE AND ITS PRODUCTS

Scientists have studied the process of generating fat and how it creates energy for the body. When the fat cells work together, they also release a cascade of compounds into the body. These compounds are being investigated for possible drug intervention. Many of the processes are not well understood. A partial list of the compounds released by fat into the bloodstream is the following:

- Tumor necrosis factor alpha (TNF-α)
- Interleukin-6 (IL-6)
- Plasminogen activator inhibitor-1 (PAI-1)
- Lipoprotein lipase
- Acylation-stimulating protein
- Cholesteryl ester transfer protein

- Retinal-binding protein
- Estrogens
- Leptin
- Angiotensin
- Adiponectin
- Insulin-like growth factor (IGF-1)
- Insulin-like growth factor-binding protein-3
- Monobutyrin

Studies of these circulating peptides have shown that concentrations of PA-I, angiotensin II, C-reacting protein (CRP), fibrinogen, and TNF-a all relate to BMI.

HYPOTHALAMUS, BOSS OF HORMONES

The hypothalamus, a tiny pea-shaped structure that is located deep within the brain, is a main player in coordinating the body's many functions. The hypothalamus controls eating and drinking, the sleep-wake cycle, body temperature, many hormones, blood sugar levels, blood pressure, heart rate, and many other functions. Also, it is involved with emotion, stress, anxiety, and feeling. In 1943, researchers using experimental animals found that destroying the part of the hypothalamus called the ventromedial nucleus made animals eat and eat until there was no food left. If another area, the lateral hypothalamus, was destroyed, the opposite would happen; the animals would starve themselves to death. Such experiments showed that one area of the brain controls the desire to eat, when to begin eating, and when to stop.

These early investigations led to an important idea about the body—set point. Just as each of us has a relatively constant level of temperature and blood pressure, we seem to also have a constant level of body weight or body fat. It appears that each person has a predetermined weight level or set point. If one attempts to go below or above this set point, the brain will adjust to return to the predetermined level. That is why people who lose weight on a diet will regain the weight and why weight is so difficult to keep off. Some people have a set point to be thin and will remain that way even if they eat. Others have a high set point. However, most people in a normal range set point can gain weight by overeating and being inactive.

In the 1940s and 1950s, researchers noted that some mice stayed at their normal weight whereas others gained weight on the same diet. The explanation was that hormones are involved. Some hormones send signals to the hypothalamus, which acts as a kind of clearinghouse; then in turn, the hypothalamus sends hormones to other parts of the body to start various behaviors, including eating. The search was on to find these hormones. Several hormones and neurotransmitters have been identified that relate to eating and fat storage:

- Leptin: In 1994, scientists found that fat cells secrete a hormone as they become full. This hormone, leptin, serves as a signal to the hypothalamus that it is time to stop eating.
- Melanocyte stimulating hormone (MSH): The hypothalamus produces this hormone in response to increases in leptin telling the body to stop eating.
- Enterostatin: The pancreas sends this hormone to the brain to stop eating. When fat is consumed, enterostatin is released. Thin people produce more enterostatin than obese people. This hormone is a hot topic for research.
- Neuropeptide-Y: This brain transmitter tells the hypothalamus the body is hungry. It seems that obese people have too much neuropeptide-Y.
- Cholecystokinin (CCK): Found in both the brain and in the intestine, CCK tells the brain when it is full, called satiation.
- Beta-3 receptors: These receptors are in BAT and have to do with thermogenesis or generation of heat. It is believed that stimulating the receptors would increase the fat-burning rate and lead to weight loss.
- Galanin: This transmitter stimulates eating behavior, especially the ingestion of fat.
- Orexins A and B: These hormones may serve as hunger signals in the hypothalamus.
- Serotonin: Some scientists believe a dysfunction of the neurotransmitter serotonin is a major cause of obesity.
- Dopamine: This neurotransmitter is involved in eating and the pleasures derived from eating. Dopamine has been called the reward system and may serve as a link to addiction.

Eating or taking in food illustrates how the body systems interact at the body level. At the sight, smell, and taste of food, the body prompts insulin release. Later in the meal, the gastrointestinal hormones, such as cholecystokinin (CCK), gastrin, gastric inhibitory polypeptide, and secretin, release a second and greater burst of insulin. Insulin is essential for the metabolism of nutrients into the cell. In normal people, insulin is the primary fat building hormone. Sensitivity of cells to insulin is a positive thing for fat loss; insulin resistance in cells can lead to increased sugar in the blood and eventually diabetes. Insulin also increases glycogen stores. When NE is released, it turns glycogen into glucose. Thus, active cells are using glucose instead of burning fat. When glucose becomes low, the energy balance drops and activates an enzyme that tells the mitochondria to burn fat for energy. At this point, the FFA produced by WAT can be burned.

Glucagon is a pancreatic hormone that increases concentration of glucose in the blood. Basically, the plasma level of glucagons increases during fasting and decreases in response to eating. The liver is glucagon's primary target and may be involved in producing the feeling of satiety, or that one has eaten enough.

Two other hormones are related to the entire body system: growth hormone and cortisol. In obesity, growth hormone (GH) is largely impaired; in starvation, GH increases. GH aids in fat loss by reducing insulin sensitivity and decreasing the action of *PPAR-γ*. GH also acts directly on fat cells to stimulate the breaking down of fat. The other hormone cortisol induces muscle loss. During a diet, cortisol levels tend to rise dramatically and reduce fat in most areas, but fat is increased in the visceral or abdominal area. Commonly known as *belly fat* or *beer belly*, this is an evolutionary safeguard because it is located near vital organs and can easily be mobilized during a period of starvation.

While dieting, generally visceral fat mass is not a problem because it is reduced as fast as cortisol can relocate it, but there are two downsides. If the individual gets off the diet and starts binging, he or she will gain weight in the abdominal area first. A second effect is that cortisol can cause muscle loss. Thus, this hormone is one that is a target for drug development. To develop a pill that could control cortisol selectively by turning it off in muscle and visceral fat but target subcutaneous fat would be a blockbuster.

Tumor necrosis factor is a cytokine, a member of a group of extracellular factors that act by changing other cells. It acts in a similar way to cortisol by increasing fat loss. TNF-α reduces calorie expenditure and possibly UCP1 and UCP2 activity resulting in reduced thermogenic activities. Like cortisol, it has the positives of fat loss and the negatives of muscle loss.

CONCLUSION

Understanding how fat is used in the body is essential to good medical treatment and emerging medical targets. As of this writing, many of the hormones and other components are being investigated as targets for pharmaceuticals. It takes many years for the actual research to be translated into use by a physician. Understanding the basic research is just the beginning. There must be many trials—some of them may provide targets; most of them will fail. Chapter 20 will include some of the new research being done on hormones and an exciting new area called intestinal microbiota or the relationship of the microbes in the gut to weight.

CHAPTER 5

The Psychological and Social Aspects of Obesity

The psychological and social aspects of obesity reflect both individual and societal issues. The thoughts and beliefs that people have about themselves and their individual choices relate to the total context of the society that they live in. As seen in Chapter 2, attitudes about weight have varied at different points in history. What society believes and accepts affects individuals. This chapter focuses on the psychology of the individual within the context of the expectations of society.

Sharon Smith, who had just completed her second year of college, needed a summer job. She has a good personality, is an excellent communicator, has excellent grades, and was highly recommended by her professors. She went to several businesses and sat in the offices and chatted in an upbeat manner with other students. But after her first interview for a job at a theme park, she knew that it might be an uphill battle. Sharon is 20 years old and weighs 230 pounds. No one ever mentioned her weight, but a look crossed the interviewer's face when she walked in. When she told the person that she loved children and would like to be one of the costumed characters at the theme park, she was told the jobs were all taken. Yet, a thin guy who went in after her interview got one of the jobs. After six grueling weeks, she finally found a job in food service, only one week before she had to go back to college. Sharon was convinced that she could have done any of these jobs, but she never got the chance.

Was Sharon discriminated against because of her size? She was convinced that she was. Sharon's dilemma represents a host of psychological and social problems that relate to obesity. Take this true-false quiz to see how you rate on psychosocial perception.

True or false:

1. Overweight people are always happy and content but lazy.
2. Overweight people are weak failures.
3. Men prefer women who are thin.
4. Thin people are healthy; fat people are unhealthy.
5. Fat people have more psychological problems than those who are thin.

All the answers are false:

1. Overweight people are no different from any one else. Like people of any size, some overweight people are happy and content; others are not. And they may be ambitious. Just because they have excess pounds does not mean they are lazy and not ambitious.
2. Only in some current Western societies has the idea developed that overweight people are weak. In history, being fat or overweight was a sign of prosperity. Thin people can be weak failures also.
3. In some parts of the world today, being thin is not in. In Western culture, it has become a fad. People are dieting more today but are fatter than ever. As for men's preference, it is strictly personal.
4. All thin people are not healthy. Those with anorexia or bulimia have serious psychological problems. All overweight people are not unhealthy. They may be fit and still never reach their ideal weight on the charts. However, the morbidly obese are at risk for serious health problems.
5. There is no psychological profile that fits all obese people. Some say they may have lower self-esteem, but this is only in certain groups that might have the problem anyway. Taunting and teasing hurt, but some obese are resilient and learn to cope. In some studies, obese people may show mild depression when compared to others, but this is not clinical depression.

Perception and attitudes of people vary greatly. The anecdote of Sharon Smith shows a person who was convinced that her weight was the problem; she did not consider other factors that might have been there. Namely, summer jobs are very competitive.

In 2004, the Hartman Group of Bellevue, Washington, surveyed 5,000 people concerning their thoughts about their own body image and obesity.

The respondents ranged from obese to thin. Called Obesity in America, the Hartman Group exploded several myths related to weight and body image. (The study's results were presented in 2004 at the First World Obesity Congress, Washington, D.C.)

- Myth #1: Most people are concerned about obesity in their everyday life.
- Reality: Most people think that their weight is average and are ambivalent about managing their weight. In other words, the way I am is normal, and I don't think much about it in my everyday life.
- Myth #2: People look to media images to set standards for their weight.
- Reality: Most people look at their social network, such as friends and relatives, to decide when it is time to lose weight. They keep an eye on their friends, and if they are trying some new or fad diet, they may join. Sometimes a decision to lose weight may come after noticing that pants are too tight. However, most just buy a larger size. One person the respondents do not look to is the physician. People do not consult their doctors about their weight problems.
- Myth #3: People blame manufacturers and retailers for their obesity problems.
- Reality: Consumers see obesity as an issue of personal responsibility. Although many scientists and health professionals view obesity as an epidemic resulting from advertising and promotion, most consumers do not see it that way.
- Myth #4: People link obesity with potential personal health issues.
- Reality: Most people do not perceive themselves at risk for health problems, regardless of their weight. They have a "not me" attitude or magical "I-don't-care-it-is." These conditions could not happen to me. The reality of potential risk is not there until something happens to their health, such as a stroke or a heart attack.
- Myth #5: People use objective measures, such as BMI and body fat, to assess weight.
- Reality: Looking in the mirror or at an old photograph is the way most people assess their weight. Most have no idea of BMI or measuring body fat.
- Myth #6: Most consumers try to lose weight by modifying food habits.
- Reality: To initially pursue weight loss, most people cite increasing physical activity rather than changing or reducing food intake.
- Myth #7: Most people are following short-term diets that allow them to lose weight rapidly.

- Reality: For successful dieting, most consumers believe the moderation principle is the best guide. They believe in making small changes over the long term.

This survey of the myths and realities of thinking about obesity reveals that a deep canyon divides the psychological and social beliefs of the general population and those of the scientific community. Many researchers, using quantitative studies, have catalogued the medical complications of obesity as well as the psychological tolls. This chapter explores what research has found about the nature of the psychological and social implications of obesity.

How America Eats: Hartman Group 2011

Building on the information from the study *Obesity in America*, the Hartman group released a study in 2011 called *How America Eats*. This report provided new insight into the status of consumers with regard to weight management and how perception of obesity has changed since the 2004 study. This sample included 1,790 adult consumers living in Chicago and Seattle.

They found thinking and obesity and weight were similar to the former report. Overweight individuals appear unable to address the problem, although they are concerned. They found the "concern" was mostly in talk but not in action. Certainly, in some circles, obesity has received a lot of attention. The concern about obesity has been touted from the White House and the 2010 new dietary guidelines that focus on foods and nutrients that consumers should eat.

Although certain groups tend to point fingers at food manufacturers, people in the study tended to blame themselves for their weight conditions. Lifestyles of eating behaviors include the key finding that consumers perceive "how" and not just "what" people eat. This encompasses food occasions such as where we eat, who we eat with, and when we eat. The social aspects of gathering and being with other eaters are exceedingly important. What we eat and emotions such as craving and indulging also influence these cultural eating habits. Following are some of the findings from the report:

- Almost half (47%) of the respondents are confused about how to manage their weight.
- Forty-two percent think childhood obesity in America is a big problem.

- Twenty-three percent of overweight consumers eat breakfast only once a week (if then).
- Fifty-five percent underestimate the number of calories they should consume by more than 200 calories.

SOCIAL FACTORS

As seen in Chapter 2, concepts of body image and attitudes toward obesity have changed over time. Currently, thin is in for women, and muscles and lean are in for men. However, as the ideals of beauty and fashion have become leaner, the Western world has become heavier. Television, newspapers, magazines, and videos portray svelte people as charming and happy; crazy commercials poke fun at obese people or portray them as unattractive. Women especially feel the pressure to be thin. Their magazines are filled with weight loss and diet articles; men's magazines have articles on general health and alcoholic beverages. Gender differences regarding concern about weight are shown in Table 5.1. Females in high school ranked weight concerns in the top four; males ranked it 13th, among the bottom three.

Table 5.1 Ranking of Concerns of Female and Male Students

Female	Male
Looks	Money
Figure	Looks
Relationships with opposite sex	Popularity with opposite sex
Weight	Relationships with opposite sex
Popularity with opposite sex	The future
The future	Physique
Money	Grades
Complexion	Sports
Grades	Complexion
Family	Family
Popularity with same sex	Health
Parents	Parents
Health	*Weight*
Nuclear war	Popularity with same sex
Sports	Nuclear war

Source: Adapted from Wadden et al. (1991).

Just about anywhere people go in the Western world, overweight people are reminded that their society hates fat. The obese are subjected to prejudice and discrimination. Beliefs are that obese individuals are ugly, sinful, psychologically impaired, self-indulgent, and undisciplined. Studies have shown that adolescents and girls who read women's magazines—especially fashion magazines—are more preoccupied with weight and more frustrated with their own bodies than those who do not read such magazines. This raises a concern that many people—especially women—tend to internalize lean weight standards and the thin ideal.

Likewise, the general public appears to internalize negative views of obesity. For example, a study of children from three to six years of age showed that these young people describe obese people as likely to be dumb, lazy, and stupid. Other research found people preferred to have handicaps, including missing hands or facial disfigurements, than to be obese. A study of college students revealed that they would rather marry embezzlers, cocaine users, shoplifters, and blind persons than obese individuals (Wadden and Stunkard 1993). Negative reviews about obesity are also ingrained in medical professionals, including physicians, nurses, medical students, counselors, and psychologists. Physicians often view obesity as a psychology-based problem and do not recognize the genetic and metabolic components.

The same feelings extend to obese people themselves. One study of formerly obese patients reported that they would rather have various disabilities—including deafness, dyslexia, diabetes, bad acne, heart disease, amputation, and blindness—rather than return to their previous state. They even preferred to be lean and poor than to be a fat millionaire. A study of a group of overweight 9- to 11-year-old children showed lower self-esteem than those children who perceived themselves as responsible for their own weight. These obese children may actually be rejected by their peers and less liked socially than nonobese children. Negative attitudes tend to pervade every aspect of the obese person.

TEASING

Negative perceptions of teasing by peers have an impact on treatment outcomes. Obese patients seeking treatment expect weight loss to be two to three times greater than the 10 percent of overall body weight that is recommended in most programs. Therefore, persons may be setting themselves up for failure by dropping out. Weight-related teasing from family members may be more detrimental than from that of friends. One study of individuals over a three-year period showed a strong relationship between negative body image and weight-teasing history by both family and friends.

Culture does play a role in attitudes about obesity. African American women equate overweight with stamina, strength, and solidarity and are less likely to connect body size to health. Compared to white women, black women have less drive and pressure to be thin, fewer incidences of weight discrimination, and greater acceptance of overweight. A 1999 study showed that, on average, African American women weighed more than 120 percent of the recommended body weight but were less likely to perceive themselves as overweight; white women indicated higher anxiety about weight but had fewer cases of chronic obesity. Asian women perceived a large body size as healthy and reported less dissatisfaction with body image. Thus, most white people in Western cultures view obesity as a social liability; ideals of beauty may vary across cultures and ethnicity and may be a factor of socioeconomic status (SES).

Social Consequences

A large body of evidence showing discrimination against obese people covers a range of life domains and affects every aspect of their lives. The effect may carry over to their professional lives. Obesity negatively affects employment, including selection, placement, compensation, promotion, discipline, and discharge. One study found that 16 percent of employers reported that they would never hire an obese individual, and 44 percent said they would hire the obese only in the rarest circumstances. This indicates that obese people may be less likely to be employed and more likely to earn lower salaries. They may then be doomed to the lower SES. Obese individuals may not get educational opportunities. They are less likely to get a higher education and encouragement and support from their parents.

Obesity is especially detrimental to females. Those who were overweight as adolescents completed fewer years of high school, had lower household incomes, and had higher levels of poverty. Studies indicate women may experience more discrimination than men.

The consequences of obesity affect both social and psychological functions. Rand and MacGregor (1991) posed questions relating to psychosocial functioning and studied responses from a group of morbidly obese persons who had bariatric surgery. More than 80 percent felt people at work were talking behind their backs and had negative attitudes because of their weight, more than 67 percent thought their weight affected their hiring, and 45 percent thought the medical profession had treated them disrespectfully because of their weight. Other researchers examined sources of weight-related mistreatment in 187 men and 800 women. In the study, 22 percent of the women reported overall mistreatment, compared to 17 percent of the men. Sources included discrimination from strangers (12.5% of women), from spouses (11.9% of women and 10.2% of men), and from friends (7.5% of men). Related abuse was nearly 10 times higher among those with the heaviest BMIs—28.5–37.5—compared to the leanest individuals, who had BMI of 21.0–24.5. These studies indicate that the obese have a number of social stigmas across a wide range of life activities.

PSYCHOLOGICAL OUTLOOK

Combine teasing, weight-related discrimination, and other negative experiences, and one might expect that overweight and obese individuals will experience psychological trauma as well. However, the general population studies in the 1990s in both Europe and the United States found no more psychological dysfunction among the overweight when compared to nonobese individuals. Some researchers question these findings and encourage more long-term, controlled studies to understand the relationship between obesity and psychopathology. There seems to be no psychological profile of an obese person. Obese people appear heterogeneous in attitude. Obesity itself is not considered a mental disorder and is not included in the *Diagnostic and Statistical Manual of Mental Disorders*, 5th edition (American Psychiatric Association 2013). This manual describes all mental disorders and is used by professionals to diagnose and clarify mental illness. It may be that the risk for psychological problems is more prevalent in certain subgroups.

Although no psychological differences in distress exist in the general population, certain subsets or groups may be associated with psychological disorders or conditions. For example, one study of people seeking weight-loss treatment showed that about half reported at least one symptom of major depression or an anxiety disorder, and 55 percent had a history of at least one personality disorder (Wadden and Stunkard 1993). Obese people appear heterogeneous in attitude and expression. A study conducted at Structure House (1999), a behavior treatment program in Raleigh, North Carolina, found food insecurity positively related to overweight in women and that men and women use food in different ways. Men use food to celebrate events or positive emotions, whereas women use food when they turn their emotions inward and seem to be depressed (see Chapter 14).

Among the group that seeks treatment, other research has found high rates of binge eating disorders (BED), low self-esteem, social avoidance, and body image dissatisfaction.

Although obese people do fit a profile, researchers have extensively studied the subgroup that has BED. These disorders are not connected with other eating disorders such as bulimia (binge and purge), excessive exercise, or anorexia nervosa. BED is characterized by consumption of large amounts of food within a certain period of time, say two hours. The most common description is that the person feels "out of control." One person with BED described it as an uncontrollable force that cannot be stopped. Others express that when this urge hits, they will do anything, such as going out in the middle of the night, to get the food they want. Compared to nonbinge eaters, these people are more likely to experience anxiety, depression, obsessive-compulsive disorders, paranoia, psychotic episodes, and borderline personality disorders. They also may experience more hostility and interpersonal sensitivity.

Social pressures to be thin and lose weight may actually cause weight gain. Several studies have shown that certain kinds of dieting over time may promote greater-than-average weight gain, especially if the person stops the diet. This is the infamous "yo-yo syndrome." (Diet. Lose weight. Stop. Gain weight back, only more than the previous weight.) For some people, overrestrictive diets can lead to binge eating or overeating.

Night eating syndrome is defined as the consumption of approximately 50 percent of the total daily calorie intake after the evening meal. Night eaters snack late into the night and then have trouble going to sleep—and that calls for more eating. One study found this may be a neuroendocrine problem and that the person may have low levels of serotonin.

Social factors also discourage physical activity in certain people, especially children. In a study of fifth- to eighth-grade students, one researcher found that weight teasing during physical activity was associated with poor attitudes toward sports and that it reduced even mild physical activity. Another researcher examined associations among self-esteem, teasing history, peer relations, and sport and game participation in clinically obese 9- to 11-year-olds. Many reported being embarrassed during physical activity and while playing sports. Seventy-two percent thought they were excluded from sports because of their size; 90 percent thought the teasing would stop if they lost weight. All the attitudes about exercise carry over into social disincentives for exercise among overweight adults.

Body Image Dissatisfaction

Body image is the perception of one's body size and appearance and the emotional response to this perception. Cultural ideas of the slim body promote dissatisfaction with body image, especially among women and girls. When compared to nonobese women, obese women are more preoccupied with their physical appearance and often avoid social situations. These individuals tend to have emotional problems and are more likely to camouflage their appearance with clothing, change posture or body movements, and avoid looking at their bodies.

In Western society, being obese and overweight appears to have a social and psychological impact on the individuals. The best ways to lose weight are the subject of strong debate and are presented in Part II of this book. Refer to Chapter 13 for a discussion of types of diets and strategies for weight loss; Chapter 16 discusses weight loss medications. Chapter 14 focuses on the issues relating to bariatric surgery, the only certain, permanent way to lose weight. Chapter 15 considers attacking social problems through legal and governmental action. All these issues are complex and rooted in the big three: environment, physiology, and genetics.

CHAPTER 6

Introduction to Genetics

The fat, little fur ball violently clawed at the bar of the food dispenser. After hours of eating, the mouse huddled in the corner to sleep. When it wasn't eating, either the mouse cowered in the corner and just sat or it slept. It did not run around the cage or play games like the other mice. Caretakers thought the mouse was pregnant, but when she turned out to be a he, they realized that here was a very different mouse—a mutant. The word *mutant* comes from the Latin word for "change." In this context, a mutant has a change in the genetic structure, which can be passed on to offspring. The mouse was originally named "obese," but this was later abbreviated as "ob" and pronounced like one who is called by his initials, O. B. The mouse O. B. and other mutants became serious subjects in the study of the genetics of obesity.

O. B. was born in 1950 at the Jackson Laboratory in Bar Harbor, Maine. He was three times larger than a normal mouse, developed diabetes, and passed the obesity trait on to his offspring.

In the 1970s, researchers found that just transfusing an obese mouse's blood into a normal mouse made the recipient gain weight. The scientists concluded that some blood-borne substance, which they called the satiety factor, normally helps control fat storage. That substance later became known as the protein leptin.

At first glance, obesity seems simple: people eat too much and they get fat; if they cut back on food and exercise enough, they will not get fat. But observe two different people who eat and exercise the same amount: one is overweight and the other is not. A simple disease is one that can be traced to a single cause. For example, the bacteria *Salmonella* is one organism that causes food poisoning. A few genetic disorders, such as Berardinelli syndrome and Prader-Willi syndrome, might be called simple because they have been traced to a single gene.

On the other hand, conditions that have many factors are complex. In obesity, lifestyle choices, such as food intake, adequate activity, environment, and family traditions, are part of the picture, but many genes are also involved. Genes may even control responses to environmental choices, such as appetite and overeating. Although news stories break about the elusive "fat gene" that holds the secret to weight and its control, in reality it is not one gene but many that affect the weight of a person. The search is on for a variety of genes with interesting names such as "couch potato gene," "stop eating gene," "can't resist gene," and even a "party platter gene," exhibited by people who follow food trays around at parties. Thus, obesity is not simple; it is a complex condition controlled not only by environmental, psychological, and social factors but also by a host of interacting genes.

Knowledge about the science of genetics is snowballing. Research into obesity is progressing so fast that it is impossible for anyone to keep up with it. The information in this chapter will probably be outdated before it goes to press. Chapter 3 presents a complex system of hormones and brain mechanisms. In this chapter, we will consider genes that relate to obesity and eating.

GENETICS IN HISTORY

To understand obesity, one must understand what is happening in the fields of genomics and proteomics. Genomics is the study of the broad set of genes that contains the information on the 23 human chromosomes; the size of the genome is measured in base pairs and is estimated to consist of about 30,000 genes. Proteomics is the cataloging and analysis of proteins in the human body; with the decoding of DNA in the genome, the next step is finding the structures and functions of proteins that are coded by DNA. Explaining proteins is much more complex.

Genetics began with the work of a patient Austrian monk, Gregor Mendel (1822–1884), who found that generations of peas in his garden seemed to follow certain rules that involved pairs of factors. These factors—later known as *genes*—determined inheritance of traits. Mendel found that some characteristics showed up in every generation; he called these traits *dominant.* However, some hidden traits were passed from generation to generation and showed up only when the factor from both parents was present. When he presented his findings to the Royal Society, no one paid much attention, and his work was forgotten in the winds and rains of time.

Around the turn of the twentieth century, Mendel's work was rediscovered. British physician Archibald Garrod (1857–1936) proposed that it was these factors, or genes, that coded for a chemical recipe for a single protein. Studying a rare condition called alkaptonuria (AKU), a disorder that darkens the urine and causes a form of arthritis, he observed that the disorder was passed from one generation to another, like the recessive traits Mendel had described. He called this a glitch in nature or "an inborn error of metabolism." In 1908, at a meeting of the Royal College of Physicians, he proposed that a missing protein caused AKU, and he speculated that other disorders, such as albinism, might be the result of defective genes that give the instruction for these proteins. No one paid much attention to his ideas either.

The thinking of both Mendel and Garrod was too far ahead of their times. Only well into the twentieth century, in 1941, did scientists George W. Beadle (1903–1989) and Edward Tatum (1909–1975) refine Garrod's ideas into "one gene, one enzyme," an explanation of how genetic information is converted or translated into proteins. In 1944, after years of serious debate, scientists agreed that the genetic material was deoxyribonucleic acid, or DNA, a relatively simple molecule made up of sugar, phosphates, and four nucleic acids: adenine (A), cytosine (C), guanine (G), and thymine (T). The letters A, C, T, and G spell out the synthesis of proteins. In 1953, James Watson (1928–) and Francis Crick (1916–2004) announced that they had deciphered the structure of DNA, which appeared like a double helix.

The human genome is an encyclopedia with 23 pairs of chromosomes as volumes. Each volume has 30,000–40,000 entries, or genes. Each entry then contains thousands of "words" written in three-letter codons. The three-letter codons grouped together form an amino acid. Two examples are CAG, which codes for the amino acid glutamine, and GGC, which codes for the amino acid glycine. Twenty of the 100 known amino acids are the main building blocks of human proteins. Of these 20, 10 are not made in the body and must be acquired in the diet. In a very complicated process within a cell, proteins are synthesized from the amino acids and fold into three-dimensional shapes according to the protein's function. The proteins then configure together to code for a trait, for example, blue eyes or curly hair.

With all the letters and processes, lots of mistakes can be made, and this does happen in nature. Switching one letter makes a difference in this sentence:

Substitute *g* for *s*.
"He looked at the *sun*" becomes "He looked at the *gun*."

The meaning is changed dramatically. The same thing happens in nature to form mutations, as in the mouse O.B.

All the information needed to build a cell is in the genes; but what information? Genes are turned off and on by circumstances or happenings in the cell. Think of it as using a switch to turn on a light. Certain genes must be turned on; this process is called expression. The genes must be turned on to be translated into proteins. Translation is the process in which genetic information directs the synthesis of proteins from amino acids. Genes are not always expressed and, even though present, may not relate to the development of the individual. This explains why some people can carry a gene that never is expressed. For example, 20 percent of women with the *BRCA1* or *BRCA2* genes for breast cancer never develop cancer. The genetic material is there for the environment to work on. In other words, genetics loads the gun, but environment pulls the trigger.

Do You Want to Know What Is in Your DNA?

Healthcare professionals may order a variety of DNA tests for a specific purpose. The tests could include the following:

- Newborn screen used after birth to identify disorders that might receive early treatment
- Diagnostic testing to rule out a genetic or chromosomal disorder
- Carrier testing to see if a couple has a risk of having a child with a serious genetic disorder, such as cystic fibrosis
- Prenatal diagnosis to check the fetus's genes before birth
- Predictive testing to see if the person has a mutation for a genetic disorder, such as the *BRCA1* gene that carries the risk of breast cancer

Others are simply curious about their DNA or ancestry and have ordered kits that will analyze DNA. These direct-to-consumer (DTC) kits have been advertised for those who want to know about their DNA or their ancestry and can bypass the health professionals.

A variety of DTC tests, ranging from tests for breast cancer alleles to mutations linked to cystic fibrosis, exist. Several benefits of the DTC testing are appealing. They promote proactive health care and encourage people to take charge of their own health. The tests are accessible and reasonably priced and are relatively private for genetic information.

Several of these kits are on the market. One approved by the U.S. Food and Drug Administration (FDA) is 23andMe. This test requires a simple saliva sample and analyzes both ancestry and certain health conditions, including body fat. Another is ancestry.com that also gives ancestry, wellness, and trait analysis.

There are possible downsides to the testing. The main objections are the lack of governmental regulation, potential for misinterpretation, and privacy. The healthcare professional especially is concerned about marketing claims and unregulated advice without medical counseling. People may misinterpret the findings and neglect getting needed health care.

TECHNIQUES FOR STUDYING OBESITY GENETICS

Three powerful techniques have contributed to the understanding of the genetics of obesity: transgenic animals, twin studies, and quantitative trait loci (QTL).

TRANSGENIC ANIMALS

Molecular biology has provided powerful tools to study genes: transgenic animals. The term *transgenics* refers to the process of transferring genetic information from one organism to another. By introducing new genetic material into a cell or individual, a transgenic organism is created that has new characteristics that it did not have before. Scientists are able to "knock out" normal genes and "knock in" a gene they may be interested in. Mice are favored animals in the study of obesity.

Studies of mice have shown us many things about genes. An old proverb says, "You are what you eat." Research has shown us that a more accurate statement is "you are what you eat after what you eat has been changed quite a bit." Genes hold the recipe for proteins that form the function of food processing. These genes direct how a single cell uses food to develop into an organized group of cells with different properties and in a unique place. This environment of the cell changes constantly.

A number of animal studies have shown that mutations in genes cause marked obesity. Agricultural scientists found that selective breeding can produce changes in food intake in animals such as pigs, salmon, mice, chickens, and ducks. These animal models are clearly genetically obese and usually overeat, a characteristic known as hyperphagia. Pioneers in the field began to look at obesity in a different manner. At Jackson Laboratory in Bar Harbor, Maine, Douglas Coleman and colleagues developed the first super-obese mice that led to the discovery of the gene *ob*.

Another institute that has gained prominence in obesity research is the Rockefeller Institute in New York. Researchers there have used genetically engineered mice with *ob* from both parents. When *ob/ob* mice were given a free choice of foods, they ate two to three times the amount eaten by the mice in the normal control group; when put on a limited diet, the *ob/ob* mice were still heavier than the normal controls. Clearly this example shows the relationship between genes and behavior.

In 1994, Jeffrey Friedman and colleagues announced they had cloned a hormone produced by fat tissues that acts on the brain to control weight. They cloned the mouse and human versions of the gene *ob*. The following year they genetically engineered the protein, which they named leptin, from the Greek word *leptos*, "thin." When leptin was injected into obese mice, they slimmed down within weeks. Leptin—the *ob* protein—is believed to act on the hypothalamus, the area of the brain that controls appetite. However, the injections had no effect on a different strain of obese mice with mutations in a gene called *diabetes* (*db*).

Although leptin has received lots of media attention, many scientists have been disappointed with the modest results found in the first human studies of leptin. In addition, many other hormones and neurotransmitters play a role in the brain. All of these are targets for research and may lead to that future breakthrough (see Chapter 19). A few promising areas of research include the following:

- *Uncoupling protein-1* and *-2* (*UCP-1* and *-2*): In 1997, researchers found a gene in obesity-resistant mice called *UCP-2*. This gene appears to raise body temperature, thus requiring more calories. Conversely, when *UCP-2* was defective, the mice accumulated fat and expended fewer calories. *UCP-1* has a minor effect on energy expenditure.
- *Mahogany* gene (*mg*): In 1999, Gregory Barsh of Stanford University identified the *mahogany* gene, which directs the production of

a receptor-like protein implicated in regulation of body weight, hair color, and the immune system. The gene appears to maintain thinness in spite of a high-fat diet. Mice with the *mg* mutation were fed a high-fat diet and did not gain weight. This gene is thought to exert control over metabolism and the rate of energy expenditure that is glucose burning.

- Cholecystokinin (CCK): This chemical is found both in the brain and in the intestine. Stimulated by eating, CCK has long been believed to signal the brain for satiation. Research with animals shows that injection of this substance reduces food intake; however, it does not seem to work the same way in humans.

- Neuropeptide-Y: This brain transmitter serves as an appetite signal to the hypothalamus. When secreted, hunger and eating behaviors follow. Leptin inhibits the release of neuropeptide-Y. If resistance to leptin is present, a person may overeat, have ravenous craving, and be hungry after eating. The gene controlling this neuropeptide has been located, and researchers are trying to develop drugs that will block its effects.

TWIN STUDIES

The genome for individual humans is about 99.9 percent identical, in contrast to the greater variety among dogs. For example, a Great Dane is very different from a miniature poodle, not only in size but also in basic body functioning. With humans, a relatively narrow range exists in weights and shapes of bodies. For example, no adults are less than 2 feet tall or greater than 10 feet. There is a normal range in which humans fall. Just how much is genetic and how much is a result of environment and behavior are debated. An estimated range of the genetic variation in humans is as low as 30 percent, but probably the range is more like 50–70 percent. Environment accounts for the difference in the range of genetic variation.

Studies of identical twins who were raised apart have contributed to the understanding of the effect of genetics and environment. Identical twins, called also monozygotic (MZ) twins, share identical heredity because one sperm from the father fertilizes one egg from the mother. After fertilization, the egg splits into two cell masses to form two zygotes that develop into two identical individuals. In contrast, fraternal, or dizygotic (DZ), twins share only half their genes. Fraternal twins are the result of two eggs and two sperm and are no more alike than any other siblings. Scientists comparing MZ twins and DZ twins have found the similarity greater among MZ twins, indicating a genetic effect. The strength of the effect is called *heritability*, an indication of the proportion of variation within a population that is due to genetics. In twins raised apart, genetics accounts for 50–80 percent of the variation in body mass, with the remaining variation attributed to environment. A finding that is common across all the age ranges of the participants is the lack of common environmental influences on body fat. When twins were placed in adoptive families, studies showed that adopted children are more similar to their biological parents than to their adoptive parents.

Another surprising finding related to body mass has come from behavioral genetics studies of twins. Studies focusing on behavior have shown genetic influences on food intake, attitude, appetite, physical activity, and even food preferences. In 1992, in one of the first behavioral studies, identical twins living separately kept a record of their food and beverage intake for seven days. The study showed that approximately 65 percent of the total calorie consumption was the same and 70–80 percent of beverage consumption. A Finnish study of the physical activity of 4,000 twin pairs found a heritability of 62 percent for physical activity.

QUANTITATIVE TRAIT LOCI

Quantitative trait loci (QTL) use maps of generations to trace and locate various genes. Using the genome of the mouse, researchers made maps of genes that are common for certain traits. QTL discovery is the first step in identifying genes that influence complex traits. The approach is tedious and limited by the low precision of the DNA region.

The human obesity gene map update for 2004 is available at http://obesitygene.pbrc.edu. This 11th update incorporates published results up to the end of October 2004. Currently, 41 Mendelian syndromes relevant to humans have led to a region on the genome and the specific genes that cause the disorders. QTL from animal models currently number 183 in certain regions of the genome. Genome-wide scans show 208 possible chromosome sites for obesity. In fact, the obesity gene map shows locations on all chromosomes except the Y chromosome. Overall, there are more than 430 genes, markers, and chromosomal regions associated or linked with human obesity. See Table 6.1 for some of these genes and their effects on obesity.

At least 30 different mapping studies for obesity are underway. Three areas on chromosomes 2 and 10 have been replicated with enough detail that researchers think they may be implicated in obesity. Replicating this complex area by different researchers is essential to arrive at conclusions.

Table 6.1 Selected Genes and Their Effects on Obesity

Gene	Mechanism	Gene Effect
Leptin (ob or LEP)	Appetite; energy expenditure	Major effect
Leptin receptor (ob-R or Lep-R)	Appetite; energy expenditure	Minor effect
Beta-2 adrenergic receptor	Energy expenditure	Probably a minor effect
Uncoupling protein-1 (UCP-1)	Energy expenditure	Minor effect
Uncoupling protein-2 (UCP-2)	Raised body temperature requiring increased need for calories	Minor effect
Proopiomelanocortin (POMC)	Appetite	Major effect
Melanocortin-4 receptor (MC4-R)	Appetite	Major effect
Peroxisome proliferator-activated receptor (PPAR-γ 1 and 2)	Adipocyte differentiation; insulin	Major effect
Hormone-sensitive lipase	Lipid traffic/metabolism	Minor effect
Low-density lipoprotein receptor	Lipid traffic/metabolism	Minor effect

These three methods—animal studies, twin studies, and QTL—have afforded a lot of information about genetics. Still, when one considers all the genetic variations that people exhibit, just the knowledge of the number of single gene mutations and rare syndromes is amazing. Then add to that all the possibilities of behavior genetics; one wonders how anyone could say that obesity is a simple condition requiring less food and more activity. Let us now consider some of the results of genetic mutations.

WHAT DOES THE STUDY OF GENETICS MEAN FOR OBESITY?

Several principles apply:

1. For those who are genetically predisposed to obesity, prevention is the best strategy. An individualized plan and greater support are required to maintain a healthy weight.
2. Obesity is a chronic, lifelong condition that is the result of an environment of abundance of calories and low physical activity, combined with genetic proclivities. Recognizing the predisposition in a family is important in developing a strategy for prevention.

3. Genes are not destiny. Obesity can be managed with a combination of diet, exercise, and medication.
4. Several drugs that will aid in losing weight have been developed and are now available. (See Chapter 17.) However, these will be for only morbidly obese cases and not be a substitute for healthy diet and activity.

CHAPTER 7

Genetic Disorders That Can Lead to Obesity

When nature skips a letter in the DNA formula or adds an extra one, a mutation results. The conditions that result are what Archibald Garrod called "inborn errors of metabolism." These errors are rare. They are usually very severe in nature and are difficult to treat. However, much of what scientists have learned about genes and metabolism has come from studying these rare diseases. The diseases have profound abnormalities and are usually so distinct that they can be deciphered more readily. Examples of the rare but highly informative inherited disorders of fat metabolism include familial hypercholesterolemia (FH), deficient fatty acid oxidation and sudden death, missing steps of mitochondrial fatty acid oxidation, and enzyme deficiency diseases in a family. Other single-cell disorders may cause syndromes characterized by morbid obesity.

HYPERCHOLESTEROLEMIA: THE BEGINNINGS OF THE STUDY OF GENES AND OBESITY

In 1938, Dr. C. Muller, a Norwegian physician, noted that several of his patients had a series of symptoms that appeared to run in families. These families had fatty deposits in tendons of the heel, hands, or fingers and sometimes yellow fat pockets on parts of the body, such as the elbows, knees, or under the eyelids. These families also had histories of heart disease and early death. After charting the families, he concluded that high cholesterol levels were a genetic condition that appeared in both males and females and must be an autosomal dominant condition.

Today, the word *cholesterol* is almost a household name. It is seen in advertisements, on television, and in the news. From these sources, we may get the impression that it is a pretty bad character. However, without cholesterol, our bodies would not function. It is essential for making cell membranes, hormones, vitamin D, and substances necessary for digestion. Although it is found in such foods as eggs, meat, dairy products, fish, and red meat, it is also made in the body.

Cholesterol is circulated in the body in little packages called lipoproteins. Two root words are in this word: *lipo* meaning "fat" and *protein*. With lipoproteins, tiny bubbles of fat are enclosed in a protein outer coat. There are two kinds of lipoproteins: low-density lipoproteins or LDLs and high-density lipoproteins or HDLs. Sometimes the cholesterol packaged as HDL is called "good cholesterol" because the liver removes the fat from the cells and processes it for body use. LDLs are referred to as "bad cholesterol." The liver does not remove the fat from the package, and it circulates in the bloodstream where it can collect in the blood vessels and cause heart problems or other disorders of circulation.

Hypercholesterolemia is the presence of excess cholesterol in the blood. When high levels of LDLs run in families, it is called familial hypercholesterolemia (FH) and has a genetic basis. When high levels of LDL cholesterol travels through the blood, the sticky residue deposits on the walls of the arteries, especially those leading to the heart. The person may experience pain or angina in the chest and risk a heart attack. The person with FH may have other health problems. Several of the other organs and tissues can be affected:

- Fatty deposits in the tendons can cause xanthomas or fatty deposits especially in the Achilles tendon or tendons of the hands and fingers. Xanthoma comes from two Greek words: *xanthos*, meaning "yellow," and *oma*, meaning "tumor or growth"
- Xanthomas on the elbows, knees, and buttocks
- Fatty deposits under the eyelids
- Cholesterol accumulation on the front surface of the cornea of the eye that appears as a gray ring

Mutations in several single genes can cause FH. The most common is the LDLR or the "low density lipoprotein receptor" gene that normally instructs for a protein called the low-density lipoprotein receptor. These receptors sit on the surface of many cells, especially the liver, waiting for the LDLs circulating in the blood to come by. Like a key fitting into a lock, the receptors then attach to the LDLs and take them into the cells, where three things can happen to the cholesterol. It can be used for cell functions, stored, or removed from the body. The LDL receptors then go back to the cell surface waiting to pick up more LDLs.

Several mutations of this gene have been found. Some of the mutations reduce the number of LDL receptors on the cells; other mutations keep the receptors from working properly. The result of the mutation is that the person will still have high cholesterol circulating in the blood. Most people with a family history inherit only one copy of the gene from a parent with FH. However, if one inherits a mutated copy from both parents, a severe form may appear in childhood. LDLR is inherited in an autosomal dominant pattern and is located on the short arm (p) of chromosome 19. Mutations in three other genes can also cause FH: *APOB, LDLRP1,* and *PCSK9.*

Discovery of the LDL Receptor

In 1964, the parents of three-year-old John D. were very concerned about the orange, fat-laden bumps on the back of his legs. When they took John to his primary care physician, he noted that his total blood cholesterol was six times higher than normal. As he got older, the bumps spread across his body, and with the slightest exertion, John told of his shortness of breath, fatigue, and chest pains. Regardless of his efforts, he continued to gain weight. At age 12, cardiologist Neil Stone at the Lurie Children's Hospital in Chicago diagnosed John with familial hypercholesterolemia (FH), a metabolic disease marked by high levels of cholesterol, artery-clogging plaques, and premature heart attacks.

In the early 1960s, FH was determined to manifest in one of two genetic forms: a less severe heterozygous form, in which patients have one copy of the mutated gene and have twice the normal blood levels of low density lipoprotein (LDL), and a homozygous form in which both copies of the gene are defective. However, no one had identified the mechanism of how these genetic forms worked. Dr. Stone sent John's skin biopsies to a pair of young researchers, Michael Brown and Joseph Goldstein at the University of Texas Southwestern Medical School in Dallas, Texas. This team had already been recognized for making inroads into the understanding of the biology of cholesterol metabolism in human cells.

The two doctors were pleased to get the cells and launched their study to locate just why the cells from this patient could not take up LDL cholesterol. This led them to the discovery of LDL receptors and the mechanism of receptor-mediated endocytosis, an idea that was not even considered worthy of investigation at the time. For their work, they received the 1985 Nobel Prize in Physiology and Medicine.

Scientists still have much to learn about fatty acid oxidation and how it is more than burning fat to keep us in shape. Fatty acid oxidation is essential for life, especially during times of fasting or starvation. The heart burns fatty acids at all times for most of its energy production.

SUDDEN INFANT DEATH SYNDROME AND DEFICIENT FATTY ACID OXIDATION

Sudden infant death syndrome (SIDS) has received a lot of attention in the media. It is not one disease but a name given to deaths from unknown causes in infants and young children. SIDS still remains a medical mystery, with many proposed answers but only a few proven.

A small portion of SIDS cases are associated with inborn errors of fatty acid oxidation. These babies die suddenly because they cannot go without food or cannot tolerate fasting. When older children and adults go without food, it usually results from a period of five or six hours without food or for at least a period of time overnight. Infants under six months must feed or nurse on demand. A defect in fatty acid metabolism may cause the infant who has not eaten for a period of time to suffer cardiac problems or death. This condition is caused by a recessive gene.

LIPODYSTROPHIES

There are several rare, single-gene obesity conditions. Some single-gene disorders are classified as lipodystrophies, which are abnormal accumulations of body fat in a certain area. For example, in one kind of lipodystrophy, obesity occurs in the lower half of the female body. The person has large deposits of subcutaneous fat in the legs, edema (collection of fluids), and varicose veins. Other lipodystrophies include the following:

- Berardinelli-Seip syndrome is caused by a rare autosomal recessive genetic disorder on chromosome 9. The condition is characterized by a lack of fatty tissue, which causes fat to go to muscles and liver. Signs and symptoms are obvious at birth. The child has a muscular look at birth, and the chin and bones around the eyes are prominent. High levels of fats are circulating in the bloodstream, and resistance to the hormone insulin is obvious.
- Dercum disease or *adiposa dolorosa* is characterized by painful fatty deposits or lumps on the back or body. The condition is more common in post-menopausal women, although men may also have the deposits. The condition may tend to run in families, although some cases appear sporadically. Although no treatment for the condition is available, painkillers or liposuction of the fat masses may give relief.
- An unnamed form of lipodystrophy has emerged in those taking a type of protease inhibitor for HIV. Deposits of fat appear in all areas of the body.
- Launois-Bensaude or Madelung disease is a rare syndrome seen in middle-aged male patients. Also called multiple symmetric lipomatosis, patients with the condition have large fat masses around the neck, shoulder, and trunk, as well as nervous system abnormalities.

Several syndromes that are associated with both obesity and mental retardation include the following:

- Prader-Willi syndrome is a condition in which children eat constantly and excessively. One mother tells of having to padlock the refrigerator and cabinets because her boy would even eat flour. Scientists have traced this genetic disorder to chromosome 15. Severe obesity, mild-to-moderate retardation, short status, lack of muscle tone, and small hands and feet characterize this disorder. Incidents are about 1 per 10,000–15,000 live births. Massive obesity develops within the first year of life.
- Bardet-Biedl syndrome is a rare autosomal recessive disease characterized by multiple fat deposits, retinal dysfunction, polydactyly, and congenital heart defects. Regions thought to be involved in the disease are located on chromosomes 11, 16, 3, and 2.
- Cohen syndrome is autosomal recessive and is characterized by facial, mouth, eye, and spinal abnormalities. An anomaly or deviation from normal is found on the long arm of chromosome 8.

- Carpenter syndrome is caused by an autosomal recessive gene. Short hands, polydactyly, coxa vara, mental retardation, hernia, heart disease, and obesity characterize this disease.
- Borjeson-Forssman-Lehmann syndrome is an X-linked syndrome, meaning it is passed only to boys from their mother. A child suffering from this syndrome has a lot of abdominal fat, a short neck, poor muscle tone, epilepsy, and mental retardation.
- Down syndrome is a genetic disorder resulting from a portion of a chromosome or an extra chromosome 21. The prevalence is 1 in 600–800 births. Signs at birth include a flat facial profile, simian hands, and suppressed immune system. Mental retardation is common in patients who are obese.

Many other very rare syndromes are associated with obesity and mental retardation.

OBESITY: COMPLEX AND POLYGENIC

Although some conditions and syndromes can be traced to certain genes and chromosomes, most cases of obesity are complex and puzzling. The monogenic forms provide insight into the interactions of specific genes and the physiology of the body. They also help researchers focus on potential therapies that may eventually be used to treat obese people. However, the abundance of factors and variations, such as the influences affecting how and why people gain weight, the degree of obesity, age at onset, ease of managing weight loss, distribution of fat, and other conditions, indicates both genetic and nongenetic factors.

The three research areas—animal studies, twin studies, and quantitative trait loci—have begun to shed light on some genetic possibilities. Although several large, well-designed studies have found a few chromosome regions that affect obesity, none is the obesity gene. Instead, it is most likely a cluster of genes combined with a permissive environment of lots of food and little exercise that lead to obesity. These are the only factors over which a person has control.

Studying the diseases with single genes has become a prototype for learning about normal biology from a disease state using a genetic approach. However, many conditions are much more complex, and many involved the interaction of several genes, including environmental factors. Obviously, medical geneticists still have much to learn about the diseases of fatty acid oxidation.

CHAPTER 8

Obesity and Health Problems

In addition to having a red face, Joe was fat—very fat. And, as it soon becomes obvious, he had some other real problems. He was traveling in a coach with Mr. Pickwick when soldiers started firing mortars at them. Joe slept the whole time. However, when the coach stopped for dinner, Joe woke up and, breathing heavily, drooled over a fat capon and veal patties. When he went back to sleep, arousing him was a task. Joe is a character in Charles Dickens's novel *The Pickwick Papers*. Named after Dickens's character Joe, Pickwickian syndrome is diagnosed in people who display a combination of obesity, sleepiness, labored breathing, and red face. This syndrome is only one of many conditions that tie obesity with a variety of health disorders.

The links between obesity and health problems are complicated and difficult to understand. Some thin people are unhealthy; some overweight people are fit and healthy. But the statistics from study after study show that obese people, in general, have more physical problems when compared to those whose weight and body fat fall into a normal range. In 1990, the National Institutes of Health (NIH) issued a summary of the conditions associated with obesity. The study compiled thousands of studies to conclude that obesity is correlated with the development of various health problems. Researchers have also found that overweight people who already have health problems benefit by losing weight. Losing weight tends to decrease health problems—especially for those who have a family history of these health problems—and increase life span.

Caution: Correlation does not imply causation. This precept is import-ant to remember when looking at obesity and diseases. The health con-ditions listed here are correlated with obesity, not caused by it. Actually, obesity causes only a few conditions. However, there is a high correlation between obesity and the conditions discussed in this chapter. The factors that make someone obese also lead to the various diseases and conditions described here.

This chapter focuses on diseases and disorders that are correlated with obesity. The NIH reports that 15–20 percent of all deaths in America are related to obesity. Using the BMI, the NIH issues risk statements in terms of how overweight a person is. For example, men who are 20 percent above their standard weights on the body mass index (BMI) chart show a lifetime 20 percent increase in death rates for any cause. This means that obese men have a 20 percent increased chance of dying in any given time period than do men whose weights are in the normal range. The following diseases and conditions have been connected to obesity:

- Heart disease
- High blood pressure/stroke
- Elevated cholesterol and triglycerides
- Type-2 diabetes
- Endocrine/thyroid abnormalities
- Cancer
- Orthopedic conditions
- Respiratory/sleep impairment
- Gallbladder conditions
- Brain conditions
- Miscellaneous conditions, such as gastroesophageal disease and falls and accidents

The medical community refers to these diseases as *comorbidities*. Accord-ing to the Centers for Disease Control and Prevention, comorbidities are conditions that occur at the same time as the primary condition in the same patient. Obese people tend to have a higher incidence of comorbidities because of their obesity.

OBESITY AND HEART DISEASE

Coronary heart disease (CHD) and obesity go together like a horse and a carriage. Major studies have revealed that obesity is an independent risk factor for CHD. This means that although smoking, high blood pressure, and high cholesterol are directly related to the condition, obesity alone stands as a top factor of heart disease. Four large, longitudinal studies have revealed this relationship:

- The Framingham Heart Study was a 26-year follow-up of 5,209 men and women (see "Findings from the Framingham Heart Study").
- The Nurses Health Studies I and II are concurrent studies that include 115,888 women.
- The Buffalo Health Study was a 29-year follow-up of 611 men and 697 women.
- The Cancer Prevention Study II is a 14-year follow-up of more than 1 million adults in the United States.

From the studies, increased BMI was the most predictive of death from heart disease, especially in males. An increased risk of death from heart disease was associated with a BMI over 25 in females and over 26.5 in males.

Findings from the Framingham Heart Study

After World War II (1941–1945), deaths from heart disease and stroke skyrocketed. In 1958, in an effort to attack the problem, the National Institutes of Health recruited 5,209 men, ages 30–62, from Framingham, Massachusetts, for an ambitious study. The men, who had never suffered a heart attack, were interviewed about their lifestyles and given lab tests and physical exams every two years. In 1971, another 5,124 people were added. From the data, evidence showed that cigarette smoking, psychological issues, heart attacks, cholesterol information, and being overweight increase the risks of heart disease. Before this study, no link was made between smoking and health. The study is ongoing.

IMPACT OF FAT ON THE HEART

Adipose tissue is not just a passive storehouse, but it is an active organ spewing compounds into the bloodstream. Many of these compounds affect the heart. For example, about 30 percent of the factor interleukin-6 (IL-6) originates in adipose tissue. IL-6 is important because it produces

C-reactive protein (CRP) in the liver that may predispose the individual to acute heart failure (see Chapter 3).

Increase in fat mass also affects circulation. An extensive network of blood vessels surrounds adipose tissue. This mass increases the demand for a supply of blood to service the expanding fat. Therefore, because of the increased metabolic demands caused by excess body weight, obesity requires the heart to pump more blood. As the blood volume and heart load increases, demands are made on the pumping side of the heart—the left ventricle. This increases the size of the left ventricle, a condition called *hypertrophy*. The enlarging of the left ventricle appears to increase in proportion to the degree of obesity and contributes to left ventricle failure. At any given level of activity, the cardiac workload is greater for obese subjects compared to lean subjects. For example, just walking is considered moderate to high intensity for most obese people.

In the fourth century BC, Hippocrates observed that sudden death is more common in those who are naturally fat than in those who are lean. Obese subjects have an increased risk of arrhythmias (irregular heartbeats) and sudden death, even when there is no evidence of heart disease. In the Framingham study, the risk of sudden death with increasing weight was seen in both men and women. In fact, compared to a nonobese population, sudden heart attacks were about 40 times higher.

High Blood Pressure and Stroke

High blood pressure (HBP)—also called *hypertension*—is related to obesity. HBP involves elevated readings of systolic and diastolic levels as measured on a sphygmomanometer (blood pressure machine). The diastolic pressure is the relaxing phase between heartbeats, normally about 80 millimeters mercury. The systolic pressure is the greatest force caused by the contraction of the left ventricle. HBP is suspected when the systolic pressure is 140 millimeters mercury or greater and the diastolic pressure is 90 millimeters mercury or greater. Evidence relates abdominal fat—or apple shapes—to elevated blood pressure. Obese adults ages 20–45 are six times more likely to have HBP than normal adults of the same age. Obese people who are 20 percent above standard weight also show a 10 percent increased risk of stroke.

Another enemy of the heart, elevated levels of serum triglycerides, called *hyperlipidemia*, has been found in obese individuals. Levels of low-density lipoprotein (LDL), the bad cholesterol, are high, and levels of high-density lipoprotein (HDL), the good cholesterol, are low.

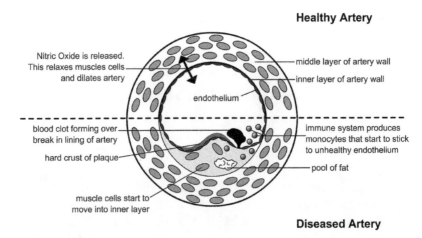

Figure 8.1 Healthy and Diseased Artery

Healthy arteries have a thin and smooth inner surface that allows blood to flow freely and deliver oxygen to the cells of the body. Compare this to the diseased artery (see Figure 8.1). The diseased inner layer consists of a pool of fat that is covered with a hard crust called *plaque* that forms inside the artery. The smooth muscle cells that have formed the active wall in a healthy artery migrate into the built-up area. A small crack may appear in the artery lining, and a blood clot adds to the mass buildup. In addition, the unhealthy, stretched endothelium lining of the artery attracts monocytes from the immune systems that stick to the mass. The abnormal deposits of fats and cholesterol grow and develop, causing the opening in the artery to get smaller and smaller. Partial blockage adds to the pressure on the heart, as blood is forced through the clogged area.

OBESITY AND DIABETES

When the word *diabetes* is mentioned, most people think of some type of blood-sugar problem. Although blood sugar is involved, this disease is insidious, affecting not only fat and protein metabolism but also almost every system of the body in detrimental ways (see "Defining Diabetes"). Two out of three people with diabetes die from heart attacks or strokes. Having diabetes in middle age raises the odds of developing Alzheimer's disease. It can also cause blindness, kidney failure, and blood-vessel problems in the extremities—especially the legs and feet, possibly leading to gangrene and possible amputation. Circulation problems can cause skin ulcers or bruises that do not heal.

Defining Diabetes

The names and terms relating to diabetes have long been misunderstood. This prompted the National Institutes of Diabetes, Digestive, and Kidney Diseases to clarify such terms in 1998.

- Type-1 diabetes: Formerly called juvenile-onset diabetes or insulin-dependent diabetes. Type-1 begins in children early in life; the person must get an injection of insulin each day.
- Type-2 diabetes: Formerly called non-insulin-dependent diabetes or adult-onset diabetes.
- Prediabetes: Individuals may have high glucose levels in the bloodstream but not enough for diagnosis; if not checked, these people may develop type-2 diabetes within 5–10 years.

Obesity is a leading cause of type-2 diabetes. This type is responsible for 90 percent of all cases and usually occurs later in life; however, it is becoming more common in obese children. With the aging of the baby boomer generation and a rise in sedentary lifestyle, the American Diabetes Association (ADA) estimates that the number of cases could climb from the 2005 level of 20.8 million to more than 30 million. About 14.6 million have been diagnosed, leaving 6.2 million people in the United States undiagnosed. Worldwide, the prevalence of both obesity and type-2 diabetes is increasing. Medical epidemiologists are predicting a major public health problem. They have labeled the phenomenon *diabesity*. Approximately 90 percent of those with type-2 diabetes are obese and have a condition called *insulin resistance*. Insulin is a hormone that transforms glucose to triglycerides and promotes fat storage. High levels of insulin in the bloodstream are associated with insulin resistance, leading to increased fat storage and weight gain. One might think of insulin as a key that fits in a lock called a receptor site. When insulin is in its receptor, it causes the cell to release a special glucose transporter that acts like a truck bringing glucose into the cell so it can be converted into energy. People with insulin resistance have a genetic defect in how the receptor site is shaped. Just a small defect prevents insulin from fitting into the receptors on the cell. Think of it as a defective lock that won't let the key in. Thus, if insulin cannot do its job because of the insulin resistance, the pancreas continues to increase the level of insulin leading to enhanced fat storage in fat cells. Insulin resistance is the main culprit that causes high levels of insulin in the bloodstream.

Recently, upper-body or central (visceral) fat was implicated as a major risk factor. The person with the apple-shaped (android) obesity has a 10-time higher chance of developing type-2 diabetes than other types. When adipose tissue releases free fatty acids into the bloodstream, the liver increases glucose production, and the pancreas, which normally produces insulin, is impaired. Adipose tissue also releases adiponectin, TNF-alpha, IL-6, leptin, and resistin, all of which could contribute to insulin resistance (see Chapter 5).

Among the hormones released by adipose tissue, leptin has specifically been connected with insulin. Researchers, using transgenic mice, have uncovered several genes responsible for excess insulin, called hyperinsulinemia. The transgenic mice have mutant leptin genes, as well as diabetes genes. Normally, leptin and insulin work together to regulate overall body weight. However, leptin resistance in both mice and humans leads to obesity, insulin resistance, and diabetes.

A key study on the Pima Indian reservation in Arizona may hold the answer to diabetes and genetics. From 1980 to 1993, approximately 300 nondiabetic Pimas participated in a study that measured insulin functioning. As the study proceeded, several of the subjects developed diabetes. When scientists compared blood samples, they found factors than indicated insulin resistance. Studying genetic samples, the researchers found a gene—the fatty-acid binding protein (*FABP-2*)—that used an amino acid called *threonine*. When the gene makes threonine, the body appears to absorb more fatty acids from the fat consumed in meals. The high level of fat and fatty acids in the blood could contribute to insulin resistance. Other studies of the Pima group include three protein phosphatase enzymes, which determine how cells respond to insulin.

Metabolic Syndrome

Some people have a cluster of major risk factors, life habits, and emerging factors called metabolic syndrome, or syndrome X. For most of these patients, the causes are improper nutrition, inadequate physical activity, and increased body weight. The following constellation of factors is present in this syndrome:

- Abdominal or visceral obesity—the apple-shaped body
- High triglyceride levels

- Decreased levels of HDL and increased levels of LDL cholesterol
- High levels of glucose
- High blood pressure
- Insulin resistance
- Kidney disorders
- Blood clots

Syndrome X is a significant factor in the development of cardiovascular disease (CVD) and is linked to gout and other diseases.

An important causal factor of Syndrome X is high alcohol consumption. Exceeding three to four drinks per day rapidly escalates the risk. Researchers have found genetic links, associated with the neurotransmitters dopamine and serotonin, that associate obesity with both alcoholism and drug addiction. The finding is especially strong among young women. In addition, anxiety and depression are linked to these neurotransmitters, and many overweight people may try to treat unpleasant moods with food. In this syndrome, as with other behaviors, genetics loads the gun, but the environment of behavior and lifestyle pulls the trigger.

ENDOCRINE ABNORMALITIES

The endocrine system is a group of glands in the body that include the pituitary, thyroid, pancreas, ovaries, and testes. These glands secrete hormones that regulate functions of metabolism, growth development, and reproduction. Largest of the endocrine glands is the thyroid, a butterfly-shaped organ that sits in the middle of the neck below the larynx or voice box. The thyroid gland produces three hormones: thyroxin (T4), triiodothyroxin (T3), and calcitonin. In the brain, the pituitary gland releases a substance called thyroid releasing hormone (TRH) that tells the thyroid to release the hormones into the bloodstream. The T4 and T3 hormones, made in the thyroid gland, play a significant role in metabolism and energy regulation in the body and act on almost every kind of body cell to increase cellular activity. If there is too much or too little, metabolism is affected.

The root word *hypo* is a Greek root word meaning "under." When combined with "thyroidism," it implies underactivity or the body's making too little of the thyroid hormones. The thyroid affects a number of functions including the modulation of carbohydrate, protein, and fat metabolism; vitamin regulation; mitochondrial function; digestive process; muscle and nerve activity; blood flow; oxygen utilization; hormone secretion;

and sexual and reproductive health. If the thyroid is underproducing hormones, a host of symptoms including weight gain and difficulty losing weight occur. The most common cause of hypothyroidism is Hashimoto's thyroiditis, an autoimmune condition in which the body's own immune system turns against itself.

Although weight gain and difficulty losing weight are strongly associated with hypothyroidism, the connection with BMI and obesity is not well understood. However, there is evidence for undiagnosed thyroid disease in one who cannot lose weight and is seriously making the effort. The most common screening is the TSH. Levels of this hormone rise when levels of T4 and T3 decrease. The American Association of Clinical Endocrinologists along with other associations released a consensus statement that the upper level of TSH should be 4.5mIU/L; another group said the upper limit for normal should be 3.0mIU/L. If the reading is between 3 and 4.5, further tests should be given.

In 2000, about 13 million Americans were estimated to have hypothyroidism. The condition is associated with weight gain, inability to lose weight, fatigue, depression, and high cholesterol. The American Thyroid Association has an excellent website for information: www.thyroid.org, or visit the website of the American Association of Clinical Endocrinologists: www.aace.com.

POLYCYSTIC OVARY SYNDROME

Obesity in women is associated with several other kinds of endocrine abnormalities. In obese women, menstrual disorders are common. Obesity appears to hasten the first menstrual period, or menarche, in young girls. Obese pregnant women have increased risk of HBP and other blood conditions. Related to menstrual irregularities is the condition polycystic ovary syndrome (PCOS). This disorder begins in puberty with weight gain, irregular monthly periods, hirsutism (excessive growth of body hair), and acne. These women are insulin resistant and usually obese. Obese women can also suffer from other endocrine abnormalities, including the fact that many obese women do not menstruate. There have been many cases of overly obese women giving birth when they didn't even know they were pregnant because their menstrual cycles are so sporadic or nonexistent. Many of these abnormalities are due to the fact that estrogen and progesterone are manufactured in the body, and the presence of excess fat is a prohibiting factor, and, in some cases, can cause a disruption in the hormone cycles that causes the excess hormonal adjustments that cause hirsutism.

OBESITY AND CANCER

Studies have linked obesity, environment, and lifestyle with a number of cancers. Many hormones involved in excess adipose tissue play a role in initiating or supporting cancer at a cellular and systemic level. Ten common forms of cancer seen in developed countries are breast, ovarian, prostate, kidney, colon, esophageal, pancreatic, lung, uterine, and gallbladder cancers.

Scientists are just beginning to understand how fat cells fuel cancer. Cancer is usually mentioned after heart disease and diabetes, perhaps because it develops more slowly than other kinds of illnesses. Being overweight can make it harder to spot tumors early, catch recurrences, determine the best chemotherapy, and even fit into radiation machines. Thus, obesity makes taking care of cancer more complicated and may even threaten survival. According to Dr. Christopher Desch, an epidemiologist, one major study estimated that excess weight accounts for 14–20 percent of all cancer deaths each year—some 90,000.

BREAST CANCER

Based on epidemiological, clinical, and experimental data, more evidence links obesity to breast cancer than to any other kinds of cancer. For example, obese women convert adrenal androgen hormones to high-level estrogen, a factor implicated in breast cancers. Many studies have suggested that drinking alcohol, even at modest levels, might also increase breast cancer risk. Also, obesity appears to be related to breast cancer in a complex way that correlates with upper-body fat (apple-shaped), especially in menopausal women.

UTERINE CANCER

Obesity's association with an increased risk of uterine cancer is well established. In obese women, estrogen directly stimulates the proliferation or enlarging of the uterine endothelium or lining through direct stimulation of estrogen receptors. Although obesity increases the risk of uterine cancer, it is strongly associated with a type of cancer that is less aggressive, endometrial cancer.

OVARIAN CANCER

Each year, approximately 26,000 women are diagnosed with ovarian cancer; 14,000 die from it. Mutations in the *BRCA1* and *BRCA2* genes are found in some cases. However, chronic hormonal stimulation from the ovarian epithelial cells, either on the surface of the ovary or within cysts in the ovaries, also plays a role. Gonadotropic hormones, produced in the hypothalamus, act on the pituitary sending hormones to release eggs (ova) from the ovaries. Although both the genes and hormones play a role in the development of ovarian cancer, obesity stimulates excessive androgen and other gonadotropic hormones on the ovarian epithelial cells that stimulate abnormal cancer cells.

PROSTATE CANCER

The prostate-specific antigen (PSA) test detects prostate cancer before it can be felt. According to the Prostate Cancer Foundation, approximately 232,000 men were diagnosed in 2005; over 30,000 men died. Prostate cancer is a combination of both heredity and environment. It is associated with aging but may be present in an inactive form in 30–40 percent of men ages 30–50. Seventy-five percent of men who have prostate cancer develop the condition by age 80. An American Cancer Society survey of 750,000 men found that obesity increased the risk of prostate cancer. Likewise, as sedentary men age, they may get fatter, have a decrease in lean body mass, and have a change in hormone levels. The culprit, dihydro-testosterone (DHT), formed from testosterone in the prostate and testes, appears to promote hyperplasia of the prostate in human, dogs, and rats. After prolonged exposure to DHT, cells may develop into prostate cancer.

KIDNEY CANCER

Obesity was also found to be a strong risk factor for renal cancer. Many mechanisms, including hormones that stimulate tumor growth, increased cytokines, and increased internal hormones, may account for the association.

COLON CANCER

Obesity increases the risk of colon cancer in men. Abnormal distribution of adenomas, precursors of cancer, increases risk and is also related to abdominal fat. A number of nutritional factors have been implicated in lowering the incidence of colon cancer, including vitamin D, calcium, and cruciferous vegetables. However, this type of cancer was rare before the advent of sedentary lifestyles and technological advances that have led to less physical activity and exercise.

ESOPHAGEAL CANCER

Most cases of cancer of the esophagus happen when stomach acid backs up into the food tube or esophagus, burning the delicate lining of the esophagus. Normally, the sphincter valve at the bottom of the esophagus closes off the stomach to keep gastric juices from leaking back up. Excess fat in the abdominal area puts stress on the valve, causing the caustic hydrochloric acid in the stomach to back up into the esophagus, and a condition known as acid reflux, or heartburn, develops. It is called heartburn because of painful symptoms similar to a heart attack. Obesity is a strong risk factor in gastroesophageal reflux disease (GERD). Although esophageal cancer is rare, there is a risk of developing cancer if GERD is not treated. Losing weight is one of the suggested treatments.

PANCREATIC CANCER

Pancreatic cancer is a lethal and quick-developing form of cancer that may be linked to fat intake, obesity, and diabetes. Fruit and vegetable consumption appear to be protective.

Obviously, cancer risks escalate as a person becomes obese and overweight. Obesity in men is related to prostate and colorectal cancer, whereas in women, it is linked to breast cancer, uterine cancer, and ovarian cancer. Upper-body fat in women, the apple shape, is strongly related to breast cancer. Research is ongoing to discover the mechanisms that operate in cancer development and obesity. However, lifestyle changes in diet and exercise do offer protection against certain forms of cancer.

ORTHOPEDIC CONDITIONS

According to the American Podiatric Medical Association, the average person will walk about 115,000 miles during a lifetime, which amounts to more than four times the distance around the equator. Each day, a person takes from 6,800 to 10,000 steps on all kinds of surfaces. With each step, gravity-induced pressure of three to four times the body's weight bears on each foot. Naturally, the more the weight, the more stress is placed on the skeletal and joint system. Therefore, obesity may lead to musculoskeletal injury and likely affects the most common forms of arthritis and lower-back pain.

Arthritis literally means "inflammation of the joints." Rheumatoid arthritis, a crippling autoimmune condition in which the body's antibodies attack its own cells, is linked to obesity. But the most common connection between obesity and arthritis is osteoarthritis, where the joints are pounded with each step. Other conditions can occur in the hips, feet, back, and spine. Weight loss appears to help these problems. However, these same women have an increase in unexplained problems in non-weight-bearing joints. Gout, another form of arthritis associated with obesity, is caused when elevated levels of uric acid crystals are deposited in the big toe and other joints, causing pain. Obesity may also cause falls, resulting from joint weakness or stumbling over feet.

RESPIRATORY AND SLEEP DISORDERS

As described in Dickens's *The Pickwick Papers*, Joe was a fat boy who had trouble breathing. In honor of Joe, the term *Pickwickian syndrome* was coined to describe those with labored breathing. Obesity may also cause shortness of breath and lowered lung capacity. Even small physical exertions and simple movement are problems. As obesity increases, the total lung volume and expansion capacity of the lungs are reduced.

Many obese people have sleep-disordered breathing, or *obstructive sleep apnea (OSA)*. OSA is characterized by episodes of not breathing, called *apnea*, which results from a collapse of the upper airway at the area at the back of the throat called the *pharynx*. During an episode of apnea, the person tries to breathe against the closed airway, but because he or she is not getting oxygen, a condition called *hypoxia* occurs in the bloodstream. The brain senses the lack of oxygen, and the person wakes up briefly to restore the upper-airway passage. After a few deep breaths, the cycle is repeated, often hundreds of times during the night, disrupting the normal sleep cycles. The person rarely remembers the awakenings, but loss of restful sleep may cause daytime drowsiness. OSA can lead to stroke, heart disease, and HBP by reducing the amount of oxygen that reaches the brain.

Obesity is one of the strongest risk factors for OSA. External neck circumference is increased in patients with OSA and may explain the link between obesity and sleep apnea. Deposits of fat pads around the pharynx area lead to airway narrowing. Imaging studies have shown these fat pads are larger in patients with OSA. Other studies have shown that obese patients with OSA have larger tongues and smaller upper-airway volumes than nonobese patients. Also, abdominal obesity tends to reduce lung volume, especially when the person is lying on the back.

Multiple studies from sleep disorders clinics have consistently shown that obesity, especially central obesity, is strongly associated with sleep-disordered breathing in adults who come for treatment in sleep clinics. However, limited data exist on the prevalence of sleep apnea in the general obese population, and it is probably more prevalent than reported. Weight loss generally helps the problem.

Recent research has correlated sleep loss and weight gain. Scientists have found that sleep deprivation increases the levels of the hunger hormone ghrelin and decreases the levels of the hormone leptin that makes one feel full. Reports from the Research Laboratory on Sleep, Chronobiology, and Neuroendocrinology at the University of Chicago School of Medicine examined the effect of sleep deprivation using 12 healthy, normal-weight men, with an average age of 22, who came to the hospital for dinner, sleep, and breakfast. On one occasion, they were limited to four hours in bed for two consecutive nights; at another session, they were allowed up to 10 hours in bed for two nights. Their blood was drawn at regular hours, and they were asked about their feelings of hunger. The results were as follows:

- Leptin levels were 18 percent lower and ghrelin levels were 26 percent higher after the men had slept four hours.
- The sleep-deprived men who had the biggest hormonal changes said they craved cakes, pies, pasties, ice cream, pasta, and bread.
- One participant said that after the four hours of sleep over two days, he was so hungry that he could eat his pillow; he had no problems with hunger after the longer nights of sleep.

A study at the University of Wisconsin and Stanford University tracked 1,024 people ages 30–60 and found that people who slept five hours a night had a 14.9 percent higher level of ghrelin and a 15.5 percent lower level of leptin than those who slept eight hours. Those who regularly slept less than 7.7 hours had a slightly higher BMI.

LIVER AND GALLBLADDER COMPLICATIONS OF OBESITY

Every year, about 750,000 gallbladder removals (cholecystectomies) are performed. Gallstones (mostly made of cholesterol) are more prevalent in women and increase with age. In the NHANES-III study, gallstone risk is related to measurements of central obesity. There are two other conditions related to obesity. The first is nonalcoholic fatty liver disease (NAFL). The second, a similar condition, is nonalcoholic steatohepatitis (NASH), in which liver cells may die and become like the cirrhosis that is seen in the livers of alcoholics. General liver conditions are seen with other problems such as diabetes and glucose intolerance. Both NAFL and NASH have been diagnosed in obese children.

OBESITY AND BRAIN SHRINKAGE

A disturbing revelation rocked researchers who had tracked the relationship of brain scans and weight gain in 290 women for over 25 years. Scientists in Sweden found that as the body gets larger, the brain gets smaller. The scientists recorded brain scans during the study and at the end of the study, when the women were between the ages of 70 and 84. Those who were overweight showed a significant loss of brain tissue in the temporal lobe, the part of the brain involved in language, comprehension, and memory. Some scientists surmise that as much as 25 percent of cases of dementia may be due to the BMI and its relationship to HBP, high cholesterol, and type-2 diabetes.

Upon reviewing the studies and the long list of diseases related to obesity, a basic premise is found: all these biological factors interact with environmental, lifestyle, and psychological factors of the individual. Thus, a variety of strategies must be used to attack the problem. Understanding biological set points, the genetically predetermined body weights that people are thought to have, leptin, insulin, hormones, and neurotransmitters can assist one in grasping the importance of setting realistic weight goals. The complexity of genes and metabolic pathways makes it unlikely that a single drug will ever be the answer to the problems of obesity. The issues involved in weight reduction and attacking these comorbidities are complex and challenging.

CHAPTER 9

Obesity, Exercise, and Energy

According to Greek mythology, a young farm boy named Milo was very pleased when his favorite cow gave birth to a new calf. He became very attached to the calf and went to the pasture every day and played with the calf by lifting him on his shoulders. As the calf grew, his muscles had to work harder and harder to lift the calf. After years of daily lifting, he could lift a full-grown bull. At the Olympic Games, Milo carried the bull around the stadium to the cheers of the crowd and was proclaimed the strongest man in the world.

Milo's story is only one example of how physical activity has been a way of life throughout history. Going back to the 1800s, the agricultural lifestyle was very labor intensive. The day began by gathering wood to start the fire so that breakfast could be prepared. Buckets of water were carried from a spring or river, or if you were lucky, a well. When breakfast was finished, a long day of hard labor began. Plowing, sowing, harvesting, and preparing food were never-ending chores and continued until sundown. There was little time for leisure or relaxation. Every day was filled with motion that required a great amount of energy.

If the people of the 1800s could be transported to today, they would be shocked to see automobiles whizzing by and planes flying overhead. An even stranger sight would be runners on a jogging path or the gym where walkers are on a tread machine walking to nowhere. In the gym, they would see both men and women lifting heavy plates of steel and looking miserable, as if they were being punished for bad behavior. The world has drastically changed since the 1800s.

Technology has proved to be a double-edged sword. Labor-saving devices have helped people avoid movement and exercise. The modern culture has come full circle in that technology has so enabled people to avoid activity that individuals must now work very hard to be active.

Although observing the jogging paths and gyms would be interesting to the citizens of the 1800s, they would be shocked to find that the exercisers are in the minority. The Behavior Risk Factor Surveillance System of the Centers for Disease Control and Prevention (CDC) reported that nearly 75 percent of Americans are at risk for health problems because they do not get enough physical activity. With 64 percent of adults considered overweight or obese according to their BMI, physical inactivity and poor dietary habits appear to be the main lifestyle factors contributing to deaths associated with obesity. Scientists have shown a correlation between physical activity or inactivity and obesity.

Numerous polls show that the majority of people recognize that a life-style of physical activity provides not only physical benefits but also mental and social benefits. But getting regular exercise is one of the hardest habits to commit to and maintain. With only 25.4 percent of U.S. adults physically active at the recommended level, it is obvious that people are simply not incorporating physical activity into their schedules. The level of physical activity contributes to body weight and body fitness and plays an important role in determining whether obesity develops.

Although many people begin an exercise and diet regimen to lose weight, they often stop when they reach their desired weight. This may cause them to regain the weight when they return to their previous life-style. This has been dubbed the "yo-yo syndrome"—losing weight and then gaining it back. The focus for diet and especially exercise must be the health connection.

The following definitions are helpful for understanding the roles of exercise, obesity, and health:

- Physical fitness is an overall term that relates to how hard the body can perform physical work and play. The components—cardiore-spiratory fitness, body composition, flexibility, muscle strength, and endurance—relate to health. Not related to health but important for sports performance are power, agility, balance, coordination, reaction time, and speed.
- Cardiorespiratory fitness has the greatest impact on health. Two types of fitness aspects are included here: cardiac (heart) and

respiratory, including the lungs, veins, and arteries. Why is cardiorespiratory fitness important? The size of the heart and the rate of contraction determine the volume and speed at which oxygen is delivered to the cells. Once inside the cells, oxygen helps convert food into energy (glucose) that cells can use. Muscles need glucose and oxygen to do work. In daily life, this type of fitness gives one the ability to work or play hard without becoming exhausted.

- Body composition is classified into two parts: lean body mass, including bones, muscles, organs, and connective tissue, and fat. As described in Chapter 3, a certain amount of fat is essential to your health, but too much is unhealthy.
- Flexibility is the ability to move a joint to its full range of motion. Muscles and connective tissues shorten from inactivity, making it difficult to do simple tasks. Individuals who are out of shape may have a hard time picking things up from the floor or even turning around in a car seat to check traffic.
- Muscular strength and endurance describe the ways muscles are used. Weight training helps develop muscular strength and endurance.

Physical Activity and Weight

The essential factor in the energy-balance equation is energy expenditure. Therefore, how active one is and how much energy one has play a critical role in weight regulation. Total daily energy expenditure includes the following:

- Resting energy expenditures—related to sleeping
- The thermic energy of food
- Energy expenditures from daily activity—the only expenditure (accounting for up to 30 percent of total expenditure) that one has control over

Overweight and obesity occur when the person consumes more than his or her average energy expenditure. Increasing physical activity can establish the negative physical energy necessary for weight loss.

However, exercise represents one of the most extreme stresses to which a body can be exposed. Consider a person who has an extremely high fever; his or her body metabolism increases about 100 percent. But a person running in a marathon increases body metabolism by 2,000 percent. So the important question is, how much exercise is enough?

Exercise is not like eating. If a person does not eat or drink, he or she will eventually die. If one does not exercise, the body soon adjusts to the sedentary lifestyle that can then foster the chronic diseases that lead to premature death. In 1990, the American College of Sports Medicine (ACSM) recommended that individuals exercise for 20–60 minutes, three to five times a week, at 60–90 percent of their maximum heart rate. To calculate your target heart rate, see the sidebar.

Calculate Your Target Heart Rate

To calculate your target heart rate range, begin by estimating your maximum heart rate. To find your maximum heart rate, subtract your age from 220:

- 220 – (your age) = _____ beats per minute

Your target heart rate range is 60–90 percent of your maximum heart rate.

- To find 60 percent, multiply your maximum heart rate by 0.6 = _____ beats per minute.
- To find 90%, multiply your maximum heart rate by 0.9 = _____ beats per minute.

Your target heart rate range is between the two numbers you just calculated.

Several recent studies have shown that exercise activity may be broken up into short segments of ten minutes each. A recommendation from the CDC and the ACSM supports that every adult should accumulate at least 30 minutes of moderate-intensity physical activity on most days, if not every day, of the week (see Figure 9.1).

New research published in the August 2004 issue of *Medicine & Science in Sports & Exercise*, the official journal of the ACSM, found that single sessions of short and continuous bouts of exercise affected postprandial lipemia, a condition characterized by an excess of fats or lipids in the blood following a meal. People who cannot exercise for long durations due to low fitness levels or busy lifestyles can take advantage of these

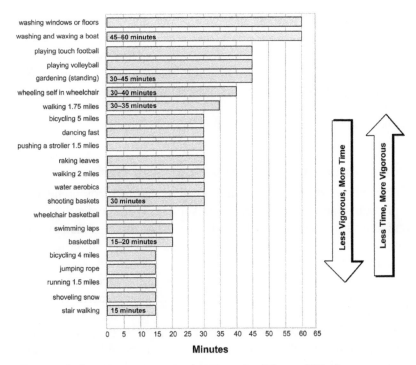

Figure 9.1 Intensity Levels and Exercise Times (CDC)

brief exercise opportunities. In the study, 18 inactive adults with normal lipid profiles were studied to compare after-meal triglyceride levels after performing a single session of continuous exercise to the triglyceride levels after a single session of accumulated short bouts of exercise. The participants ate a high-fat meal of known fat composition after jogging on a treadmill in a continuous session and in intermittent bouts. Blood samples were collected prior to activity and every two hours during the activity to determine the lipid level. Results indicated that the intermittent bouts of exercise reduced the blood levels of triglycerides more effectively than continuous exercise. The reason for these results could be that each short exercise bout may provide a slight increase in metabolism. Other medical groups suggest even more exercise, varying from 60 to 90 minutes per day. The letters FIT describe the scope of exercise activity:

- *F*requency: Plan for exercise on most days, if not every day, of the week.
- *I*ntensity: Activity should be moderate; this measures the work of the cardiovascular system. Low- to moderate-intensity activity includes

pleasure walking, climbing stairs, gardening, and yard work. Moderate- to heavy-intensity activity includes heavy housework, dancing, and home exercise. Vigorous aerobic exercise includes brisk walking, running, swimming, bicycling, rollerblading, and jumping rope. Vigorous activity should be done for 30 minutes, three to four times a week.

- *Time*: Total time each week should be 60–90 minutes of exercise.

EXERCISE PHYSIOLOGY: USING FUEL AND ENERGY

Two basic types of exercise are important as part of a comprehensive health program—aerobic and anaerobic. Aerobic (with oxygen) exercise is a continuous form that allows the body to consistently replenish oxygen to the working muscles. Light exercise, such as walking or light jogging, uses a lot of skeletal muscle cells. These cells have a good blood supply and have access to fuel and oxygen. An increase in the pace of exercising results in an increased rate of fuel consumption, an increased release of fatty acids, and an increased rate of muscle fatty acid oxidation. However, if the intensity of exercise is increased further, the rate of fatty acid oxidation becomes limited. This is now anaerobic exercise. Anaerobic (without oxygen) exercise utilizes oxygen at a faster rate than your body can replenish it. This type of exercise is intense and usually short in duration. Moving weights through repetitive motion is anaerobic as it burns fat and builds muscle mass.

What happens to the body during exercise? Regardless of intensity, at the start of exercise, a cascade of biochemical actions begins. Hormones and neurotransmitters are essential for *glycolysis*—an anaerobic means of adenosine triphosphate energy provision fueled by carbohydrates. Low- to moderate-intensity exercise meets energy demands by using fat in the form of muscle triglycerides and plasma-free fatty acids. If the exercise is high intensity, energy from carbohydrate-derived fuels is used.

Shifting from fat to carbohydrate oxidation during high-intensity exercise is essential to increase the amount and rate of release. Muscle can extract more energy per liter of oxygen from carbohydrate than from fat. However, the only reliable route to weight loss is to take in less energy from food than is expended in activity. Two components are involved in the total energy cost of exercise:

- Energy expended during the activity itself that accounts for most of the calories used.

- Energy expended in recovery while the metabolic rate remains elevated above the resting level. This excess postexercise oxygen consumption (EPOC) is fueled by fat.

EXERCISE AND WEIGHT LOSS

Many people who want to lose weight look for the magic bullet. They try modifying diet without exercising. Although losing a mere ten pounds may increase health benefits, without exercise, there will be no effect on muscle tone and there is a greater likelihood of regaining weight. Exercise is the leading predictor of long-term weight maintenance. However, without dietary intervention, a higher level of activity must be performed for even a small weight loss. For weight loss, exercise or activity must be performed most days of the week, with aerobic exercise increasing to at least 45 minutes per day, with 60–90 minutes recommended.

Although energy expenditure is an important component in the energy balance equation, the results from exercise alone show a modest loss of 1–3 kilograms (2.2–6.6 pounds) per week. When combined with dietary change, exercise training increases total body fat loss and has favorable effects on the fat-free mass. No consistent studies suggest that exercise training alone produces significant changes in energy or nutrient intake; exercise must be combined with proper food intake.

LONG-TERM MAINTENANCE

One of the most important roles that physical activity plays in the treatment of overweight and obesity is in the long-term maintenance of weight loss. Consistent follow-up studies of weight-loss program participants show a strong correlation between exercise and the ability to keep the weight off, as compared to diet alone. For example, a study reported in the National Weight Control Registry (NWCR) surveyed 800 men and women who had successfully lost 30 kilograms (60.6 pounds) or more and who maintained the loss for an average of five years. Ninety percent of the successful maintainers reported both changes in diet and continuing physical activity. Thus, the long-term commitment to physical activity is important.

EXERCISE AND SKELETAL MUSCLES

Skeletal muscle is the single-largest type of tissue in the human body. More than 640 muscles account for between 30 and 40 percent of body weight. The importance of exercising skeletal muscles extends beyond athletics. Although Olympic athletes are considered as being in top condition, most of our hunting and gathering ancestors had bodies that were almost as fit. The metabolic characteristics of modern humans have evolved to support high levels of physical activity. This fact contributes to the prevalence of health problems seen in inactive twenty-first-century humans. The underutilization of skeletal muscles may play a role in the rise of chronic diseases.

Skeletal muscles have plasticity, meaning they adjust to meet acute or chronic demands placed on them. To illustrate plasticity, consider what happens to a person whose leg is immobilized from an accident. Because the person is not putting any weight on the limb, the leg loses one-third of the skeletal muscle within weeks. It appears that the muscle realizes that it is not needed and changes itself into a weak muscle. The opposite is true when a couch potato increases activity for relatively short periods each day—as in beginning an exercise program. Now the plastic muscle will adapt its proteins to be more efficient when contracting.

What happens to skeletal muscle during exercise? Inside the skeletal cells, mitochondria, the powerhouses of the cell, use oxygen to make *adenosine triphosphate (ATP)* by breaking down the products of glucose and fatty acid. Capillaries—the connectors between the arteries and veins—supply the necessary oxygen to the mitochondria. Frank Booth and his colleagues at Washington University in St. Louis performed an experiment using rats that were trained in a progressive four-month running program. When compared to their sedentary cage mates, the rat marathon runners had increased mitochondrial content density and capillary density—skeletal muscle was nearly doubled. The doubling of mitochondria and capillaries also doubled the capacity of the muscle to make ATP with oxygen—the aerobic capacity. Muscles then can work longer before tiring.

For muscles to show this plasticity, certain genes must act. These genes in the muscle sense the change in use and send messages to produce certain proteins. The genes are classified in three categories:

- Stress-response genes are activated during the later phases of endurance exercise. These genes also appear as a general response to stress in all types of cells. The proteins produced here increase to high levels and then return to normal levels when exercise stops. Two types of proteins are in this category: heat shock proteins, such as uncoupling protein-3 (UCP-3) and heme oxygenase-1, and early transcription factors, which are proteins that tell the cell what to do.

- Metabolic-priority genes make proteins that respond to a problem. They may be thought of as the body's paramedics, responding when blood glucose or muscle glycogen become low. One of these genes codes for protein pyruvate dehydrogenase kinase-4 (PDK-4), which keeps the cell from breaking down the products of glycolysis (glucose breakdown) and prevents them from entering the mitochondria to form ATP. Thus, they limit the amount of energy available from carbohydrates. Does this shutting down of a major source of energy make sense when the muscle needs it during a period of stress? Yes. The fact is that glucose is the only fuel that the brain uses to make ATP, and the brain must have priority over muscles. If blood glucose is low during prolonged exercise or fasting, the body cannot afford to let the skeletal muscles gobble up the oxygen needed by the brain. So instead of going into the mitochondria, the breakdown products travel to the liver when they are turned into new molecules to be utilized by the brain.
- Metabolic and mitochondrial enzyme genes produce proteins that convert food to energy. Although activated slowly, they tend to remain for a long period of time.

Calculating calorie intake can be as simple as using a calorie chart to add up all the food that was consumed, but calculating the actual calorie expenditure is much more complex. Four factors are involved:

- The minimum energy required to keep cells, tissues, and organs alive when the body is at rest. This is called *basal metabolism*. This can be compared to the idling of an automobile engine
- The energy required for digesting food
- The energy required to heat the body
- The energy required for movement or physical activity

In a human being, the first three are fixed; the last is a matter of choice and control. Thus, the skeletal muscles play a key role in obesity.

Any reduction in activity leads to weight gain. For example, if a 70-kilogram (154-pound) woman reduces the distance that she walks each day for a year, she would add a pound of fat if she remained on the same calorie intake.

WHAT IS THE PRICE OF INACTIVITY?

Obesity and inactivity take a heavy toll on the human body. Physical activity plays an important role not only in weight management but also in reducing the risk of the diseases and conditions caused by obesity.

As part of a vicious cycle, obese people who are inactive and do not exercise have problems not only with exercise performance but also in daily living. Following are some mechanisms affected by inactivity:

- Respiratory function: Obesity increases the mechanical work of breathing. Associated with higher normal levels of pulmonary ventilation, oxygen consumption, and carbon dioxide production, obesity compounds problems during exercise. Deposits of fat on the lungs and abdomen and around the diaphragm and ribs cause breathing to be labored.
- Insulin action and glucose tolerance: Studies have shown that physical activity improves insulin action and reduces insulin resistance, thus improving glucose tolerance in obese people. Conversely, when compared to the physically fit, people with low fitness have three times the risk for developing type-2 diabetes. Two studies, the Diabetic Prevention Program and the Finnish Diabetic Prevention Study, reported that physical activity combined with weight-reducing diet can prevent the transition from glucose intolerance to type-2 diabetes.
- Blood pressure: Exercise training alone does not appear to lower blood pressure when compared to diet alone. However, many studies support the notion that the combination of exercise and diet is best.

Clearly, regular activity is helpful not only for weight control but, more important, for health. Numerous studies have documented the effects of exercise. From these studies, the following is a list of the benefits of exercise:

- Reduces the risk of cardiovascular disease
- Lowers blood pressure and some cancer risks
- Helps people with type-2 diabetes manage symptoms
- Reduces the risk of developing diabetes
- Reduces the risk of osteoporosis
- Delays many health-related problems of aging
- Promotes endurance and strength
- Increases total body flexibility
- Improves mood and sleep quality
- Reduces stress
- Helps thinking ability
- Reduces body fat percentage

Yet exercise and physical activity remain critical problems in all age groups.

How Much Exercise?

According to the National Institutes of Health, studies suggest that staying active may lower a person's chance of getting heart disease, stroke, some cancers, type-2 diabetes, and other conditions. Researchers believe that some physical activity is better than none, and extra health benefits can be gained by increasing how often and intensely one exercises and how long each session lasts.

Government guidelines recommend that healthy adults take part in aerobic activity of moderate intensity for at least 150 minutes a week or vigorous intensity for 75 minutes a week. Aerobic activity uses large muscles such as the legs and back and makes the heart beat faster. Also, the guidelines recommend that people do activities that strengthen muscles, such as weight training or push-ups, at least twice a week. One study found that only 3–5 percent of adults meet these recommendations.

PART II

Issues and Controversies

CHAPTER 10

Is Obesity a Disease?

Part I, consisting of Chapters 1 through 9, presented the foundation information about obesity and its physiological, psychological, social, and genetic background. Part II, Chapters 10 through 20, presents issues relating to obesity. Both sides of each issue are presented. Many of the issues are debated only in medical circles. Others issues, such as which diet is best, are seen every day in the news media. It is not the intent of this book to make a judgment on the value of the arguments but to present the debates in a nonbiased manner.

The debate is raging among government and medical communities: Is obesity a disease or not? This discussion has been going on for more than 100 years. For most lay people, it does not matter what obesity is called. However, whether obesity is a disease or whether it is termed a condition has important implications for several reasons. The official designation determines the following:

- The approach that is taken to treatment
- The regulation of medicines used for treatment
- Who is going to pay for health care

Throughout most of history, obesity has been a stigmatized condition. During the Middle Ages especially, those who were obese were considered immoral, lazy gluttons. This thinking is still prevalent today. "If these people would only exhibit self-control and push themselves away from the table, they would solve all their problems." "If they do not care about themselves, why should others?" Such an interpretation makes obese people unlikely candidates for sympathy. Thus, a large segment of the public, the medical profession, and, especially, medical regulators ignore and even disdain obese people.

This chapter will present both sides of the debate regarding whether obesity is a disease or a condition. The debate will probably continue for many more years. However, as the epidemic of obesity expands worldwide, some resolution of the debate is imperative.

On June 18, 2013, Dr. Patrice Harris, a board member of the American Medical Association, issued a statement that sent shock waves through the medical community. The organization was recognizing obesity as a disease. Harris stated that recognizing obesity as a disease will help change the way the medical community tackles the complex issues that affect about one in three Americans.

WHAT IS A DISEASE?

Ideas about the meaning of disease have changed over the centuries as people pondered the mysteries of life. Early societies explained disease as the result of evil spirits, the devil, or sin. Some early societies, such as the Incas in Peru, trepanned, or punched holes, in the skull to let the evil spirits out. The Greeks proposed that diseases were the result of an imbalance of the four humors, an idea that held on for centuries.

Today, to classify a disease, a pathological basis is needed. Conditions for diagnosis must be well defined. For example, in diagnosing measles, rheumatoid arthritis, or hepatitis C, criteria are established that give the doctor a solid indication of the disease. Obesity is defined by body mass index (BMI), an increase in fat-cell size, or an increase in fat-cell numbers. Yet, at present, these parameters are vague. If the volume of increase in these cells is necessary for diagnosis, the criteria using the numbers have not been established. Also, a person may have a BMI of less than 25 but have more adipocytes in certain parts of the body than is normal. The use of the number of fat cells for diagnosis is difficult because the fat cells themselves get larger before they begin to divide. An important point here is that the criteria to label obesity as a disease has not yet been established.

OBESITY IS A DISEASE: FIVE PRO ARGUMENTS

Pro 1: Obesity Meets the Definition of Disease

In 2013, the American Medical Association (AMA) identified three criteria to define disease:

- An impairment to normal functioning of some aspect of the body
- Characteristic signs and symptoms
- Harm or morbidity

According to the AMA's Council on Science and Public Health report, obesity does all three of these things. Other doctors and organizations chimed in and agreed that obesity satisfies all the definitions and criteria of a disease and medical condition.

The position that obesity is a disease is recent in history, perhaps a result of the influence of eighteenth-century Enlightenment thinking on medicine. One of the earliest monographs suggesting that obesity is a disease was published in 1760 by M. Flemyng, a Dutch doctor, who said that corpulency may be reckoned as a disease that has a tendency to shorten life. A half-century later in 1810, William Wadd labeled obesity (corpulence) a disease that is increasing in frequency. In the early 1900s, the first clear-cut evidence for physical factors relating to obesity appeared. Babinski and Frohlich published papers describing two cases of obesity associated with injury to the hypothalamus. In the twentieth century, obesity became recognized as a condition that may accompany other conditions rather than as a disease in its own right.

As early as 1985, the National Institutes of Health held a Consensus Development Conference on the Health Implications of Obesity. Nineteen experts in diverse areas of obesity science presented relevant information, and 15 of these scientists concluded that obesity is a disease. They found that a body weight of 20 percent or more above the recommended BMI is associated with a number of other diseases leading to death and that it is therefore a hazard to health. The panel did note that precise measurement of body fat is not available to most physicians and that use of the BMI as an indicator is far from exact and has many problems for precise diagnosis. The study from this conference is often used to support the idea that obesity is a disease, although the word *disease* is not used in the document.

The American Obesity Association also has been an organization that is actively working to have obesity recognized and regarded as a major epidemic in the United States and abroad. They argue that *obesity* has

a definition—"an abnormal increase in fat in the subcutaneous connective tissue"—and that it can be measured by a BMI over 30. A *disease*
is defined as "an interruption, cessation, or disorder of bodily function,
systems, or organs."

Pro 2: Obesity Impairs Normal Functioning of the Body

Several body functions are abnormal because the person is obese. For
example, obese people have excess adipose or fat tissue that causes the
overproduction of leptin, a molecule that regulates food intake and energy
expenditure. This condition leads to abnormal regulation. The person who
is obese may have impaired mobility and range of motion. Also, obesity
may affect the reproductive systems of both men and women.

G.A. Bray, director of the Pennington Biomedical Research Center
in Baton Rouge, Louisiana, is a strong proponent of classifying obesity
as a disease. He believes that obesity is a disease that has a pathology
that can be traced. He reasons that as the pathological description of disease has advanced, so has our understanding of biology. When the first
anatomy texts were printed about 450 years ago, people used gross anatomy to identify diseased organs. Later, differences in tissues were recognized, which enabled the classification of disease by identifying tissues.
In the mid-nineteenth century, microscopes—although crude by current
standards—enabled scientists to look at cells and establish a cellular basis
for understanding disease. Now, the tools of molecular biology and genetics have changed many of our perceptions. The understanding of fat cells
and adipose tissue acting as an endocrine organ sending hormones that
affect many body processes lays the foundation for obesity as a disease.

Pro 3: Obesity Decreases Life Expectancy and Can Cause Death

Obesity has been suspected to correlate with decreased life expectancy
for many years. *Lancet* (July 13, 2016), a British medical journal, published a meta-analysis of 239 prospective studies in four continents. The
researchers found that even moderate obesity led to an increased chance
of early death: 29.5 percent of men as compared to 19 percent of men
with normal BMI weight. For women, the increase was 14.6 percent as
compared to 11 percent. The authors calculated that one in five premature
deaths in North America could be avoided if obese people had normal
BMI weights.

Earlier, a 2009 study of 900,000 patients in a meta-analysis published
in *Lancet* found that obesity in adults can lead to three years' loss of life.

Extreme obesity is correlated with a shorter life expectancy of 10 years. Could one in five early deaths in North America be avoided if people had normal BMI weights? Yes, according to a Centers for Disease Control and Prevention (CDC) 2013 report. People who are obese have a 50–100 percent increase in risk of death from all causes.

Pro 4: Obesity Can Be a Genetic Disorder

In May 2016, a study in the *Journal of Molecular Psychology* showed that higher rates of obesity may be linked to the fat mass and obesity association or *FTO* gene. This gene may lower the activity in the area of the brain that controls impulses and responses to taste and texture of food. People with this gene may desire and eat more fatty foods and also eat more impulsively.

The important twin studies as recounted in Chapter 5 showed that twins who were raised apart with different food and eating styles still showed a genetic influence on BMI. Also, the 2013 surgeon general's report states that in addition to genetic predisposition, about 10 percent of morbid obese people have defects in genes that regulate food and body metabolism.

Pro 5: Major Organizations Recognize Obesity as a Disease

Several other prestigious organizations have fought to recognize obesity as a disease, including the National Academy of Sciences, World Health Organization, International Classification of Diseases #278, Food and Drug Administration, Federal Trade Commission, and the Social Security Administration. Certain organizations and others related to the medical profession also recognize the disease designation. These include the American Medical Association; American Heart Association; American Dietetic Association; the National Heart, Lung, and Blood Institute; and American College of Gastroenterology, in addition to numerous medical encyclopedias, medical textbooks, and medical journals. Even the Internal Revenue Service in 2002 recognized obesity as a disease so that people could take off medical expenses for treatment from taxes.

OBESITY IS NOT A DISEASE

Others argue that obesity should not be considered a disease and give several arguments for their reasoning.

Con 1: Obesity Is Not a Disease But a Survival Mechanism

The proponents of this position argue that obesity is not a disease but a condition that is an adaptation for survival. Although the health problems of obesity are evident, history illustrates that adipose tissue is the predominant means for storing energy, in the form of fatty acids. Fat tissue has many other important bodily functions, such as the synthesis and secretion of certain proteins that regulate fuel flux, insulin sensitivity, motor tone, cell turnover, inflammation, coagulation, and conversion of certain hormones. Many of these responses are related to the survival advantage of obesity. When the body is deprived of food, such as during a time of starvation, or during pregnancy or lactation, adipose tissue provides body energy. Fat also acts as insulation and protects against the adverse effects of cold air or water. Although the exact role of fat for the reproductive function is controversial, leptin appears to be important. A study of rats showed that loss of adipose mass alters sexual function. The point here is that such a natural occurrence is not a disease.

Con 2: Obesity Is a Result of the Present Environment and Is Preventable

The present environment (in much of the world) of increased food availability and decreased physical activity causes people to get fat. Although evidence from adoption and twin studies supports a genetic basis for the accumulation of body fat, the fact that the gene pool has changed little does not explain the epidemic of overweight individuals and increased obesity in the past few decades. Thus, the environment must be examined as the cause.

Evidence from migratory patterns of populations shows the influence of environmental changes on obesity. Samoans, Hawaiians, Pima Indians of Mexico and Arizona, Japanese American immigrants, and West African immigrants to Western countries show that overweight results when the stresses of life in a deprived setting are replaced by the conveniences of the modern world. Thus, one concludes that the body creates a fat reservoir in preparation for times when the environment will be less favorable.

Experiments in forced overfeeding may be unrealistic when compared to everyday eating patterns, but they may support the view that obesity is a condition for adaptation by showing how the subjects returned to normal when forced overfeeding stopped. In experiments in which monkeys were overfed, weight gain depended on the species. Monkeys that gained weight returned to their normal weight when overfeeding stopped. This indicates a genetic connection. Studies involving twins have provided some insight. In one study, 12 pairs of identical twins were overfed by 84,000 calories over a span of 100 days. The average weight gain was 8.1 kilograms, but a range of 4.3–13.3 kilograms was observed. About 63 percent of the excess calories were stored; the remaining excess calories were not stored, which implies that the bodies were using the excess food for heat generation. Twin pairs were similar in their responses. There was three times more variance in weight gain among the entire group than within the pairs. Within four months of the conclusion of the overfeeding experiment, 82 percent of the gained body weight was lost.

Losing weight is difficult for obese patients, and it is even more difficult to sustain. In general, the adaptations of the reduced weight appear to work against weight loss in a manner that causes the individual to gain the weight back. After successful weight reduction and months sustaining the lost weight, forces come into play that cause weight to creep back up. Increases in appetite and the strong urge for energy-dense foods, such as those containing sugar and fat, are observed. This may be partially related to decreases in leptin. Another study indicates that the changes in the gastrointestinal hormone ghrelin may contribute to weight gain after successful diet-induced weight reduction. Regain of weight is also related to changes in energy expenditure. The basal metabolic rate falls in proportion to the loss of lean body mass. Many people do not increase their physical activity. One researcher found that of those registered in the National Weight Loss Registry, more than 90 percent of the subjects who lost weight required a combination of a diet restricted in fat and daily exercise to maintain a BMI of 25. The problem of maintaining weight loss is related to the adaptation for survival.

In extreme situations, obesity can promote survival. Autopsies of people who have died from starvation show a body with marked or complete loss of adipose tissue. For example, studies of those who died during the Irish famine of 1847, World War I, and World War II, in addition to studies of the children of Kharkov, Russia, show that loss of subcutaneous fat precedes the loss of fat located elsewhere or loss of muscle mass. Men who lose as little as 4 percent of fat mass reach a level that is inconsistent with good health; women show more variability in their ability to survive. More recent data from the famine in Somalia suggest that a BMI of less than 10 can support life if the individual receives special care. However, males had more severe edema and a poorer prognosis for surviving than females at any given level of starvation. Women appear to withstand starvation better than men, perhaps because of the increased fat stores in women. The shape of the pear, versus the apple or android shape of men, appears to be related to the metabolic activity of the pelvic area.

Con 3: Not All Obese People Have a Shortened Life Expectancy

Not all people who have a high BMI die early. In fact, in a 2013 *Lancet* article, Dr. Frank Hu of Harvard School of Public Health said some people may be healthy and have a high BMI. BMI is not a perfect measure of obesity. It often defines people who are muscular as obese because muscle is denser than fat. Hu identified characteristics of some obese people who are indeed healthy. They may have:

- a waist size of no more than 40 inches for a man or 35 inches for a woman;
- normal blood pressure, cholesterol, and blood sugar;
- normal sensitivity to insulin; and
- good physical fitness.

Con 4: Obesity Is the Result of Eating Too Much and Sedentary Lifestyles

A U.S. Department of Agriculture (USDA) bulletin called "Choose My Plate" recommends that the daily intake of 31- to 50-year-olds should be 1,800 calories for women and 2,200 calories for men. However, the National Health and Nutrition Examination Survey (NHANES) of 2009–2010 revealed women aged 30–39 consumed an average of 1,831 calories, which is 1.7 percent over the recommendation; men consumed an average of 2,736 calories or 22 percent over the recommendation. A study of the average American restaurant meal portion showed the average size. Wu and Sturm in a review of the energy and nutritional content of U.S. chain restaurant menus found food portions in 2013 four times as large as the potions in the 1950s, and 96 percent of the chain restaurant entrees exceeded dietary guideline for fat, sodium, and especially saturated fat. The CDC recommends reducing consumption of sugary drinks and changing diets that are high in calories.

In addition to consuming too many calories, the sedentary lifestyles of people today add to obesity. In 1960, 50 percent of the jobs required moderate physical activity compared to just 20 percent of jobs in 2011; the other 80 percent required little or no physical activity. This shift shows 120–140 fewer calories burned per day.

Con 5: Obesity Is a Side Effect, Not a Disease

Obesity correlates with many diseases but does not cause them directly. In fact, some conditions such as hypothyroidism or Cushing syndrome may cause obesity. Drugs such as antidepressants, steroids, beta-blockers, and contraceptives can cause obesity.

Does It Make a Difference?

Is obesity a disease or isn't it? Does it really matter? The answer is yes. The impact of the environment is the same with either view. However, the impact on healthcare professionals and consumers may be strongly influenced by definition and outlook. The outlook affects scientists, government, healthcare reimbursement organizations, and the marketplace that includes pharmaceutical companies, weight-loss programs, and over-the-counter products.

Those who support the disease theory disagree with the position that it is simply a matter of personal choice and argue over the question of personal responsibility. They ask the question: personal responsibility compared to what? They assert that hypertension, diabetes, HIV/AIDS, high cholesterol, sexually transmitted diseases, and lung cancer are diseases that involve an element of choice and lifestyle. Participating in sports and the likelihood of injury involve personal responsibility. They also point to conditions like skin cancer, which involves genetic inheritance or fair skin, environmental exposure to the sun, and failure to take the protective steps of using sunblock or wearing long-sleeved shirts. The disease advocates say that the suspension of compassion is unreasonable. Any other condition that causes 300,000 deaths a year, millions of cases of pain and disability, and related to 30 or more health problems would be a disease.

The Centers for Medicare and Medicaid Services distributes funds from the federal government. Medicare provides certain health services to older adults and to some people with disabilities. Medicaid provides health care for people who qualify according to poverty guidelines. The healthcare budget in the United States is about $190 billion. About 6.7 percent (about $12.7 billion) of this budget is obesity-related. Some conditions are presently covered under obesity-related comorbidities, but many are not. For example, each year Americans spend about $33 billion on weight-loss programs that include diet, exercise, and behavior modification. In 2004, Medicare was given the directive to reimburse obesity treatments for treatment types that were proven to be successful. Groups that fall into the nonrecognition category include the general public, Medicare, Medicaid, private insurance, and some physicians. Claiming that obesity is not a disease, members of these groups believe that eating or overeating is a personal responsibility that includes genes, environment, and behavior.

They believe that obesity is self-inflicted and that people should not be sympathetic to a self-inflicted condition.

If obesity is not a disease but a metabolic adaptation for survival, would this affect the view of health economists? The answer is probably yes. And not only the payers but also the pharmaceutical companies and the multitude of healthcare businesses related to obesity are affected.

There is also a human psychological component to this debate. Crystal Hoyt and colleagues published an article in *Psychological Science* in which they found that obese people described more dissatisfaction with their own bodies. Reading a fictional news story about "obesity genes" led participants to eat more cookies because they had a disease. Thus, there were decreased feelings of control and responsibility.

The debate will probably continue for several years, with an uncertain outcome. Additional research and data collection must be done before we find an answer: Is obesity a disease or is it something else?

CHAPTER 11

Are We Creating Generations of Couch Potatoes?

On Sundays and Mondays during the fall, millions of fans are glued to their television sets watching their favorite NFL bruisers slug it out for championship hopes. We cheer the huge linemen who intimidate quarterbacks and running backs.

However, a study conducted in the 2003–2004 season and published in the *Journal of the American Medical Association* (*JAMA*) found that almost all the 2,168 players had BMIs that qualified them as overweight. Fifty-six percent were considered obese, and a small percentage had BMIs over 40. The study concluded that although strength training had increased muscle mass, some of the players' body weight is also fat.

John Jurkovich, a former defensive tackle, described his problem. He weighed 272 pounds in the mid-1990s, which was hefty on his six-foot-two frame. He said the coach pressured him to balloon up to 328, which is morbidly obese on the BMI scale. Because he had maxed out on his weightlifting, most of the weight was packed on by gorging. Now 37 and retired, he is down to 295, but he has problems with his knees and other joints because of his weight. The *JAMA* study questioned what will happen to young men like Jurkovich when they retire in their midthirties. Are these larger bodies putting young men at risk for cardiovascular and other problems as they age? What will happen to the hosts of young men who play sports and aspire to play professional sports?

NFL spokespeople quickly responded that the study was not scientific. They said that there's no proof that the NFL is worse than society in general, where about 30 percent of adults are obese, according to the BMI scale. Other representatives of the sports industry denied that obesity is a major problem among athletes.

This controversy illustrates only one aspect of the issue: Is obesity increasing in every age group? Are we raising generations of couch potatoes? Some argue yes, and others argue no. Some groups and factions believe that the problem of overweight is blown out of proportion. This chapter will look at obesity issues in the various stages of life: childhood, adolescence, young adulthood, pregnancy, and older adulthood. It will consider whether an individual can be overweight or obese and fit and healthy as one progresses through life stages. The chapter quotes many statistics and studies relating to weight gain over the years.

BODY WEIGHT GAIN OVER TIME

Nutritionists tell us there are sensitive periods when food affects obesity development. This programming may be changes in gene expression, in the cloning of cells in specific tissues, or in the growth of tissue cell types. Identifying these key periods of life for the development of obesity may allow us to develop strategies for prevention and treatment of the disease.

Obesity is a lifelong issue beginning in early childhood and continuing through older adulthood. In Part I, several correlates of the relationship between overweight and obesity and body-fat gain over time were discussed. These predictors are the following:

- Age: As people grow into adulthood, their body-fat content tends to increase. Generally maximal rates of overweight and obesity are attained from 55 to 65 years. People who are obese in childhood are at risk for adult obesity.
- Sex: Women tend to have more body fat, but differences in obesity vary among ethnic groups.
- Socioeconomic status (SES): In poor countries, the upper classes are more obese; in Western countries, people with low SES are more often overweight.
- Energy intake: Overeating causes people to gain weight.
- Fat intake: Studies show eating a high-fat diet is related to overweight; eating a low-fat diet often reduces body weight.
- Physical activity level: A low level of physical activity is a risk factor for weight gain. Obese people tend to lead more sedentary lives. Regular physical activity can change body composition and lead to weight loss and weight maintenance.

- Insulin sensitivity: Obese people are often insulin resistant and have high amounts of insulin in the bloodstream.
- Cortisol levels: Obese people produce the stress hormone cortisol at higher rates; their bodies tend to degrade or get rid of it more slowly.
- Sex hormones: Obese men have low levels of androgen, a male sex hormone; obese women often have high androgen levels.
- Smoking: The habit is associated with lower body weight; stopping smoking increases body weight in most people.

Overweight and obesity are problems at various stages of life. Children, teenagers, young adults (especially women during pregnancy), middle-aged adults, and older adults must fight against lapsing into the unhealthy habits that are creating generations of couch potatoes.

CHILDHOOD OBESITY

According to the Centers for Disease Control and Prevention (CDC), the percentage of children and adolescents who are defined as overweight has more than doubled since the early 1970s; about 15 percent of children and adolescents are now overweight. These figures indicate that about 9 million children are in the category of overweight or obese. Although these conditions certainly have an impact on public health, they have not been a major public health priority in the past.

There are three periods of childhood that are critical to the development of obesity: the intrauterine period, the period between the ages of four to six, and adolescence.

The problem appears to start early. Some evidence shows that the developing fetus may show signs of future heart disease. Some miscarried fetuses have shown fatty streaks in the heart, indicating the beginning stage of heart disease, which may be genetic but is also related to the nutritional status of the mother.

Data from a study in Holland during World War II found that when mothers were starving during the last trimester, the infant was protected from obesity. This period when the infant is adding fat tissue possibly influences adipose tissue cells. In contrast, starvation during the first two trimesters promoted obesity in the offspring, perhaps due to impairment in food intake regulation. This seems to indicate that limiting weight gain during the last trimester may be beneficial to the offspring.

A 2004 report by the American Heart Association showed that more than 10 percent of U.S. children ages two to five are overweight. These data, collected in 2002, showed a 7 percent increase since 1994. And the situation worsens each year. These findings among preschoolers strongly indicate that the couch potato syndrome is beginning early in life. Another period of rapid fat growth begins at about five to six years of age. Three mechanisms may explain why adiposity rebounds during this period, and this contributes to adult obesity: this period is critical for learning diet and exercise behaviors; early adiposity may reflect early maturation; children with early adiposity may be those who were exposed to gestational diabetes.

Other statistics focus on older children. Between 1980 and 1994, the number of obese 6- to 11-year-olds increased from 5.7 percent to 10.6 percent.

Why is childhood obesity a problem? A fat body in childhood increases the risk factors for adult obesity, and that increases the risk of many health conditions in adulthood. However, some overweight children experience weight-related health problems before adulthood. Hypertension or an abnormal lipid profile is present in most overweight children as young as 5–10 years of age. Fat around the middle, or central adiposity, is associated with higher cardiovascular risk-factor levels, even in children. Life-threatening complications, such as sleep apnea, also affect children. In children ages 8–10, there has been an alarming increase of type-2 diabetes, a disease that was once called adult-onset diabetes.

Not only health but also learning tends to be affected. A report from the National Education Association showed that sedentary kids who eat high-sugar, high-fat meals may have poorer cognitive skills, higher anxiety levels, and problems with hyperactivity. Although the epidemic touches all cultures, a disproportionate number of Hispanic and African American children are overweight.

Children become overweight for a variety of reasons. Although underlying causes may be genetic, lack of physical activity and unhealthy eating patterns provide the environment for obesity. The social influences from parents and family are prime causes. In rare cases, an endocrine problem may cause a child to be overweight.

The third stage associated with greater obesity is adolescence; thus the importance of the following statistics of the rising percentage of overweight adolescents. A 1990–1994 study found that overweight among young people ages 12–17 increased from 5.7 to 10.6 percent. The 1999–2000 data showed that 15.3 percent were overweight. Obesity in adolescence— especially in girls—tends to affect self-esteem and mood disorders; however, this varies by age and ethnic background. Especially for males, being overweight as an adolescent was associated with increased mortality later in life from a variety of conditions, including cardiovascular diseases and colorectal cancer. It is possible that the increased risk related to the central deposition of body fat takes place in males during early adolescence. Effective interventions to treat childhood obesity and to prevent its development would have major health and economic benefits now and in the future. Some argue against treatment of childhood obesity because those children who will "outgrow" the obesity will receive unnecessary treatment and may be harmed by being labeled obese. Although this argument may have merit, peers of children who are obese can be cruel and may have already labeled them. However, the rising prevalence of obesity and the consequences of serious medical problems make doing nothing increasingly hard to justify.

Although treatment of children is not always successful, studies have shown good short-term and long-term outcomes. Programs involving both parents and children in weight-loss efforts have found that the children's changes were better than the weight changes in their parents. Successful initiatives used behavior modification for both parents and children (see Chapter 11).

Leonard H. Epstein's work represents the largest and longest studies in this field. Children from 6 to 12 years of age who were 20–100 percent overweight participated in a series of studies for 8–12 weeks and then monthly for 6–12 months. Families followed a balanced low-fat diet with moderate calorie restriction. Parent participation and type of physical activity were also factors. At the end of the treatment period, children in the most successful groups of each study attained a 15–20 percent weight loss. Ten years after the treatment programs, 30 percent of all children in the trial were nonobese. A multifaceted approach to modifying behavior has been most successful in treating childhood obesity.

School-based interventions are attractive because they can address the problem of overweight in a place where children spend much of their time. In 2005, the only state that required daily physical education was Illinois. Because of the emphasis on reading and math, some school districts have neglected health and physical activity. Students who are required to undergo remedial instruction because they have not met standards are sometimes pulled out of physical education for extra academic help.

However, some districts have seen the value of educational programs and have implemented nutrition and activity programs. A controversial idea emerging in some states and districts is sending letters to parents about the BMI of their child, encouraging them to take action. One study in schools compared two types of weight-loss programs: one that included exercise and nutrition education and another that focused on a balanced low-calorie diet. First, for a period of two to three months, students followed an exercise and nutrition education program. The study found that the weight of participants decreased about 5 percent after two to three months of weekly sessions. Then, when students followed a balanced low-calorie diet for six months, a decrease of 24 percent of ideal body weight was seen. Rather than targeting overweight children, some school-based programs have made changes throughout a school or throughout a specific grade. For example, a program called Planet Health for six and seventh graders encourages decreased television time, increased physical activity, and a lower-fat diet with increased fruit and vegetable intake.

Several commercial weight-loss programs target teens. Examples include Shapedown and Way to Go Kids. Shapedown is a three-month program for adolescents that uses behavioral techniques to change diet and exercise. A program called Committed to Kids also demonstrated significant weight loss using a very-low-calorie, high-protein diet. Some adult commercial programs, like Weight Watchers and Jenny Craig, accept 15-year-olds.

Multidisciplinary care and family support can help young people lose weight and maintain the loss. However, these programs face many obstacles such as high costs, poor reimbursement, high attrition rates, poor adherence, and weight-loss maintenance after the program ends. New medications, better integration of primary and tertiary care, greater connection within the community, and new uses of technology could help in many instances.

ADULT COUCH POTATOES

In 1951, the Pentagon dispatched physicians to Korea to perform autopsies of 2,000 young men killed in battle. The doctors were shocked when they found that these young, athletic men showed signs of heart disease, a condition thought only to afflict older adults, not 22-year-old men. Instead of finding smooth heart muscle in the soldiers, the researchers found fatty streaks and abnormal deposits of cholesterol in 77 percent of these Korean casualties; 30 percent had vessels that were more than half closed. Since the Korean War, many studies have shown that healthy-looking young adults carry the beginning signs of heart disease as well as other conditions.

Young and middle adulthood—especially after marriage—appears to be a time when people become so busy with career and family that they get into habits of unhealthy eating and reduced physical activity. It is much easier to take the family to a fast-food restaurant than to plan and cook a nutritious meal for them. Exercise becomes something that one can do without. Lack of time is the most common reason cited for individuals

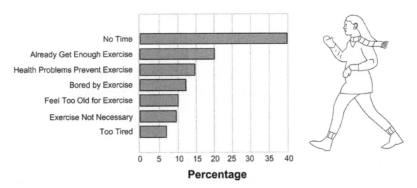

Figure 11.1 Why Don't We Exercise? (President's Council on Physical Fitness and Sports)

not to engage in physical activity (see Figure 11.1). Patterns set in young adulthood and young families become even more complex when these families get very busy during middle adulthood.

Pregnancy often represents a risk period for obesity development in adult women. Excessive weight is correlated with increased labor problems, cesarean section, and large babies. Each pregnancy may lead to permanent weight gains of 1.5–5 kilograms.

The most important prevention of cardiovascular (CV) disease, peripheral vascular disease, and obesity is exercise. Previously, sedentary men who adopted regular physical activity during a four-year period showed risk reduction of 44 percent for all causes of mortality and 52 percent for CV-related mortality during a subsequent five-year period. One study predicted that if just 30 percent of the adult population were to adopt regular physical activity, 30,000 lives would be saved each year due to reductions in coronary disease and diabetes alone.

In 1998, the U.S. surgeon general reported that 60 percent of the adult population is not active enough to get health benefits. Other surveys pinpoint that African American adults, those in lower socioeconomic classes, and especially older adults are less likely to engage in regular exercise and physical activity.

OLDER ADULTS: PHYSICAL ACTIVITY AND WEIGHT CONTROL

In 1900, only 4 percent of the total population was over 65 years of age. Now this rapidly growing segment comprises about 12 percent of the total population, or about 30 million people. Further projection indicates that by 2025, older adults will account for 17–20 percent of the population. The fastest growing segment of the population is adults 85 years and older.

As one ages, the likelihood of physical activity declines. Like all people, older individuals gain weight when their energy intake chronically exceeds energy expenditure. Older adulthood and retirement is a time when people must work hard to overcome the couch potato syndrome. As many as 250,000 deaths each year are attributed to physical inactivity. With the increase in the older population that is expected as the baby boomers age, the numbers of deaths related to physical inactivity will spiral upward.

Although weight gain during menopause is commonly reported and assumed to be a problem, studies of overweight and obesity during this stage of life have conflicting conclusions. Some studies have not confirmed menopausal weight gain but rather have found a change in the body-fat mass and body-fat distribution. The fat distribution tends to increase in the central part of the body. A high waist-to-hip ratio is positively associated with risk of mortality. Hormone replacement therapy, commonly used to alleviate the symptoms of menopause, appears to prevent the redistribution of body fat.

One major difference between overweight younger adults and overweight older adults is that the young adults have elevated levels of both fat mass and fat-free mass, but the older people have high levels of fat mass and lower levels of fat-free mass. When the fat-free mass erodes, the individual experiences higher rates of disability and a general decline in quality of life. Examples of fat-free mass are muscles and bones. Thus, any strategy that seeks to reduce body fat and preserve fat-free mass is important. Encouraging older people to increase their activity levels even moderately will likely improve their overall health and functional independence. Studies have shown that regular physical activity can enhance fat oxidation and prevent age-related increase in central-body fatness. As the population ages, this area of study will likely get more attention.

Are we developing generations of couch potatoes? Considering the life span as a whole, there definitely seem to be critical times when putting on weight is more likely and meaningful. Before a child is born, maternal diet affects development of fat tissue. From ages of four to six, children begin to make choices about food preferences and physical activity. During adolescence, the body is growing and changing, so this is another critical time for weight gain. When young adults gain weight, they gain both fat and fat-free mass. During pregnancy, women put on weight and tend to keep some of this weight as they return to normal life. In older adulthood, people tend to gain weight but lose fat-free mass such as bone and muscle.

Understanding the relationship of obesity and health is crucial. In the media, maintaining weight by eating properly and physical activity has been framed as looking good, appealing to our sense of vanity. Although better looks may be a consequence, the main reason to avoid the couch potato syndrome at any stage is health.

CHAPTER 12

The Great Diet Debate

In 2002, Americans spent over $400 billion on diet-related programs, books, foods, and beverages. Visitors to Amazon.com spend $120,000 a day on diet books. For example, diet books by Dr. Robert Atkins, promoter of the low-carbohydrate, high-fat diet, have sold more than 15 million copies. Magazines, news reports, and the Internet are replete with diets and weight-loss information. Exciting new ways to lose weight are hawked through television. To sort through all the information is quite a challenging task.

This chapter presents various approaches to dieting and eating for weight loss. It is designed neither to evaluate diets nor to encourage use of any one diet plan. Rather, the goal of this chapter is to present the issues in the great diet debate. One can readily see that experts disagree on which diet mode is best for prevention, maintenance, and loss of weight. One perspective that must be remembered is that a person may lose weight on any plan, but the important thing is to keep the weight off and remain healthy.

OBESITY AND DIET COMPOSITION

The current U.S. food supply produces 3,700 calories per person per day, far more than the estimated energy needs for a typical man, woman, or child. Although energy imbalance is the chief reason for weight gain, studies have sought to link obesity with specific nutrients or foods. Some studies have suggested that certain nutrients influence the brain chemistry

Table 12.1 Food Composition and Obesity

Component of Diet (macronutrient)	Suggested Relationship to Obesity	Diet for Weight Loss
Carbohydrates	Regardless of total energy intake, excessive consumption of starches and simple sugars leads to obesity. Excessive insulin caused by carbohydrates, such as those low in fiber, causes storage of fat in adipose tissue. Just eating excess sugar is thought to cause weight gain.	Eat a low-carbohydrate diet, focusing on eliminating simple sugars.
Protein	Obesity is due to excess protein consumption in early childhood, regardless of calories. Early high-protein intakes may account for increases in stature and muscle mass. This may involve hormonal changes, particularly insulin-like growth factor-1 and growth hormone.	Avoid excess protein, especially at early ages.
Fat	Excessive consumption of fat energy leads to obesity, regardless of total energy intake. High energy of fat (9 kcal/g) is responsible for "passive overeating."	Eat a low-fat diet to assist with calorie restriction.

of only the obese but not the lean. Table 12.1 shows how proposed mechanisms link certain dietary macronutrients—carbohydrates, protein, and dietary fat—or a given food with excess weight gain. In most cases, obese persons are said to choose foods high in sugar, fats, or energy instead of the more nutritious fruits and vegetables. Constant snacking and inappropriate food choices are usually driven by metabolic events, food compulsions, or food cravings.

A study by the American Physiological Society (2002) found that all animals, including humans, have an innate physiological ability to seek out sources of nutrients, such as minerals, that are deficient in the major food sources available to them. The researchers tested the animals' ability to choose from containers of various nutrients. The tests showed that there is a natural predisposition to select a balanced diet with all the necessary nutrients when these foods are present. Experiments of this type led to the concept of "nutritional wisdom" about the needs of each species. This idea states that given a choice, animals will choose foods that have the nutrients they need. However, the study found that nutritional wisdom is abandoned when unhealthy choices are more available than the healthy choices. The studies may point to a model for human obesity in which the wrong foods can override wise choices. The study concluded that the availability of food—and not the physiological needs of the body—is the culprit of obesity by choice.

Each macronutrient has been implicated in weight gain. According to some researchers, excessive intake of carbohydrates leads to weight gain, regardless of total calories consumed. This group believes that excess insulin caused by carbohydrates, especially those low in fiber, increases adipose tissue. Elevated sugar levels alone are thought to cause weight gain. For example, pediatric studies attribute excess weight gain in children to an elevated intake of fruit juice with fructose and juice-based drinks containing fructose and sucrose. Weight gain in adolescents is attributed to sweetened soft drinks. The potential mechanism here is the *glycemic index (GI)* of foods, a scale that ranks foods based on how much they raise blood-glucose levels. In this view, the GI plays an important role in the development of obesity, diabetes, and cardiovascular disease. Measuring foods by their GI is not universally accepted, and no long-term studies have been done on the topic. Some investigators call for an increased consumption of whole grains and complex carbohydrates as a way to reduce energy intakes through improved diet choices.

Other researchers believe obesity is due to consuming excess protein in early childhood, regardless of calories. High intake of protein may account for increases in muscle mass and stature and contributes to hormonal changes involving insulin-like growth factor-1 and growth hormone. Diets that are high in protein also tend to be rich in fat. In the United States, red meat—the major protein-rich food—is a major source of fat.

Another group of scientists hypothesizes that excessive fat consumption is the key to obesity. At 9 calories per gram, fat is highest in energy density of all nutrients. According to their rationale, the rising obesity rates are associated with increased consumption of dietary fat.

Diets fall into the following categories: fasting, low-fat, and very low-fat diets; low-carbohydrate diets; and low-calorie diets.

FASTING

Voluntary fasting, or abstinence from food, has been a tradition in most religions and is viewed as a spiritual purification rite. Many religions, including Christianity, Judaism, and the Eastern religions, encourage fasting for penitence, preparation for ceremony, mourning, and enhancement of knowledge and powers. Moses, Elijah, Daniel, and Jesus communed with God with fasts lasting as long as 40 days. Ancient philosophers and physicians, such as Socrates, Aristotle, Galen, and Hippocrates, believed in therapeutic fasting as a natural method of healing. They pointed to the fact that when animals are sick, they fast and suggested that fasting is a way to increase our natural resistance to disease.

A modern proponent of a modified version of fasting is Elson M. Haas, MD. His book *Staying Healthy with Nutrition: The Complete Guide to Diet and Nutritional Medicine* (2002) promotes the idea that fasting is a natural way to remedy obesity but that over a long period of time, it must be combined with protein drinks. A short fast of 5–10 days can be a useful motivator for those wanting to make necessary dietary changes and new commitments.

Very obese patients have been monitored in hospitals while on water fasts and have shed as much as 100 pounds without any medical consequences. Other patients have had their jaws wired shut so they can only take liquids through straws.

In the 1920s and 1930s, fasting became very popular as a weight-loss treatment. In the 1950s, a series of studies were conducted on hospitalized obese persons to see how well a diet of only water worked. Fasting patients reported a feeling of well-being and even euphoria, and they did not feel hungry after the first day. However, this study did show that there were some physiological disturbances during the fast and concluded that fasts were ineffective in the long term.

HIGH-PROTEIN DIETS AND LIQUID PROTEIN DIETS

To combat the problem of muscle loss caused by fasting, some doctors administered injections of glucose, a strategy that did not work. When they tried low-calorie protein supplements, the muscle loss stopped. High levels of protein resulted in elevated levels of ketones in the bloodstream. However, adding glucose to the protein supplement reduced these ketone levels. In the 1970s, various research groups administered protein-glucose mixes to obese patients. Liquid protein diets were also investigated. A book published in 1976, *The Last Chance Diet* by Dr. Robert Linn, proved to be fatal for many who tried protein supplements during fasts. Several people developed heart arrhythmias. For more than 60 people who died on the diet, it did prove to be their last chance.

Newer fasting programs substitute a variety of protein-rich powders for meals. These medically supervised diets—which are for people who are at least 30–50 pounds overweight—use prepackaged powders such as Optifast or Medifast. The high-protein, low-calorie shakes replace for at least one meal per day, and they enable patients to burn fat and provide the needed vitamins, minerals, and amino acids to sustain life. A doctor must supervise this diet for possible damage to kidneys caused by ketones or depletion of potassium.

SINGLE-FOOD DIETS

For many years, diets focusing on a single food have appealed to those wanting to lose weight fast. These diets are not nutritionally balanced, but they are easy to do. Many kinds of single-food diets have been popular. Usually, they will appear as a sensational media story. In the 1930s, the grapefruit diet began as the Hollywood diet. This plan combined eating a few vegetables with eating a grapefruit before every meal. The cabbage soup diet has had many versions over the years. Current cabbage soup diets add a few vegetables and meat. Other single-food diets may include the Duke University rice diet, comprised of beans, apples, and other low-calorie foods. On these diets, one may lose weight rapidly but then gain all the weight back upon resuming normal eating.

LOW-CARBOHYDRATE DIETS

The diet industry bombards us with new and revolutionary miracle approaches to weight loss. Many of these diets have recycled over a number of years. One such type of diet is the low-carbohydrate diet. In 1961, Herman Taller, a physician, wrote *Calories Don't Count*, a book that described obesity as a metabolic disorder. He said that this metabolic disorder appeared in three ways:

- The body produces fat at a higher than normal rate.
- The body stores fat at a higher than normal rate.
- The body releases fat for metabolism at a slower than normal rate.

Although some of his assumptions are not exactly correct according to recent research, his observation that obesity is a metabolic disease forms the foundation for the low-carbohydrate theory. Taller believed that pyruvic acid, a by-product of carbohydrate breakdown, inhibits the body from burning stored fat and then becomes fat. To combat this effect, he recommended that fat be balanced by limiting carbohydrate and saturated fat. His low-carbohydrate, high-fat, high-protein diet became very popular in the 1960s, and this approach is seen today in many popular diets.

In 1967, Irving Stillman published *The Doctor's Quick Weight Loss Diet*, which described a low-carbohydrate diet. He thought that protein was difficult for the body to digest and that by consuming protein and fat and restricting carbohydrates, body fat would be lost.

In 1972, cardiologist Robert Atkins issued the book *Dr. Atkins' New Diet Revolution* that recommended low or zero carbohydrates with fat and protein as the primary source of food. This book started a low-carb craze that is continuing. Estimates are that in any quarter of 2003, almost 35 million Americans were on a low-carbohydrate diet. Dr. Atkins created his own food pyramid that begins with meats. Information, including the Atkins food pyramid, may be accessed at http://www.atkins.com.

Low-carb diets have fueled fiery debates among scientists. Most nutritionists state that a calorie—the amount of energy needed to heat 1 kilogram of water 1 degree centigrade. A calorie is a calorie regardless of where it comes from. But two scientists, Richard Feinman of the State University of New York and Eugene Fine of Jacobi Medical Center in New York, have turned to physics to assert that calories differ. In an article in *Nature* (August 16, 2004), they agree with the first law of thermodynamics that states that energy is always conserved. In weight-loss terms, that means that protein, fat, and carbohydrate calories are equivalent because none of their energy is destroyed when you eat them. However, the second law of thermodynamics says that energy spontaneously disperses if not hindered. They point out that protein and carbohydrates are metabolized in different ways, and their energy is dispersed in different forms. When the body breaks down protein, more energy is released as heat than is converted to chemical energy. This means that a piece of steak and slice of bread may have an equal number of calories, but the energy that the body gets from them, to move or to store as fat, is different. Of course, other scientists disagree and argue that, although people on a low-carb, high-protein diet shed three times as much weight in the beginning, after a year, there was little or no difference when compared to those who count calories.

Other diet plans that are versions of low-carbohydrate diets are found in the South Beach Diet, The Zone, and the glycemic index.

Some experts from the federally appointed Calorie Control Council believe that the low-carb craze hit its peak in 2005. The council's 2004 consumer survey indicated that respondents believed that cutting carbohydrates was important but that it was also important to reduce calories.

The low-carbohydrate diets are appealing to people because meat, cream, eggs, and other high-fat foods are satisfying. Usually, there is rapid weight loss. Some individuals have experienced certain side effects, such as hair loss and stomach and intestinal problems, when following a low-carbohydrate diet for long periods of time.

LOW-FAT AND NO-FAT DIETS WITH HIGH CARBOHYDRATES

In 1955, 40-year-old Nathan Pritikin was diagnosed with serious heart trouble and cholesterol levels of 280. The doctor told him to avoid all exertion. Doubting the doctor's advice, Pritikin combined exercise with a diet of fruits, vegetables, and grains. Eleven years later, that same doctor proclaimed that he showed no signs of heart abnormality. In 1979, Pritikin wrote a book designed for patients with heart disease, high blood pressure, and diabetes, called the *Pritikin Program for Diet and Exercise*. Following Pritikin's death, cardiologist Dean Ornish took up his ideas and wrote *Eat More, Weigh Less* (1993), in which he recommended that fat calories be less than 10 percent of the diet. Ornish believes that on this diet, which he says is important for everyone, you can eat beans and legumes, fruits, greens, and vegetables until you are full but not stuffed. The diet demands avoiding meat (including chicken and fish), avocados, olives, oils, seeds, any dairy products, sugar, alcohol, and any commercial product with more than 2 grams of fat per serving. He also adds meditation, exercise, and stress reduction techniques.

Susan Powter is a fitness guru who believes in low-fat diets. Her book *Stop the Insanity* (2002) aggressively pursues this type of diet developed by Pritikin and Ornish; it also recommends rigorous exercise.

Mark Mattson of the National Institute of Aging presented information at a forum discussion in 2005. Mattson showed the converging lines of evidence from studies of human populations, patients, and animal models that suggest a diet low in calories and saturated fats can protect against neurodegenerative diseases like Alzheimer's disease, Parkinson's disease, and stroke. Calorie restriction and intermittent fasting may reduce oxidative stress and induce beneficial cellular stress resistance responses.

Critics of this diet contend that a low-fat diet without a decrease in total calorie intake does not promote weight loss. The very-low-fat diets of Pritikin and Ornish promote weight loss only if calories are also decreased.

CALORIE COUNTING

Calorie counting for weight loss has been around since the idea of the calorie was introduced. The Food and Drug Administration (FDA) has a new campaign called "Calories Count" that focuses on educating people about the importance of counting calories. Dr. Barbara Rolls, a professor of nutritional sciences at Pennsylvania State University, presented new research at the North American Association for the Study of Obesity (NAASO) on an initiative called "The Volumetrics Eating Plan: Techniques and Recipes for Feeling Full on Fewer Calories." This plan encourages people to fill up and replace high-calorie food with lower-calorie items. Examples are incorporating more fruits and vegetables and using lower- and reduced-calorie versions of foods. By filling up on fruits and vegetables and reducing portions, approximately 800 calories can be eliminated from the daily diet.

The program Calories Count can be accessed through http://www .caloriescount.com, a website that offers a free diet assessment and other tools for weight loss. A free, award-winning website is http://www .caloriecontrol.com, which has a BMI calculator as well as information on how to cut calories in a sensible manner. This site also has a downloadable brochure, "Winning by Losing."

Examples of low-calorie, nutritionally balanced diets are Weight Watchers, Jenny Craig, Nutrisystem, the National Cholesterol Education Program Step I and Step II diets, and the Dietary Approaches to Stop Hypertension (DASH) diet. Low-calorie diets provide 800–1,500 calories per day. Very-low-calorie diets of 400–500 calories per day may increase rates of weight loss initially, but at one year, results are similar to those of low-calorie diets.

PYRAMIDS AND PLATES

In recent years, the government, medical associations, and nutritionists have tried to give reliable information on eating. The Food Guide Pyramid has been given several faces over the years. About 80 percent of the populace recognized the 1992 Food Pyramid, but the government acknowledged that few followed its recommendation. The pyramid outlined the portions that Americans should eat with grains at the base; moved through fruits, vegetables, and meats; and reached fats, oils, and sugars at the apex. Critics said that the plan was too broad and vague. For example, people were told to eat 6–12 servings of grains, without an explanation of who should eat 6 and who should eat 12. Also, no information about serving size was provided.

MyPyramid.gov
STEPS TO A HEALTHIER YOU

Figure 12.1 MyPyramid, the 2005 Revision of the Food Pyramid (U.S. Department of Agriculture)

On April 19, 2005, the old Food Pyramid was turned on its side and outfitted with stairs, as the federal government offered a new effort to help Americans make proper food choices. The new program, called MyPyramid, was an interactive, customized food guidance system that also incorporated activity (see Figure 12.1). The recommendations were based on the 2005 Dietary Guidelines for Americans, published by the Department of Health and Human Services and the Department of Agriculture (USDA). This time the pyramid was a series of vertical color bands of varying widths. The band of fruits and vegetables took up most of the space; the grains followed, with fats, sugar, and oils being the narrowest. A stick figure to the left of the pyramid walked up the left side of the pyramid to match the guide's slogan, "Steps to a healthier you." The new pyramid also came in 12 variations, depending on a person's activity level and caloric needs.

The goal of the pyramid was to give the public a graphic of the 70-page document in a way that would be useful to them. However, critics said that it was likely to be as ineffective as the older models.

On June 2, 2011, the USDA replaced MyPyramid with MyPlate. The new pictorial guidelines featured a circle (representative of a dinner plate) with color-coded sections for different food groups. It is divided into four sections: approximately 40 percent vegetables, 30 percent grains, 20 percent protein, and 10 percent fruits. To the side of the large circle is a

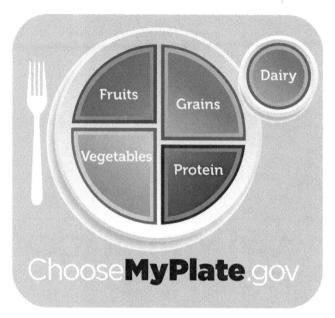

Figure 12.2 MyPlate (U.S. Department of Agriculture)

smaller circle (representing a glass of milk or cup of yogurt) to indicate recommendations for dairy. (See Figure 12.2.)

The new graphic's plate-based design has been praised for being more intuitive and user-friendly than MyPyramid. As with other incarnations of the USDA's guidelines, however, some have criticized the amount of space given (or not given) to certain food groups. In response to some of these criticisms, the Harvard School of Public Health released its own altered version of MyPlate, called the Harvard Healthy Eating Plate.

USING FOOD LABELS

Under regulations from the FDA and the USDA, food labels must be placed on all processed foods (see Figure 12.3). At the top of the label is the serving size, which is the basis for all the nutrient amounts listed on the panel and the number of servings that are in the package. This is very important for understanding the rest of the label. For example, if one cup is listed in a serving, and the package contains two servings, you double the calories and other nutrient numbers if you eat the whole package. Many items that are sold as a single product contain two or more servings. The next items are the total fat, cholesterol, and sodium. On the right side of the

Sample label for
Macaroni & Cheese

① Start Here ➡

② **Check Calories**

③ Limit these
Nutrients

④ Get Enough
of these
Nutrients

⑤ **Footnote**

⑥ Quick Guide
to % DV

● **5% or less
is Low**

● **20% or more
is High**

Nutrition Facts

Serving Size 1 cup (228g)
Servings Per Container 2

Amount Per Serving

Calories 250   Calories from Fat 110

	% Daily Value*
Total Fat 12g	18%
Saturated Fat 3g	15%
Trans Fat 3g	
Cholesterol 30mg	10%
Sodium 470mg	20%
Total Carbohydrate 31g	10%
Dietary Fiber 0g	0%
Sugars 5g	
Protein 5g	

Vitamin A	4%
Vitamin C	2%
Calcium	20%
Iron	4%

* Percent Daily Values are based on a 2,000 calorie diet.
Your Daily Values may be higher or lower depending on
your calorie needs.

	Calories	2,000	2,500
Total Fat	Less than	65g	80g
Sat Fat	Less than	20g	25g
Cholesterol	Less than	300mg	300mg
Sodium	Less than	2,400mg	2,400mg
Total Carbohydrate		300g	375g
Dietary Fiber		25g	30g

Figure 12.3 How to Read a Food Label (U.S. Food and Drug Administration)

label is a quick guide to the percent of daily value (DV). This shows how a serving fits in with recommendations for a healthful diet and allows consumers to compare the product with other foods. The panel also shows how much dietary fiber, vitamins A and C, calcium, and iron are in the package. If an individual wants to determine which frozen dinner is lower in saturated fat, he or she can look at the percent of DV to see which is higher or lower in the nutrient of interest. A host of other information is also on the label.

In 2014, the FDA began considering revisions for a new nutrition facts panel, the design for which was finalized in May 2016. The new label will feature several key changes, including a larger font size for total calories, removal of the "calories from fat" information, more realistic serving sizes, and inclusion of information on added sugars. Initially intended to

Table 12.2 Fat-Free Foods versus Regular-Calorie Foods

Regular Food	Calories	Fat-Free or Reduced-Calorie Food	Calories
Regular chocolate chip cookies (3 cookies)	142	Reduced-fat chocolate chip cookies (3 cookies)	118
Regular peanut butter (2 tablespoons)	191	Reduced-fat peanut butter (2 tablespoons)	187
Regular fig cookies (2 cookies)	111	Fat-free fig cookies (2 cookies)	102
Regular whole milk vanilla frozen yogurt, 3–4% fat (1 cup)	104	Nonfat frozen yogurt, less than 1% fat (1cup)	100
Regular vanilla ice cream, 11% fat (1cup)	133	Light vanilla ice cream, 7% fat (1 cup)	111
Regular blueberry muffin (1 small, 2 inch)	138	Low-fat blueberry muffin (1 small, 2 inch)	131
Regular tortilla chips (1 ounce)	143	Baked tortilla chips (1 ounce)	113
Regular cereal bar (1.3 ounce)	140	Low-fat cereal bar (1.3 ounce)	130

Source: National Heart, Lung, and Blood Institute.

go into effect in 2018, the FDA has extended the deadline for compliance because of industry pressures.

One way of reducing calories is to cut the amount of total fat and limit the overall caloric intake. However, eating fat-free or reduced-fat food is not always the solution that it seems to be (see Table 12.2). Checking the labels will help the consumer assess if there is a difference in value. Because a product is labeled as fat-free or reduced-fat does not mean that it is calorie free.

Just losing weight for vanity is not a viable goal and generally will not succeed. The basic premise is that a healthy eating style must become ingrained as a permanent life change in behavior and attitudes about eating.

2015–2020 DIETARY GUIDELINES

This revision is updating the guidelines in addition to the ones that were promoted in the past years. It does take time for people to know of guidelines and to make changes. The core of the new guidelines is developing healthy eating habits. The goal of the 2015–2020 Dietary Guidelines for Americans is for individuals throughout all stages of the life span to have eating patterns that promote overall health and help prevent chronic disease. Major guidelines include focusing on food variety and nutrient density, avoiding added sugars and saturated fat, and watching portion sizes. The guidelines can be found at https://healthy.gov/dietary guideline/2015/guidelines.

CHAPTER 13

Can Behavioral Strategies Result in Weight Loss?

Diet, exercise, and surgery have been touted as ways to lose weight. More drastic strategies include hypnosis, voluntary incarceration, and jaw wiring. However, some specialists believe that procedures will not be effective unless the psychological aspects of weight loss are considered. These scientists are convinced that people must make up their minds for a complete change and that determination is not only to lose weight but also to improve health for life.

One of the keys to battling obesity is a technique used in working with many other addictions, such as smoking or drugs, called behavior modification. In this technique, persons are aware of the environment and context of their lives and the elements that feed the addiction. Personal responsibility is emphasized.

The psychological foundations are based on the concept of self-efficacy, which was defined by Stanford psychologist Albert Bandura in 1977. He theorized that people's perceptions of their abilities to be effective influence whether they will act and how they will act. It will affect how much effort they expend and how long they will sustain their efforts in face of challenges. If a person believes that he or she lives in a diseased state, can that person have the confidence in his or her ability to change the predicament? People are often encouraged to try to lose weight using various weight-loss fads as cure-alls rather than through self-mastery. Although participating in short-term diets may lead to some success, it does not attack the root of the problem. When the diet fails, the person may become convinced that he or she is powerless and cannot control the situation. Behaviorists view efforts to sue food establishments, demonize various industries, and rid schools of vending machines as simplistic Band-Aids. By blaming these institutions, society makes individuals who have no confidence in their ability to lose weight. Accordingly, frivolous lawsuits against the food industry and classifying obesity as a disease only reinforce the idea that obesity is something that people cannot control.

RECOGNITION AND ACTION

In looking at the problem of obesity for the individual as well as society, one must recognize that no single industry, group, or food is to blame. A person cannot blame his or her genes or have the attitude that he or she is helpless because of heredity. The responsibility is put back into the hands of the individual. The worst thing that can happen here is to make the person a victim. Also, behaviorists recognize that obesity is a very complex problem and is not simply a matter of pushing away from the table.

Gerard Musante, PhD, founder of Structure House in Durham, North Carolina, uses this evidence-based, cognitive-behavioral approach to treating obese patients. Musante has created a broad definition of behavioral modification based on research and includes the following items:

- Advertising: There is a link between obesity and "preference manipulation," or advertising. But people must recognize ads for what they are: efforts to influence or manipulate preferences or buying habits. The consumer must be discriminating and recognize advertising for what it is.
- Parental influence: When parents change how the family eats and offer children wholesome rewards, obese children shed pounds quickly.
- Environmental influences: A direct link exists between urban sprawl and health: people walk less, weigh more, and suffer from elevated blood pressure. A direct correlation exists between television watching and obesity among children: the more TV a child watches, the more likely he or she is overweight. Physical education is no longer a mainstay in schools throughout the country; Illinois is the only state to require daily physical education.
- Psychological factors: Food insecurity is positively associated with overweight in women. Men and women use food in different ways: men celebrate situations of positive emotions and conflict, whereas women turn their emotions inward and become depressed.

- Physiological factors: The endocrine system is closely linked to obesity, with leptin, ghrelin, and other hormones and proteins influencing obesity. Genetic factors also play a role.

Despite all of these physical and psychological factors, most people lack self-awareness; they do not want to accept blame for their obesity. They do not realize that they overindulge in food for psychological reasons. They may realize that they do not devote enough time to physical activity, but they feel they have good reasons or excuses for not participating. They are not aware of the complex problem rooted in their relationships with food. One of the keys is helping people understand how they are eating for emotional needs, not for nutritional needs.

A Universal McCann Global Study released in July 2004 showed the difference between the attitudes of the people in the United Kingdom and the United States. The study revealed that 83 percent of American adults believe that it is the responsibility of individuals who choose to overeat. Sixty-eight percent of American respondents believed that lack of exercise is the main cause of obesity, whereas 32 percent believed eating too much was the main cause. In the United States, only 26 percent blame the food companies and advertising for obesity problems. Also, 65 percent of Americans in the study said advertisers were not to blame. When asked about the role of intervention of government agencies as a solution to the problem, 22 percent of Americans thought the government should step in, whereas 30 percent of the British were in favor of government intervention. In spite of publicity about the influence of advertising, most Americans believe in accepting responsibility for the choices that they make.

Musante noted that this attitude of personal responsibility is the first that must be faced when struggling with weight loss. The blame cannot be assigned to the fast-food, soda, and snack-food industries. His facility in Durham focuses on the psychology of overeating and encourages participants to examine their relationships with food. He deplores the stories that emerge almost daily and lawsuits that tend to point fingers at fast-food restaurants, sodas, snack food, television, and computers. Restricting these items is only the tip of the iceberg when it comes to attacking the complex problem of weight loss. According to Musante, maintaining a healthy weight and a healthy lifestyle is not easy, and there is no quick fix.

The attitude of behavior therapy is to manage or control food cues and identify trigger points that relate to food. For example, if the candy aisle at the grocery store is tempting, do not go through that aisle, and be sure not to go to the store on an empty stomach. If watching television entices you to snack on high-calorie foods, keep healthy snacks on hand to avoid bingeing without thinking, or shift your evening activities to something else, such as reading or exercising. The individual is in charge of the choices made and has the capacity to change these habits to make better choices.

HISTORY OF BEHAVIORAL TREATMENT

In the 1960s, behavioral techniques rose out of a learning theory that emphasized the importance of focusing on eating and exercise behaviors, changing the circumstances that preceded these two behaviors, and looking at the reinforcers or consequences that controlled these behaviors. In early programs, the goal was to make patients aware of their behaviors and to change the harmful patterns. For example, the participant would be aware of when and where food was eaten rather than monitoring the actual calories eaten. Strategies included self-monitoring, in which clients wrote down what they ate and the circumstances surrounding eating. Stimulus control emphasized removing cues for inappropriate eating, eating only in one place, and slowing down the act of eating. Participants were taught to identify alternative sources of reinforcement. They may increase lifestyle activity, but the focus was on behavioral patterns, not on the calories used in the activity.

At first, the programs were individual, but they soon moved to group interventions. Programs lasted 10–12 weeks, and participants lost an average of 3.8–4.2 kilograms. When followed up after 15 weeks, the average weight loss was an additional 4 kilograms. These weight losses were shown to be greater than those achieved by nutrition or psychotherapy interventions.

From 1970 to 1990, the programs evolved to include heavier patients for longer periods of times and longer follow-up. The programs began to focus on energy balance, and people were given specific goals for eating and exercise. Stimulus-control approaches added physical cues related to eating and also addressed the psychological and social cues. The result improved to an average weight loss of 8.5 kilograms at 21 weeks.

Since 1990, programs have strengthened behavioral approaches aimed at improving both initial weight loss and long-term maintenance.

CURRENT BEHAVIORAL APPROACHES

Most behavioral programs are in a group format with six months of weekly meetings followed by six months of biweekly meeting and then six more months of monthly meetings. Usually 10–20 participants meet in a closed session and remain together as they proceed through the program. A multidisciplinary team made up of therapists, nutritionists, exercise physiologists, and clinical psychologists leads the program. Lessons are designed to teach participants to modify their diet and behavior.

Self-monitoring is a key component of these programs, and it is often the single most important part of the program. Participants are given calorie- and fat-intake goals and are taught to write down everything they eat. Keeping track of food intake helps the participants ensure that they stay within their calorie and fat goals. Dietary intake is recorded each day for six months and then periodically after that. A nutritionist reviews the records and makes recommendations for food choices and offers supportive feedback. Also, for the first six months of the program, participants self-monitor physical activity by recording either calories per activity or minutes of activity. Obviously, self-monitoring is not always completely accurate. In fact, the program team expects that participants underestimate their own weight loss by about 30 percent. Consequently, the technique is looked upon as more of a tool for behavioral change rather than an assessment tool.

Patients must change the negative aspects of the environment in which they live. Unhealthy eating habits arise from cues in the environment, such as servings of large portion sizes, friends going out for a meal, and enticing television ads. The programs teach stimulus-response controls to reduce cues for inappropriate behavior and encourage activity, such as removing high-calorie foods from their shelves and keeping a variety of low-calorie foods readily available.

Important, especially in the later weeks of a behavioral program, are problem-solving techniques. Participants are given scenarios to brainstorm for solutions and choose one of the best solutions for implementation. Problems that occur most frequently are eating in restaurants, lack of time for exercise, and dealing with unsupportive family members. Participants are taught to expect and plan for relapses.

SPECIFIC STRATEGIES TO IMPROVE OUTCOME

Physical Activity

Almost all current behavioral weight-loss programs include exercise or physical activity as a key component, and their goal is to increase the proportion of participants who adopt and maintain their exercise behaviors for the long term. To improve adoption and maintenance of physical activity, behavioral programs encourage a combination of lifestyle exercise and programmed or structured exercise. Lifestyle activities include taking the stairs rather than the elevator, parking at the far end of the lot, walking from store to store, and getting off the bus one stop earlier. These types of activities can easily become part of a daily routine. However, most of these activities are not enough to achieve marked increases in overall energy expenditures. Structured exercise involves setting aside times specifically for the purpose of exercise. Examples are participating in an aerobics class three days per week or walking a two-mile route five days per week.

Behavioral programs encourage participants to gradually increase the level of activity to 1,000 calories per week. This level would be achieved by walking two miles on five days each week. Some researchers do not think this recommendation is enough. Participants in the National Weight Control Registry who have succeeded in losing 60 pounds or more and have kept it off for six years report that they expend an average of 2,800 calories per week. They achieve this through a combination of activities, such as walking, bicycling, strength training, or aerobic dance. About 500 calories per week are expended in medium-intensity activities, and 800 calories are expended in high-intensity activities. The important factor is selecting a type of physical activity that the individual enjoys. Enjoying a type of activity increases the likelihood of adherence over a long period of time.

Behavioral programs have studied strategies to increase participation in exercise. Most people note that lack of time is a major barrier to increasing exercise. One approach has been to divide exercise into multiple short sessions each day rather than one extended session. Several studies have compared the effects of exercising in one daily 40-minute bout or in four 10-minute bouts. The short-bout prescription led to better adherence and better weight loss at the end of six months. Participants who were given a treadmill for home use were found to have the best overall outcome in the study. Making exercise equipment easily accessible appeared to influence long-term outcomes. The key is setting realistic goals that work for the individual.

Studies in exercise motivation have shown that changes to the environment and community offerings make exercise easier. Many communities are building parks and walking paths to encourage people to make small changes that get them physically active. James O. Hill, codirector of the National Weight Control Registry, tells people to start on programs that begin with small daily goals, like walking an extra 2,000 steps (about a mile) and cutting out about 200 calories a day (or one soda). Wearing a pedometer, a device to measure how many steps a person takes, is an excellent way to keep track. Once people reach 2,000 steps comfortably, they are encouraged to add 2,000 more. Hill encourages people to drive less and walk more.

A study from the Mayo Clinic in Rochester, Minnesota, compared total activity of 10 lean people and 10 mildly obese people for 10-day periods. The lean people spent two hours on average each day doing nonpurposeful activity, such as going to the water cooler, pacing, and fidgeting. That extra activity added up to 350 calories burned each day, which would total about 30 pounds over the course of a year. This study encourages small bursts of activity in daily life to change the balance of energy expenditure.

MODIFYING DIETARY INTAKE

Behavioral researchers have studied the type of diet that is most effective for long-term weight loss. The issues are related to the amount of calorie restriction, composition of the diet, and strategies that promote adherence to new eating patterns.

Calorie restriction is a key element of a weight-loss program. Typically, behavioral programs recommend diets of approximately 1,200–1,500 calories per day. The baseline estimate of how many calories a person should consume per day is found by multiplying weight in pounds by 12 to 15. Then, 1,000 calories per day is subtracted to estimate weight loss of about 2 pounds per week.

Structured meal plans have been studied as a means for weight loss. The reasoning behind these meal plans is that if people were provided with food or a liquid formula, they would find it easier to remain on the diet. One study divided participants into four groups: group 1 received a standard behavioral weight-loss program with a prescribed calorie goal; group 2 received the same plan but was given meal plans for five breakfasts and five dinners each week and a grocery list to help with purchasing the required foods; group 3 received a box of food with these meals provided and shared the cost of food with the study; and group 4 received free food. Weight losses at the end of eight months averaged 8, 12, 11.7, and 11.4 kilograms, respectively, for groups 1 through 4.

Almost all the studies in the weight-loss literature show that patients achieve maximum loss at about six months, followed by weight regain. Maintenance of weight loss remains difficult for several reasons:

- Physiological changes occur with the weight loss, such as lower metabolic rate and lower leptin levels, which promote weight gain.
- Reinforcement associated with weight loss, such as fitting into smaller-size clothes, attention from others, and improvements in

certain risk factors, is greater for the period of weight loss than for weight management.
- Many people do not achieve their desired weight loss and thus give up on the program.
- Boredom is the most reported explanation for failure to maintain behavior changes and weight loss in the long term.

Ongoing contact with a physician or therapy specialist appears to be the most effective approach to continued weight maintenance.

PREDICTORS OF WEIGHT LOSS

The great variability of weight loss makes predicting success difficult; thus, studies are mixed. The average patient in a behavioral weight-control study is white, middle aged, middle income, and female. Studies have found no long-term predictive difference between men and women and no relationship between age and treatment outcomes. Marital status, education, and employment do not appear to predict treatment outcomes. Ethnic differences in weight-loss treatments are fairly consistent. In several programs, black participants appear to have less success because of poor attendance and greater weight gain in the latter six months of a program. Generally, the only demographic characteristics that predict positive outcome are initial body weight and race. Patients who are heavier lose more weight than those who are lighter, and whites lose more than blacks. Patients with binge eating, depression, major stress, and major medical problems are at a greater risk for attrition and should be in contact with their physician or counselor.

The amount of sleep that one gets may be correlated to weight loss. J. O. Hill (2003) monitored the sleep of 1,001 patients and found that patients with normal body mass indices slept 16 minutes longer than those classified as overweight or obese. Although this was only a causal relationship, a clear trend exists that Americans now sleep less and weigh more. Something as simple as adding 20 extra minutes of sleep per night may add to the list of behavioral modifications for combating obesity.

BEHAVIOR AND THE OBESITY DILEMMA

In a study on behavioral therapies, Eric Finkelstein, PhD, MHA, of RTI International categorizes obese consumers into three subgroups: the overweight by choice, the uninformed, and those with self-control problems. Interventions need to be tailored to each group.

- Overweight by choice: From the demographics of the increase in obesity over the past 30 years, it seems that a greater fraction of people prefer a lifestyle that leads to excess weight. Even when informed about the adverse effects of obesity, these individuals could weigh less, but it is just too hard in their current environment. They will not make the lifestyle changes until something catastrophic happens—and maybe not even then. Because many of their medical expenses are financed through insurance or by the government, individuals do not bear the full costs of their decisions. This implies a role for government in this subset and also provides motivation for employers to adopt a healthy lifestyle. Interventions that do not affect the costs or benefits of obesity-related behaviors will not be effective for this group.
- The uninformed consumer: This subset lacks information or has misinformation about food consumption and physical activity. Because of the plethora of information available, it is hard to imagine that a large group such as this one exists. Finding the most effective way to reach them is the challenge.
- Those with self-control problems: Even when provided complete information, the self-control group does not embrace a positive lifestyle. This is a large group, evidenced by the existence of the more than 55 million Americans who spend $40 billion per year fueling the diet industry. Providing only information is not effective with this group, but other intervention strategies that include behavior modification may be more successful.

Effective patient education can improve the quality of health care a patient receives. Because of the lack of time with physicians, programs that involve creative ways of communication can be effective. Doctors targeting obesity could set up a program similar to the University of Pittsburgh Medical Center's Internet portal, which allows diabetes patients to talk remotely with their physicians. Launched in 2003, the program now has more than 1,000 patients who can communicate with doctors and their staffs, receive alerts about appointments, and submit requests for refills and referrals.

Various media have been used for direct-to-consumer marketing: physician office flyers and materials, advertisements in pharmacies, e-mail, direct mail, branded web, spot TV, print, radio, national TV, and banner ads. Optas, located in Woburn, Massachusetts, performed a survey of 150 manufacturers and agencies. According to Paul Buta of Optas, 47 percent of the respondents thought more money should be spent on materials in the doctor's office, whereas 42 percent believed advertising money should be spend on unbranded websites like WebMD. Weight loss, diet, and exercise are the most sought-after subjects. However, television advertising of over-the-counter weight-loss products has skyrocketed. People are interested in buying herbal-type weight-loss products because of these advertisements. Is behavior therapy that seeks life changes effective in controlling weight? The issues are related to changing the mind-set of people who seek to lose weight not for their health but because of their vanity. Diet fads are appealing because they make it possible for dieters to quickly lose weight. However, the problem is maintenance and weight gain after ending the diet. It is possible for a dieter to gain more weight back than he or she lost. Behaviorists know that expecting and preparing for weight relapse provides dieters with a realistic way to overcome the setbacks. Behaviorists believe that changing lifestyle behaviors is the only logical way to maintain permanent weight loss, but it is precisely this method that is the most difficult.

CHAPTER 14

Should Surgery Be Used as a Weight-Control Method?

The causes of severe obesity are many and complex, but the published success rates for all medical approaches for the morbidly obese are poor. These medical approaches include the use of drugs, diet, hypnosis, voluntary incarceration, jaw wiring, intragastric balloons, and behavioral modification. An estimated 95 percent of morbidly obese patients subjected to medical weight-reduction programs regain all the lost weight, as well as additional weight, within two years of the onset of therapy.

In 1991, scientists at the National Institutes of Health (NIH) Consensus Conference used medical evidence to conclude that surgical treatment was a logical therapy for patients with a BMI of more than 40 or a BMI of more than 35 with certain conditions. These conditions include type-2 diabetes, severe degenerative joint pain, severe sleep apnea, severe reflux esophagitis, polycystic ovary syndrome, and nonalcoholic liver disease.

Surgical treatment of obesity designed to restrict food passage, nutrient absorption, or both. This group of procedures, called bariatric—meaning obese—surgery, has gained acceptance among surgeons, physicians, and the public. No long-term weight program has as solid a track record for maintenance of weight as surgery. Most insurance companies require that patients have attempted but failed with nonsurgical attempts to reduce weight. However, after surgery, the patient must still make lifestyle changes that include exercise and dietary education.

To understand the surgical issues, a brief look at the digestive system is essential:

- Mouth and esophagus: Food enters the mouth, where chewing and enzymes in saliva begin the process of digestion; swallowing takes the food into the food tube, or esophagus. The delicate lining of the esophagus is like the skin on the back of the hand. It is protected from the strong gastric acid by a valve that lets food pass into the stomach but keeps acid and gastric juices from flowing back into the esophagus.
- Stomach: The food enters through the esophagus and exits through the pyloric valve. In the stomach, the enzyme pepsin, hydrochloric acid, and mucus begin to break down protein and churn food into a liquid-like state. The stomach holds about three pints of food at a time.
- Liver: Located next to the stomach, this large organ produces bile that is stored in the gallbladder. Bile is secreted into the small intestine for the digestion of fats.
- Pancreas: Located between the stomach and small intestine, this triangular-shaped organ produces enzymes that break down proteins, starches, and fats.
- Small intestine: The major digestive action takes place here, where nutrients are absorbed into the bloodstream. Most of the action is in the first 30 centimeters (12 inches) called the duodenum. Bile and pancreatic enzymes speed up the process. Most of the calcium and iron is absorbed in the duodenum. Digested food is absorbed here through finger-like projections called villi into a network of blood vessels that carry nutrients to all parts of the body. The second part of the small intestine is the jejunum, and the lower end of this six-meter (20-foot) structure is called the ileum.
- Large intestine (colon): In the large intestine, water is absorbed and solid waste is held for elimination.

Bariatric surgery alters or affects the process of normal digestion.

THE HISTORY OF BARIATRIC SURGERY

Over the last half of the twentieth century, surgical treatment evolved and is still characterized by exploration, investigation, innovation, and revisions of surgical procedures. In 1952, Victor Henriksson of Gothenberg, Sweden, reported the first surgical treatment for obesity in a Scandinavian medical journal. Henriksson had cut out a portion of the small intestine. In the early 1950s, A. J. Kremen and John Linner joined a section of the jejunum to the lower ileum of the small intestine in animals. The procedure, called the jejunoileal bypass (JIB), took out a large segment of the small bowel that absorbed nutrients from food. They presented their work to a surgical society and in a peer-reviewed journal in 1954.

In 1963, J. H. Payne and L. T. Dewind reported results of 10 patients who had received an end-to-end jejunocolic shunt. The upper bowel was joined even farther down the intestinal tract to the colon. This surgery, called jejunum *anastomosis*, caused uncontrollable diarrhea, dehydration, and electrolyte imbalance in patients, and it was soon abandoned. The term *anastomosis* means "joining two structures."

In 1969, Payne and Dewind developed the end-to-side jejunoileostomy, or the 14 + 4 operation, which created a blind segment of the intestine. In this procedure, 14 inches of jejunum were joined to the terminal 4 inches of the ileum. It became known as the jejunoileal bypass (JIB). In this procedure, an extensive length of the small intestine is bypassed—not cut out—but is still excluded from the alimentary canal, or digestive system. Later, Scott and Dean performed an end-to-end anastomosis of the proximal jejunum to the distal ileum. Both variants left only about 35 centimeters (18 inches) of unaltered absorptive small intestine, compared to the normal length of about seven meters (20 feet). The procedure became popular with general surgeons interested in bariatric surgery. However, the unused or blind portion of the intestine was prone to bacterial growth and other serious complications such as malabsorption (preventing nutrients from entering the bloodstream), leading to nutrient deficiencies and diarrhea. The JIB had excellent weight-loss results, but because of these complications, it is no longer recommended. Patients who have a JIB that is intact are advised to have it taken down and converted to one of the less restrictive gastric procedures.

Types of Bariatric Surgery

Two types of obesity surgery are performed today: restrictive and a combined restrictive with malabsorption. Different operative procedures have been developed for each type, and each type has its own positive factors as well as risks. Restrictive procedures are vertical banded gastroplasty, gastric binding, and laparoscopic gastric banding (lap band). Combined restrictive and malabsorptive surgery includes Roux-en-Y (RNY) gastric bypass and biliopancreatic diversion. Surgeons decide the best procedure for an individual patient. Procedures that are not recommended are intestinal bypass, jaw wiring, and liposuction.

RESTRICTIVE PROCEDURES

Gastroplasty

The word *gastroplasty* is a combination of two Greek roots: *gastro*, meaning "stomach," and *plast*, meaning "to form." During World War II, Russian scientists developed a series of surgical instruments for stapling various body tissues together simply and rapidly. After the war, this concept was adapted and refined by American surgical-instrument makers. The concept today is known as surgical stapling. The instrument places four parallel rows of staples to create the partition; some staplers have a knife blade that will cut between the staple rows, dividing and sealing the staples.

Gastric Bypass

Dr. Edward E. Mason of the University of Iowa noted that females who had undergone partial removal of the stomach for ulcers tended to remain underweight. When studying obese women who had undergone this surgery, he found that they too lost weight and kept it off. With the availability of surgical staples, he introduced gastric bypass (GBP), in which an area of the upper part of the stomach is partitioned into a small pouch and then connected to the jejunum by a direct loop. This decreases the size of the stomach so that only about one ounce of food can be held. Over time, the amount the stomach can hold may expand to two to three ounces. The pouch's lower outlet has an opening, called a stoma, which is about a one-quarter inch in diameter. This procedure does not require removal of any of the stomach.

Complications of GBP are much less severe than those of intestinal bypass. The most common complication occurs shortly after surgery when the patient may experience leaks at the junction of stomach and small intestine. The person will have to return to surgery for repair. After the incision has healed, the development of scar tissue squeezing the opening is a common complication and may affect the patient's eating. The problem is usually corrected by endoscopic balloon dilatation. Anemia may be common in younger women. Extra iron, vitamin, and calcium supplements are essential.

After the procedure, a problem sometimes occurs when the muscular walls of the stomach have a tendency to stretch and the stoma, or opening, would enlarge. Patients would lose weight the first few months when the stoma was small, but they soon stopped losing and frequently regained all the weight they had lost.

Vertical Banded Gastroplasty

In 1982, Mason realized that the lesser curvature part of the stomach had the thickest wall and introduced vertical banded gastroplasty (VBGP). In this procedure, the stomach is compartmentalized with the use of lines of vertical staples parallel with the curve of the stomach. Mason was very meticulous in measuring and defining the size of the pouch. He also placed a polypropylene band (Marlex mesh) around the lower end of the pouch to act as the stoma, a measure that prevents stretching. When this procedure is performed correctly, significant weight loss results.

This procedure is purely restrictive—meaning that it keeps the person from eating large amounts of food because an area is partitioned. It was introduced to avoid adverse long-term nutritional consequences and the possible formation of ulcers. In VBGP, a 15–20 milliliter upper stomach pouch is created that empties into the remainder of the stomach. This approach keeps the gastrointestinal tract in continuity and is a safe and easy way to reduce food intake with few metabolic complications. Because the procedure is located near the valve that keeps stomach acid from leaking back into the esophagus, the patient may develop reflux or severe heartburn. Advantages of VBGP are that it is completely reversible, and the body anatomy is left intact. There is also no dumping syndrome or nutritional deficiencies. Disadvantages are it demands strict patient compliance. Vomiting may occur if food is not chewed well or is eaten too quickly. However, VBGP seems to be less effective for weight loss than GBP. Patients who enjoy sweets will have to avoid these foods after the procedure, and they must learn to chew their food carefully. A variant of this is Silastic ring vertical gastroplasty (SRVG), which uses a pliable, plastic ring to control the stoma size. This, along with RNY, is one operation that is recognized by NIH as best for treatment of severe obesity.

Adjustable Gastric Binding

Another way to limit food intake is adjustable gastric binding (AGB), in which a constricting ring is placed completely around the top end, or fundus, of the stomach (see Figure 14.1). The ring is placed near the upper end of the stomach below the junction with the esophagus. The idea has been around for a number of years, especially in Europe, but it became

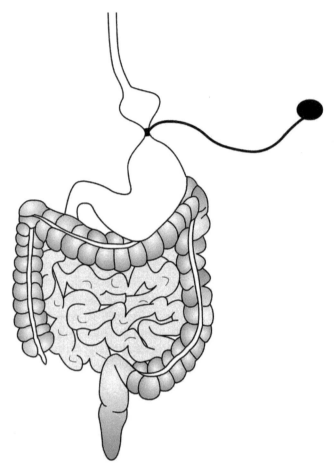

Figure 14.1 Adjustable Gastric Binding

popular in the United States only after the development of more effective bands. In 1990, Dr. L. I. Kuzmak devised a band with an inflatable balloon at its lining. The balloon is connected to a small reservoir placed under the skin of the abdomen through which the balloon can be inflated to reduce the size of the stoma or deflated to increase the size of the stoma. Because the hourglass configuration constricts only the upper stomach, the problems of malabsorption and anemia are avoided. The main disadvantage is that the patient must strictly comply with instructions for care and lifestyle. Results of long-term studies are not yet available. Two devices are manufactured for use in this procedure: the LapBand and a Swedish device called the Obtech. Trials with the LapBand have been completed, and the product has been approved by the FDA. Some models can be inserted laparoscopically to avoid making a large incision.

Advantages of this procedure are that it is simple and relatively safe with a short recovery period and the complication rate is low. There is no opening or removal of any part of the stomach or intestines or altering of the body's natural immunity. Recovery periods are very short. The major disadvantage is that about 5 percent of the procedures fail due to balloon leakage, band erosion or movement, or deep infection.

COMBINED RESTRICTIVE AND MALABSORPTIVE SURGERY

Roux-en-Y

The RNY operation is the most common GBP surgery. A portion of the stomach is sectioned creating a small pouch for reduced food intake. This usually holds only about one ounce or food, and the patient feels full after just a few bites. The size of the pouch is determined by the surgeon. Advantages are that the amount of food taken in is controlled and that it is reversible in an emergency. The term *dumping syndrome* is used to describe the release of the stomach contents into the small intestine. Small meals alleviate this syndrome, but the condition is still present to control the intake of sweets. Disadvantages are the possible failure of the staple line, ulcers, narrowing or blockage of the stoma, and vomiting, which can occur if food is not processed well or is eaten too quickly.

The Sapala-Wood Micropouch RNY GBP completely divides off the top of the stomach and creates a tiny pouch separate from the stomach. The pouch is about the size of a grape (1–2 cubic centimeters). The small intestine is divided into two ends. One intestinal section is connected to the micropouch. The other end is attached to the side of the distal small intestine to complete the circuit. Food travels down the esophagus, into the micropouch, and into the intestine, bypassing the stomach entirely. The bottom of the stomach no longer receives any food or liquids, but it still functions because the nerves and blood vessels are intact. Advantages are that food is greatly controlled and that the patient is less susceptible to ulcers. Disadvantages are narrowing and blockage of the pouch and vomiting if food is not prepared properly or is eaten too quickly. The amount of food that can be absorbed by the GI tract is limited.

Currently, most bariatric surgeons in North America and Europe perform RNY, VBGP, or AGB. Many of the procedures now can be performed by laparoscopic surgery.

Biliopancreatic Diversion

In 1969, Nicola Scopinaro and his colleagues at the University of Genoa, Italy, introduced the partial biliopancreatic diversion (BPD), a technique for creating a stomach pouch. The procedure was different from the JIB in that the function of the small intestine is not affected. The procedure has two components. First, a small part of the stomach is taken out, resulting in reduced intake of food. Second, doctors create a long-limb RNY anastomosis with a short digestive channel of 50 centimeters (19.7 inches). *Roux-en-Y* is the term used for the joining of the distal end of the small intestine to the stomach or esophagus. This procedure creates an important malabsorptive component that maintains long-term weight loss. Recently, Dr. Scopinaro reported long-term results of this procedure in which 72 percent of excess body fat was lost and kept off for 18 years. In terms of weight loss and duration, these are the best results in bariatric surgical literature to date.

From the patients' perspective, this procedure has some great advantages. They may eat large quantities of food and still achieve excellent, long-term weight results. Malabsorption is significant. The disadvantages are loose stools, chronic ulcers, and foul-smelling stools and gas. Protein malnutrition has been the most common complication, so BPD patients must take calcium and vitamins, particularly vitamin D, for life. Also, because of potential complications, patients require lifelong follow-up.

Duodenal Switch

In 1988, D.S. Hess used a combination of Scopinaro's BPD and the duodenal switch (DS). This switch was originally designed for patients with reflux gastritis. It connects the duodenum to the jejunum, allowing the first portion of the duodenum to remain intact. The hybrid procedure has advantages of BPD but avoids some of its problems. First presented in 1993, the procedure is known as biliopancreatic diversion with duodenal switch (BPDDS). Both of these procedures are major surgery, and prospective patients must seek experienced surgeons with lifelong follow-up programs.

CURRENT TRENDS IN BARIATRIC SURGERY

According to a study by the University of Wisconsin surgery department in 2014, nearly 95 percent of bariatric operations are performed laparoscopically as opposed to traditional open surgery. Three operations are commonly performed in the United States today:

- Laparoscopic RNY GBP
- Laparoscopic gastric sleeve resection
- Laparoscopic adjustable gastric banding

At most medical centers across the country, GBP is the most common followed by gastric sleeve resection. Some patients have very good results with gastric banding, but it is the least common performed at many institutions because of band erosion, slippage, and infection.

FUTURE PROCEDURES

Stomach Pacemakers

A new procedure that involves an implant may reduce hunger and pose less risk than other weight-loss surgeries. This experimental procedure involves a pacemaker for the stomach that reduces hunger pangs. Similar to the heart pacemaker, a matchbox-size battery-powered device is implanted under the skin of the abdomen. The device emits a mild electrical signal that creates the feeling that the person is full. Called the *implantable gastric stimulator*, it may provide a safer alternative to radical weight-loss surgeries that shrink the stomach or alter the digestive tract.

Liposuction

Liposuction is a procedure that removes fat cells beneath the skin. It is considered cosmetic surgery rather than weight-loss surgery. The procedure typically removes five or six pounds of fat per surgery. A series of small incisions about an inch long are made in the skin, and a device for suctioning out the fat is inserted. Results may not be obvious for six months because of the swelling and tissue trauma that occurs. People who have had liposuction can regain all the weight, not in the fat cells that were removed but elsewhere in the body.

CONTROVERSIAL QUESTIONS

The question of bariatric surgery for treatment of obesity is controversial in many quarters. The procedures came about because of the discouraging results of conservative medical treatment, which may cause initial weight loss but the loss is not maintained. At present, surgery is the only method of keeping weight off in the long term. Currently, the gastric restrictive measures are the most popular surgical methods for obesity therapy, but, because there are no long-term studies, some questions about their lasting effectiveness have emerged.

SURGERY AS A TREATMENT OPTION FOR CHILDREN

Although the issues of childhood obesity are discussed in Congress and government agencies, children who are morbidly obese have limited treatment options. Recent studies have shown that the use of bariatric surgery for severely obese teenagers is safe and is associated with significant weight loss. Having obese teens undergo bariatric treatment resulted in a reduction of conditions comorbid with obesity. Teens also experienced an improvement in self-image. Another investigation supported the use of laparoscopic GBP surgery as an option for adolescents. Also, a multidisciplinary team of pediatric specialists and bariatric surgeons found that GBP surgery is a safe and effective treatment but that it warrants further study.

The American Academy of Pediatrics (AAP) takes a more conservative approach and encourages many other approaches before considering bariatric surgery. The American Pediatric Surgical Association (ASPA) applauded the AAP position and encouraged more clinical research to address the comparison of the methods of GBP or adjustable banding and the measure of the quality of life in the postoperative patient.

The American Society for Bariatric Surgery (ASBS) encourages the following considerations in considering surgery for children and teenagers:

- The surgery must be performed by an experienced bariatric surgeon who has performed at least 100 bariatric procedures or who has had a year-long bariatric surgery fellowship.
- Adolescents with a BMI of 35 or more with significant comorbidities should be considered.
- Age limits should not be considered because no evidence exists that, even with balanced nutrition, there will be impaired growth or development of early osteoporosis in the younger patient.
- All surgical options should be considered.
- Practicing institutions must have a standardized plan for collecting data that goes beyond collecting short-term mortality and morbidity data.
- Institutions must have a standardized plan for the bariatric patient that includes every step of the operative procedure.

The National Association to Advance Fat Acceptance (NAAFA) strongly opposes the use of bariatric surgery for children. Some broadcasters have documented the emergence of weight-loss surgery for children. NAAFA claims that these stories focus on success anecdotes that picture proud surgeons holding up large pairs of pants or displaying before-and-after pictures. NAAFA believes that performing these procedures on children under 18 is dangerous. They cite that 60 serious complications may result, and the side effects may be particularly disturbing for children. NAAFA claims that fat people who undergo weight-loss surgery have not been shown to live longer and with fewer diseases than those who do not have the surgery. They claim that people who have diabetes and other conditions can control these with medications and do not have to resort to surgery.

BARIATRIC SURGERY SUMMARY

As has been presented in this chapter, there are several kinds of weight-loss surgery. There is none that one can call the best. Surgery is recommended only for those who are 100 pounds or more overweight or who have high BMI with certain conditions like diabetes or high blood pressure. As has been indicated, all procedures have advantages and disadvantages.

It is important to remember that risk exists with any surgery. Bariatric surgery has some specific risks:

- Ten to 20 percent of patients require follow-up operations for complications. Abdominal hernias that require surgery are common. Less common problems are the breakdown of the staple line and stretched stomach outlets.
- More than one-third of patients who have GBP surgery develop gallstones. These can be prevented with supplemental bile salts after surgery. Some surgeons remove the gallbladder during surgery.
- Nearly 30 percent of patients who have weight-loss surgery develop nutritional deficiencies such as anemia, osteoporosis, and metabolic bone disease. Vitamins and minerals must be taken.
- Women of childbearing age should avoid pregnancy until their weight is stable. Rapid weight loss and nutritional deficiencies can harm a developing fetus.

Even with surgery, it is important that the patient follow very strict rules provided by the surgeon. Behavior modification and lifestyle changes, especially the ones that the patient avoided before surgery, are also important for success.

Who is going to pay for the surgery is another problem. Like any major surgery, bariatric surgery is very expensive. Many insurance companies will not pay for it unless the person has documentation proving that other methods have been tried and failed. This documentation may be difficult to obtain. Some insurance companies deny all procedures. If it is an adaptive condition for patients, then changing their lifestyles should cause weight loss—if that person was disciplined and tried hard enough. If obesity is deemed a disease, then would the payer for the surgery—which could be the government under Medicare or Medicaid—have the money to meet the demand? Another important issue for consideration is that the relationship between surgery and morbidity has not been studied. Is there a connection between surgery and extension of the life of the individual? Should the person who is obese just be able to enjoy life without the discrimination or condemnation of being fat? Does the government have an obligation to pass laws against fat discrimination, or should it pay for corrective programs such as surgery? These are issues that relate to our basic philosophies of the rights of the individual versus responsibilities of government.

CHAPTER 15

What Should Be the Government's Role in the Obesity Crisis?

Christina Corrigan was a bright and friendly child. She read, swam, and collected music boxes. Her dream to visit Australia was cut short when she died at the age of 13. Her weight was 680 pounds. About eight months after her death, her mother, Marlene, was charged with felony child abuse and endangerment for allowing her child to suffer physical and mental pain and for permitting her child to be injured. Under the California Penal Code, if convicted, she could be imprisoned for six years. Was Marlene guilty of a crime because of her daughter's overweight condition? Should the government prosecute parents of morbidly obese children for neglect? When parents fail to change their children's damaging lifestyles, do they expose their children to ridicule that could be otherwise avoided? Are the parents responsible for the endangerment of their children's health?

This chapter will pose questions that relate to role of government in the obesity epidemic. It will look at questions such as the following: Are fat people discriminated against, and should governments pass laws against discrimination? Are governmental prevention strategies ethical and worth the effort? Is childhood obesity a problem, and what are the roles of government agencies in dealing with the issue? Should governments intervene in controlling the food industry? Is fat tax a recipe for a healthy population? Granted that most people who lose weight gain it back within a year or two, should the government waste money on a seemingly lost cause? Should people who are fat just enjoy life and accept themselves as they are? This is the position of certain organizations, such as the National

Association to Advance Fat Acceptance (NAAFA). The issues in this chapter are subjects of debates that will continue for years.

SHOULD LAWS PROTECT OBESE PEOPLE AGAINST DISCRIMINATION?

The setting is San Francisco in the year 2001. A large number of people appeared before the San Francisco Board of Supervisors presenting the case that they must add height and weight to the list of ordinances that make it unlawful to discriminate. First to appear was an articulate spokesperson who presented scenarios of insults and discrimination about people because they are fat. For example, a health club put up a billboard that pictured a hungry space alien with the caption, "When they come, they will eat the fat ones first." Marilyn Wann led 30 large people to protest with signs that said "Eat me." Her demonstration got international coverage and caused the club to pull the ad. A parade of others tugged at the hearts of the supervisors. A 16-year-old girl told them about receiving ego-bruising comments about her size from a nurse practitioner. Others told of losing insurance or being passed over for jobs because of their sizes. Author Sondra Solvay spoke of working undercover for the U.S. Department of Housing and Urban Development and found blatant weight discrimination in housing. Some landlords would not make eye contact with her because she was fat.

Wann assured the board that the cost would be little—perhaps only a couple of armless chairs for overweight people. The fat activists expounded the point that fat is immutable—that is, it cannot be changed—and that diets do not work. They claimed that all diets are money-making schemes. They also referred to the 1986 studies of Danish twins that surmised heredity determined 80 percent of body weight. Wann's efforts led the San Francisco Board of Supervisors to add weight and height to existing city ordinances that made it unlawful to discriminate in employment, housing, public accommodations, business, and social activities. The administrators were convinced that such discrimination posed a substantial threat to the health, safety, and general welfare of the community.

According to Wann, a professional fighter for fat acceptance and board member of NAAFA, the ordinance was a great victory against fat discrimination. The NAAFA is celebrating 35 years of promoting plus-size fashion, fitness, and fun. For them, *fat* is not a dirty word; the dirty word is *diet*. Wann is convinced that the medical establishment has a propaganda campaign and a lot of hysteria about an obesity epidemic that is unwarranted. Author of *Fat! SO?* Wann tells a host of horror stories about people who lost or were refused jobs, not because of their ability but because of their size.

Is such a law necessary? "No," said a variety of legal scholars who presented their case to the San Francisco board. Beginning in the 1950s, the general precepts of American antidiscrimination laws were aimed at protecting individuals from significant unfair social or economic treatment that is based on personal characteristics over which the individuals have no control. Discrimination must be proven or based on immutable circumstances. The opponents claimed that the evidence presented by the pro-ordinance group was entirely anecdotal and statistically meaningless. San Francisco adopted these provisions for height and weight, although Wann and her group provided no scientific basis that obesity is immutable. Additionally, more current genetics studies agree that heredity accounts for only about 30 percent of variability. Although the move seemed to be a logical, reasonable, and humane reaction, according to the opponents, they were creating a legal monster. If fully implemented, private-sector businesses may suffer, and strong legal protection is given to a condition that, in the view of nutritionists and many scientists, would damage public health.

The first people to take advantage of the new San Francisco ordinance were eight-year-old Fredrika Keefer and her mother, Krissy. They filed a complaint with the San Francisco Human Rights Commission that a ballet school required that students have a slender, well-proportioned body with feet that are able to arch and turn out like the feet of penguins. The plaintiffs claimed that this violated the ordinance against size discrimination. The school had to accept the girl and put her in a ballet that had a role for an overweight participant. See "Fat-Discrimination Lawsuits" for other cases.

Fat-Discrimination Lawsuits

- *Greene v. Seminole Electric Cooperative, Inc.* So.2d 646 (Fla.197): A plaintiff was allowed to file a hostile work environment claim under the Americans with Disabilities Act (ADA) and the Rehabilitation Act because he was harassed and ridiculed about his weight.

- *McDermott v. Xerox Corp.* (1985): Xerox refused to hire Catherine McDermott because of her weight. A court of appeals upheld an earlier ruling that she was discriminated against on the basis of a disability unrelated to her employment. Xerox was ordered to offer her a position with back pay.
- *English v. Philadelphia Electric Company* (1981): After passing several preemployment tests, a company doctor deemed Joyce English unfit for employment because of her weight. The Pennsylvania Human Relations Commission found that morbid obesity was a handicap or disability within the meaning of the Pennsylvania Human Relations Act and ordered the company to pay $20,000 and offer English the next available position.
- *Pan American Airways* (1989): The company agreed to pay $2.35 million to 116 female flight attendants who were disciplined, denied promotion, forced to resign, or fired for being overweight. This class action suit determined that the weight-restriction policy constituted sex discrimination and violated the U.S. Civil Rights Act. Pan Am agreed to drop appeals, pay union legal fees, and institute a new weight policy.
- *Cook v. Rhode Island Department of Mental Health, Retardation, and Hospitals* (1989): Cook had worked for this department until 1986, when she resigned for personal reasons. When she reapplied for a similar position in 1988, she was denied employment and told her application would not be considered until she got her weight down to 299 pounds. Cook's attorneys argued that this decision violated federal laws prohibiting discrimination against the handicapped. A federal jury upheld the decision of the lower court that she should receive $100,000 award and ordered the state to give Cook the next available job and retroactive seniority.

For other law cases relating to obesity discrimination, refer to the NAAFA's website, http://www.naafa.org. to FindLaw, http://www.findlaw.com, and type "obesity discrimination laws."

Michigan is the only state with an anti-size-discrimination law on its books. In addition to San Francisco, Washington, D.C., and Santa Cruz, California has formal bans on weight discrimination.

How Pervasive Is Weight Discrimination?

Empirical data reveal discrimination against those who are morbidly obese (see Chapter 4). According to Marianne Bodolay of the NAAFA, workplace discrimination is the most prevalent type of discrimination. A typical scenario might go like this: A well-qualified person interviews over the telephone and is called in for an interview. When the personnel director meets the person, the tone starts to change. All of the sudden, the person is no longer qualified. One study found that 16 percent of employers admitted they wouldn't hire an obese person in any circumstance; another 44 percent said they would hire them only under certain circumstances. A Western Michigan University professor analyzed 29 studies and found that when obese people are hired, they are paid less than their leaner counterparts.

A 1994 study by the National Education Association found that fat students experience ongoing prejudice in school. From nursery school through college, they experience ostracism, discouragement, and sometimes violence. When they get out of college and into the workforce, overweight people face similar circumstances everywhere.

An attorney for the Obesity Law and Advocacy Center states that appropriate health care and accessing public facilities are two pressing areas of weight discrimination. Although insurance companies do not refuse to cover conditions like AIDS or cancer, many may refuse to cover morbidly obese persons. Southwest Airlines charges morbidly obese people for two seats. The companies may use a "fault-based paradigm" to justify refusing the overweight. After all, in the airline's thinking, it is the obese person's fault.

This brings up the question: Is weighing 300 pounds OK? Is the genetic argument strong enough to convince people that nothing can be or should be done about weight? Is the fact that most people who lose weight soon gain it back strong enough to lead people to accept their bodies as they are?

Wann and the NAAFA are proponents of accepting fat as a fact of life. Members of the NAAFA are quick to praise eating nutritious food and engaging in regular aerobic exercise. They blame certain diet gurus and the medical establishment for causing a climate of fat phobia. In her book, Solovay laments that prejudice against fat people is just as bad as that of racial prejudice and that fat people are an oppressed biological minority. She believes that discrimination against fat people will be the prevailing civil rights issue in the twenty-first century.

Weighing 300 pounds is not OK, according to a group of health experts and nutritionists. Dr. Dean Ornish, a professor at the University of California–San Francisco, disagrees with such claims. He is famous for his research showing that changing your lifestyle can reverse heart disease. His diet of eating grains, vegetables, and fruits, combined with exercising regularly, not only helps the heart but also has an effect on weight. He contends that if weight is caused by genetics, then why is there a greater percentage of obese people in the population than ever before?

Another perspective might fall in between the two extremes. Emphasizing the prominence of environmental and lifestyle factors, Dr. Joanne Ikeda, codirector of the Center for Weight and Health at the University of California–Berkeley, describes metabolic defects that make weight loss difficult. She refers to these as "set points." Eating habits and physical activity regulate these set points. Exercise has been shown to lower set points, but eating saturated fat may raise them. Obese people often suffer from an imbalance of these set points, but they can manipulate these points with exercise and a nutritious diet. Likewise, when the person diets, a sudden loss of weight can trigger the body to create a set point above the dieter's previous weight. If the diet is broken, the weight will be regained.

SHOULD GOVERNMENTS PASS ANTIDISCRIMINATION LAWS?

In the United States, laws relating to employment discrimination are complicated and conflicting. The laws can be federal, state, or local rulings. Any of the three branches of government—executive, legislative, or judicial—can create employment protections.

The Civil Rights Act of 1964 (Title VII; 42 U.S.C.2000 et seq.) established basic federal law on employment discrimination. It does not identify weight as a protected characteristic, and as a result, it does not provide direct protection for obese individuals who have been discriminated against by their employers due to weight.

In 1990, the ADA was passed to ensure that merit, rather than bias, was used for judging people with disabilities. The definition of a disability has the following components:

- A physical or mental impairment that substantially limits one or more of major life activities
- A record of such impairment; the person must have a history of the impairment
- Is regarded as having such an impairment; in all their life tasks, the person is regarded by the community as having an impairment

The Equal Protection Clauses of the Constitution (Article IV and Amendment XIV), as well as clauses in state constitutions, may protect fat people from discrimination. However, the court system may make the judgment of whether the claim of obesity discrimination falls within the guidelines of federal, state, or local rulings. These determinations about when obesity becomes an impairment are based on many factors, including the language of the ADA, ADA and disability interpretive guidelines, the courts' own beliefs, popular culture, other courts' determinations, academic opinions, and medical views. In dealing with a case in court, there must be a specific case brought by specific individuals. The case must include all the circumstances relating to a specific case of the impairment caused by obesity. In other words, cases cannot be a general idea but must have a plaintiff who has been offended and is seeking a remedy.

A physical impairment is defined as any physiological disorder or condition, cosmetic disfigurement, or anatomical loss affecting one or more of the body systems. In general, the rulings thus far have determined that fatness is mutable and remediable, so such rulings basically eliminate the use of disability laws by fat people. There are two potential arguments that may be used to challenge the claim of mutability:

- When using medications or certain types of low-fat foods, dieters experience many side effects such as diarrhea, memory loss, concentration problems, weakness, and dizziness.
- The court does not require mitigating devices like wheelchairs; however, if these devices are used, their impact must be assessed as important.

Many fat people feel limited because of society's feelings and assumptions about their condition rather than feeling limited by the condition itself. These prejudices can be just as handicapping, according to the ADA. Legal protections apply in two situations. First, there is a mistaken belief that an impairment limits a major life activity. Second, when there is an impairment coupled with the mistaken belief that the impairment substantially limits major life activities, according to the ADA's equal employment opportunity provisions, it is impermissible to make negative decisions based on unfounded fears. For example, one cannot assume that just because a person is fat, he or she cannot be a newspaper reporter, TV analyst, or physical education instructor.

SHOULD OBESE INDIVIDUALS USE DISABILITY LAWS?

Many fat people have accepted themselves as normal and do not think it is their bodies that are disabled, but that society's treatment of them as unable, different, undeserving, and inferior. They maintain they can do the same jobs and have the same abilities as thin people despite stereotypes to the contrary. Some consider it an insult to be labeled as disabled or to call obesity a disease.

There are inconsistencies at all levels of law related to body weight. The Department of Justice found that morbid obesity—defined as 100 pounds overweight—is an impairment. However, the New York Court of Appeals held that obesity itself does not meet the statutory definition of disability, even if it is mutable. Possible reasons why this is so confusing is that mainstream medicine regards the whole range of obesity as a dangerous condition.

ARE GOVERNMENT PREVENTION STRATEGIES ETHICAL AND WORTH THE EFFORT?

In 2001, the surgeon general issued a call to action to prevent and decrease overweight and obesity and identified obesity as a key public health priority for the United States. Some governments have launched broad, population-based prevention strategies against obesity, similar to seat belt and antismoking campaigns in the United States. In France, the Ministry of Health noticed a rise in the prevalence of obesity among young French people. The ministry recommended handing out free fruit and installing more water fountains to encourage kids to stay away from soft drinks. The Australian government is encouraging broader school programs involving diet and physical exercise. Singapore (a society under an authoritarian government) has had greater success in attacking the epidemic. According to the minister of defense, if new military inductees are obese, they are required to attend special basic training lasting 6 weeks longer than the normal 10-week course. This is an incentive to be in shape when they enlist. After completing the two-year stint, most remain in the reserve capacity for years and must pass an annual basic fitness test. Some agree this is the only society that has successfully managed the outbreak of the epidemic.

In the United States, a wide range of government policies and programs have been implemented in recent years. These include national clinical guidelines, nutrition labeling on packaged foods, education and social marketing efforts, and financing for fresh fruits and vegetables. Most of these, however, have rarely addressed the environmental drivers of obesity.

Several efforts are being made to combat the epidemic in response to concerns about obesity. On August 24, 2004, the U.S. National Institutes of Health (NIH) launched a systematic campaign to fight overweight and obesity, which, according to its figures, now affects close to two-thirds of the population. The plan calls for targeting obesity on several levels and aims for both behavioral and environmental changes. Some of the goals include better city planning to encourage exercise, developing better drugs and surgical approaches, and finding out how obesity causes diabetes, heart disease, and certain cancers. The research will be translated into information that the general American public can use. The plan recognizes that accomplishing this appears simple—eat less and exercise more—but in reality, the charge is difficult to accomplish. The NIH believes that research is essential to address the issues successfully.

One effort to make enable lifestyle changes involves communities. Convinced that the car-dependent society can be broken, some cities have decided to design activity back into people's lives. Stapleton, Colorado, is a community that has been built on the remnants of Denver's old airport. Some of the solutions include bike paths and pedestrian-friendly policies to compete with driving. The new community is designed around active living. Worksite changes encourage employees to get up from their desks more often. Sidewalks are inviting, as are the neighborhood storefronts, mini-parks, main street shops, and a town green, which are all connected by sidewalks and greenways. The goal is for the neighborhood paths to lead to real destinations such as playgrounds, schools, and grocery stores. Specific destination strategies are essential; people are not just walking to walk; rather, they walk with a purpose.

The question is whether people will take advantage of the changes. Preliminary studies indicate that they will. The National Institute of Environmental Health Sciences in North Carolina plans to evaluate 25 communities like Stapleton during the next five years to compare the residents' fitness to those in 10 control communities. The study will look for a causal connection between environment, transportation, and health.

Some private-sector corporations have addressed concerns about health. In 1999, the new Sprint Corporation headquarters in Overland Park, Kansas, was built to encourage more physical activity. The parking lot is a five-minute walk away from the campus buildings. Elevators are deliberately slow to encourage use of stairs, and there is also a walking trail and a sports field. Because of privacy reasons, Sprint does not track employee health, but indications are that those who take advantage of the walking path have dropped weight. Some meetings are even held on the walking path.

Are all these efforts worth it? Do people take advantage of these facilities when they are available, or is the car culture too engrained to change people's habits? L. D. Frank (2004) released one of the first studies to objectively study the relationship between neighborhood walkability and physical fitness. The researchers tracked the activity levels of 357 people in the Atlanta area by using pedometers to measured walking. They then calculated the walkability of an area. People who live in walkable areas are 2.5 times more likely to get 30 minutes of exercise than those who are in areas with poor walking possibilities. However, only about 37 percent of the neighborhoods were walkable. Frank is convinced that the ways that communities are designed are important.

ARE ANTI-OBESITY PROGRAMS THE RESPONSIBILITY OF SCHOOL DISTRICTS?

One issue that is consistently emerging is the role of schools—especially public schools—in the obesity question. Beleaguered with accountability and testing that has been federally mandated by the No Child Left Behind Act of 2001, schools have focused on raising student performance. To prepare students to pass high-stakes tests, districts have substituted remediation and extra academic courses for those that engaged students in physical activity. According to 2004 data from the National Association of State Boards of Education, only 8 percent of elementary schools, 6.4 percent of middle schools, and 5.8 percent of high schools have daily physical education. Illinois is the only state that mandates daily physical education. Yet 9 million children over age six are obese, and another 15 percent are borderline. Exercise in school and home has been sidelined. Video games have replaced the playground as kids' favorite pastime, and more than 50 percent of the nation's schools have eliminated physical education (PE). Once a part of nearly every school day, PE programs have become rare to nonexistent in many parts of the country, although many believe that just one additional hour of PE per week is significant in addressing obesity for five- and six-year-olds, especially girls.

School lunches are traditional whipping boys for students and teachers. The typical criticism of hot dogs that resemble rubber dolls' legs and tater tots that bounce off of the floor have been standing jokes for years. In the spirit of the new FDA guidelines, some districts are seeking changes in lunchroom procedures and perceptions. One such effort has been made by New York City public schools. Concerned about childhood obesity, Chef Jorge, or Jorge Leon Collazo, is determined to improve the nutritional quality, taste, presentation, and perception of food served in the nation's largest school district. He has revamped the menus and reduced fat, sugar, and salt in recipes and also substituted whole-grain breads, pasta, and cereal for less nutritious options. He has implemented salad bars, even though the USDA National Lunch Program only reimburses for one fruit and one vegetable per student. Surprisingly, he found the salad bar as one of the most popular innovations.

Vending machines are increasingly drawing fire in the obesity battles. School districts strapped for money have used the machines to fund activities and programs. In May 2004, the Center for Science in the Public Interest (CSPI) found that 70 percent of the 9,723 vending machines surveyed held soft drinks with sugar. Forty-two percent of the machines held candy, and 5 percent of the milk that is offered is low-fat. Some health experts claim that these vending machines are a direct assault on attempts to improve breakfast and food programs in the schools.

Taxpayers generally agree. A study conducted by RTI found that although the public overwhelmingly supports adding nutrition curricula to the schools and likes the idea of healthy food in vending machines, less than 50 percent were willing to pay more than an additional $100 per year in taxes to support anti-obesity efforts. Meanwhile, many administrators and athletic directors claim that the vending machines make funding available for sports and other events.

In some districts, administrators are finding ways to make good nutrition pay. *Making It Happen! School Nutrition Success Stories* is a book that highlights 16 schools that have changed vending machine content and experienced no decrease in revenue. A school in Southington, Connecticut, installed a milk-vending machine with low-fat and fat-free choices and maintained its revenue by cutting a deal with the vendor to keep 20 percent of monthly sales. At Hampden Academy in Maine, administrators let kids taste-test low-fat yogurt and other choices for the vending machines. A middle school in Westerly, Rhode Island, gave the vendors strict calorie and fat limits. Coke machines that once supported the sports booster programs now offer only water. However, these programs are only in about 30 of the 90,000 nation's districts.

Responding to statistics that more than 15 percent of American children and teens ages 6 through 19 are overweight, Senate Majority Leader Bill Frist introduced the Childhood Obesity Reduction Act to recognize schools that voluntarily increase physical activity and promote nutritional choices. The bill authorized a Congressional Council to Combat Childhood Obesity that will, in two years, create a public-private foundation to award grants to schools to implement model anti-obesity programs.

In January 2005, the U.S. government issued its latest dietary guidelines, a joint effort by the Department of Health and Human Services (HHS) and the USDA. The biggest change in the new guidelines is the emphasis on restoring energy balance to people's diets. If calorie intake exceeds energy output, a person gains weight. Thus, these guidelines advise 30–60 minutes of exercise most days of the week. Also new is the emphasis on fiber- and nutrient-rich whole grains instead of refined grains and a recommendation to eat nearly twice the quantity of fruit and vegetables recommended by older versions. The guidelines also distinguish among types of fat. Although this is the latest government issue, it is obvious that Americans are hungry for food advice, as indicated by the $2 million spent last year on diet books.

Is This Government Intervention Necessary?—"No," Says NAAFA

The NAAFA believes that fat people must be presented with alternatives to drastic weight-loss measures. Its focus is helping people live an active lifestyle and to focus on their health, but it believes that one can be fat, healthy, and happy. NAAFA is against the word *diet* because of its association with efforts that do not work. The organization supports this with statistics showing that people who lose weight gain it back. NAAFA also opposes weight-loss surgery, declaring that such surgery interferes with the body's ability to absorb many nutrients. It claims that weight loss peaks after two years and that fat is gradually put back on as the stomach regrows. The group condemns weight-loss surgery for children, and it strongly claims that medical science has not produced convincing evidence that fat people who undergo this surgery live longer with fewer diseases than those who do not have the surgery. NAAFA says that if a person has diabetes, high cholesterol, or high blood pressure, then his or her malady should be controlled with medication.

Should the Government Intervene in the Food Industry?

Another debate that is emerging is the role of government in controlling the food industry. In 2004, Kelly Brownell and Katherine Horgen wrote *Food Fight: America's Obesity Crisis and What We Can Do about It*. This book described the obesity epidemic that has developed over the past decade. The book sought to persuade, through emphasis on death and disease, that "big food" is the convenient demon. It is not our fault that we are fat, but we are the victims of preference manipulation—or advertising—that we can no longer be responsible for what we are eating. The authors also introduced the idea that food is addictive. Brownell said that overconsumption has replaced malnutrition as the world's top food problem. If the food industry will not change voluntarily, then the government should step in. The threat of regulation might help the food industry change its ways.

One of the most popular targets of finger-pointing is the fast-food industry. At a 2004 conference of Chain Exchange Operators in Miami Beach, product liability attorneys warned food-chain operators that they must be proactive to eliminate the threat of obesity-related tort lawsuits against their companies. Attorneys warned the operators to expect claims that food is addictive and that litigators are planning to use the same arguments used in winning judgments against tobacco manufacturers. The attorneys blamed the media and public-health advocates for creating the perception that the food industry is responsible for the country's obesity problems. These advocates are developing an argument that the food industry is deliberately deceiving the consumer with their techniques of preference manipulation. Following is a list of accusations of the deceptions that opponents of food chains see as issues:

- Promoting and marketing food in enticing ways makes people eat too much
- Claiming that certain foods are addictive; promotion pushes this addiction
- Accusing food companies of putting profits ahead of public health
- Asserting that restaurants serve excessive portions
- Targeting vulnerable groups, including children, the poor, and the less educated

The attorneys for the food marketers mentioned two lawsuits that lost against the deception argument. McDonald has settled for $10 million concerning a secretive use of beef-based flavoring in french fries. Twenty years ago, General Foods had to pay out $20 million to settle a lawsuit in California. The plaintiffs claimed that a Saturday morning TV commercial for one of the company's cereals led children to believe that eating the cereal would make them strong and invincible. The attorneys at the conference encouraged the manufacturers to be proactive in promoting balance and moderation.

However, current studies do not support the arguments of the antifood industry lobby. An April 2004 study by Context Marketing of Sausalito, California, found that Americans generally place the blame for the obesity epidemic on consumers, not the food and beverage industry. Some 90 percent of those surveyed absolve food and beverage companies, and

77 percent of respondents believe that food and beverage companies should not be held accountable for the problem.

Is a "Fat Tax" a Recipe for a Healthy Population?

An advertisement in a popular magazine showed a picture of California governor Arnold Schwarzenegger with the caption "Actor, Governor, Fatso?" The ad continued, "According to the U.S. government, the Governor, Tom Cruise, and Sammy Sosa are all obese." The ad criticized trial lawyers and activists for using these flawed standards to sue food companies and call for higher food taxes. The ad was paid for by the Center for Consumer Freedom, which fights trial lawyers and the food police.

Taxation of fat is an idea that has been tossed around on both sides of the Atlantic for a few years. Some people, especially in the United Kingdom, are promoting the taxing of items that contain fat. Arguments for a fat tax include the following:

- Making items that have a high fat content very expensive would discourage people from buying them and make consumers aware that these are targeted items.
- Foods high in saturated fats contribute to strokes and heart attacks.
- If people avoid fat, then they will be healthier, and thus, the burden on health care is reduced.
- Money from the tax could be used for other public services.
- Only cakes and cookies without saturated fat should be exempt from tax.

Opponents of the fat tax say the idea is riddled with problems. Arguments against the fat tax include the following:

- Problem 1: Health information has focused on saturated fats as the demon, but cholesterol-free cakes would be just as fattening as cakes. The caloric value per unit weight of saturated and unsaturated fat is virtually identical.
- Problem 2: Using taxation for behavior management is doubtful. Smoking is heavily taxed, but in the United Kingdom, it is on the rise, especially among young women.
- Problem 3: The target is slippery. Smoking causes harm in a cumulative way, but no case can be built for the harm of junk foods, such as chips or cookies. The harm is the habit of consumption.

- Problem 4: Fat content cannot be accurately targeted. Some foods, such as avocados and nuts are high in fat, but healthful. Thus, how can you determine the difference if a pure fat content is established?
- Problem 5: Why fats? Why not target carbohydrates? It is possible to become obese from eating excessive sugar.

Despite the disagreements among factions about the obesity epidemic, the U.S. government in 2004 launched a systematic campaign to fight obesity. The plan calls for targeting obesity at several levels, including both behavioral and environmental changes. The plan calls for better city planning to support exercise; better drug and surgical approaches; finding the ways obesity causes diabetes, heart disease, and certain cancers; and translating research into something that is applicable to the everyday lives of people. The emphasis on research is essential. The NIH has plans to increase the $440.3 million investment in the next several years.

Current thinking from the 2010 Assessing Cost-effectiveness (ACE) studies of obesity identified three of the most cost-effective interventions:

- A tax on unhealthy foods and beverages
- A front-of-the pack "traffic light" nutrition labeling system
- Reduction of marketing unhealthy foods and beverages to children

Other recent policies show federal legislation to help make healthy choices. In 2009, $183 million was allocated for Safe Routes to School, a project that promotes bike lanes, trails, and sidewalks. First Lady Michelle Obama in 2010 launched an effort called Let's Move! Federal menu-labeling legislation was passed in 2010 as part of the Patient Protection and Affordable Care Act. Evaluations of these programs have had mixed results, and it is not clear that they have had an impact on weight reduction. Political opposition to these programs has been strong and effective.

The role of governmental intervention in the problem continues to be a hot topic. Obviously, there are different approaches to the same problem, and the debate will continue for many years in the future.

CHAPTER **16**

Weight-Loss Medications: Is There a Miracle Pill?

According to a 1990 Gallup poll called "Mirror of America," 62 percent of women and 42 percent of men had a desire to lose weight, but only about 18 percent were making the effort. Popular magazines and news outlets began to tout a new hot "miracle pill" that was guaranteed for quick weight loss. The name was fen-phen. The public, especially women, wanted to improve their body image and weight, and not having to diet or exercise seemed appealing. The stage was set for the "miracle pill" as more popular than the latest rock star.

Diet pills were not high on the public radar. In the 1960s, a pill containing amphetamine had been prescribed for weight loss, but it was soon determined to be addictive and found disfavor quickly. In the 1980s, researchers had formulated a new drug that contained a combination of two drugs: fenfluramine that suppressed the appetite and phentermine that prevented drowsiness. The medical community and the public were concerned about the rising tide of obesity and began to prescribe pills containing the fen-phen cocktail off label (meaning it was not approved by the FDA). Fenfluramine was marketed by American Home Products as Pondimin. Pressure was put on the FDA to put Redux, a European version of the drug, on the market.

Healthcare professionals had warned that the pill should be used only for those who were seriously overweight, but it was so popular that it was soon taken by millions. Several researchers were very much opposed to approval and presented strong evidence to the FDA, but in spite of impassioned testimony, the agency approved dexfenfluramine in April 1996. An advertising frenzy and a $52 million marketing campaign ensued, and American Home Products, which changed the name to Wyeth Pharmaceuticals, had a bonanza.

But all was not well. In an August 1997 issue of *New England Journal of Medicine*, Dr. Heidi Connelly of Mayo Clinic reported some unusual findings. Women were appearing with pulmonary hypertension and heart-valve problems, and these were linked to the use of fen-phen. The heart-valve problems required extensive, risky surgery; there was no cure for pulmonary hypertension (PPH). Finally, the FDA removed the drug from the market on September 15, 1997.

YEARS AFTER THE FALLOUT

Over the years, most of the weight-loss medications have been withdrawn for serious adverse effects. However, recently the FDA has approved several agents to be used in combination with other therapies such as reduced-calorie diet, increased exercise, and behavior modification.

SHORT-TERM AGENTS

The following four short-term agents have been approved for weight management for use only about 12 weeks or less:

- Phentermine: Brand names are Adipex-P, Oby-Cap, Suprenza, T-Diet, and Zantryl. This preparation is a stimulant similar to amphetamine, which acts as an appetite suppressant and affects the central nervous system
- Diethylpropion: Brand names are Tenuate and Tenuate Dospan. This compound is an appetite suppressant.
- Phendimetrazine: Brand names are Bontril, Bontril PDM, Bontril Slow-Release, Melfiat, Obezine, Phendiet, Phendiet-105, and Prelu-2. This drug is an appetite suppressant.
- Benzphetamine: Brand names are Didrex and Regimex. This drug is also an appetite suppressant.

All the above short-term drugs are available only through doctor's prescriptions. All may have side effects that are listed in the National Institutes of Health Library of Medicine and on their approval websites. They are recommended only for a short period of time and only if the person follows a reduced-calorie diet and increases physical activity. They are all classified as appetite suppressants.

Long-Term Agents

Following is the list of long-term agents that the FDA has approved:

- Orlistat
- Phentermine hydrochloride/topiramate
- Lorcaserin hydrochloride
- Naltrexone hydrochloride/buproprion hydrochloride
- Liraglutide (rDNA origin)

Researchers have developed the above drugs that have been approved for long-term use, still in combination with diet, exercise, and behavioral change. Instead of just working as an appetite suppressor, many of them work in different ways. Understanding of how fat is made, how it works, and how the cycle of feeding and satisfaction affects weight loss has provided several targets for therapeutic agents.

The above drugs with the exception of orlistat have been approved since 2012. They have been on the market only recently.

Approved Medications and How They Work

Orlistat (Xenical)

Orlistat is a gastrointestinal and pancreatic inhibitor of lipase, the hormone that creates fat. It was approved in 1999. Orlistat is an anomaly among the weight-loss agents in that it does not directly target appetite mechanisms but prevents fat from being absorbed. It must be taken one hour after eating a meal that contains fat.

There are several downsides to this agent. It may reduce absorption of certain essential fat-soluble vitamins, such as vitamins A, D, E, and K. Also, it may interfere with medications that the person is taking for other conditions, especially the blood thinner warfarin.

A person taking orlistat or Xenical three times a day may experience certain gastrointestinal disturbances, such as flatulence (gas), oily stools, diarrhea, and fecal incontinence. Many of these adverse events are the result of the misconception that people may eat all the fatty meals they desire. Those taking orlistat must be cautioned that it is extremely essential to consume only a low-fat diet.

An over-the-counter product called Alli, which has a smaller dose of orlistat, is available. It may not have the extreme adverse events, but it also is not as effective in weight loss.

PHENTERMINE/TOPIRAMATE (QSYMIA)

Approved in 2012, this drug includes a low dose of phentermine that acts as a sympathomimetic amine (a compound that evokes a response similar to epinephrine or ephedrine, known agents to reduce appetite). Phentermine is combined with extended-release topiramate, a drug that reduces appetite and enhances a feeling of fullness or satiety. The agent is administered in a step-wise procedure to determine tolerance and effectiveness. Common side effects include paresthesia, dizziness, bad taste in mouth, insomnia, constipation, and dry mouth. Doctors who prescribe this medication also watch closely for other side effects. It must be used in conjunction with reduced-calorie diet and increased physical activity.

LORCASERIN (BELVIQ)

Approved in 2012, lorcaserin suppresses appetite by decreasing appetite and promoting a feeling of fullness (satiety) by activating the serotonin 2C receptor (5-HT2C) on neurons called pro-opiomelanocortin (POMC) located in the hypothalamus. Common adverse events were headache, depression, and dizziness. It is not recommended for anyone who had renal (kidney) problems.

NALTREXONE HYDROCHLORIDE/BUPROPION HYDROCHLORIDE (CONTRAVE)

Two agents are combined: bupropion and naltrexone. Bupropion increases dopamine activity in the brain to reduce appetite and activates the POMC neurons to increase energy. Naltrexone blocks opioid receptors on the POMC neurons. The combination appears to regulate the activity of the dopamine reward system of the brain that helps control food cravings and overeating behaviors. There are several precautions in the use of this drug. One is called a boxed warning, which includes suicidal thoughts and behaviors and neuropsychiatric reactions.

LIRAGLUTIDE (SAXENDA, VICTOZA)

Although approved for diabetes in 2012, liraglutide was approved for chronic weight-loss management in 2014. It is a glucagonlike peptide-1 (GLP-1) analog that regulates the appetite and caloric intake. The GLP-1 receptor is present in several areas of the brain. The agent is recommended for those with a BMI 30 or over or one of 27 or higher with at least one weight-related comorbidity. A boxed warning on the prescribing medication tells of risk of thyroid C-cell tumors and possible acute pancreatitis, gallbladder, and other conditions.

2016 META-ANALYSIS OF DRUG EFFECTIVENESS

How do these drugs compare with safety and effectiveness? A meta-analysis is a comprehensive study of all the studies of a particular drug or agent and may give healthcare professionals information to help them make decisions about which drug to prescribe. Khera et al. (2016) compared weight loss and adverse events among the five approved drugs. They used 28 random controlled trials that included 29,018 patients. The study had the following key findings:

1. With one year of treatments, all the five drugs are associated with higher loss of weight compared with placebo (a pill that does not have the drug).
2. Phentermine-topiramate combination was associated with higher odds of achieving weight loss of at least 5 percent and 10 percent when compared to other active agents. No difference in the odds of adverse events or drug discontinuation was found.
3. Liraglutide was associated with higher odds of weight loss of at least 5 percent and weight loss of 10 percent compared to orlistat, lorcaserin, and naltrexone-bupropion; however, higher odds of discontinuation due to adverse events were seen.
4. Lorcaserin and orlistat were associated with lower rates of adverse advents but were also associated with achieving lower rates of weight-loss outcomes.

The study did emphasize that because of other medical conditions, certain treatments may be more appropriate than others. For example, liraglutide may be more appropriate for people with diabetes because it lowers glucose. Naltroxene-bupropion should not be considered for use with patients who have alcohol or opiate dependence problems because of neuropsychiatric complications.

Several other strategies are in the pipeline. One is not a drug but a hormone (GLP-1) that has been researched as an antidiabetic drug. Chapter 20 will consider several strategies that are being investigated for obesity intervention.

Chapter 17

How to Avoid Food Scams and Fad Diets

The thin, gorgeous singer, a top performer in Las Vegas, appears in an appealing television ad. A picture of her before she started on the lose-weight system is shown. She compares her body with "belly fat" before and after eating the food on the "plan"; she has lost 50 pounds in just a few months. Several former football all-stars tout the program for men. Your food is packaged and sent to the door, and all you have to do is eat. It is all so easy. And it sounds so reasonable for people struggling with weight. Everything is beautiful and appealing, and they may fall into the trap.

Advertisers for products that are part of the weight-loss industry know exactly how to make individuals sit up and listen and perhaps make that important step of buying the product. When they lose weight easily and quickly, they become part of the story that ends there. Here is where the diet will backfire. It falls in the category of a fad diet.

What Is a Scam?

People looking for that quick fix or magic diet are easy targets for scam artists and fad diets. Some of these diets sound credible but are clearly based on bad science. There are basically five scams that have been recycled through the years:

- Metabolism-boosting pills: Many diet pills are based on herbal ingredients that promised to help you burn fat faster. The FDA does not monitor or regulate herbs, so these products are advertised and sold. One such product is ephedra, a substance that was banned in February 2003 due to the risk of illness. This herb is related to methamphetamine, or speed, and can cause high blood pressure, irregular heartbeat, insomnia, nervousness, and even death. Another supplement contains kava, a plant from the islands of the South Pacific that may cause liver damage.

- Fat- and carb-blocking pills: These pills claim to absorb fat and carbs. Problems like diarrhea, bloating, and gas may arise, and the pills may also block the absorption of vitamins.
- Weight-loss teas: Teas are usually herb based and have caffeine, a diuretic (which aids water loss). A possible benefit of these teas is that they might keep an individual from drinking high-calorie sweetened drinks and possibly curb late-night bingeing.
- Diet patches: Although some patches help smokers quit or deliver hormones for birth control, no effective diet drug has been developed to be used as a patch. Similar to this scam is weight-loss jewelry, such as earrings or bracelets.
- Body wraps or slim suits: This scam has been around a long time. The old sweat suits have changed to silver slim suits that promise to lock in heat and melt away body fat. The only thing one loses while wearing one of these suits is water, and that weight quickly returns when one takes a drink.

The Federal Trade Commission (FTC) warns that anything that looks too good to be true probably is. To lose weight, there is no magic bullet. Consumers should be aware of extravagant claims of dramatic, rapid weight loss; testimonials from famous doctors; dramatic before-and-after pictures; ads that promote the latest trendy ingredient; and a tiny footnote that says diet and exercise are required.

What Is a Fad Diet?

A fad diet is one that promises weight loss and longer life without any solitary backing of science. The diet may refer to one study or have a doctor promote it as "proven." The word *proven* in science is not used because nothing is ever proven. Sometimes, the diet may restrict certain foods or use unusual foods. Frequently, celebrities endorse the program, and the individuals who develop it profit from it.

Following are signs of a fad diet:

- A celebrity appears as the spokesperson or a doctor has written a book, which has become a best seller.
- No plan exists to keep the weight off after you reach a weight-loss goal. The diet lasts only a certain number of weeks, and you have not learned the behaviors to keep the weight off. Most people gain the weight back within a short period after stopping the diet.
- Only a few foods are allowed. The diet may be restrictive to only certain foods and ban others. For example, on the cabbage diet, in addition to cabbage soup that you make, you eat the soup plus all the fruits that you desire, with the exception of bananas. The diet may be exciting for a few days, and then it becomes quite boring.
- You are guaranteed to lose a certain amount of weight in a given amount of time. Such promises can lead to loss of not weight but of muscle mass. If you lose more than two pounds a week, you may slow metabolism down making it more difficult to lose the additional pounds.
- You are promised to lose weight in certain body parts, especially "belly fat." Nutritionists say that people do not lose fat in only one part of the body. Weight loss occurs throughout the body. If you want to lose weight in one body part, it is wise to combine exercise focusing on that part of the body with a sensible eating plan.
- You may be hungry. If one decides that the only way to lose weight is to go hungry, that person may experience fatigue and other disruption of body functions. Women need about 1,200 calories per day, and men need about 1,400. If one eats less, he or she may not be meeting nutritional needs.
- You may be asked to invest in certain food plans, pills, or other supplements. Many of these diet aides are not proven, and some may be even harmful causing such problems as constipation or diarrhea.
- Read the fine print. The disclaimer may say this does not work for all people or must be combined with exercise and healthy living.

Almost any magazine, television ads or programs, and news articles have a new diet designed and "proven" by science to make you lose weight faster and easier than ever before. The diets may claim certain magic power that will be your answer to weight loss without giving up a lot of your lifestyle. And some of them do work for a short period of time.

There is a long list of these diets. Many are recycled from one period of time to another and given new names or new twists. Many of the diets are harmless, but a few of them could put your health in danger.

Following are 10 current diets that are in the popular press and some perspectives about the diet:

1. The blood type diet: Basically, there are four blood types: O (the most common), A, B, and AB (the rarest form). In 1996, Dr. Peter D'Adamo, a naturopathic physician, wrote a diet book called *Eat Right for Your Type* in which he claimed that the best diet for human being was based on the person's blood type. This book became a *New York Times* best seller, selling millions of copies. This book convinced many people that the genetic traits of their ancestors can determine what they should eat.

- Type A are the farmers or agrarians who live close to the land. They should eat plants and never any red meat. This diet is close to that of a vegetarian.
- Type B are the nomads. These people can eat plants and most meats except chicken and pork. Certain foods like wheat, corn, and tomatoes should be avoided.
- Type AB are a puzzle because they are a mixture of two types. They can eat seafood, tofu, dairy, beans, and grains but must avoid kidney beans, corn, beef, and chicken.
- Type O are the hunters. They can eat a high-protein diet with lots of meat, fruits, and vegetables but limit grains, legumes, and dairy. This is similar to the paleo diet.

Many of these diets or ways of eating do have some healthy aspects because it steers the person from the Western fast food and processed junk food. Following some of the patterns could be an improvement regardless of the blood type. However, there is no scientific proof that your blood type affects weight loss and what your ancestors did does not affect the decisions that one makes today.

2. The perfect gene diet: In 2007, Pamela Anderson, a nurse practitioner, wrote *The Perfect Gene Diet*, a book that purports that one uses the body's *ApoE* gene type to treat high cholesterol, weight problems, heart disease, and Alzheimer. Find out your *ApoE* genotype, and use it to make the necessary changes that will prolong your health. The book is not just changing one's life but changing the lifestyle. There is a lot of genetic information, which makes the book sound quite scientific. However, similar to the blood

type diet, the suggestions that were made of sensible diet, exercise, and balanced eating can be helpful regardless of one's gene type. Research into the *ApoE* gene is interesting and an important part of scientific investigation, but this diet with its emphasis on lifestyle change would be just as effective without knowing one's gene type.

3. Paleo diet: This diet, also called the Paleolithic diet, caveman diet, or Stone-Age diet, is based on foods that a caveman would have access to and eat. Basically, the diet consists of vegetables, fruits, nuts, roots, and meat but avoids dairy products, grains, sugar, legumes, processed oil, salt, alcohol, and coffee. The diet has been touted in several best-selling books. Like many diets, it is promoted for good health, and some evidence does exist that it may improve health when compared to the Western diet of fast foods and high-sugar snacks. However, assuming the digestion system of the modern person is the same as Paleolithic humans is stretching facts of evolution and assuming that people have not changed over time. There is little scientific data on the metabolic effects of people eating a paleo diet. Limiting oneself to such a restrictive intake can lead to certain nutritional deficiencies, such as those of calcium and vitamin D.

4. Werewolf diet: This fad diet, also called the moon diet or lunar diet, instructs people to fast and eat according to the phases of the moon. There are two parts to this diet: A basic moon phase in which the person drinks only water and freshly squeezed juice for a 24-hour period during the full or new moon. The extended phase instructs people to fast during the full moon and then follow a series of eating plans based on the moon. With this diet, you many lose weight, but it has nothing to do with the moon.

5. Cookie diets: This diet promotes several types of cookies that one eats for breaks, lunch, and snacks, and then one eats a normal dinner for a total of 1,000–1,200 calories a day. These cookies are sold as Dr. Siegal's Cookie Diet, the Hollywood Cookie Diet, and the Smart for Life Cookie Diet. The only thing is that you do not eat just any cookie but ones that sell, supposedly with high fiber and high protein. On this diet, you may lose weight but by dinner, you may be so hungry that you will binge.

6. The five-bite diet: On this diet created by Dr. Alwin Lewis, you can eat anything you like but only five bites. You skip breakfast, have five bites for lunch, and five bites for dinner. Eating smaller

portions is a good idea, but even if you take monster bites, you will only consume about 900–1,000 calories per day. This diet may work a few days, but the suggestions are rather bizarre for today's lifestyle.

7. The cabbage soup diet: This diet has been around for a long time and consists of fat-free cabbage soup eaten whenever you are hungry and all the fruit you want except bananas. During the week, you may add vegetables except no baked potato. Later in the week, you add beef, chicken, and brown rice. One of the main problems with this diet is bloating and excess gas. It is also lacking in protein, which leads to loss of lean body mass.

8. The grapefruit diet: This fad diet has been around since the 1930s. Dieters have a half-grapefruit before every meal, which supposedly contains enzymes that break up fat. Different versions exist. With some plans, you can eat all you want as long as you have grapefruit; others limit it to a low-calorie regime along with the grapefruit. Some versions require eating very hot or very cold foods, using aluminum pans to prepare the food, or spacing certain kinds of meals four hours apart. On a low-calorie diet, people do lose weight but usually gain it back when they cannot avoid the taste of grapefruit any more. And there may be some danger of its interfering with certain medications such as statins.

9. The HCG diet: HCG stands for human chorionic gonadotropin, a hormone that is supposedly an appetite suppressant. The doctor gives you an injection and then limits you to 500 calories per day. One may lose weight, but it is not related to the injection, which has no more than a placebo effect. HCG is used to treat women with fertility issues and has not been approved by the FDA for weight loss.

10. The tapeworm diet: Probably the most bizarre of all fad diets is the tapeworm diet. Tapeworms are parasites that inhabit the intestines and eat the food of their host. Weight loss is one of the signs of the parasite. A person desperate to lose weight can purchase the eggs of the tapeworm from Internet sources. The eggs hatch and the tapeworm eats the food that you eat. When you reach the desired weight, you then take an antihelminthic (antiworm) medication to kill the worm. In the meantime, the worm can migrate to other parts of the body and cause health issues. This diet obviously is not one for a healthy lifestyle.

If you have followed a fad diet at some time in your life, you are not alone. They are appealing and usually promoted by some enthusiastic friend or advertisement. Fad diets usually do not work in the long term, and the weight may return when you do not stay on a boring diet for a period of time.

Think of your body as a car. You need the proper ingredients to make it run. Those ingredients include a balance of protein, carbohydrates, fat, and other nutrients. Fad diets usually focus on one or two things and then ignore certain balanced nutrients. You may not notice the problem immediately, but over a period of time, your health will suffer.

Following are some ideas on how to avoid diet mistakes:

- Control portions. Food amounts in restaurants are supersized and so may the portions placed on the plates before us.
- Plan for a variety of foods. Make sure that you include basic food groups in your everyday diet. A fad diet will not have the necessary ingredients to run the body efficiently.
- Avoid snacks as a habit. Sometimes a snack makes us happy and is satisfying but minimize these for only certain times.
- Serve meals on smaller salad plates.
- When you go out, share your food with a friend.
- Eat at least five servings of fruits and vegetables a day.
- And avoid empty calories such as sugar-containing sodas and fruit drinks.

Most experts agree that no single nutritional solution exists for Americans battling overweight, diabetes, and heart disease. Studying nutrition in humans is difficult because of our complicated lifestyles and individual differences. Studies that involve nutrition in animal models may not exactly equate the nutritional effects on a human being. However, the general agreement is that one must take responsibility for health decisions. One food-science researcher, Dr. Donald Layman of Illinois State University, said that different diets suit different people. He indicates that decisions about which diet regime is most appropriate will be based on health factors, such as risk of heart disease or diabetes. Like personalized medicine, personalized nutrition will be the direction of the future.

CHAPTER 18

Alternative and Complementary Obesity Therapies

Throughout her life, Marjorie had struggled with her weight. She had tried the latest diet plans and experimented with the latest fads. Exercise did not seem to work for her. It bored her, and although she tried different ways of getting exercise, she never enjoyed them. While reading or looking at television, she heard of other ways to lose weight that were not the old diet and exercise routine. These strategies are called alternative or complementary treatments.

But what are these treatments?

The National Center for Complementary and Integrative Health (NCCIH), an agency of the federal government, lists them as follows:

- *Alternative* medicine is a practice that is out of the mainstream of conventional medicine. National Institute of Child Care Management (NICCM) estimates that more than 30 percent of adults and 12 percent of children use healthcare approaches developed outside Western or conventional medicine.
- *Complementary medicine*—the practice uses Western medicine, together with conventional medicine.
- *Integrative medicine*—this approach brings conventional and complementary approaches together in a coordinated way.

Although many diet and exercise programs are available for losing and maintaining weight, over the years, interest in alternative treatments and complementary medicine (CAM) for obesity has greatly increased. NCCIH defines alternative and complementary medicine (CAM) as "a group of varied and medical and healthcare systems, practices, and products that are not considered to be part of any current Western health care system." *Western medicine* is defined as that used in conventional medical practice and has generally been tested through scientific investigation and approved by the Food and Drug Administration (FDA). These methods include herbal supplements, acupuncture, and mind-body therapies such as mindfulness, meditation, and yoga.

Some of these treatments have been practiced for centuries. For example, various herbal remedies and acupuncture are mainstays of traditional Chinese medicine (TCM). Some individuals have tried these types of treatments for obesity, and some have had success at least for the short term. Most of these therapies are promoted by word of mouth or by anecdotal testimonies. However, questions persist about the efficacy and especially safety. In Western medicine, for a medication or procedure to be approved, it must go through a long period of scrutiny and testing. Many of the alternative methods have not been studied or have fallen short when compared to placebo. Esteghamati et al. (2015) published a comprehensive review of studies in the 2015 *International Journal of Endocrinology Metabolism*. The team found the following shortcomings in the trials of alternative therapies: no controls, subjects are not randomized, a small number of patients enrolled in the studies, and short or no follow-up of the lasting success of the treatment. Side effects and potential harm are not usually included in the studies. They concluded that further investigations are necessary to determine the safety and efficacy of the various CAM methods in use.

This chapter considers these therapies, describing the nature of the therapy and results of some of the studies as found by the meta-analysis of Esteghamati et al. The intent of this chapter is to increase awareness of the many types of treatments that are outside of the thinking of Western medicine. For any treatment about the safety or effectiveness of the product or procedure, please contact your healthcare professional.

WHAT IS THE HISTORY OF ALTERNATIVE MEDICINE?

In order to understand alternative medicine, one must look at TCM and the Indian system of Ayurvedic medicine. Both of these philosophies treat the body as a whole. Both Chinese and Indian medicines draw upon plants, animals, and minerals to provide treatment for disease of the whole person.

In the latter part of the twentieth century, the self-help movement developed as a reaction to the image of Western medicine in which doctors dehumanize patients. The "counterculture" movement of the 1960s questioned all kinds of traditional thinking, including medicine, which the proponents believed to be concerned only with disease and pills and not interested in prevention or in health. Therefore, the groups were attracted to alternative therapies that emphasize the physical, mental, emotional, and spiritual aspects of the person and stress prevention and good health practices.

HERBAL SUPPLEMENTS

One of the fastest-growing methods for weight loss is the use of medicinal plant extracts. Research is being done into how suitable and safe certain herbals are for efficacy, long-term uses, optimal dosage, side effects, and mechanism of action. The following are eight of the most popular plants used and seen in health food stores.

Garcinia Cambogia

Garcinia cambogia is extracted from the dehydrated rind of a tropical fruit known as Malabar tamarind. It is a popular weight-loss supplement because users think it blocks the body's ability to make fat and suppresses appetite. It also is reputed to keep blood sugar and cholesterol levels low. The active ingredient in the rind is called hydroxycitric acid or HCA. Experiments in rats have shown that Garcinia prevents activity of ATP-dependent citrate lyase, an enzyme that breaks down oxaloacetate and acetyl-CoA. By blocking this enzyme citrate lipase, which the body uses to make fat, HCA could be useful in weight loss. It also appears to raise level of the neurotransmitter serotonin, which gives the feeling of satiety. However, results from nine human trials have not shown a significant difference between the action of HCA and a placebo for sustained weight loss.

Garcinia has always been considered safe. However, the scientific studies in humans did reveal a number of side effects such as dizziness, dry mouth, headache, and upset stomach and diarrhea. In 2009, the FDA warned people not to take this herbal because some individuals developed serious liver problems. It may also interact with other medications used for asthma, diabetes, iron for anemia, pain medications, statins that lower cholesterol, and warfarin, a blood thinner.

Camellia Sinensis (Green Tea)

Camellia sinensis or green tea originated in China and has spread to other Asian countries. People over the centuries have used the leaves of this plant for various health issues. However, recently it has become a popular remedy for obesity. The active ingredient of green tea is a type of polyphenol, a catechin, which affects the sympathetic nervous system. This system regulates the consumption of energy and oxidation of fat. Green tea also contains caffeine, which increases alertness.

Green tea has been suggested in many forms for weight loss. According to a meta-analysis by Esteghamati et al. in the 2015 *International Journal of Endocrinology Metabolism*, several studies showed there was no significant difference in the effect of *C. sinensis* on appetite reduction or energy consumption when compared to placebo. However, the studies did conclude that other mechanisms such as increased energy expenditure may help reduce body weight when used in combination with other strategies such as diet and exercise.

The FDA has not reviewed this product for safety or effectiveness. Some herbal/diet supplement products have harmful impurities or additives. The substance may cause withdrawal reactions if used regularly for a long time or in high doses. Some side effects may include nausea, diarrhea, upset stomach, headache, and dizziness. People are advised to follow all directions on the package or bottle for preparation and let their health advisor be aware they are using green tea.

Chromium Picolinate

The element chromium is a trace mineral that the body uses in small quantities to help insulin use glucose. When combined with picolinic acid, the bright red compound is used to assist people with type-2 diabetes. In 1989, a study suggested that it might be effective in weight loss and in producing muscle mass. The product claims to stimulate neurotransmitters that regulate food cravings and mood and eating behaviors. This product has been sold over the counter in both the United States and Europe and is one of the most popular supplements.

A systematic review of nine trials of chromium picolinate involving 622 subjects found no significant differences between graduated doses and placebo for weight loss. Likewise, because of the small number of participants and duration of the trials, safety and long-term effects of this dietary supplement could not be established in overweight and obese adults.

Conjugated Linoleic Acid

Conjugated Linoleic Acid (CLA) belongs to a family of about 28 isomers of linoleic acid found mostly in meat and dairy products. A number of weight-loss products containing CLA are advertised and marketed claiming to reduce fat mass. Onakpoya et al. in a 2012 meta-analysis found four of the seven clinical trials studying CLA and weight loss were flawed statistically. Thus, there is insufficient evidence that CLA is useful for overweight or obesity reduction as it has no long-term effect on body composition. It has shown to affect the insulin response in rats, but as of 2017, no evidence is there of the effect in humans.

Hoodia gordonii

Hoodia, also known as Bushman's hat, is one of the most popular anti-obesity products. It is a succulent plant grown naturally in Botswana, South Africa, and Namibia. For centuries, the Khoisan people of South Africa have nibbled on this native plant of the Kalahari Desert to suppress appetite and to treat many illnesses. In 1977, a group isolated the active ingredient, a substance called P57, and marketing campaigns began promoting its ability to suppress appetite. Little is known about how *Hoodia* works, but it does seem that P57 alters the neuropeptide-mediated pathways of the central nervous system associated with inhibiting appetite, at least in mice. Human trials have not been so hopeful.

Hoodia has received lots of media coverage. In 2004, *60 Minutes* aired a report on how this plant is a native appetite reducer. In 2007, over 300 products were being sold as *Hoodia*. In spite of reports that no scientific evidence supports the claims of efficacy and safety, the supplement is still being sold. It has been marketed as capsules, tablets, tinctures, tea, coffee, syrup, protein shakes, diet fruit bars, and even a lollipop called Power Pops.

Cynanchum auriculatum

This plant species is native to China but is also found in other mountainous regions of Asia. The roots are used in TCM to enhance immunity and longevity. The bioactive ingredient of the plant is called a pregnane glycoside and is similar to that of P57 found in *Hoodia gordonii*. In animal trials, it has shown to reduce appetite. Although both the efficacy and safety need further investigation, *C. auriculatum* may be under serious consideration for various medical treatments, including cancer and appetite suppression. The plant is more readily available than *Hoodia*, which may soon become endangered.

Chitosan

This substance is a polysaccharide made from the chitin of shells of certain crustaceans that have been treated with sodium hydroxide. It has been used widely in agriculture and even in the production of bandages but is now marketed for weight loss. It appears to work by binding fat, which restricts the absorption from the gastrointestinal tract. Experiments with mice have shown reduction of food intake.

In humans, 15 randomized trials were recorded with a total of 1,219 subjects. Some low-quality trials showed that the substance was effective. However, other high-quality trials questioned the obesity effect as minimal and not significant.

Gambisan

Gambisan is a novel formula developed at Kyung Hee University and Korean Medical Center, Seoul, South Korea. Called HH911G, the plant and its mechanism of action has not been fully investigated. However, it has been used as a popular supplement with extensive worldwide sales. It may have the potential for weight loss, but clinical trials are needed before efficacy and safety are determined.

Many herbal remedies for weight loss are on the market in health stores and other places. They may be promoted on television and other advertisements with anecdotal testimonies. Lots of fraud have been reported especially if people are buying the items from the Internet. Herbals are not regulated by the FDA and are considered food supplements. Before any of these products are tried, one should always consult his or her healthcare professional. Although many are harmless, others may be dangerous to one's health as they interact with other medications or harm certain body organs.

There is another group of alternative/complementary treatments that involve mind-body interactions. Many of these strategies come from Eastern practices and are outside the scientific probing of Western medicine.

Acupuncture

Acupuncture, the insertion of fine needles into the body for medical treatment, is of Chinese origin. Around 2500 BC, the practice grew out of the cosmic theory of yin and yang, whose imbalance causes a disruption of the life force or chi. The life force flows through 12 pathways or meridians in the body. Trained practitioners insert the needles over the 12 bases or acupoints. Applications of acupuncture have supplemented Western medical practice and over recent years have come under consideration for the treatment of obesity. Studies of both animals and humans have suggested how acupuncture may work to reduce weight. One theory is that acupuncture regulates obesity-related neuropeptides in the central nervous system. Another idea is that it may regulate the hypothalamus-pituitary-adrenal cortex axis, which is involved in body composition. A number of studies indicate a reduction of triglycerides and total cholesterol. A last idea is the bacteroides, a group of gram-negative rod-shaped bacteria that are part of the normal flora of the gastrointestinal system and are plentiful in people who are obese. Acupuncture may reduce bacteroides.

Several systematic reviews have indicated that acupuncture is more effective than conventional medicine for both body-weight reduction and obesity treatment. In fact, acupuncture probably has been one of the most studied of these procedures. One of the leading institutes of study is at Kyung Hee University in Seoul. Researchers found that using the ear points (auricular acupuncture) has resulted in 6 percent BMI decrease over eight weeks. Although with more study the procedure may be promising, small-size and non-random trials limit the validity of conclusions.

NONINVASIVE BODY CONTOURING

Invasive methods of weight loss include bariatric surgery and liposuction, which is the most common plastic surgery procedure used around the world. However, this popular method still raises serious concerns about complications and recovery time. Several noninvasive methods have emerged and have gained popularity. These methods include high-intensity-focused ultrasound, cryolipolysis, and low-level laser therapy.

High-Intensity-Focused Ultrasound

High-intensity-focused ultrasound (HIFU) is a novel therapeutic method that uses hyperthermia (excess heat) and mechanical action on the tissue. It has been especially effective in prostate surgery. For obesity treatment, the noninvasive technique affects the subcutaneous fat deposits by ablating (destroying) the adipose tissue. Ultrasonic waves are emitted through a device called a traducer along with a coupling gel to the desired target. No harm is done to the adjacent cells. At present, the technique appears to be more effective in those with less than a BMI of 30.

Low-Level Laser Therapy

Another novel non-invasive therapy is low-level laser or light therapy (LLLT). A device called the Zerona LipoLaser has five rotating independent diode laser heads that emit laser light. This laser was the first to receive market clearance in the United States in 2006. The procedure has been effective in reduction of fat in certain areas, such has hips, waist, thighs, and upper arms. There are two theories of the underlying mechanism: pores are made in the fat cell that allow fat to leak out, and some biochemical cascade could active cell death and release lipids. Although there have been initial successes, additional research on LLLT is required to determine efficacy and safety protocols.

Cryolipolysis

This procedure has been advertised often on television as a novel method of fat reduction. The method uses controlled cooling to target fat. Several studies have assessed that there is clinical evidence to support the efficacy and safety. The exact mechanism of how it works is not completely understood. A 2009 review of four clinical studies found evidence to support safety and efficacy. However, additional studies are needed to determine the long-term effects.

Radiofrequency

Another method for body contouring is radiofrequency (RF). Based on heat that changes the layers of subcutaneous fat, the procedure causes fat turnover that leads to fat cell shrinkage. At present, RF is one of the most common devices, and many articles support its efficacy and safety.

MIND-BODY PRACTICES

Mind-body therapies may complement other obesity treatments. Most of these strategies have not been well studied for obesity treatment but are based on commonsense appeals or anecdotal experiences of people. Some individuals find these practices support the positive changes needed for better eating. These therapies include meditation, mindfulness, yoga, and hypnosis.

MEDITATION/YOGA

Meditation is the practice of focusing your attention to find calm and clarity. It is believed to lower blood pressure by lowering stress, which drives many people to eat. Dr. Adam Perlman, director of Duke Integrative Medicine, believes that people put on weight by just trying to comfort themselves with food. Meditation and the other strategies of mind-body practices have not been studied directly, but it can help one become more aware of thoughts and actions when it comes to food.

There are many ways that one can practice meditation. The Centers for Disease Control and Prevention (CDC) lists the things they have in common:

- Find a quiet location. It can be on a walk or in your favorite chair.
- Assume a comfortable posture. No slouching, but sit, lie down, stand, or walk in a comfortable way.
- Focus your attention. One can focus on a word or phrase, breathing, or something else. Your attention must be on the area you are in. You are stopping to look within and not be concerned about the world around you.
- Maintain an open attitude. When one is meditating, it is easy to think about other thoughts, such as what happened at school or work. Put these thoughts aside, and focus on breathing, a phrase, or a word.

Dr. Perlman urges people to set a goal to get calmer so you can make better food choices. Reducing stress and managing blood pressure would eliminate emotional eating.

Yoga is another strategy that people are practicing for health benefits. There are many types of yoga. The general consensus is that regular yoga practice can influence weight loss but not in the traditional sense of how we link physical activity to weight loss. The practices probably burn fewer calories than jogging or brisk walking, but yoga can help one focus on the way to relate to the body

MINDFULNESS

Very similar to meditating is mindfulness, a strategy that is being used in many areas such as education, medicine, and social work. It is defined as a state of complete attention to the present. Being mindful means that you observe what you are thinking and feeling without judging them as good thoughts or bad thoughts. It means living in the moment and not thinking about the past or worrying about the future.

Researchers are referring to a change in the way we eat as a mindfulness diet. For example, you may have the habit of eating three meals a day or a habit of nibbling on something throughout the day. Mindfulness practices use tools of thought and rationality to improve health and reduce stress. Because stress is the root of overeating, being mindful of what and why we are eating can help us make better choices and lose weight without dieting.

The definition of *mindfulness* involves the act of focusing on present-moment experiences. Apply that to a meal you are eating. Michael Mantzios is a mindfulness researcher at Birmingham City University in the United Kingdom. His research shows how mindfulness brings one back to the present moment and to the present meal. Mindfulness can reduce that appeal of unhealthy foods. For example, smelling the food to see if really it does bring joy can determine whether we will eat the food or not. Mantzios recommends creating a food diary with questions such as the following: How does this meal smell? What are the colors and textures of it? Am I really hungry? Pay attention to each bite by taking small ones, and chew slowly savoring your food.

Hypnosis

Hypnosis has been used to help people stop smoking or other addictions. Although it is not shown to be a weight-loss solution on its own, it may help you stick to your diet or exercise plan.

Biofeedback

This strategy has helped people manage blood pressure and stress but has not been shown to assist in weight loss.

As we have outlined in this chapter, CAM is a broad term that has one thing in common: they do not conform to the principles and ideas of Western medicine. This fact has not affected their popularity as more and more people are seeking alternative means to lose weight. They are highly advertised and commercialized. However, it must be remembered that the scientific evidence supporting their efficacy and safety is limited.

An institute of the National Institutes of Health, the National Center for Complementary and Integrative Health (NCCIH), is the federal government's lead agency for scientific research on complementary and integrative health approaches. At present, the agency urges more strict protocols for herbal supplements, acupuncture, and other noninvasive strategies for weight loss. Until these are available, healthy nutrition and physical activity are still the mainstays for weight loss.

CHAPTER 19

Can People Be Healthy at Any Size?

In the 1960s, several individuals became concerned that the prevalent beauty standards and emphasis on thinness were having negative consequences on the psyche of Americans who were overweight. They questioned the idea that the slim and fit body type was the standard for health and well-being. They contended that some people naturally have a larger body type and that the culture focusing on losing an amount of weight to adhere to some artificial measure like body mass index (BMI) was harmful. The movement was dubbed "Health at Every Size" (HAES©) and generally was not taken too seriously for many years.

However, today some researchers have emphasized that a person can be fit and overweight. The situation of John Jurkovich, the NFL player, is an example. Many athletes are over the BMI ratio considered healthy. The Aerobics Center Longitudinal Study (ACLS) found that higher levels of physical activity may protect against mortality in certain subgroups of overweight individuals. The protective effects of physical activity appear to benefit both healthy and unhealthy individuals, smokers and nonsmokers, those who are hypertensive and those who are not, those with a family history of early congenital heart disease death, and those with elevated cholesterol or glucose. Even those who are overweight do benefit from increases in physical activity. Suzanne Brodney of the Cooper Institute in Dallas, Texas (which conducted the ACLS study), said that she believes that public health would better be served with more attempts to increase physical activity rather than emphasizing ideal weight ranges and raising an alarm about the prevalence of obesity.

THE DEBATE OVER BEING MODERATELY OVERWEIGHT

In April 2005, national debates over the dangers of fat erupted when Katherine Flegal and other statisticians of the National Center for Health Statistics (NCHS), a branch of the Centers for Disease Control and Prevention (CDC), reported that overweight people actually have a lower risk of death than people whose weight is in the normal range. Publishing their findings in the *Journal of the American Medical Association* (April 20, 2005), the authors supported the view that overweight people actually have a lower risk of death than people whose weight is in the normal range. And even the moderately obese are not at much risk. Deaths occur more frequently at the extreme ends of the weight spectrum—among the extremely obese and also among the extremely thin. Flegal also found that very heavy people with a BMI of about 35 had only a slightly increased risk of dying. For example, a five-foot-six person who weighs 217 pounds and does not smoke would have a smaller risk of dying than a person of the same height who has a normal BMI but who smokes. The study is one of the most quantitatively sound to date and uses only documented heights and weights, not self-reported statistics. She claims that the current standard for overweight, a BMI of 25–30, is actually the healthiest category. This conflicts with the CDC's healthy weight category of 22–25 BMI.

Only 13 months before, the CDC had published a paper warning that obesity was the cause of 400,000 deaths a year. This figure is 14 times higher than Flegal's finding. Flegal's study concluded that 112,000 deaths each year are attributed to obesity, but she also believes that being overweight prevents 86,000 deaths each year—making the net death toll 26,000.

The report generated controversy immediately. Some scientists supported the idea that a healthy person who is overweight and does not have hypertension, diabetes, or heart disease should not worry that his or her weight is dangerous. Some commentators attacked the talk about the "food police," and the food and beverage industries mounted a $600,000 media campaign that declared that Americans have been fed a steady diet of obesity myths.

Other scientists disagreed, saying that a seemingly healthy overweight person should worry because excessive fat contributes to health problems. An overweight person who is healthy at a given point in time is more likely to develop conditions in the future. They condemned Flegal's study as contradicting four major recent studies:

- A 1998 *New England Journal of Medicine* (*NEJM*) study of 300,000 men and women found the minimal risk to be a BMI of 19.0–21.9. Being very lean seems to be associated with better survival.
- In 1999, a study of more than a million men and women (the largest such study ever conducted) put the optimum BMI for longer life at 23.5–25 in whites and at 23–30 for blacks.
- A December 2004 report in the *NEJM* evaluated 116,000 women over a 24-year period and found that the lowest mortality rate among women was for those with a BMI of less than 23.

Longevity specialists have studied every species from worms to monkeys and found that calorie restriction increases length of life.

CAN PEOPLE BE BOTH FAT AND FIT?

Yes, Say Proponents of Health at Every Size©

The HAES movement focuses on health rather than weight. They claim that this emphasis on dieting has caused many people to develop serious emotional and physical problems. Emphasis on health will allow these habitual dieters to reshape their thinking, shed unhealthy habits, adopt new patterns of eating, become more physically active, and increase their self-esteem. Many of habitual dieters have tried a sequence of diets and failed. This movement is an alternative to conventional dieting.

HAES© is an approach supported by the Association for Size Diversity and Health (ASDAH). This association emphasizes a holistic definition of health: the absence of physical or mental illness, imitation, or disease. Health exists on a continuum that changes with times and circumstances for each person. Regardless of the condition or disease, one must not pursue health as a moral imperative or obligation. Health should never be used to judge or define an individual. For example, one is not a cancer patient but a person with cancer. One is not an arthritic, disabled, crippled, or demented, but a person with the condition. This approach is person-centered, not diseases-centered.

The proponents of HAES have consulted a number of healthcare workers, consumers, and activists. They shared a mutual concern about using weight, size, and BMI to define a person as healthy. The first principles of HAES were developed in 2003, but in 2013, a new task force was formed to renew and enhance the principles. According to the ASDAH website, the five following principles guide both policy and practice:

- Accept the diversity of people. Respect and accept different body shapes and sizes. Reject idealizing and pathologizing specific weights that do not conform to others' ideals. ASDAH principles emphasize that the focus should be not on the weight but respecting the individual's circumstances, helping them to make choices for health and well-being.
- Enhance health. Support policies that improve and equalize access to information and services. This will lead to personal practices that improve human well-being, with special attention to physical, economic, social, spiritual, emotional, and other needs.
- Practice respectful care. Acknowledge the biases against people who are overweight and work to end this discrimination. Even members of the healthcare profession appear to have these biases. Identify all ideas that impact weight. Here the dangers of dieting for weight loss are emphasized. People who lose weight on a diet and then return to former weight begin to question their strength and self-image.
- Eat for well-being. Adopt flexible and individual eating plans based on hunger, nutritional needs, and pleasure rather than some externally focused plan based on weight control. Here is the importance of relaxed eating in response to body cues.
- Enhance life. Support the physical activities that allow people of all sizes, abilities, or interests to engage in enjoyable movement, to the degree that they choose. (https://www.sizediversityandhealth.org/content.asp?id=76)

Books and Articles Support

Probably one of the first articles to appear with this idea appeared in the *Saturday Evening Post*. In the November 1967 issue, Lew Louderback wrote, "More People Should Be Fat." He was angry and enraged at the treatment that both he and his wife received from society because they were overweight but healthy. In the article, he outlined the following reasons:

- "Thin fat" people suffer physically and emotionally when they must diet below their natural body weight.

- Dieting forces changes in weight that are likely to be temporary.
- Dieting unleashes destructive emotional forces.
- When Louderback and his wife ate without dieting, they found that they were able to better relax and still maintain their same weight.

This article with the position about fat people was quite unique in the 1960s because it was a period when "thin was in." Later, Louderback wrote a book with his ideas and experiences called *Fat Power*. As of 2017, Louderback is alive and well in his 80s.

Louderback's article found fertile ground among all the causes of the 1960s such as race, sex, war, and feminism. So why would it not be logical for the fat to co-opt the ideas and stage their own "fat-in" event in Central Park in New York City. They ate ice cream and burned posters of the thin model Twiggy. One of those who read Louderback's article was Bill Fabrey, a young engineer, whose wife had been discriminated against all her life. In 1969, Fabrey organized a group called the National Association to Aid Fat Americans (NAAFA). In the 1970s, some members split from the group and formed an alliance called the Fat Underground, which took their cue from the radical Left and harassed weight-loss groups. However, the group never gained much power. In the mid-1980s, the main group changed their name to the National Association to Advance Fat Acceptance, a not-for-profit human rights group.

Several other books came out in the next decade. In 1982, Dr. Bob Schwartz wrote *Diets Don't Work*. The basic premise was to eat the way thin people eat and listen to your body, an approach that he dubbed "intuitive eating." He advocated eating an unrestrictive diet as a way of losing weight. Another author, Molly Groger, espoused the same idea in her training program, Eating Awareness Training.

Other books included *The Dieter's Dilemma* by William Bennet, MD, and Joel Gurin and *Breaking the Diet Habit* by Jane Povlivy and Peter Herman. Both the books reframed dieting as "restrained eating." The themes of all the books are similar; do not be guided by some outside scale like BMI or some restricted diet that must be followed, but respond to one's internal cues about health.

Jon Robison, PhD, MS, has called HAES approach a new paradigm of weight and health. He declares that promoting exercise, dietary restriction, and behavior modification rarely succeeds and leads to body hatred, dangerous eating disorders, or exercise addiction.

Pro Arguments

Numerous books and articles have been written to support the HAES position. Most of these focus on the principles of self-reliance and self-determination for health rather than depending on some outside measure.

ARS at UC Davis Controlled Experiment

A team of scientists at the Agricultural Research Center Western Human Nutrition Research Center at Davis, California, collaborated to study the HAES approach. Marta van Loan, Judith Stern, and Linda Bacon said this novel experiment is one of the most rigorous comparisons of conventional dieting versus every size lifestyle.

The team chose 78 obese women, ages 30–45, assigning them to either the health-centered approach or traditional diet. The teams met for 90-minute educational sessions every week for the first six months of the year-long study and then for six once-a-month sessions. Both groups were instructed in nutrition basics. The conventional track learned about topics covered in typical weight-loss programs, such as how to monitor their weight, control their eating, and brisk exercise. The HAES group learned how to build their self-esteem, follow their body's natural and internal cues to hunger and satiety, make healthy choices at mealtime, and enjoy some form of physical activity—an approach that is different from exercising mainly to lose weight.

Two years later, 38 women, 19 from each team, were part of a panel of follow-up exams, lab tests, and questionnaires. Results: HAES had kept their weight stable, not gaining or losing a significant number of pounds. In contrast, the dieters had lost weight by the six-month benchmark but had regained it by the two-year checkpoint. Their beginning weights and those two years later were not significantly different. At the start, total cholesterol and blood pressure were in normal range for all women. The HAES group had made progress in health risk factors, such as cholesterol levels and systolic blood pressure. In contrast, the dieters did not lower their total cholesterol at any point and did not maintain what they had achieved after the six-month dieting.

What about physical activity? HAES team had quadrupled the time spent in moderate or hard physical activity. The dieters started out well and were doing fine at one point, but at the end, they did not sustain the level.

The researchers also monitored depression, a common problem among large-sized women whose self-esteem is related to body image.

Both groups made progress, but the HAES women had a more optimistic outlook.

Although this was a very small sample, the researchers concluded that focusing on health and on changing behavior was the key to success for the HAES team. The HAES strategy could break the cycle of unsuccessful dieting and open the door to happier, healthier lives. The study was published in the 2005 *Journal of the American Dietetic Association.*

The most current book on the topic is *Fat Activism: A Radical Social Movement* by Charlotte Cooper. Published in January 2016, Cooper has been a fat activist for more than 30 years and described the activist methods and approaches for over 40 years.

Con Arguments

Most health professionals acknowledge the large number of health problems correlated with obesity. Remember that correlation does not mean causation, but according to the evidence and a number of studies, obesity has significant measures in many diseases and illnesses. The list of correlative studies is long: congestive heart failure, high blood pressure, deep vein thrombosis, type-2 diabetes, infertility, birth defects, stroke, dementia, cancer, asthma, and erectile dysfunction.

A 2017 study presented at the European Congress said emphatically no. In a statement released to the *Telegraph* (the United Kingdom), researchers from the University of Birmingham stated, "Fat but fit is a myth, and big is not beautiful—so stop making excuses for obesity." These researchers studied the records of 3.5 million people who had no evidence of cardiovascular disease at start of the study (1975–2014), dividing them into groups according to their BMI > 30. The study found that individuals who were overweight but metabolically healthy had the higher risk of coronary disease, heart failure, and stroke compared to the people without obesity. They encouraged practitioners to adhere to accepted standards of weight loss, BMI, and so forth. However, one must remember this was an observational study and not a clinical trial.

Another researcher, Australian Amanda Sainbury-Salis, believes that HAES is not correct in interpreting healthy at every size. She thinks that this may encourage people to ignore weight gain and be careless in their thinking about the relationship of health and size.

Dr. David Katz is a critic of the movement. In his article "Why I Can't Quite Be Okay with Okay at Any Size," published in the *Huffington Post*, he regrets that this movement seems to be gathering pop culture momentum.

He declared that epidemic obesity *is* the reason for the diabetes epidemic and that it is the known reason for the increase in cardiac risk in even younger people. It is true that people can be fat and fit, but in reality few of us are. It is not the size that inspires my opposition to this movement, but it is what the consequences are.

CHAPTER 20

Can There Be a Fat-Free Future?

The two obese children could barely totter into the University of Cambridge Hospital in Cambridge, England. An eight-year-old girl weighed 190 pounds, and her cousin, a boy of two, was a hefty 63 pounds. The children were the victims of a metabolic disease that caused them to be hungry all the time; nothing the parents or doctors did kept them from gorging. The doctors at the hospital injected the children with a genetically engineered hormone that controls appetite and metabolism. Within days, their hunger subsided, and after only two weeks, they were eating 90 percent fewer calories. The fat began to melt off. By the end of a year, the children were the normal size for their age and height.

Although such a treatment may be the dream of every person who wants to lose weight, these children at Cambridge had a rare condition that affected their ability to make leptin, a hormone that regulates body fat and hunger. When this worked with the children, jubilant scientists thought they had found that magic potion for dieters. Instead, they found just how rare extreme leptin deficiency is. Experiments later showed that many fat people are insensitive to leptin and would not respond to treatment with the hormone.

Historically, the world has seen a host of nonscientific treatments, such as fat-reducing soaps, massages, and body wraps. Most people agree that weight loss and maintenance are very difficult. That observation, and the reality of the multi-billion-dollar diet industry, suggests that researchers need to think differently about treatment options. However, success of this extraordinary case involving the children at Cambridge shows just how far science has come in understanding obesity and points to treatments of the future. "Personalized medicine" is getting a lot of attention in scientific circles. This treatment means that an individual's genetic makeup is analyzed and drugs are matched to that person's profile. Although still in the developmental stage, personalized medicine could be a trend. The latest insights into genetics, proteins, hormones, and viruses may point to an era of personalized weight loss involving injections, pills, inhalers, and nanorobotics.

The chapters of this book have established a foundation for understanding the complexities of research into the genetics and physiology of fat. The relationship between genetics and environment has been explored in relationship to the treatment of obesity as a disease or a condition adapted for survival. At this point, the future of the treatment of obesity is debatable. It is obvious that there is a rising tide of obesity throughout the world. Although some question calling it an epidemic, there is no doubt that two issues establish the framework for the possibility of a fat-free future: to treat those who are currently obese and to prevent obesity in those who are currently lean.

Strategies for treatment and prevention are very different, but both are doomed to fail if our understanding of the problem is not adequate. Presently, standard treatment programs have not had much success, and public health programs for prevention have been ineffective. Reexamining the theories upon which these two are built is essential.

To start, we need to shift away from the paradigm of the static energy-balance equation:

$$\text{energy intake} = \text{energy expenditure}$$

This model assumes that the origins of obesity lie only in metabolic defects, psychological abnormalities, or genetic mutations in the individual. Should a new paradigm assume that differences among individuals represent the normal spectrum of physiological or genetic variance and that the problem is not individual but environmental? For example, the epidemic has emerged at the same time as an increase in dietary fat intake and a reduction of physical activity—both environmental factors. Should the new paradigm frame obesity as both an individual and a societal problem?

In history, epidemics have been controlled only when environmental causes are addressed. For example, draining swamps and spraying for mosquitoes control the spread of malaria. To cut down on automobile accidents, medians are built and police monitoring is increased. To address smoking, legislation has implemented taxation and smoke-free zones. Does the obesity epidemic need a similar environmental approach to complement the current educational, behavioral, genetic, pharmacological, and surgical approaches? Although the issue is debatable, thinking outside the box is essential to solving some of the problems.

Although five new drugs have been approved and many more are in the pipeline, no one can look into a crystal ball and predict which drugs will be successful. The shift to a medical model of obesity and scientific breakthroughs has spurred the development of several therapeutic drug classes, with 15 compounds in clinical trials. A lot of research on treating obesity is forthcoming. Research in this complex area has revealed new targets for the possible treatments. Future pharmaceutical targets might include adipose or fat tissues signals, brain or neuropeptide regulators of energy balance, signals from the gastrointestinal tract, hormones that control feeding efficiency, proteins related to thermogenesis (heat production), hormones from the adrenal glands, and a variety of other actions that have yet to be explored.

ADIPOSE SIGNALS

Insulin and Leptin

Two major hormonal signals of adiposity are insulin and leptin. Both enter the brain and reduce energy intake; both circulate in the bloodstream in proportion to the amount of body fat and enter the central nervous system (CNS) in proportion to their blood plasma levels. A deficiency of both hormones increases food intake. The majority of obese people have elevated leptin compared to lean people, suggesting that some resistance to leptin exists at the brain level. However, the children in Cambridge appeared to be deficient in leptin, a rare condition. Although their treatment was an exciting breakthrough, the results of trials with human subjects with leptin resistance have been disappointing. Research is proceeding in the area of recombinant leptin therapy. Trials with eight subjects who received leptin were compared to 12 subjects on placebo; the trial showed that the leptin level had to be 19 times the placebo level to be effective. Such high pharmaceutical levels make it unlikely to be cost-effective, and the safety of such high levels beyond six months is unknown. Several pharmaceutical companies have various preclinical projects on leptin, and there may be a breakthrough with additional studies of biochemical pathways and how the hormone enters the brain.

Resistin

Resistin is a peptide produced by adipocytes and secreted into circulation from adipose tissue to modulate insulin resistance. As might be suspected from its name, resistin enhances insulin resistance. Studies suggest that this peptide is the missing link between fat cells and the control of peripheral insulin. Control of resistin may open new avenues for the treatment of obesity and type-2 diabetes.

Perilipin

Perilipin is an adipocyte protein encoded by the gene *plin*. Mice without the *plin* gene have reduced fat deposits, increased muscle mass, and elevated metabolism rates, which allow for higher food intake. Agents that inactivate perilipin may ultimately prove to be useful as anti-obesity medication.

NEUROPEPTIDE MODULATORS OF ENERGY BALANCE

When leptin receptors are activated, neuron signals alter food intake and expenditure of energy. Failure of one of these signals may cause leptin resistance and hold a clue to future drug therapy. The signals are linked to several important peptides in the hypothalamus.

Neuropeptide Y

At one time, neuropeptide Y (NPY) was thought of as an important target. NPY injected into the hypothalamus of mice stimulates food intake and decreases energy expenditure. NPY appears to be important during periods of starvation but possibly not during periods of normal nutrition. At present, scientists believe this neuropeptide has some potential for treatment of hypertension, but it will probably be of limited use with obesity.

Proopiomelanocortin and Melanocortin-4 Receptor

Two peptides, proopiomelanocortin (POMC) and melanocortin-4 receptor (MC4-R), appear to be involved in the feeding process and obesity in human beings. Although most people with a BMI over 40 have a form of the MC4-R mutation, not all people who have the mutation are obese, indicating that knowing an individual's genetic makeup will someday play an important role in obesity treatment. In two German patients who are not related, specific mutations have been described associated with an unusual adrenal hormone deficiency, red hair pigmentation, excessive eating, and severe early-onset obesity. One family with MC4-R known mutations was very tall and morbidly obese and ate excessively. Synthetic agonists of

MC4-R may prove useful in the treatment of obesity in those who possess the specific genetic mutation.

Agouti-Related Peptide and the *Mahogany Gene*

The agouti mouse is a fat, yellow fur ball. Its obesity appears to be due to the overexpression of a protein called *agouti*, which is produced by the *agouti* gene. An agouti-related peptide (AGRP) is found in humans and has a similar action in the brain to the agouti peptide in mice. Another gene in mice is called the *mahogany gene* because it darkens the coat color of the agouti mice and appears to prevent obesity by increasing energy expenditure rather than by reducing food intake. Finding answers about the expression of these genes may provide targets for pharmaceutical development.

Melanin-Concentrating Hormone and the Orexins

Melanin-concentrating hormone (MCH) injected into the brains of rats increases food intake, whereas MCH knockout mice (those genetically engineered not to express the gene) have reduced food intake and are excessively thin. The area of the brain that is closely related to MCH orchestrates smell. This has led to the concept that MCH is involved in the "pizza effect." If a person is full and not hungry, MCH level is low, but the smell of appetizing food cooking, such as pizza, will increase the level of MCH. Smell supposedly overwhelms satiety by the release of MCH. Research is underway to find a blocking agent for MCH that might be useful in obesity therapy. Two other peptides, orexins A and B, are also related to food intake. However, deletion of the *orexin* gene in mice induced narcolepsy, causing the mice to sleep all the time. Obviously, this is not a strong target.

Galanin

This peptide released from both the gastrointestinal tract and the brain is related to food intake, especially of fatty foods. Three galanin protein-linked receptor subtypes have been cloned. One peptide, M40, is a selective antagonist that blocks the action of galanin. Such compounds may have potential in controlling the desire for fatty foods.

Calcitonin Gene–Related Peptide and Amylin

Both of these peptides reduce food intake. Especially, Salmon calcitonin is a potent suppressor of food, and it lasts longer than amylin. This suggests that another receptor system is mediating the suppression of food intake that can be activated by calcitonin and amylin.

Neuromedin U Receptor

Neuromedin U (NMU) is a peptide widely expressed in the gut and CNS. When injected in the hypothalamus, it reduces food intake, suggesting another strategy for drugs to treat obesity.

GASTROINTESTINAL SIGNALING

Islet and gut peptide hormones seem to be involved in how much food is eaten and how food is processed. Granted, food intake is a complex behavior involving sensory, cognitive, postingestive, and postabsorptive processes. However, the gut hormones have received a lot of media attention proclaiming that they may be answer to overeating and even calling them the "eat-less hormones." Mechanical and chemical stimulation of the stomach and gut initiates the feeling of fullness or satiety signals. Several hormones are active here. It may be that a cocktail of drugs will be required to target multiple sites if sustained weight loss is to ever be achieved.

Peptide YY

Peptide YY (PYY) hormones are 36 amino-acid intestinal peptide hormones that are produced in the depths of the human colon. They are secreted in response to meals and control satiety. This hormone is a strong candidate as an anti-obesity drug.

Nastech Pharmaceuticals is rapidly developing a pipeline of peptides including PYY and its analogues for the treatment of obesity. The company is developing also PPY-36 combined with GLP-1 or other compounds that may produce greater efficacy than either product independently. Early clinical trials have shown promise for safety and efficacy. In partnership with Merck, Nastech is developing an intranasal version of PYY-36 that may emerge as a future treatment for obesity.

Cholecystokinin

The major biological functions of cholecystokinin (CCK) are to provide for contraction of biliary smooth muscle, reduction of food intake, and induction of anxiety-related behavior. Two types of CCK have been cloned—A and B. Information in the literature on both satiety and behavior is mixed; however, GlaxoSmithKline, a British pharmaceutical company, is now in phase III testing of a CCK-A agonist compound for increasing satiety.

Glucagon-Like Peptide 1

Glucagon-like peptide 1 (GLP1) may decrease diet-induced thermogenesis in humans by 47 percent, with a decrease in carbohydrate oxidation. It also increases the desire to eat food. Inhibiting GLP1 might be a treatment for obesity for those with a certain genetic makeup.

Enterostatin

This last gut hormone has been shown to decrease hunger, but it has not been shown to reduce food intake.

FEEDING EFFICIENCY

In the hypothalamus, leptin induces the expression of POMC, which then is broken down to MSH. This compound is the agonist for two forms: MC4-R and MC3-R. While MCR-4 regulates food intake and possibly energy expenditure, MC3-R influences feeding efficiency and portioning of food into fat. These receptors are promising targets for anti-obesity therapy. The locus encoding MCR-3 is located on the human chromosome 20q, and it has been linked to the regulation of body mass, subcutaneous fat mass, and fasting insulin levels.

Ghrelin

This peptide hormone releases growth hormone, and it appears to encourage the use of carbohydrates as an energy source by converting fat into adipose tissue for later use. Fasting increases ghrelin levels, possibly indicating its role in shifting to efficient use of energy during starvation. Various preclinical studies are looking at ghrelin to stimulate hunger.

Athersys is developing small-molecule pharmaceuticals that relate to the hypothalamus and the regulation of appetite and body weight. Using a system called Random Activation Gene Expression (RAGE), the company has created human cell lines that express the ghrelin receptors and other receptors in the hypothalamus. These molecules have been shown to reduce food consumption and body weight in animal models when doses are administered by mouth; the compounds are scheduled for clinical tests.

Growth Hormone

A deficiency of growth hormone is associated with moderate obesity and visceral deposition of fat. It has successfully treated some people but is not consistent. The high cost of growth hormone limits its role in treatment.

CENTRAL NEUROTRANSMITTERS

Dopamine

This neurotransmitter plays a role in food intake, but the actual role is difficult to distinguish from motor impairments brought on by dopamine deficiency. Two dopamine receptors are divided into two groups, D1/D5 and D2/D3/D4, which have been involved in altering food intake. Several pharmaceutical companies have clinical trials on this agent.

Serotonin

The serotonin system has been a primary target for anti-obesity research with drugs like dexfenfluramine and sibutramine. These drugs have suppressed appetite, but side effects make serotonin a debatable candidate.

Antidepressants

Two antidepressants of the selective serotonin reuptake inhibitor (SSRI) family, fluoxetine and sertraline, produce modest weight loss that fades away after some 20 weeks of treatment.

Gamma-Aminobutyric Acid and Topiramate

Gamma-aminobutyric acid (GABA) may have a role in modulating food intake. Topiramate is an agonist of GABA activity and is used to treat convulsions, especially in epilepsy. Although trials in animals to control weight loss have been successful, most of these compounds have been withdrawn from consideration because of side effects in the human trials.

ADRENAL HORMONES

Cortisol

This adrenal hormone plays an important role in the distribution of body fat, especially in the abdominal area. One hypothesis suggests that poor nutrition in utero and in early life programs an infant for later cardio-vascular problems, hypertension, and obesity; cortisol is involved in this process. New medications that act on the cortisol receptors may have some potential as anti-obesity agents.

KETONES AND FATTY-ACID SYNTHASE INHIBITION

The ketone in the brain, 3-hydroxybutyrate, depresses the food intake in lean animals. Recent research on fatty-acid synthase (FAS), another ketone, shows the role of fatty acids in the control of food intake. FAS cat-alyzes the reductive synthesis of long-chain fatty acids from acetyl coen-zyme A (acetyl CoA) and malonyl CoA. When the body stores fats, FAS makes the long-chained fatty acids that are required. In November 2004, Xenon Pharmaceuticals and Novartis signed an agreement to develop drugs treating obesity using stearoyl-CoA desaturase 1 (SCD1). The com-panies will target this regulatory enzyme in fatty acid metabolism to fight obesity by increasing metabolic rate.

Peroxisome Proliferator-Activated Receptors

The peroxisome proliferator-activated receptor (PPAR) family is involved in burning and storage of fatty acids. Found primarily in adipose tissue, muscle, and heart tissue, a subtype, PPAR-g, is known to regulate fat release and consumption in response to exercise and exposure to the cold. Scientists at the Salk Institute have found that this receptor could be turned on in genetically altered mice, increasing metabolic activity. In studying muscle tissues, where 80 percent of all the body's glucose is used, they emphasized why muscle tissue is so significant in obesity. When the body has excess calories, it burns fat, not glucose, leaving excess glucose. But most obese people do not exercise. By activating PPAR-g, the scientists caused a change in muscle fiber, similar to prolonged periods of exercise. They created a "marathon mouse" that was capable of running long dis-tances. Reengineering muscles like this could help very overweight people who have trouble exercising. Medication could make exercising easier. GlaxoSmithKline has a PPAR-g agonist now in phase II trials.

Thermogenesis

Adaptive thermogenesis has many areas of interest in the development of obesity therapy. Uncoupling proteins (UCP) generate heat without pro-ducing adenosine triphosphate (ATP) so that diversion of fat to uncoupled heat production remains an option for reducing body fat. UCP-1 is mainly expressed in brown adipocytes, and UCP-2 is expressed in many tissues. UCP-3, which is expressed in skeletal muscle in humans, is the primary target for pharmaceuticals. Amylin, Novartis, and SmithKlineBeecham are some companies involved in investigating these proteins.

NOVEL STRATEGIES

Gene Therapy

Gene therapy is a procedure that seeks to alter faulty genes. Although some trials have had some well-publicized failures, gene therapy has had successes also. Scientists are still hopeful that the process will improve, and they are working on several strategies. Obesity researchers are hoping that someday people will benefit from gene therapy research. Two obesity researchers at the University of Florida studying obese, diabetic adult rats showed that gene therapy helped animals shed weight and eat less. The scientists stimulated production of a brain protein called proopiomelanocortin (POMC) and showed that this POMC system may be important in combating obesity. The study sidestepped a major problem in obesity: the body's resistance to leptin (the hormone produced in fat tissues), that initiates a biochemical chain reaction controlling appetite and energy expenditure. Overweight mammals produce so much of the hormone that the brain resists its effects. The researchers decided to get around leptin resistance by stimulating downstream in the leptin pathway, and one of the substances that leptin activates is POMC. In these studies, POMC was released directly into the rats' brains, but improved methods might make it possible to send genes through less critical parts or the body and direct them to specific parts of the brain. Some of their research suggests that POMC deficiencies may actually cause age-related obesity rather than leptin resistance. Gene therapy to boost POMC production might have an advantage over weight-loss drugs.

Targeting Fat Tissue

AdipoGenix has a unique technology that includes a proprietary collection of human fat-cell precursors (preadipocytes) isolated from subcutaneous, mesenteric, and omental fat deposits from more than 250 individuals. Using high-throughput techniques that enable the testing of thousands of specimens at once, the scientists can identify compounds that can reduce the fat content of human fat. They collect a portfolio of assays and pharmacological tolls that identify the mechanism of action and molecular targets for active compounds. This far, the company has identified low-molecular-weight compounds that reduce the number of mature fat cells formed from precursor cells, decrease the synthesis and storage of fat in the mature cell, increase the breakdown and release of stored fat, and enhance the burning of stored fat to produce energy.

HMGene, a company that develops therapies for metabolic disorders, is targeting adipose tissue. Using a technique called Adiposense platform, the company has identified and prioritized 139 obesity genes. They have found that HM-21, an endogenous secreted protein that signals in a known adipogenic pathway, is highly expressed in fat tissue. As a drug candidate, HM-21 shows preclinical therapeutic potential. The company intends to file with the FDA within two years. Already, it has HM-12 as a validated obesity target. Individuals with decreased HM-12 expression have lower BMI, reduced prevalence of obesity, and decreased abdominal fat.

Natural Products

An untapped market in the past has been the scientific investigation of natural products. PhytoLogix is a technology platform of Unigen Pharmaceuticals that has led to the investigation of more than 5,900 medicinal plants and 6,500 extracts. UP120 is a novel composition of free-b-ring flavonoids and flavans from two plants that, in a double-blind placebo-controlled study, led to a 9 percent weight reduction in 90 days.

Obesity Vaccine

In May 2005, the Swiss biotechnology firm Cytos announced the enrollment of 112 obese individuals for the first human trial of an obesity vaccine. The test is designed to trigger antibodies to ghrelin, a human hormone that stimulates appetite. The volunteers, who must have a BMI between 30 and 35, receive monthly shots for six months. A control group will receive a placebo. Both groups will receive counseling on diet and exercise. The vaccination aims to induce antibodies that will bind ghrelin in the blood system so that it does not enter the brain and induce hunger. Scientists identified ghrelin in 1999 and found that it increases before a meal and decreases after a meal. The peptide appears to have a role in long-term weight regulation. When weight loss occurs, blood levels of ghrelin rise, probably explaining why so many dieters regain weight quickly after losing weight.

The Obesity Virus

The possibility that fat may be an infection with a virus is a novel idea. Infection with human adenovirus-36 (Ad-36) causes dramatic changes in body composition and serum lipids in animals and is associated with differences in body weight in humans. Ad-36 has been inoculated into chickens, mice, and monkeys, and it has produced a 50–100 percent increase in body fat. Two human studies have been performed. The presence of Ad-36 antibodies in body serum denotes a previous infection of the virus. In more than 500 people from New York to Naples, Florida, the prevalence of the antibodies was 30 percent in obese subjects and 11 percent in nonobese subjects. Those with the antibodies were, on average, nine BMI units larger than those without. Obtech Obesity Research Center has patented assays to detect the presence of Ad-36 antibodies in serum and the presence of Ad-36 DNA in tissues.

Zinc Deficiency in Obesity

Obesity is associated with low zinc levels in many populations of the world. Zinc supplements appear to relieve sucrose- or sugar-induced obesity in animals. Preventive Nutrient Company has found that cyclo (his-pro), or CHP, stimulates intestinal zinc absorption and muscle-cell zinc uptake. CHP facilitates zinc transport across the lining of the intestine. Zinc is an integral part of an insulin-degrading enzyme, which helps to maintain normal insulin levels in the body. CHP plus zinc was found to reduce more than 10 percent of body weight in obese rats.

Nasal Sprays

A few companies are experimenting with nasal sprays as a method of delivering drugs to suppress appetite. Compellis Pharmaceutical has found that using the novel target of olfactory perception, volatile compounds pass over the olfactory epithelium and directly stimulate a nerve impulse that reaches the brain. Using already-approved calcium-channel blockers, such as diltiazem, the scientists found significant appetite suppression in preclinical trials. The company has designed phase I trials with 50 trial subjects in eight different groups. Other companies are investigating this strategy.

Designer Foods and Devices

Genetically engineered foods that have fewer calories are being developed. For example, a potato that has less starch but still has "potato" characteristics is on the market. Monsanto is applying breeding tech-niques to produce a soybean high in oleic acid and low in linolenic acid. The company has developed a trans-fat-free soybean, which can produce the first natural, trans- and saturated-fat-free oil. The company made its Vistive-brand soybean seeds with this trait available in 2005.

Nanotechnology

The hottest topic of the twenty-first century is nanotechnology. Nano is a Greek prefix that means one-billionth of something, such as a second, liter, or meter. In the nanoworld, the laws of physics are turned upside down, and inertia, friction, and gravity do not matter. Nanomedicine now involves hundreds of scientists working to develop effective drugs that work on the cellular level. Cell surgery, a new area of research, seeks to understand how to change cell processes. Nanomedical technology could be applied to surgery of fat cells, as well as the delivery of targeted drugs by nanorobots.

WHAT ABOUT THE FUTURE?

Will there be a fat-free future? Do we want a fat-free society? Or should we be focused on a healthful society? In 1995, two demographers predicted that the whole U.S. population would be overweight by 2230. However, with average weight increasing about 1 percent per year, the demographers now predict that the entire U.S. population will be overweight by 2040 and obese by 2100. The figures indicate what a difficult problem is facing the United States and the international community.

In treating obesity, current options are not sufficient. Successful manage-ment of these diseases depends on novel, improved therapeutic strategies, targeting early intervention in the disease progression. The complexity of contributing environmental and genetic factors has hampered the discov-ery of novel metabolic targets. But scientists and researchers are looking for the great breakthrough, which will more likely be a series of small breakthroughs targeting individual needs.

The research and possibilities cited in this chapter have highlighted why an effective anti-obesity agent still eludes us. The mechanism of control of intake, expenditure, and body weight is complex and involves many genes and biochemical pathways. Only by understanding the rules of this effec-tive human system that has survived over the ages can the scientist find breakthrough anti-obesity agents. It is likely that one agent will not be the answer for everyone. The personalized package will probably be tailored for each individual's specific requirements. On the other hand, researchers may eventually find a common pathway or pathways with one or more agents that are useful to everyone with weight problems. However, it will probably be several decades before this elusive therapy will be discovered. Most scientists agree that conquering cancer will come before the answers to the difficult problem of weight loss and maintenance.

Ultimately, it is the individual who must make the choice of whether to live a healthy lifestyle; however, social and environmental pulls are working against that individual. Because of the many implications for the healthcare system, the philosophical question of whether obesity is a disease or a disorder resulting from evolution is an issue that must be resolved—but will probably not be in the near future. The question of whether government has a role in prevention of obesity has strong proponents on each side of the debate. Would establishing and enforcing rigorous policies be feasible? How much would government regulation limit individual freedom and personal choice? Questions of money and finance are involved. How much will it cost to establish activity-friendly communities, and who should pay for them? All these issues must be worked out in the arena of public debate and opinion.

Obesity is both a societal and individual problem. Answers to the many questions posed in this book must come from both the individual and society. However, after years of neglect, the problem of obesity and the issues surrounding it have experienced a renaissance in this twenty-first century. Is this the century in which a fat-free society will come about?

PART III

Scenarios

CHAPTER **21**

Case Illustrations

CASE STUDY 1: BRYAN AND THE ROLE OF FAMILY IN MANAGING WEIGHT

Bryan is a 16-year-old junior at Central High School. The first time that his parents noted that he was somewhat overweight was when he was about 5. He was gaining about three pounds a month. By the time he was in the fourth grade, he had to wear men's clothing. He even overheard an insensitive family doctor say to his mother, "How can he be so fat when you are so thin? He needs to lose weight." Both of Bryan's parents were thin, although several members of the extended family had weight problems.

Bryan's parents were concerned about his weight. His mother was exceedingly worried. She even said to a friend, "If he needed new shoes, I would buy them; if he needed school supplies, I would have them the next day. But what do you do when your child is fat, and you feel there is nothing you can do?" However, they tried to show that they were not too concerned and always told him how good he looked.

Bryan was miserable. Other children in school and in the neighborhood taunted him and called him names like "Fatso" and "Fatty." He often cried to his mom about how he was being treated at school. When he was nine, the family brought home a new baby boy. Bryan kissed the new baby and said to him, "When you grow up, I hope you will not be fat like me."

The school district had developed a health program in which they evaluated the BMI of students and sent home letters encouraging parents to help children lose weight. It was a well-intentioned program, but Bryan's parents were furious at the letter and complained to the school board that such letters were damaging their child's self-esteem. The district eventually dropped the program.

The frustrated parents then decided to "help" Bryan lose weight. His mother, Sue, heard that Weight Watchers had an excellent program for losing weight, and she enrolled him in the program. But Bryan did not feel comfortable in the program with all the ladies and would not go to meetings. He sat outside while she attended the meetings. Obviously, this strategy did not work. Even a program called T.O.P.S (Taking Pounds Off Sensibly) held at their church met the same fate. He would not attend meetings. Next, the parents thought of taking him to a gym for workouts, but none of local gyms would take a client under 16. They encouraged him to become active in sports, but he was just too much out of shape. No one wanted him on their team.

After trying several strategies, the family tried a new strategy of nagging and shaming. They said to him, "Just look at yourself in the mirror; all the kids will call you fat and not want to have anything to do with you." Or, "Don't you want to lose weight so you can look nice in your clothes?" When they told him to only eat one piece of pizza, he would eat two or three just to spite them. The weight-loss game became a tug of war with neither side winning.

When Bryan was 14, he and his family went to the beach on vacation. They took many pictures. When Bryan looked at the pictures, it was a moment of truth. He did not want to look like that. He started crying and said to his parents, "Please help me." It was the opening they had awaiting, but they were still not sure where to turn.

Sue began to look for a program that they would go to together. She began researching various options. After scouring the Internet and talking with several physicians, she came across a program recommended specifically for teens who are overweight. It was worth a try. Although the program was designed for a group, Dr. Timothy Jones thought it best to work individually with Bryan and his mom. The program cost was $2,000. They would meet for 10 weeks of private consultations and then participate in a maintenance program for 10 months.

Throughout the program, Sue learned that nagging about food and exercise was counterproductive. She learned that she could not be the "food police." With the guidance of Dr. Jones, she learned herself about healthy choices and then involved Bryan in making the decisions about the meals. She did not tell him what to eat but offered choices. She found that the less aggressive she was about his weight, the more positively he responded.

Bryan liked Dr. Jones's approach and enjoyed meeting with him. "He does not just nag you about food and exercise," he said. "It is much more mental." Dr. Jones encouraged him to think of himself and his image. He asked him, "What do you really want for yourself?" He helped him set goals based on health. The word *diet* was never used. Everything was based on health and the future, not on appearance.

The family also appreciated Dr. Jones's approach to open communication. He did not just tell him to lose weight but sat down with him and the family to make a plan with goals. For example, he set a goal to exercise half an hour each day. He even gave him a journal to enter items daily and for a weekly review. If he met a weekly goal, he received $5 to spend on something that he really wanted.

The parents also helped by changing their own eating habits. All the snacks and "junk food" were left off the shopping lists. Bryan even asked his mom not to bring his favorite kind of cookies into the house. All this really paid off; Bryan joined the tennis team and is having fun with friends and family.

Bryan will soon be going to college where he has lots of control over his choices without the parents being there. He intends to keep the new lifestyle. Sue, who once felt powerless and frustrated, now feels she has not only learned to empower her son but has made her own better choices as well.

Analysis

This case shows how well-meaning parents can help or hinder weight-loss efforts. Like many modern parents, Sue wanted Bryan to be likeable and popular and was concerned about his weight. Sue realized that he had problems when Bryan came home crying about the mean things other children were saying to him.

Bryan's parents learned quickly what did not work and then had to readjust their thinking to find what would work. They realized that shaming and nagging would not work. When they tried to take him to places like Weight Watchers, he felt out of place and rebelled.

When the school district tried to intervene by sending letters to parents whose students had high BMIs, they rebelled and worked against the program. Some districts have these types of initiatives and have counselors and advisors to assist families and children. They missed the well-intentioned opportunity here.

No one can tell exactly when the point of realization will occur. For Bryan, it was the pictures at the beach. He knew that he did not want to look that way. He had to accept that he must want to make the effort not to just lose weight but to become healthy. It now has become an issue of self-esteem. He realized that no one can force you to lose weight and keep it off. The individual must believe in himself or herself and understand who he or she is and who he or she wants to be.

One of the first things recommended to Bryan was for him to figure out his goals and write them down. The goals should include weight and fitness and also must establish goals beyond just looks and health.

Dr. Jones recommended that he keep his achievement in a diary. The diary or journal included a page for each day divided into morning, afternoon, and evening. The person records the food/beverage and amount, the hunger level, the calories, and mood or feelings. There is a space for exercise, plan for tomorrow, today's success, and random thoughts. At the end of the week is a page for review. He reflected on what helped this week, such as goals met that were met, things to work on, reminders of why I want to get to a healthier weight, and reminders of how my life is better. Weight is recorded weekly.

This strategy helped Bryan achieve and then establish habits that will be with him throughout life.

The families of teens can play a major role. Nagging them about the way they look is discouraging and destructive. Success was centered on the following themes:

- They encouraged and praised the person. They just did not tell them to eat right; they set the example for healthy eating.
- They provided materially for weight loss. They made sure that the right foods were available and paid for exercise programs if necessary.
- They themselves planned and ate healthier meals.
- Families work together for better health.

CASE STUDY 2: KEVIN AND THE POWER OF MOTIVATIONAL INTERVIEWING

Kevin has just finished a milestone in his education. He has graduated from the University of Florida Medical School. But he knows the long road is still ahead of him. He has chosen a field in which he sees himself as a pioneer. That field is tackling the problem of obesity in America by being a specialist in weight-loss counseling.

Kevin entered life 25 years ago as a healthy baby boy and the apple of his parents' eyes. Being an only child, he had lots of toys and adoration. He was also surrounded by lots of food; Oreos and chocolate chip cookies were his favorite treats. His parents were raised in the Southern tradition of fried chicken, mashed potatoes with gravy, and pecan pie. The favorite family outing involved church picnics with sumptuous spreads of food topped off with a peanut boiling. Food in this traditional Southern family was an important part of life, and if you loved people, you fed them. From the beginning of his life, Kevin was surrounded by love and food.

Kevin was overweight, but he was in good company because his parents, cousins, aunts, and uncles were also overweight. The pediatrician, Dr. Smith, told his mother that six-month-old Kevin was overweight. She was insulted and decided to leave Dr. Smith. Over the years, his mother, who also struggled with weight issues, took him to many doctors who told him to lose weight and get more exercise—period. The doctors appeared to have little empathy for either of them and briskly told them that "you both are too fat" or sometimes used the *O* word—*obese*. They ignored the "insulting doctors" and celebrated by going to the local buffet dinner where you can eat all you want.

The year that Kevin graduated from college and began medical school, his dad had a massive heart attack and died at the age of 57. Devastated, he and his mother knew that their lifestyle and eating habits were greatly responsible for their loss. Looking at themselves, they made a pact that they would lose weight. Their problem was that they did not know where to turn.

He and his mother were disappointed with the advice from their family doctor. They both asked where they should go and how to go about doing it but got little assistance other than a couple of brochures. They tried to lose weight on their own by cutting calories and going on the latest fad diet. They lost weight but soon gained it back. They both decided that losing weight was hopeless.

As a medical student, he began to realize that such defeatist attitudes were devastating. He became concerned about what could be done to help people like his mother and him, who were frustrated about what to do. He talked with other students and even some of the doctors in the field about what they were doing to help and counsel patients about weight loss. He found that most of the students and clinicians said they were not at all confident about counseling to address nutrition, exercise, and especially drugs or pharmaceuticals that may help them. They admitted they did very little except to give them a booklet or refer them to a nutritionist. Even people who had serious comorbidity problems associated with weight, such as cardiovascular issues or diabetes, were given little information about weight loss.

He and his mother made a pact. They would study nutrition and change the lifelong habits that were so traditional in Southern families. He read about an idea that has especially been used to help other people with unhealthful habits, such as smoking. The technique is called motivational interviewing. In motivational interviewing, one is just not given booklet or a pamphlet and told to lose weight and exercise more. With more research, he was fortunate to find Dr. Ayala, a professor in the medical school who is an advocate of motivational interviewing. He and his mom both made appointments. Dr. Ayala realized they were serious about their weight loss and were highly motivated. He actually helped them set goals. They would see him each month for several months. In the meantime, a member of his staff would follow up with encouragement and assistance.

Kevin was pleased with Dr. Ayala's approach. He and his mom set their goals and worked to carefully follow directives. When they were discouraged, Dr. Ayala was there to support and encourage them. Kevin began studying how such a program can be implemented into a busy practitioner's practice. He called practices that implemented such a program into their office practices. All of them possessed effective leadership and determination and set a priority for preventive services. The physicians, staff, and office administration would plan jointly. Cooperation and teamwork are essential. For example, each person's role to implement counseling within the office would be defined. It could be a physician's assistant, a nurse practitioner, or health educator.

Kevin knows his future and his excitement to help people will not be easy. It will involve changing the way that things in the medical profession are done, and this is neither quick nor simple. Tackling any changes of negative attitudes toward people who are obese is a challenge. He can point to the success that both he and his mom have had in changing their lifestyles and eating habits.

He will do a residency in internal medicine and then specialize in a weight-loss practice using motivational interviewing and good preventive practices. In addition, he hopes to challenge the negative attitudes that many in the health profession have about individuals who are overweight.

Analysis

Because of his personal experience with weight and the difficulties involved in being overweight, Kevin has chosen a field in which he is ideally suited. Kevin has been introduced to a counseling technique called motivational interviewing. Discussing a person's weight is a sensitive subject for most people. Physicians also are not comfortable and may avoid the topics because they want their patients to like them. Steeves et al. (2015) reported in the journal *Obesity Research Clinical Practice* that nearly half of all clinicians indicated they were "not at all" or were only "somewhat" confident in their ability to counsel patients about weight loss. They stated that psychological issues were the most challenging but also felt completely inadequate in conveying knowledge about nutrition, exercise, and pharmacotherapy. Steeves also found that most clinicians were not educated about motivational interviewing techniques or considered that counseling was "fluff" and ineffective.

Jackson (2013) found that in a cross-sectional survey of patients, fewer than half recalled their family practitioners providing weight loss counseling. Another researcher, Glauser (2015), found that many physicians had negative attitudes about overweight patients and believed that obesity is self-inflicted from laziness and overindulging. Such barriers to addressing the obesity epidemic and attitudes must be overcome for the good of patients and society as a whole.

The U.S. Public Health Service has implemented an approach for tobacco cessation that has become the foundation of motivational interviewing. This technique enables physicians to deliver brief, individually tailored messages to patients. Called the 5A's protocol, the points are the foundation of motivational interviewing:

Assess: check the understanding of the severity of the condition and readiness to change
Advise: clear, specific, personalized behavioral change
Agree: plan together on a program of action
Assist: looking at the goals and develop the skills to achieve goals
Arrange: follow-up in person or telephone to discuss barriers, adjusting the plan if necessary

Motivational interviewing uses nonjudgmental, nondirective questions and comments. For example, the doctor may say to the patient, "Your BMI is above the 95th percentile, what concerns do you have about your weight?" In order to establish rapport with the patient, the doctor looks into the patient's eyes to express empathy. This technique is called active listening. From there, he or she asks questions and listens to uncover beliefs and values. "It looks like you have a good idea of the effect of weight on your health; would you like to talk about some ways you could get to a healthier weight?" With the patient, the doctor and patient set goals and make a realistic plan to achieve the goals. This is called shared decision making. The final stage is to arrange a follow-up by a visit, telephone call, or e-mail. This important step is often left out, and the person is left on his or her own.

We can all agree with Kevin that poor health choices are a great burden to individuals and to the entire health system. When the people are involved, know what to do, and are encouraged and choose to be involved in their health care, they have the opportunity to respond. Motivational interviewing is a technique to help them set and attain those goals.

CASE STUDY 3: SUSAN AND THE "FRESHMAN 15"

Susan F. was so excited. She graduated from high school and was among the top 10 percent of her class. As an active high schooler, she ran track, worked hard in her studies, and was a member of student council. Her plans were to go to the same state university that her dad and all her relatives had graduated from, major in political science, and then go to law school. She never had a problem with weight.

That summer, she made great plans. She bought the latest trendy clothes and kept in touch with her friends. She did not continue to run track but did get a lot of exercise swimming, hiking, and dancing.

The big day came. Moving into the freshman dormitory was exciting. For the first time in her life, she was on her own and could go and come as she chose. Because she was in a campus dormitory, she bought a meal plan but soon joined the group that grumbled about the food. The salads were boring, and she was tired of baked chicken and yogurt. According to her friends, the breakfasts were tasteless, so she began skipping breakfast.

As part of the meal plan, they could go to the local pizza shop and enjoy pizza with extra cheese and toppings. She did not realize how great fast-food hamburgers with french fries tasted. She especially liked shakes. She enjoyed her classes, although they were so large and pretty overwhelming.

Campus life in the fall was exciting. There were football games with lots of tailgate parties and good tasty food cooked on the grill. Fraternity parties were also fun, and there were always lots to eat and drink.

This was the first time in her life that she could do really what she wanted to do, and it was great! She found herself getting little sleep. The world was too exciting, and it was fun to brag about all-nighters. Although there was a lot of stress trying to keep up with grades, she was coping well and having a good time.

She found some real strategies that worked to help her cope better. Although she never had been a coffee drinker, she found that coffee and other caffeine/high-sugar energy drinks could provide the fuel that she needed. The dorm was so great. There was a small refrigerator, so she could buy cartons of soft drinks, with sugar to provide quick energy. Someone always had great snacks, such as potato chips and cookies.

Although running track was lots of fun in high school, she did not think she was good enough for college competition, so her former sports activities and exercise were greatly curtailed. She had little time with the demands of studying and socializing to find a new replacement for running track. She considered exercising boring and did not care for tennis or swimming.

Her parents asked about the meal plan that she had purchased. She told them that the food was fine, but with her busy schedule, she had trouble getting to the cafeteria when it was open. She suggested that for the next semester, she would not do the plan, but they could just send her money and she could get a few things to eat in the dorm; there was a place to cook in a common area. Her parents willingly agreed. Eating out with friends was always so much more fun than going to the boring cafeteria. Susan had always been very conscious of her appearance and her clothes. She bought the trendy clothes from the fashion places in the mall. The size-nine jeans fit her snugly, but that was always a comforting feeling. One Saturday morning, when football season was over, she slept late and then planned to get dressed to meet two of her new friends. She had bought a neat pair of jeans that had sequins all up and down the legs and on the back. When she put one leg in the jeans, she noticed that it was a little tight. The other one felt the same. But when she tried to put them up, the zipper would not meet. She was surprised and put that trendy pair away and wore the old pair that had stretched to meet her form.

She began to notice that her stomach was getting a little pouch. She thought that she must go on a diet to lose a few pounds, but going out with her friends was so much more appealing. When she weighed herself, she had added 15 pounds. She thought that she really must consider going on a diet and got advice from friends about the latest trends. One had tried the cabbage diet. Another told her of a fasting diet. None of these diets were very appealing. Of course, she had studied nutrition in health class, but that food pyramid never meant much to her and seemed so vague. Some of the girls had tried making themselves throw up after eating a delightful meal, but that did not appeal to her either. She had to concentrate on the new classes that she would be taking in the spring.

Spring came, and she went to the mall to buy the latest trend in clothes that she had seen in fashion magazines. She was surprised when her old size nine did not fit. The clerk laughed and told her she was a victim of the Freshman 15.

Everyone laughed about the famous Freshman 15, which students derided as a myth. After the comment from the clerk in the mall, she was determined to lose weight again. She bought a book on the Atkins diet and said she would try it. But the food was boring. She soon gave this diet up and returned to her pizza and hamburgers — this time without the fries. She soon decided that she could not do without the fries.

The end of her freshman year was great and full of terrific memories. Her only one point of sadness was that when she stepped on the scales, she had not gained 15 pounds but 30 pounds.

Ignoring the Freshman 15 talk, she just bought some new clothes a size larger and enjoyed baggy tops and stretchy pants, without zippers. For Susan, Freshman 15 was a myth; she could have said Freshman 30.

Analysis

Is the Freshman 15 a reality or a myth? There are arguments on each side. However, most researchers declare that freshmen do tend to gain weight during that first year and may continue to increase the weight during college. Researchers at Auburn University in Alabama followed 131 students during their four years of college and found that 70 percent of them gained weight during the four years. Published in *Applied Physiology, Nutrition, and Metabolism*, the researchers found that by graduation, students had added an average of 12 and up to 37 pounds, thus increasing their weight by 18–31 percent. They attributed the weight gain to late-night study habits, vending-machine snacks, fattening choices in college cafeterias, and lack of activity.

Poor sleep may also spur college weight gain. A study in the *Journal Behavioral Sleep Medicine* looked at the sleep habits of 132 first-year students at Brown University. On average, they went to bed around 1:30 a.m. Optimally, teenagers need about nine hours and 15 minutes a night. These freshmen averaged about seven hours and 15 minutes. When people are sleep deprived, they more readily reach for candy and desserts.

Other studies debunk Freshman 15 as a myth. A 2013 study in the *New England Journal of Medicine* found that students may gain weight but far less than the reported 15 pounds. The study said this was erroneously reported and caused great fear among college students but was really nothing more than an urban myth. They noted a danger in the preoccupation with gaining weight that might lead to severe eating disorders, such as bulimia and anorexia nervosa.

There are several things that Susan and other college students can do to keep that weight off. One strategy is to keep a log of both food and activity by writing down daily meals, snacks, beverages, and activity.

Other tips include:

- Do not skip meals, especially breakfast, which gets your metabolism humming and decreases overeating.
- Keep healthy snacks handy. Stock the dorm-room refrigerator with fruit, string cheese, Greek yogurt, hummus, baby carrots, and so on.
- Watch portions.
- Choose fats wisely.
- Drink water and low-calorie beverages.
- Stay active. Walk to class, and find some sport that you enjoy participating in.
- Get enough sleep. Less than six hours each night affects hormones that control appetite, cravings, and metabolism. People not getting enough sleep will depend on high sugar and junk foods for quick energy.

It does take a lot of willpower to go out on your own for the first time. Colleges can help by providing information about what can happen when poor diet and no exercise become the lifestyle.

CASE STUDY 4: MARIA AND THE RISKS OF EATING DISORDERS

A native-born Texan of Mexican heritage, Maria was raised in a happy home with parents who worked very hard. Her mother was a maid at a famous hotel chain, and her dad, Juan, had a successful lawn business. Her parents were very active in their church, and as a teenager, Maria was active in the youth group. Her parents provided well for their family of four, and Maria loved preparing the tamales, tacos, enchiladas, beans, and rice for daily meals with her mother and grandmother. They also had expansive spreads on feast days and holidays. Her parents were proud of their heritage and also joked quite a bit about their big meals and their family fat genes. Her parents were not what you would call "gordito," but being short and stocky probably would qualify them as obese on the BMI scale. But Maria seemed to have more of the weight problem than either of her parents. Her grandmother, who lived with them, weighed 200 pounds.

Maria went to an elementary school in an affluent community. At nine, some of the boys at the school teased her and called her "hefty lefty" when she played softball on the playground. She just laughed but began to internalize that she was "fat." She buried herself in her school work and became an outstanding student. She continued thinking of her worth in terms of her body image throughout middle school.

One day at the age of 10 after a second helping of dessert at a huge family feast, she felt very full. She ran outside, bent over, and threw up in the bushes. She then ran back into the house to eat some more dessert. It felt good.

In the eighth grade, Lisa, one of her friends in algebra class, told how she read about a way she could eat all that she wanted and lose weight. She was interested. Also, she noticed that her body was changing and that her big breasts and hips were making her into a shape like her 200-pound grandmother. She did not want that.

She decided that she would diet by saying no to any food that came her way. She lost weight but could not abide the constant hunger pangs gnawing at her stomach. She remembered the casual words of her algebra friend and the new way to lose weight. Eat all you want, and then make yourself throw it up. You will never be hungry again, and you feel great.

She was determined that she would never be called "hefty lefty" again. Losing weight would give her this great body, and she would be extremely happy. She did lose weight, but she was not happy.

As the years faded from middle to high school, Maria became utterly obsessed with food. At age 16, she found herself eating all day. If there was no food available at the time, she had anxiety attacks. She must have food for the next binge and purge.

Now became the great performances that would even qualify her for Hollywood. With her beautiful hair and eyes and new perfect body, she was the envy of classmates and very popular with the boys. She became a cheerleader, the ultimate for popularity in the school. She was good at sports and an honor student. Her teachers and classmates admired her energy and enthusiasm. She was awarded a scholarship to the state university.

This picture shielded her real internal self. She was falling apart. She had to hide the fact that she was so obsessed with food that she would eat anything, even things that classmates would throw away. When no one was looking, she raided the cafeteria garbage looking for sweet delicacies. Her opinion of herself was low. She even thought that perhaps she was crazy and needed to be locked up.

Entering the university at 18 was exciting and gave her new opportunities to binge, purge, and hide it. She found herself binging and purging over 10 times a day. Outside, she was the happy beauty queen; inside, she was a seething pot of frustration and confusion.

During the spring of her sophomore year, she noticed a problem with her teeth. The enamel was thin and decaying. And another symptom arose. She began to feel like butterflies were fluttering inside her chest. One day she had such severe chest pains that she fell to the floor. Her great way of eating and vomiting was catching up with her. She could not hide her secret much longer.

Maria realized that she must change this terrible cycle of binge and purge. Her body and mind were on the verge of collapse. It would be only time until she would die. She knew that she needed help and went back to her original support group—her parents and members of the church. The pastor recommended her to a counselor, who worked out a plan.

The road to recovery was very rocky. It did not happen overnight. In fact, it took about eight months before she had one complete day without binge and purge. Now at the age of 20, she has been completely free for nearly over a year. For her, life is beautiful, and she now has inner peace with herself.

Analysis

This vignette shows a person who sought to control her weight by eating all she wanted and then making herself throw it all up. Maria had a clinical case of bulimia nervosa. She met the criteria described in *The Diagnostic and Statistical Manual*, Fifth Edition, published in 2013. With this condition, the person evaluates self-worth by body shape. He or she eats a large amount of food and then compensates by vomiting up the food, fasting, using laxatives or diuretics, or exercising excessively. The incident occurs at least once a week for three months.

Maria was from a family in which eating was pleasurable and lots of starchy and rich foods were available. Eating was a meaningful experience for the family and part of their culture and heritage. She learned early to overeat to the point of fullness. When the boys in the softball game called her "hefty lefty," she began to think of herself as "fat." The incidence when she purged was the beginning of the realization that she could enjoy food and lose weight. Purging at this early age is unusual, but this one-time event established the memory of how good it felt to be able to eat all she wanted.

It is usually in middle school that girls begin to think about body image. It is also an important time to make healthy or unhealthy decisions. When her body began to change, she developed large breasts and hips like her grandmother. She knew that was not what she wanted. The most successful way of losing weight was dieting, but the overwhelming hunger pangs made her unhappy and uncomfortable.

Like many young people, information from friends is important. When a friend told her casually that she had heard of a painless way in which one can lose weight and eat all he or she wants, she was interested. She learned to keep her obsession with food a secret. She was an ideal student. Although she became very thin, she still thought that she was fat. Her own evaluation of herself was based on body shape and weight.

Going away to school helped a lot. She was in circumstances that she could get away from people. She even carried a small bottle with her so she could go into restrooms or corners and purge the latest package of cookies.

The two physical events—decaying teeth and heart pain and palpitations—were a frightening warning. Many people ignore these signs, but Maria knew something had to change. She could not live this way forever.

She found she must tell and seek help. Fortunately, she had a supportive and understanding family and community who engaged a counselor. She had to reorganize her thinking patterns, or neural pathways, from the binge eater to a normal eater. The counselor worked with her and kept in touch weekly with her. It was a rocky road to recovery, but with persistence, she was successful. Today, she has developed an online Bulimia Recovery Program, in which she helps people with bulimia find help and self-love.

Many young people with bulimia are not quite as successful. Maria had the family support and intelligence to realize that something was wrong. Others find themselves unable through counseling to break the binge habit and must be put in residential treatment. Even with such treatments, some are not able to break the cycle that will eventually lead to death.

CASE HISTORY 5: AMY AND BARIATRIC SURGERY

Amy B. had been overweight as a child and young teenager and endured being called names like "fatty" or "hefty." At the age of 13, she visited her family doctor who expressed grave concern that she was 100 pounds overweight and had a BMI of 35. The doctor suggested exercise and diet programs, but these were only vague suggestions. She tried several of the diet plans, but they never seemed to work. Amy did not stick with them and continued through the teen years to gain weight.

Amy loved junk food, rich desserts, fast foods, and her favorite pizza. After a routine blood test, her doctor told her that she had very high glucose and cholesterol readings and that eventually she may have health problems. He gave her a brochure on healthy eating and told her to get more exercise. Amy did not take this seriously. After all, both her mom and dad were from families with histories of heart conditions and diabetes, and nothing had happened to them. This magical thinking gave her the excuse to continue her eating and sedentary lifestyle. At age 16, she read about weight-loss surgery, but somehow the idea did not appeal to her. She had never had surgery and was frightened at the prospect. Amy was a bright girl and an excellent student. She really disliked the required health class in school and believed that all this information about the food pyramid and exercise was for other people. She had no interest until she saw a film about how fat affects the body systems and how important it is to live a healthy lifestyle. She thought that maybe her attitude was wrong and she should explore dieting. She tried to lose weight on her own, but the most she ever lost was about 40 pounds. However, over time, she gained that weight back and added a few more pounds. She went to several programs in the community. Those also worked for a while and then the weight returned.

Amy began investigating weight loss on the Internet. There were many doctors who promised to help. She read many of the entries and considered diets of all kind. She even tried the cabbage diet and the new gene diet. One day, Amy found an article on bariatric surgery. Maybe this was an answer. She did not take the site too seriously but thought that she could at least go to a seminar presented at the local hospital. Along with her mother, she attended the first seminar. The doctors explained the procedure and showed some of the people who had success with this procedure when dieting and exercise had failed. Her interest was heightened. She attended a second seminar and then a third. She talked privately with the doctor to see if this approach was right for her. She found that she must have a letter from her primary care physician that the surgery was a medical necessity and also that she had been a part of a nutrition/exercise program for about three months but failed to lose weight. Now was the time for her to seriously look at specific recommended programs. She found that she was one who had the "yo-yo syndrome." She would lose weight and then gain it back.

She attended another seminar on surgery that the local hospital provided. She found that currently there are two effective bariatric procedures, gastric bypass and sleeve gastrectomy. The doctors carefully explained the benefits and drawbacks of each one of the procedures. They were not high pressure but emphasized that even with the surgery, the person must still eat properly and exercise.

She did not make the decision quickly, as she was still frightened of the prospect of the hospital and pain after surgery. She made a list of all the pros and cons. She knew she would have to give up the double cheeseburger and life on the couch. At age 17, she was now 150 pounds overweight. Great events were happening in her life. She would soon graduate from high school and attend community college in the fall. She realized that she could not live through life as she was and bravely decided that surgery was the right path. The day of decision had arrived. Assessing the information she received, she decided that the gastric sleeve surgery appealed to her more because it could be done laparoscopically, with minimum invasive surgery.

She met with the surgeon and his team. They were very supportive of her decision and explained the details of the surgery. On that day, she calmly walked into the hospital and bravely faced the surgery. She was given a general anesthetic and was basically comfortable during a four-day hospital stay. All her friends came to visit, and she commented that she didn't know she had so many friends.

Amy still has to drastically change her lifestyle, including avoiding certain foods and adding exercise to her daily routine. She had no side effects from the surgery but was warned that with this procedure, she would not lose weight as quickly as other types.

Now four years have passed. She is still overweight but not morbidly obese. However, the best results were the decrease in blood glucose and cholesterol. The risk of diabetes and heart trouble that had plagued other family members was now decreased. Amy, now 21, reflects on that health class that she did not want to take. It helped her realize that her unhealthy lifestyle could be deadly. She does not regret having the surgery and feels very confident and amazing now. She still is conscious of what she eats and does exercise, although that is not her favorite thing. She is committed to follow-up appointments and checkups—a strategy that she says keeps her on her toes knowing that she will be accountable.

Analysis

Many people like Amy have struggled with weight and then come to the decision that surgery is the only way to go. According to a study by Dr. Thomas Inge, Cincinnati Children's Hospital Medical Center, some 4.6 million children and teens in the United States are severely obese—defined as 100 pounds or more overweight. A study published in the January 5, 2017, news release from *The Lancet Diabetes & Endocrinology* showed how weight-loss surgery can offer long-term benefit to very overweight teens with significant maintenance for over five years. Two strategies appear to work best for young people: gastric bypass surgery and vertical sleeve gastrectomy.

In gastric bypass surgery, the stomach is divided into a small upper pouch and the small intestine then attached to a remnant pouch. The volume of the stomach is reduced, and food is then processed differently.

A newer procedure called vertical sleeve gastrectomy reduces the stomach about 15 percent of its original size, by removing a large portion of the stomach along the greater curvature. A tube-like structure or sleeve is the result. The doctor usually uses a laparoscope and makes several tiny incisions. The American Society for Metabolic and Bariatric Surgery endorses the procedure and notes that it is gaining in popularity, especially for treating children and adolescents. Reports do show that progress in growth is unaffected after sleeve gastrectomy in children younger than 14 years of age.

Dr. Michael Roslin, chief of obesity surgery at Lenox Hill Hospital in New York, agreed with findings of this study and underscored the benefit of surgery for severely obese young patients. He believes that once obesity reaches this level in teens, it affects future success more than drug addiction, alcohol, or poverty. He believes that more teens should be rescued through weight-loss surgery. He also added that access to surgery should be more easily provided.

The study also emphasized that despite some dramatic weight loss, many of the teens were still obese afterward but not as severely. Monitoring and follow-ups are very important not only to encourage the patients but also to check for a major downside of gastrointestinal issues and monitor for appearance of comorbidities such as diabetes, high blood pressure, or heart trouble that may need to be treated.

Amy was happy that she had the surgery. She realizes that it gives her the motivation to eat proper food and exercise. Because she does follow directions and instructions, for her, it has been a success.

GLOSSARY

Adenosine triphosphate (ATP): The chemical that is the main source of energy for the body.

Adipocyte: The individual mature fat cell that stores lipid, also known to be an endocrine cell.

Adiponectin: A chemical that makes the body more sensitive to insulin.

Adipose tissue: A collection of fat cells.

Adrenoreceptor: Area on the cells that responds to chemical neurotransmitters.

Aerobic : Means "with oxygen"; used in the context of exercise to describe the first system that delivers oxygen to the cell to meet energy production.

Anaerobic: Means "without oxygen"; used in the context of oxygen to produce ATP for energy inside the cell but outside of the mitochondria.

Anastomosis: The joining of two body parts as in bariatric surgery.

Android obesity: People with apple shapes who have fat concentrated in the upper part and midsection of the body; found mostly in men.

Bariatric: Obese, from the Greek meaning "heavy."

Basal metabolism: The minimum energy required to keep cells, tissues, and organs alive at rest; this can be compared to the idling of an automobile engine.

Binge eating disorder (BED): A condition in which individuals cannot control what they eat. They may have more difficulty losing weight and keeping it off than those without BED.

Bioelectrical impedance: A body measurement using electrodes placed on the body that uses conduction of body fat as an indicator of obesity.

Body mass index (BMI): BMI is calculated as the weight in kilograms divided by height in meters squared. The National Institutes of Health defines a BMI of 25–29.9 as overweight, BMI of 30 or above as obese, and BMI over 40 as morbidly obese.

Brown adipose tissue (BAT): Fat that derives its characteristic color from high concentration of mitochondria; used for heat-production via nonshivering thermogenesis.

Caliper: Calibrated device used to measure body fat by pinching the fat in the arm or other areas and then calculating the measurement from a standardized chart.

Catecholamine: Chemical neurotransmitter from the brain.

Centers for Disease Control and Prevention (CDC): Located in Atlanta, Georgia, an agency of the U.S. government focused on the prevention and control of disease.

Cholesterol: A waxy substance similar to fats; a major difference is that the cells do not burn cholesterol for energy.

Corpulence: An archaic word for overweight or obesity; not politically correct to use at present.

Cushing's syndrome: A condition caused by the hypersecretion of the adrenal glands, resulting in obesity and other conditions.

Endocrine gland: Ductless gland that secretes hormones that may have a specific effect on a tissue or organ into the bloodstream or lymph.

Essential fatty acids: Omega-3 and omega-6 are necessary for good health and are not made in the body.

Expression (gene): Process in which genes are turned on or used.

Fat-cell differentiation: The process of making new fat cells.

Fat-free mass: Parts of the body other than fat; includes bone, organs, and blood.

Fatty acids: Three building blocks of a triglyceride molecule that differ in their length of carbon chains (from 4 to 22) and the number of double bonds they contain.

Genomics: Study of the genome, or complete genetic profile, of a living organism.

Glycemic index (GI): A scale that ranks food by how much the food raises glucose levels.

Glycerol: An alcohol present in chemical combination in all fats.

Glycogen: A polysaccharide commonly called animal starch; formed from carbohydrate sources.

Glycolysis: The anaerobic means of ATP energy provision fueled by carbohydrates.

Gynecoid obesity: Body type shaped like a pear; usually found in women.

Heritability: An indication of the proportion of variation within a population that is due to genetics.

High-density lipoprotein (HDL): Often called good cholesterol, HDL carries cholesterol back to the liver where it is processed into bile and excreted.

Hydrogenation: A process that modifies oils so that they will be hard.

Hyperlipidemia: Elevated levels of serum triglyceride levels.

Hyperphagia: Overeating.

Hypertension: High blood pressure (HBP).

Hypertrophy: Enlarged in size.

Hypothalamus: A tiny pea-shaped structure within the brain that coordinates many bodily functions.

Hypothyroidism: A malfunction of the thyroid due to secretion of thyroid hormone, resulting in lowered basal metabolism and possible obesity.

Interstitial fat tissue: Fat that is so tightly interspersed in the cells that it becomes part of the body tissue and is hard to separate.

Leptin: A hormone that signals to the brain how much fat the body has.

Ligand: A molecule that binds to another chemical group.

Lipids: A specific term used referring to all material extracted with certain lipid solvents like ether or chloroform; lipids are made of triglycerides, phospholipids, and other small lipids.

Lipogenesis: The process of making fat cells.

Lipolysis: Breaking down of fat cells.

Lipoprotein: Protein-coated packages that carry fat and cholesterol through the bloodstream; classes are high-density, low-density, and very low-density.

Low-density lipoproteins (LDL): Often called bad cholesterol because it carries cholesterol to the tissues of the body, especially the arteries.

Macronutrients: Important nutrients like carbohydrates, protein, and dietary fat.

Mesenteric: Area surrounding the viscera or abdominal area.

Mitochondria: Bean-like structures that are the powerhouses that produce energy in cells and are involved in protein synthesis and lipid metabolism.

Monounsaturated fats: Fats that have one double bond and are more stable; moderate amounts help maintain HDL.

Mutant: Literally means "change"; in genetics, it refers to a change in the genetic makeup of an organism that can be passed on to offspring.

Neurotransmitters: Chemicals that are released when the axon of a neuron is excited.

Norepinephrine (NE): A neurotransmitter.

Obstructive sleep apnea (OSA): Sleep is characterized by episodes of patient not breathing.

Omega-3 fatty acids: Have the first double bonds as the third atom along the chain and appear to protect against heart disease.

Omega-6 fatty acids: Have the first double bond in the sixth carbon atom and tend to have potent LDL-lowering properties to protect against heart disease.

Omentum: Area surrounding the small intestine.

Organization for Economic Cooperation and Development (OECD): An organization based in Paris that watches worldwide health trends and the impact on the future.

Peroxisome proliferator-activated receptor (or PPAR-g): A protein that acts as a master switch driving the formation of fat and regulating the storage of fat.

Phospholipids: Fats that have a phosphorous molecule.

Polyunsaturated fats: Those with more than one double bond.

Proteomics: Study of the proteins in a living organism.

Quantitative trait loci (QTL): Use of maps of generations to trace genetic conditions.

Resistin: A molecule that makes the body more resistant to insulin; thought to be the link between obesity and diabetes.

Roux-en-Y (RNY): Joining the distal end of the small intestine to the stomach or esophagus in bariatric surgery.

Satiety: The feeling of fullness—that one has had enough to eat.

Saturated fats : Fatty acids with no double bonds with a high melting point at room temperature; has great influence on total and LDL cholesterol.

Serotonin: A neurotransmitter.

Set point: The genetically determined body weight each person is thought to have.

Socioeconomic status (SES): The social and economic status of an individual.

Thermogenesis: The body's heat producing mechanism produced by brown adipose tissue.

Third National Health and Nutrition Examination (NHANES III): A study conducted by the National Institutes of Health between 1988 and 1994 that revealed overweight conditions of groups of Americans.

Trans-fatty acids: The bent form of unsaturated fatty acids found in hydrogenated vegetable oils.

Transgenic animals: Animals that have been genetically engineered to express certain traits.

Translation: The process in which genetic information directs the synthesis of proteins from amino acids.

Triglycerides : Refers to a family of lipids found almost entirely in fat cells; when the term *fat* is used, it refers to triglycerides.

Uncoupling : Breaking down of ATP to produce heat.

Visceral: Pertaining to the stomach and intestines.

White adipose tissue (WAT): Used as an energy store, also an endocrine organ, the majority of adipose tissue in the body is this type.

World Health Organization (WHO): A unit of the United Nations committed to international health problems.

TIMELINE

25,000 years ago	Paleolithic humans carve fat figurines that represented an idealized female body.
1552 BCE	The Egyptian compilation of medical texts known as the Ebers Papyrus addresses the problem of fat in the "Book of the Stomach."
377 BCE	Hippocrates, the Greek physician, observes that sudden death is more common in those who are naturally fat than in those who are lean.
199	Galen, the Roman physician, divides obesity into types: moderate obesity, a result of life and aging and is acceptable, and immoderate obesity, which is a character flaw from a life of overindulgence and lust.
430	Saint Augustine, a Christian philosopher, ranks gluttony as one of the seven deadly sins.
600–c. 1400	During the Middle Ages, peasants had to live on meager diets and were thin; the nobility and clergy are pictured as hefty in Chaucer's *Canterbury Tales*.
1037	Ibn Sina, or Avicenna, an Islamic physician, writes in *Kitab al-Qānūn fī al-tibb* that obesity is a disease and suggested treating it with hard exercise and lean foods.
1600–1700	Painters of the Renaissance or Baroque Period show individuals with BMIs of 30 or more.
1636	Santorio Santorio, a doctor at the medical school in Padua, Italy, weighs himself in a hanging chair and is the first to discover that body mass can be quantified.

1800	Malcolm Flemyng, a Dutch physician, first suggests that some fat people inherited a predisposition for the condition that they might not be able to control.
1829	William Wadd disagrees with Flemyng and promotes the idea that people had only to change their diets to food that has little nutrition in order to lose weight.
1834	Sylvester Graham, a minister in Maine, lectures on the evils of gluttony and promotes a plain diet of whole grains, vegetables, and pure water. His followers become the first "weight-watchers."
1853	William Beaumont, a frontier doctor, studies the process of digestion.
1870–1900	Stores of body fat are desirable.
1874	A Belgian scholar, Adolphe Quetelet, measures Scottish and French soldiers, plots the results on a normal curve, and develops the idea of an "average man."
1878	William Banting, a London undertaker, loses weight on a diet of meat, fruit, and alcohol. He writes the first diet book, which sold over 60,000 copies, and originates the term *to bant*, which means "to diet."
	Horace Fletcher promotes chewing each bite at least 100 times for weight loss.
1880	German physiologist Max Hubner discovers the calorimeter, a device to measure metabolic rate.
1890s	Lillian Russell, an actress, sets the stage for beauty. She weighs 250 pounds.
1900	Charles Dana Gibson introduces his "Gibson Girl," a look that changes the standards of beauty to large breasts, slim waist, and big hips.
1907	Russell Chittenden, a Yale professor, argues that food intake should be calculated by counting calories; thus, Americans are introduced to calorie-counting.
1908	French designer Paul Poiret introduces a new line of clothing that emphasizes a slim body.
1909	Oscar Rogers of New York Life Insurance warns that being 10 pounds overweight shortens one's lifespan; concern for weight comes not from physicians but from the insurance industry.
1910	Prescriptions, patent medicines, and home remedies emerge to get rid of fat; pharmaceuticals are untested and primitive.
1940s	Metropolitan Life Company designs ideal weight charts that declare it unhealthy to gain weight with age.

	Albert Stunkard, a psychiatrist, shows how emotions affect digestion and become preoccupied with obesity.
1944	The term *yo-yo dieting* is used to describe diets that cause people to lose weight and then gain it right back again.
1945, July 5	Louis Reard, a Paris fashion designer, invents the bikini. The bikini became popular with the advent of beach-party movies, and its popularity continues today.
1948	The famous Framingham Heart Study begins.
1950s	Doctors begin to redefine *obesity* as a medical condition that requires intervention. They abandon the idea that it is a moral problem and now believe it to be a malady or sickness.
1954	Jules Hirsh, an investigator at Rockefeller Institute, begins to study lipids and finds that obese people have more fat cells than an average person.
	Kremen publishes the first study of a bariatric surgery procedure.
1960	A thin model named Twiggy becomes popular, and many women seek to emulate her look.
1960, January	Three people in Southern California begin meeting for the purpose of helping each other with their eating problems, patterning their efforts after the Alcoholics Anonymous 12-step program. The program is called Overeaters Anonymous.
1963	Jean Nidetch, a Long Island housewife, starts Weight Watchers International.
1963	J. H. Payne and L. T. DeWind report results of an end-to-side jejunocolic shunt.
1968	Dr. Erwin Stillman writes *The Doctor's Quick Weight Loss Diet*, which becomes a best seller and the first of many diet fads.
1972	Robert Atkins writes *Dr. Atkins' Diet Revolution*; it becomes a best seller.
1994	Teams of researchers from Rockefeller University make headlines when they report that they have discovered and cloned a gene that regulates appetite and metabolism.
	The American Society of Plastic and Reconstructive Surgeons reports that 51,072 liposuction procedures have been conducted.

1995	FDA advisory panel votes to support Redux, a sensational new diet aid.
1996	Body mass index emerges as the standard definition of obesity.
1997	Fen-phen is pulled from the market when reports of an unusual heart-valve problem surface.
1999	Researchers are investigating more than 15 drugs for obesity.
	Weight-loss medication Orlistat approved by FDA.
2012	Medications Phentermine/topiramate, Locaserin, Naltroxin HCL/bupropion HCL approved.
2014	Liraglutide approved.
2018	Many new drug investigations target genetic and biochemical pathways.

Sources for Further Information

Books and Articles

Aelianes, C. 1666. *Various History*, Book IX. London: Thomas Dung. Quoted in Meir H. Kyger. 1993. "Sleep Apnea from the Needles of Dionysius to Continuous Positive Airway Pressure." *Archives of Internal Medicine* 143: 2301–2303.

Akers, Charlene. 2000. *Obesity*. San Diego: Lucent Books.

Aldana, Steven. 2005. *The Culprit and the Cure*. Mapleton, UT: Maple Mountain Press.

Allison, David B., Patty E. Matz, Angelo Pietrobelli, Raffaella Zannolli, and Myles S. Faith. 1994. "Genetic Influences on Obesity." American Obesity Association. AOA Fact Sheets. http://www.obesity.org/subs/fastfacts/obesity_global_epidemic.shtml.

American College of Sports Medicine. 2004. "Short Bouts of Exercise Reduce Fat in the Bloodstream after Meals," news release. https://www.exercisedaily.org/cgi-bin/details.pl?article_id=343.

American Physiological Society. 2002. "Obesity ... By Choice." www.physiology.org/doi/abs/10.1152/ajpregu.00739.2001.

Andersen, Ross E., ed. 2003. *Obesity Etiology Assessment: Treatment and Prevention*. Champaign, IL: Human Kinetics.

ASDAH. "HAES Principles." Accessed August 16, 2017. https://www.sizediversityandhealth.org/content.asp?id=76.

"Bariatric Surgery as a Treatment Option for Children." 2005. Accessed June 25, 2005. http://www.medscape.com/viewarticle/501526_4.

Barlow, Sarah. 2003. "Treatment of Childhood Obesity." In *Obesity: Mechanisms and Clinical Management*, edited by Robert H. Eckel, 13–29. Philadelphia: Lippincott Williams & Wilkins.

Blackburn, George L., and Laura Bevis. 2003. "The Obesity Epidemic: Prevention and Treatment of the Metabolic Syndrome." http://www.medscape.com/viewprogram/2015_pnt.

Bliss, Rosalie. 2004. "Watch Your Waistline." *Agricultural Research* 52 (6): 8–9.

"Blue Cross Blue Shield of Michigan Helps Schools Launch or Expand Fitness Programs." 2004. Accessed July 30, 2004. http://media.prnewswire.com/en/jsp/latest.jsp;jsessionid =33810598A26C26A56CAAB4D4.

Booth, Frank W., and P. Darrell Neufer. 2005. "Exercise Controls Gene Expression." *American Scientist* 93: 29–35.

Bouchard, Claude, ed. 2002. *Physical Activity and Obesity*. Champaign, IL: Human Kinetics.

Bray, George. 1998. "Historical Framework for the Development of Ideas about Obesity." In *Handbook of Obesity*, edited by George Bray, Claude Bouchard, and W. P. T. James, 1–29. New York: Marcel Dekker.

Bray, George A. 2003. "Treatment of Obesity with Drugs in the New Millennium." In *Obesity: Mechanisms and Clinical Management*, edited by Robert H. Eckel, 449–475. Philadelphia: Lippincott Williams & Wilkins.

Bray, George A. 2004. "Obesity Is a Chronic, Relapsing Neurochemical Disease." *International Journal of Obesity* 28(1): 34–38.

Bren, Linda. 2003. "Losing Weight: More Than Counting Calories." Reprint from FDA Consumer, printed March 2003. Publication no. FDA 03–1303.

Brody, Jane. 2004. "TV's Toll on Young Minds and Bodies." Accessed August 3, 2004. http://www.nytimes.com/2004/08/03/health/03brod.html?pagewanted=print&position=.

Byrne, Peter. 2004. "As a Matter of Fat." Accessed December 20, 2004. http://www.sfweekly.com/issues/2001-01-17/news/feature_print.html.

Clevinger-Firley, Ellen. 2003. "Highlights from the North American Society for the Study of Obesity Annual Meeting: A Registered Dietician's View." *Medscape Diabetes & Endocrinology* 5 (2). Accessed July 5, 2004. www.medscape.com/viewarticle/463887.

Cotton, Richard, ed. 1992. *Personal Trainer Manual*. San Diego: American Council on Education.

Critser, Greg. 2003. *Fat Land: How Americans Became the Fattest People in the World*. Boston: Houghton Mifflin.

Dohrman, Cord E. 2004. "Target Discovery in Metabolic Disease." *Drug Discovery Today* 9 (18): 785–790.

Drewnowski, Adam, and Vicoria A. Warren-Mears. 2003. "Nutrition and Obesity." In *Obesity: Mechanisms and Clinical Management*, edited by Robert Eckel, 436–448. Philadelphia: Lippincott Williams & Wilkins.

Ebert, Jessica. 2005. "Americans Face Drop in Life Expectancy." *Nature*. Accessed March 29, 2005. www.nature.com/news/2005/050314/full/050314-11.html.

Eckel, Robert H. 2003. "Obesity: A Disease or a Physiologic Adaptation for Survival?" In *Obesity: Mechanisms and Clinical Management*, edited by Robert H. Eckel, 3–29. Philadelphia: Lippincott Williams & Wilkins.

Eckel, Robert H., ed. 2003. *Obesity: Mechanisms and Clinical Management.* Philadelphia: Lippincott Williams & Wilkins.

Egyptian Ebers Papers. Accessed July 6, 2004. www.crystalinks.com/egyptmedicine.html.

Esteghamati, A., M. Marmot, T. Atinmo, T. Byers, J. Chen, T. Hirohata, and A. Jackson. 2015. "Complementary and Alternative Medicine for the Treatment of Obesity: A Critical Review." *International Journal of Endocrinology* and *Metabolism.* Accessed August 31, 2017. https://www.ncbi.nlm.nih.gov/pmc/articles/PMC4386228/.

"Facts about Fats." Nutrition and the Genome. Accessed August 2, 2004. http://www.eufic.org/gb/heal/ heal/10.htm.

Faith, Myles S., Patty E. Matz, and David B. Allison. 2003. "Psychosocial Correlates and Consequences of Obesity." In *Obesity Etiology Assessment: Treatment and Prevention,* edited by Ross E. Andersen. Champaign, IL: Human Kinetics.

Fauber, John. 2004. "Obesity Can Lead to Brain Loss, Study Finds." *Milwaukee Journal Sentinel,* November 23.

Felson, David T., and Susan L. Edmond. 2003. "Orthopedic Complications." In *Obesity: Mechanisms and Clinical Management,* edited by Robert H. Eckel, 399–411. Philadelphia: Lippincott Williams & Wilkins.

Frank, L. D. 2004. "Relationship between a Neighborhood's Walkability and Physical Fitness." *American Journal of Preventive Medicine* 27: 87–96.

Fraser, Laura. 1998. *Losing It: False Hope and Fat Profits in the Diet Industry.* New York: Plume.

Fumento, Michael. 1995. "Obesity Myths? Fat Chance." Accessed May 5, 2005. http://www.townhall.com/columnists/GuestColumns/printFumento20050505.shtml.

Glauser, T. A., N. Roepke, B. Stevenin, A. M. Dubois, and S. M. Ahn. 2015. "Physician Knowledge about and Perceptions of Obesity Management." *Obesity Research and Clinical Practice* 9(6) (November–December): 573–583.

Global Business Research LTD. 2004. World Obesity Congress and Expo. July 12–13. Washington Hilton, Washington, DC.

Grady, Denise. 2004. "Fat: The Secret Life of a Potent Cell." *New York Times.* Accessed July 6, 2004. http://www.nytimes.com/2004/07/06/science/06fat.html?th=&pagewanted=print&positions=.

Haas, Elson. 1992. *Staying Healthy with Nutrition.* Berkeley, CA: Celestial Arts.

Heber, David. 2003. "Cancer." In *Obesity: Mechanisms and Clinical Management,* edited by Robert H. Eckel, 75–87. Philadelphia: Lippincott Williams & Wilkins.

Henry, Robert, and Sunder Mundaliar. 2003. "Obesity and Type II Diabetes Mellitus." In *Obesity: Mechanisms and Clinical Management,* edited by Robert H. Eckel, 229–265. Philadelphia: Lippincott Williams & Wilkins.

Hill, J. O., James F. Sallis, and John C. Peters. 2004. "Economic Analysis of Eating and Physical Activity: A Next Step for Research and Policy Change." *American Journal of Preventive Medicine* 27 (October): 111–116.

Huggins, Charmicia. 2005. "Experts Advise Elderly to Continue Exercising." Accessed March 29, 2005. nih.gov/medlineplus/print/news/fullstory_23733.html.

Hunter, Philip. 2004. "Fat Tax, a Recipe for a Healthy Population." *The Scientist* 18 (10): 68.

Jackson, S. E., Sarah E. Jackson, Jane Wardle, Fiona Johnson, Nicholas Finer, and Rebecca J. Beeken. 2013. "The Impact of a Health Professional Recommendation on Weight Loss Attempts in Overweight and Obese British Adults: A Cross-Sectional Analysis." *BMJ* 3:11. http://bmjopen.bmj.com/content/3/11/e003693.

Jandacek, Ronald J., and Stephen C. Woods. 2004. "Pharmaceutical Approaches to the Treatment of Obesity." *Drug Discovery Today* 9 (20): 874–879.

Kelly, Evelyn. 2000. "Trends in Alternative Medicine." In *Science and Its Times*, edited by Neil Schlager, 7: 339–341. Farmington Hills, MI: Gale Group.

Kelly, Evelyn B. 2004 "The Business of Obesity: Trends in Developing and Commercializing Therapeutics for the Worldwide Marketplace." *Drug and Market Development*: 720–727.

Khera, I., M. H. Murad, A. K. Chandar, P. S. Dulai, Z. Wang, L. J. Prokop, R. Loomba, M. Camilleri, . . ., J. Singh. 2016. "Treatment for Obesity with Weight Loss and Adverse Events: A Systematic Review." *JAMA* 315(22): 2424–2434.

Kolata, Gina. 2005. "CDC Team Investigates an Outbreak of Obesity." Accessed June 3, 2005. http://www.nytimes.com/2005/6/03/health/03obese.html?th=& emc=th& pagewanted=print.

Kolata, Gina. 2005. "A Matter of Fat." *AARP Bulletin*: 12–15.

The Krentzman Obesity Newsletter. 2005. 12 (3). Accessed January 30, 2006. http://home.comcast.net/~bkrentzman/articles/krentzman.obesity.newsletter/2005/newsletter.3.1.05.

Latifi, Rifat, and Harvey J. Sugerman. 2003. "Surgical Treatment of Obesity." In *Obesity: Mechanisms and Clinical Management*, edited by Robert H. Eckel, 503–521. Philadelphia: Lippincott Williams & Wilkins.

Lerner, K. Lee, and Brenda W. Lerner, eds. 2002. *World of Genetics*, vols. 1 and 2. Detroit, MI: Gale Group/Thomson.

Lewis, Ricki. 1997. *Human Genetics: Concepts and Applications*. Dubuque, IA: Wm. C. Brown.

MacGregor, Alex. 2002. "The Story of Obesity Surgery." Accessed May 5, 2005. https://asmbs.org/resources/story-of-obesity-surgery.

"Making the Case for Size Acceptance." 2005. Accessed May 5, 2005. http://www.bodypositive.com/argument.htm.

Mangold, Sam. 2003. "Sampling the Kalahari Cactus Diet." BBC News. Accessed June 25, 2005 news.bbc.co.uk.

Mark, David H. 2005. "Being Obese, Underweight Associated with Increased Risk of Death." *JAMA* News Releases. Accessed April 5, 2005. http://pubs.ama-assn.org/media/2005j/0419.dtl.

Markus, Annette. 2005. "Neurobiology of Obesity." *Nature Neuroscience* 8: 551, 505–551.

Mattson, Mark. 2005. "Forum Discussion: Caloric Restriction: Eat Less, Live Longer!" Accessed January 24, 2005. http://www.alzforum.or.

McWhirter, Norris. 1988. *The Guinness Book of World Records, 1988.* New York: Sterling Publications.

Milner, J. Purvis. 2000. *It Can Break Your Heart.* Memphis, TN: Eagle Wing Books.

"Molecular Genetics of Obesity." 2004. Accessed October 4, 2004. https://www.ncbi.nlm.nih.gov/pmc/articles/PMC1642700/.

Moyad, Mark A. 2004. "Fad Diets and Obesity—Part I: Measuring Weight in a Clinical Setting." *Urology Nursing* 24 (2): 114–119.

Musante, Gerard. 2004. "Triumph of the Individual." Accessed January 14, 2005. http://www.techcentralstation.com/072604C.htm.

"NAAFA Speaks Out against Weight Loss Surgery for Children." 2002. Accessed May 5, 2005. http://naafa.org.

Newman, Cathy. 2004. "Why Are We So Fat?" *National Geographic* 206 (2): 46–61.

"New Obesity Research Highlighted at ENDO2004." 2004. Accessed June 17, 2004. https://www.eurekalert.org/pub_releases/2004-06/es-nor061604.php.

Novotny, Monica. 2004. "Hungry for Acceptance: Fat Is Not a Four-Letter Word." Accessed May 5, 2005. http://msnbe.msn.com/id/5664075/print/1/displaymode/1098/.

Onakpoya, I. J., P. P. Posadzki, L. K. Watson, L. A. Davies, and E. Ernst. 2012. "The Efficacy of Long-Term Conjugated Linoleic Acid (CLA) Supplementation on Body Composition in Overweight and Obese Individuals: A Systematic Review and Meta-Analysis of Randomized Clinical Trials." *European Journal of Nutrition* 51(2): 127–134.

Pearson, Helen. 2004. "Low-Carb Diets Get Thermodynamic Defense." *News@Nature*, August 16. Accessed August 24, 2004. www.nature.com/news/2004/040816/full/040816-2.html.

Pietrobelli, A., and K. S. Steinbeck. 2004. "Pediatric Obesity: What Do We Know and Are We Doing the Right Thing?" *International Journal of Obesity* 28 (1): 2–3.

Porter, Roy. 1997. *The Greatest Benefit to Mankind: A Medical History of Humanity.* New York: W. W. Norton.

Powell, Kendall. 2005. "One Step at a Time." *Nature Medicine* 11 (4): 363–364.

Powter, Susan. 1993. *Stop the Insanity!* New York: Simon & Schuster.

Precope, J. 1952. *Hippocrates on Diet and Hygiene.* London: Zeno.

Rand, C. S., and A. M. MacGregor. 1991. "Successful Weight Loss Following Obesity Surgery and Perceived Liability of Morbid Obesity." *International Journal of Obesity Related Metabolic Disorders* 15: 577–579.

Rashid, Mitchell, Francisco Fuentes, Robert C. Touchon, and Paulette S. Wehner. 2003. "Obesity and the Risk for Cardiovascular Disease." *Preventive Cardiology* 6 (1): 42–47.

"Recent Lawsuits about Fat Discrimination." 2002. Accessed May 5, 2005. http://www.naafa.org.

Robinson, Tracey D., and Ronald R. Grunstein. 2003. "Sleep-Disordered Breathing." In *Obesity: Mechanisms and Clinical Management*, edited by Robert H. Eckel, 202–225. Philadelphia: Lippincott Williams & Wilkins.

Robison, Jon. 1999. "Weight, Health, and Culture: Shifting the Paradigm for Alternative Healthcare." *Alternative Health Practitioner* 5: 1–24.

Rossner, Stephan. 2002. "Obesity through the Ages." *International Journal of Obesity* 25 (January): S29–S33. Accessed January 30, 2006. http://www. nature.com/ijo/journal/v25/n4s/pdf/0801936a.pdf.

Schwartz, Hillel. 1986. *Never Satisfied: A Cultural History of Diets, Fantasies, and Fat*. New York: The Free Press.

"Set Point Theory." 2000. *The Krentzman Obesity Newsletter* 7 (4). Accessed June 13, 2004. http://home. comcast.net/bkerntzman/articles.obesity. newletter/newsletter.500.1.

Shell, Ellen. 2002. *The Hungry Gene: The Science of Fat and the Future of Thin*. New York: Atlantic Monthly Press.

Sherman, Mark. 2004. "Medicare Seeks Weight Loss Plans That Work." Accessed July 23, 2004. www.hateweight.com/news/. . ./news_medicare_seeks_%20 weight_%20loss_20july04.ht. . .

Shi, Yuguang, and Paul Burn. 2004. "Lipid Metabolic Enzymes: Emerging Drug Targets for the Treatment of Obesity." *Nature Reviews Drug Discovery* 3 (8): 695–710.

Simopoulas, Artemis P., ed. 1992. *Metabolic Control of Eating: Energy Expenditures and the Bioenergetics of Obesity*. Basel, Switzerland: Karger.

"Sizing Up Weight-Based Discrimination." 2002. Accessed May 5, 2005. http:// www.tolerance.org.

Solovay, Sondra. 2000. *Tipping the Scales of Justice*. Amherst, NY: Prometheus Books.

Spake, Amanda. 2005. "The World of Chef Jorge." *U.S. News & World Report*. Accessed January 30, 2006. http://www.usnews.com/usnews/health/articles/ 050509/9chef.htm.

Spiegel, Allen, Elizabeth Nabel Nora Volkow, Story Landis, Ting-Kai Li. 2005. "Obesity on the Brain." *Nature Neuroscience* 8: 552–553.

Steeves, J. A., D. R. Bassett, Jr., D. L. Thompson, and E. C. Fitzhugh. 2015. "Relationships of Occupational and Non-Occupational Physical Activity to Abdominal Obesity." *Obesity Research Clinical Practice* 9(3): 243–255.

Structure House. 2003. "Pointing Fingers Is Not the Answer to Solving America's Obesity Epidemic," press release. Accessed July 5, 2005. http://www. structurehouse.com.

Suleman, Amer et al. "Exercise Physiology." Accessed January 27, 2005. http:// www.emedicine.com/sports/topic145.htm.

Underwood, Anne, and Jerry Adler. 2004. "What You Don't Know about Fat." *Newsweek*. Accessed January 30, 2006. http://www.msnbc.msn.com/ id/5709350/site/newsweek/print/1/displaymode/1098.

"Universal McCann Global Study on the Obesity Epidemic," press release. 2004. Accessed July 7, 2004. http://media.prnewswire.com/en/jsp/latest. jsp?resourceod=2720304&access=EHget%20usr=ek.

USDA. 2005. "Health at Every Size: New Hope for Obese Americans. http://agresearchmag.ars.usda.gov/2006/mar/health.

Wadden, T. A., and A. J. Stunkard. 1993. "Psychosocial Consequences of Obesity and Dieting—Research and Clinical Findings." In *Obesity Theory and Therapy*, edited by A. J. Stunkard and T. A. Wadden, 163–177. New York: Raven Press.

Wadden, Thomas, Gary Brown, Gary D. Foster, and Jan R. Linowitz. 1991. "Salience of Weight-Related Worries in Adolescent Males and Females." *International Journal of Eating Disorders* 10: 407–414.

Warner, Jennifer. 2005. "The Skinny on Diet Scams." Accessed April 4, 2005. http://aolsvc.health.webmd.aol.com/content/Article/103/107165.htm?printing.

Wilkinson, William J., and Steven N. Blair. 2003. "Exercise." In *Obesity: Mechanisms and Clinical Management*, edited by Robert H. Eckel, 476–499. Philadelphia: Lippincott Williams & Wilkins.

Wing, Rena R., and Suzanne Phelan. 2003. "Behavioral Treatment of Obesity: Strategies to Improve Outcome and Predictors of Success." In *Obesity: Mechanisms and Clinical Management*, edited by Robert H. Eckel, 415–425. Philadelphia: Lippincott Williams & Wilkins.

ORGANIZATIONS AND WEB SOURCES

American College of Sports Medicine. http://www.acsm.org. This organization is the largest sports medicine and exercise-science organization in the world, with more than 20,000 members.

American Obesity Association. http://www.obesity.org. This advocacy organization disseminates information about obesity and seeks to influence public policy.

American Society for Bariatric Surgery. http://www.asbs.org. The society of bariatric surgeons supports the group with education, a journal, and conferences.

America on the Move. http://www.americanonthemove.org. This website was founded by J. O. Hill, a recognized exercise expert.

Association for Morbid Obesity Support. http://www.obesityhelp.com. A group for support of those who are obese and have problems with discrimination and other issues.

Atkins Medical Service. http://www.atkins.com. This is the website of Atkins Health and Medical Services.

Boston Obesity/Nutrition Research Center. http://www.bmc.org/bonrc. Suggestions for diet and exercise are given on this site.

CaloriesCount. http://www.caloriescount.com. This site is a valuable resource but charges $45 per year for tools, calculators, and information needed to lose weight.

Center for the Study of Nutrition Medicine, Beth Israel Deaconess Medical Center, Harvard Medical School, Boston, Massachusetts. www.bidmc.org/Research/. . ./Center-for-the-Study-of-Nutrition-Medicine.aspx. Suggestions for diet and exercise are given on this site.

Food and Drug Administration Obesity Initiative. https://www.fda.gov/Food/FoodScienceResearch/. . ./ucm081696.htm. The FDA has jurisdiction over the content and labeling of foods, drugs, and medical devices.

Food Pyramid. https://www.cnpp.usda.gov/FGP. This is the government site of the 2005 food pyramid; it asks for information about gender, age, and activity level and designs a pyramid for the individual.

Genome News Network. http://www.genomenewsnetwork.org. The network presents news about genetics by topic and with book reviews.

Health Politics. https://www.ncbi.nlm.nih.gov/pmc/articles/PMC2652986/. This website provides information about political involvement in health, with obesity as a hot topic in the national and state governments.

National Association to Advance Fat Acceptance. https://www.naaf.org. The NAAFA is an advocacy group for acceptance of fat; it is involved in political issues of discrimination.

National Education Association. http://www.nea.org/ The NEA is a group of educators interested in issues that relate to children and students.

National Institutes of Health Obesity Research. http://obesityresearch.nih.gov.

National Sleep Foundation, 2004 Sleep in America Poll. http://www.sleepfoundation.org. This study reveals the relationship between obesity and sleep.

National Weight Control Registry. 800–606–6927. http://www.nwcr.ws. This study gathers information from people who have successfully lost weight and kept it off. They would like to hear from anyone 18 years or older who has lost at least 30 pounds and maintained that weight loss for at least a year.

North American Association for the Study of Obesity. http://www.obesityresearch.org. This is a group dedicated to the study of obesity and influencing public policy.

Obesity Education Initiative, National Heart, Lung, and Blood Institute. 301–592–8573. https://www.nhlbi.nih.gov/science/obesity-nutrition-and-physical-activity. This study reveals the relationship between obesity and sleep.

Physical Activity Readiness Questionnaire. http://www.d.umn.edu/student/loon/soc/phys/par-q.html. This study reveals the relationship between obesity and sleep.

President's Council on Physical Fitness and Sports. http://www.fitness.gov. Shapedown is a program for children and teens created 25 years ago at the University of California–San Francisco and is used by a number of collegiate centers like Vanderbilt. Shapedown emphasizes self-esteem and adopting healthier life habits.

Shape Up America! https://www.shapeamerica.org/

Steps to a Healthier U.S. Initiative. www.cdc.gov/nccdphp/dch/programs/healthy-communitiesprogram/. . ./steps/index.htm

Take Off Pounds Sensibly. http://www.tops.org.

U.S. Department of Agriculture Calorie Control Council. https://caloriecontrol.org/. This Calorie Control Council website gives information in an interactive format.

Weight-Control Information Network, National Institute of Diabetes and Digestive and Kidney Diseases. 877–946–4627. http://win.niddk.nih.gov/.

INDEX

About the Author

Evelyn B. Kelly, PhD, is a professor at Saint Leo University, San Antonio, Florida, and a medical writer. She has authored 18 books and over 400 articles. Her other books with ABC-CLIO/Greenwood include *The 101 Most Unusual Diseases and Disorders* (2015), the two-volume *Encyclopedia of Human Genetics and Disease* (2013), *Gene Therapy* (2007), *Stem Cells* (2006), and *The Skeletal System* (2004).